MW00980052

# SCRIBBLERS
# FOR BREAD

# SCRIBBLERS FOR BREAD

## Aspects of the English Novel Since 1945

# GEORGE GREENFIELD

Hodder & Stoughton
LONDON SYDNEY AUCKLAND TORONTO

British Library Cataloguing in Publication Data
Greenfield, George
  Scribblers for bread: aspects of the English
  novel since 1945
  1. Fiction in English 1945–1988. Forms.
  Novels. Critical studies
  I. Title
  823′.009

ISBN 0-340-49656-8

First published in Great Britain 1989

Published by Hodder and Stoughton,
a division of Hodder and Stoughton Ltd,
Mill Road, Dunton Green, Sevenoaks, Kent TN13 2YA.
Editorial Office: 47 Bedford Square, London WC1B 3DP.

Typeset by Hewer Text Composition Services, Edinburgh.
Printed in Great Britain by St Edmundsbury Press Ltd, Bury St Edmunds, Suffolk.

'I speak not of the scribblers for bread, who tease the press with their perishable trash. It was not for gain that Bacon, Newton, Milton and Locke instructed and delighted the world; it would be unworthy of such men to traffic with a dirty bookseller.'

Earl Camden, Lord High Chancellor,
in a parliamentary debate on copyright, 1774

Page 278, third paragraph

The last sentence is incorrect and must be disregarded. Gollancz did not let their hard cover edition(s) go out of print during the period in which they held volume rights.

The Author

# Contents

| | | |
|---|---|---|
| | Acknowledgments | ix |
| | An Explanation | xi |
| | Introduction | 1 |
| CHAPTER I | Danger – Writers at Work | 7 |
| CHAPTER II | Bestsellers – Born or Made? | 20 |
| CHAPTER III | Still at Work | 34 |
| CHAPTER IV | Enter the Literary Agent | 50 |
| CHAPTER V | The Way It Was | 74 |
| CHAPTER VI | Censorship and the Novel | 92 |
| CHAPTER VII | Early Years and the Rise of the Paperback | 107 |
| CHAPTER VIII | The 1960s and 1970s | 123 |
| CHAPTER IX | Conglomerates and Aggregates | 136 |
| CHAPTER X | Fiction Publishing in the 1980s | 153 |
| CHAPTER XI | The Editorial Function Today | 168 |
| CHAPTER XII | The Crunch | 187 |
| CHAPTER XIII | Films and Television | 201 |
| CHAPTER XIV | Trade Winds | 223 |
| | Publicity and Advertising – Book Clubs – The Net Book Agreement – Public Libraries – The Public Lending Right – The Arts Council – Prizes and Awards – The Society of Authors and the Writers' Guild – The Inland Revenue and its Effect | |
| CHAPTER XV | 'Once upon a future time' | 290 |
| APPENDIX A | Some Thoughts on Auctions *by Scott Meredith* | 311 |
| APPENDIX B | Subsidiary Rights – the American Way *by Paul S. Nathan* | 315 |
| APPENDIX C | Acquisition Statistics on Selected Quoted and Unquoted Companies | 323 |
| APPENDIX D | Select Bibliography | 325 |
| | Index | 327 |

# Acknowledgments

My grateful thanks are due to:

the literary agents, Giles Gordon, Douglas Rae, Deborah Rogers, Michael Shaw, Carol Smith and Ed Victor: and the editors, Mark Barty-King, Liz Calder, Rosemary Cheetham, Richard Cohen, James Hale, Harold Harris, Chris Holifield and Robert McCrum – all of whom gave unstintingly of their time and expertise in the interviews included in this book;

the authors, Jeffrey Archer, A. S. Byatt and Jon Cleary, for sharing with me their thoughts on novel-writing, which also appear as interviews;

Scott Meredith, the doyen of New York agents, and Paul S. Nathan of *Publishers Weekly*, New York, both of whom produced expert insights into 'the American way';

Lord Hardinge of Penshurst for his constructive comments and John Bright-Holmes, whose editorial advice was invaluable;

Louis Baum, editor of the *Bookseller*, and Clare Dupernex, archivist, for allowing me to clutter their offices every Wednesday for over fifteen months;

and finally a specially warm tribute to Michael Geare, joint deputy editor of the *Bookseller*, who each week throughout that period poured out for me in equally generous measure his wide knowledge of the book trade and libations from the office bottle.

# An Explanation

It was a golden evening in June 1939. The Foundation Dinner at Downing College, Cambridge, had just ended and I found myself in a champagne haze strolling on the lawns – rare privilege – with my tutor, Bill Cuttle. Although he knew I was committed to the University Diploma of Education for the year ahead, he thought he could wangle me out of that and into a research fellowship. F. R. Leavis, my supervisor, would be well disposed, he felt. Twenty-two years old and pleasantly drunk, I was flattered to be shown the keys of the academic kingdom. Ten weeks later, I did apply – but it was to enlist in the infantry.

There followed six years of war, seven years in publishing and nearly thirty-five as a literary agent; but I never quite forgot the evening of the Foundation Dinner. In October 1986, two days after retiring from the John Farquharson agency and fifty years almost to the day since I first went up to Cambridge, I enrolled as a post-graduate student at University College, London, to attempt a Ph.D. thesis.

By its very nature, of course, a thesis sets out to prove something. After a happy year of researching and interviewing, I discovered that mine was likely to prove nothing except that of making many books, there is no end – a fact already well established. So with the helpful intervention of Dan Jacobson, my supervisor at UCL, the College authorities have given me leave of absence to write this book.

# Introduction

In the forty years to the end of 1987, discounting reprints, new editions and translations, 90,859 novels were published in the United Kingdom. If the average thickness were an inch and the titles were stacked one on top of the other, the column would rise to a height of over 7,500 feet. But in case the reader might think that the great expansion of post-war fiction writing occurred in the early days and has been dwindling ever since, the facts are surprising. In the period 1946–50, 10,345 novels were published; in 1983–87, 14,762 novels appeared, an increase of nearly 43 per cent.

Literary critics have long prophesied the demise of the novel. Q. D. Leavis, writing in 1980, mentioned

> what is generally recognised to be the decay and approaching death of the English novel as a major art (though not of course of English fiction as commercial entertainment).

Later in the same volume (*Collected Essays*), she says, 'Our novelists seem to have abdicated from moral responsibility, to have become sub-human'. At around the same time, George Steiner stated,

> Like many of its institutions and forms of expression, the novel can also survive over a long period, both in a sad and parodic way. But its vitality is no longer great.

When interviewing Antonia Byatt on various aspects of the novel and novel-writing, I asked for her views on 'the early demise of the serious novel'. She replied, 'I don't think it's in question any more. There *are* serious novels and people are writing them; not, on the whole, the English . . . They may not like his work but no one can say that Salman Rushdie isn't a serious novelist. He's written a large

1

book about the nature of India [*Midnight's Children*] and it's a *big* book. A large number of English writers are writing pale imitations of the big Victorian novels . . . I do think that television is having a terrible effect . . . through causing people to get out of the habit of reading and paying sustained attention to the written word.'

Per Gedin anticipated George Steiner's theme in *Literature in the Market Place* (1977):

> Culture is not only relatively uninteresting from a political point of view, it is also unimportant economically. The frenetic recreation industry finds it more profitable to sell travel and hobby articles rather than books.

Prophecy is a form of betting and hindsight makes fools of many. In the decade after Mr Gedin's utterance, the British book industry quadrupled its volume from around £500 million* to about £2 billion and appeared to be on an upward curve.

The English novel is certainly alive and kicking 'as commercial entertainment'. And, when one takes into account such living novelists as William Golding, Graham Greene, Doris Lessing, Iris Murdoch, Patrick White and Angus Wilson, can it be accurate to say that the novel is dead as an art form?

To earn one's living by writing novels is not an unworthy aim. To succeed, the author has to go to the market; in a few special cases, as with Ian Fleming and Peter Benchley, the market will occasionally come to him. The purpose of this study is to set out the conditions since 1945 – the outlets, the commercial aspects – that may have influenced his aim and his achievement. The main outlets available to the professional novelist in the forty or so years since the Second World War will be discussed. Other sections of the book will deal with the effect or influence, if any, of publishing editors and literary agents in persuading novelists in one direction or another, either positively or negatively: positively in suggesting themes or events considered to have a sales appeal or, negatively, in dissuading the author from tackling 'uncommercial' themes or even characters that might not appeal to a wide readership.

Further chapters will deal with such topics as the effects of public libraries and the Public Lending Right, of how changes in the structure of the publishing industry may have influenced full-time novelists,

---

* In present values, about £1.3 billion but, even so, the increase would be about 54 per cent.

the very limited help provided by state sponsorship through the Arts Council and the results of high taxation. Mention must also be made of the gallant and, at length, successful battle, led by Sir Alan Herbert and Mr Roy (now Lord) Jenkins in their Obscene Publications Bill of 1959, to bring the then prevailing Victorian law on obscenity into a more modern and more tolerant form.

The scope is limited to the influences of the market on professional novelists and, in some rare cases, vice versa. For instance, it can be argued that Ian Fleming spawned numerous imitators of his glittering spy fiction; or in more recent years that the wake of *Jaws* washed up various wild creatures – a rabid dog, a killer whale and a giant conger-eel, among others – on to the wilder shores of fiction. The definition of the professional novelist used throughout is that of the writer who earns a reasonable income mainly from his books, at least the equivalent of a fairly senior manager in industry or a middle-grade civil servant. (It is difficult to strike close parallels because the industrial manager may receive various 'perks' – the use of a company car, private health insurance – not reflected in his salary and the civil servant can look to an index-linked pension, whereas the writer through a judicious application of Schedule D may charge legitimate expenses including a share of his rent, rates, heating etc, against his writing income, if he works from home.)

For the sake of convenience, I shall usually refer to authors in the masculine gender but, as I hope to show, women writers are of at least equal importance to the study. The professional novelist may well earn additional income through writing articles or from appearing on television and radio programmes but the present test is that the income from his books should provide him with a sufficiency.

For my purpose, a novel is any work of fiction of not less than 40,000 words, whether it be a 'straight' novel or a 'category' novel. These are definitions commonly used in the book trade: 'category' is the term usually applied to romances, Westerns (now virtually defunct), crime novels (which can be subdivided into 'thrillers' and 'whodunits'), horror novels, and science-fiction stories, whereas a 'straight' novel is a piece of general fiction that does not fall into one or other of those specific types. The term 'category' is not used in any pejorative sense. Ray Bradbury and Frank Herbert as science-fiction writers or Patricia Highsmith, Eric Ambler and Ruth Rendell as crime writers would each occupy a distinguished place in any listing of the best modern novelists. But, in the main, as category fiction tends to obey

3

narrower limits, my references to 'the novel' will apply to straight or general fiction for adult readers, unless otherwise stated.

In a 1953 article in the *Author*, the quarterly journal published by the Society of Authors, C. P. Snow claimed that there were more than 300 novelists in the United Kingdom earning a professional income of over £750 a year from novel-writing alone; a further 600 who reached that level by combining writing with literary journalism; and 1,500 earning that much from 'all kinds of literary activity'. The comparable figures he gave for the United States were 250, 1,000 and 2,000; for France 50, 350 and 750. He concluded,

> Writers in this country do not realise how lucky they are . . . Life is not easy for a writer in England today but it is a good deal easier than anywhere else.

A young reader may be struck by the humble figures of earnings he cited. Older readers will recall that in the years from 1945 to 1960 there was little inflation in Britain – an annual increase of 1.44 per cent. Not long after Harold Macmillan told us ungrammatically that we had never had it so good, Britain began to discover it was about to have it much worse than before. To find the present-day equivalent of C. P. Snow's £750, we need to multiply by a factor of almost 11. There are probably fewer than 1,000 British novelists today earning over £8,000 from their book advances and royalties alone. (In this context, 'British' novelists are those who were born and spent their formative years in the United Kingdom or in the Commonwealth.)

Whenever discussing inflationary effects or presenting historic values in current terms, I have throughout made use of the Retail Price Index figures and internal purchasing power appendices issued by the Central Statistical Office. For convenience, when using the term 'one billion pounds', I have adopted the American definition of 'one thousand million pounds', not the original British definition of 'one million million pounds'.

Over the period under review, the American market has been a major influence on the earning capacity of the British novelist. Indeed, up to September 1949, the reverse was true. Till then, the prevailing rate of exchange was $4 to the £1, which compensated the American novelist for the fact that the total British readership was only about a quarter of his domestic readership. In 1949 the pound was devalued to a rate of $3 and was subsequently stabilised for nearly twenty years at \$2.80. The present (September 1988) floating rate has dropped to around 60 per cent of that level. So while the British market has become a useful additional source of income for the American novelist, the American market has become a vitally important source to the British novelist.

Nevertheless, although I refer to influential events in the American publishing trade throughout the post-war period, it will be impossible to cover the American scene over so many years in equal detail. One special difference between the two markets for much of this period is neatly summed up by J. A. Sutherland in his *Fiction and the Fiction Industry* (1978):

> There is something characteristically premature about the way in which Americans put their books out. Books are often paid for before they are written; editors interfere with them before they are complete; the Kirkus Book Service (a system which has no equivalent in Britain) offers a 'tipsheet' assessment of books months before their publication – for professional 'previews' are thus much more important than reviews; often before books are in print they are sold to bookclubs and paperback firms. The sums made in this way are released to impress the public.

Had Mr Sutherland written his book a decade later, he might very well have omitted or qualified that passage for, influenced partly by those American practices and partly through the aggregation of power into fewer and larger groups, British publishing in the 1980s has itself adopted and deployed most of the same characteristics and techniques.

The sheer size of the US market with its potential adult readership of nearly 185 million, allied to the fact that the public library system there is tiny on a per capita basis compared with the British version, has made it an Eldorado for the aspiring British novelist. It has no protectionism in the shape of a Net Book Agreement and this has led to aggressive discounting in the major bookselling chains. Book stores occupy prime sites in metropolitan areas; within a couple of hundred yards on central Fifth Avenue, New York, there are at least four large and brightly displayed book stores. Several of them, as in other important American cities, stay open until late at night. Drugstores in shopping malls throughout the USA contain racks of popular paperback titles. Although demand often creates an over-supply and the shelf life of a paperback edition can vary from three to six weeks at the most, the American public contains enough book buyers – not all of them necessarily book *readers* – to make publishing there 'big business'.

Late in 1986, William Morrow Inc. paid an advance on royalties of over $5 million for US hard- and softcover rights in *Whirlwind* by James Clavell. To 'earn back' that advance and assuming top royalty rates for both editions, a net hardcover sale of over 750,000 copies and a net paperback sale of more than 5 million copies (or various adjustments either way) would be required, leaving aside income from book club sales. (The net sales in both cases were most likely under 40 per cent of the target sales figures.) No British novelist, however successful, could reasonably expect trade sales in the UK and Commonwealth market to exceed 150,000 hardcover copies and more than 1.5 million in paperback. The sternly ambitious, therefore, have to look westward for their main sales outlet.

CHAPTER I

# Danger – Writers at Work

About 99 per cent of the population, regardless of age,
is incapable of equating writing with work, not real work.
Peter Dobereiner, the *Observer*

American insurance man: 'Well, what do you do?'
Irwin Shaw: 'I'm a writer.'
American insurance man: 'Yes, I know. But what do
you do for a *living*?'

In the general view of the British public, a miner or a nurse does real
work and so to a lesser degree does a nine-to-five office worker or a
postman or the ticket collector on the Underground. But someone
who sits at home, perhaps even in a dressing-gown and slippers,
and between cups of coffee puts words on to paper must be having
a fine old lazy time. Only those with the compulsion to express
themselves through the printed word and those with the education
and the understanding to realise why this should be will know the
strains and pressures that arise from the apparently simple task of
putting black marks on to white paper.

Authors themselves are often ruefully aware of these attitudes.
Jeffrey Archer has said to me, 'Authors are mad. They ought to
do "a proper job", as my wife says. Or as my son said, when he
was six or seven and I used to take him to school every morning,
"Could you stop taking me to school, Dad, in the mornings?" And I
asked, rather hurt, "Why?" He said, "Because the boys think you're
out of work."'

Even someone who has made a close study of literature will
sometimes fail to understand what compels a novelist to write. For
example, J. A. Sutherland in *Fiction and the Fiction Industry* cites the
case of Heinemann's generous and far-sighted gesture in the early
1930s in paying Graham Greene £600 a year for three years after the

7

success of *The Man Within* (1929), thus freeing him to write full-time. Mr Sutherland goes on to say:

> Without the salary there is a strong likelihood that Greene would eventually have found his destiny as the letters editor of *The Times*, unable in his spare time to concentrate on sweating out his stylistic infection.

Can one really imagine that the author of *The Power and the Glory*, *Brighton Rock*, *The Heart of the Matter*, *The End of the Affair* and a dozen other highly notable novels would have tamely given up writing without Heinemann's subsidy? And what of the converse? If Graham Greene had only been interested in a comfortable stipend, why has he gone on writing novels and novellas into his eighties when he could have retired many years ago on the income from his existing work?

In the same study Mr Sutherland states that certain novelists have been forced to over-produce through economic factors. He cites Iris Murdoch (18 novels in 20 years), Melvyn Bragg (9 novels in 9 years), Simon Raven (14 novels in 15 years) and Anthony Burgess (19 novels in 10 years, with the use of a pen-name as well). But the point he misses is that some novelists are prolific by nature; they are bursting with ideas and concepts and either by temperament write quickly or have managed to train themselves to a high output. After all, Iris Murdoch, an Oxford don married to another Oxford don, can hardly have been close enough to the breadline to be forced to write beyond her natural speed. Nor would the other writers mentioned in Mr Sutherland's study have been driven to 'scribble for bread'.

A novelist who worked four hours a day over a five-day week and averaged 200 words an hour (less than an A4 page double spaced) would produce 4,000 words a week. If he maintained that rate for six months, he would have amassed over 100,000 words, approximately equivalent to a full-length novel. Several novelists of my acquaintance, when in full flow, would think little of averaging 500 words an hour over a five-hour stretch and keep up that level of output for the two or three months required to complete the first draft of a long novel. Dashiell Hammett wrote the last third of *The Glass Key* (over 20,000 words) in one thirty-hour stretch. He later had the grace to admit, 'Ever since then, I've told myself, "I could do it again if I had to." Of course, I never did.'

The only thing that matters are the words that end up on paper.

It is immaterial how quickly or how slowly they arrived there. Yet the reading public – and often critics who ought to know better – fall into the trap of thinking that a novel that has taken five or ten years in the writing may well be a masterpiece, whereas they consider the writer who publishes two or three novels a year must be *ipso facto* a pot-boiler. For a long time, Simenon was underrated merely because of his uncanny speed of output. The very prolific novelist often *is* superficial, shuffling cardboard characters through implausible plots where only the speed of action deceives the reader's eye. But the reader must judge the results on paper, not the length of time the writing took.

And yet Martin Amis, reviewing in the *New Statesman* Iris Murdoch's *The Sacred and Profane Love Machine*, took her to task for writing too quickly:

> Were she to slow down – were she to allow one of those ominous 'silences' to gather, silences such as more tight-lipped novelists periodically 'break' – she would be accepting a different kind of responsibility to her critics and to her own prodigious talents.

The undeniable master of the 'quick and often' was John Creasey, who died in June 1973 aged sixty-four. His obituary noted that he received 743 rejection slips before any one of his novels was accepted for publication – a breathtaking mixture of hope and stubbornness. In 1937 he wrote two books in one week and still found time to play a half-day's cricket. The year 1946 saw his peak of production: his Stakhanovite output that year was twenty-four novels. In all, he was the author of 560 novels, published under his own name and twenty-five pseudonyms. Over ten years before he died, his books were selling almost 2 million copies a year worldwide; his estimated sales up to 1962 were 25 million. Hodder & Stoughton arranged to reprint ten titles every year for the foreseeable future. Not long afterwards, they announced in a trade advertisement that they were about to publish his 101st title under their imprint.

But time has not been kind to John Creasey's memory. At December 1987, less than a decade and a half since his death, Hodder had only two paperback titles of his in stock – and even those two were 'static'. Had the mass market tastes changed so much in such a short time or had the back sales been maintained during his lifetime only by his prodigious output and energetic self-publicity?

The other hugely prolific author of recent times was Georges Simenon. He once wrote a novel in exactly twenty-five hours; his output includes 150 novels under his own name and 350 under various pseudonyms. It is unsurprising, perhaps, that he once said, 'Writing is not a profession but a vocation of unhappiness'. His preparations, according to the *Paris Review Writers at Work* (1st Series), were obsessively detailed. He would clear his diary of appointments for eleven consecutive days and, just before starting a new novel, would have a thorough medical check-up (and another at the end of the intensive writing stretch; usually, the doctor would find that his blood pressure had gone down). Then he would begin.

> On the eve of the first day I know what will happen in the first chapter. Then, day after day, chapter after chapter, I find what comes later. After I have started a novel I write a chapter each day, without ever missing a day. Because it is a strain, I have to keep pace with the novel. If, for example, I am ill for forty-eight hours, I have to throw away the previous chapters. And I never return to that novel.

The other multi-volume writers, apart from Enid Blyton, many of whose 400-plus books for children were either short or were compilations of her magazine stories, fade far into the background when compared with Creasey and Simenon. Eden Philpotts had more than 250 novels published, the majority under the Hutchinson imprint to which he remained loyal for more than fifty years. But his writing career spanned almost seventy years; he started at the age of twenty-six and delivered his last novel to Hutchinson when he was ninety-five, three years before he died in 1960.

Barbara Cartland published her first novel, *Jigsaw*, sixty-five years ago and, according to her *Who's Who* entry, has since produced a further 360 novels, a third of which contain the word 'Love' (or a derivative) in the title. She has also published 44 volumes of non-fiction and verse, including no fewer than five autobiographies – a busy, if hardly self-effacing, career. She was quoted in the 21 January 1978 issue of the *Bookseller* as saying,

> I write every day, 750 words an hour . . . I dictate everything to a secretary who is good at punctuation. Then a schoolmaster friend reads it all again, for grammar *and* punctuation . . .

I find Ginseng so wonderful. It was entirely because I was taking 400 mg of Ginseng every day, I broke the world record by writing those 20 books (in one year).*

Another prolific living novelist is Christopher Nicole. Over a thirty-year writing spell, he has published close on 100 novels under his own name and various pseudonyms. That seems a modest total, compared to the output of a Creasey or a Cartland, but many of Mr Nicole's novels are between 125,000 and 150,000 words in length. In any one year, his *published* wordage will exceed 500,000, so that in the last twenty years he will have seen in print over 10 million words, the equivalent of nearly 200 novels by Georges Simenon.

It must not be thought that John Creasey and the other frequent writers have treated their vast output with a cynical shrug. Creasey attacked Julian Symons sharply in the columns of the *Bookseller* when the latter hinted that anyone who wrote twelve or more novels a year could not be much good. Pride is not an up-market prerogative.

Daily or weekly output of words will obviously vary from one author to another but by studying individual comments we can begin to sketch something of a pattern. In his autobiography, *Against the Wind*, published in 1958, Geoffrey Household, describing a writer's methods, said,

His working day is short, for no man can drive imagination more than five hours.

A five-hour day, between morning and evening, will produce anything between seven hundred and a thousand words.

Also in 1958, R. H. Mottram, who reckoned to write 200,000 words a year and who had had twenty-seven novels published in thirty-five years, said, 'I have for over twenty-five years averaged four mornings a week, producing about 1,000 words in each.'

Sheila Hailey, writing in 1978 about her husband Arthur, said:

His target is 600 [words] a day, and as each paragraph is completed he deducts the number of words it contains from that target. Occasionally, on a bad day when progress is slow, he will go back to his study after dinner to make up those 600 words.

* Alas, in spite of the ginseng, she did not break the world record. Cf. John Creasey's output of 24 novels in 1946, cited on page 9.

She added that it took him about eighteen months to write a 500-page novel. During that time, they would live a very disciplined life with no social engagements except at weekends.

In the same month of September 1978, the *Sunday Times* reported that Nicholas Monsarrat produced *exactly* 600 words a day, working from 4 a.m. to 12 noon, then lunch and a siesta, then again from 9 p.m. to 1 a.m. seven days a week.

Angus Wilson, interviewed in the *Paris Review Writers at Work* series, said:

> I write very easily . . . *Hemlock* took four weeks. *Anglo-Saxon Attitudes* took four months, and an awful lot of that time was taken up just with thinking . . . I usually work from eight to two, but if it's going well I may go on to four. Only, if I do, I'm extremely exhausted. In fact, when the book is going well the only thing that stops me is sheer exhaustion.

He writes in longhand and, when working on a novel, would expect to average 1,000–2,000 words a day.

William Styron is another longhand performer, who expects to finish two and a half to three pages a day. He will spend five hours at a time at his desk, working in

> the afternoon. I like to stay up late at night and get drunk and sleep late. I wish I could break the habit but I can't. The afternoon is the only time I have left and I try to use it to the best advantage, with a hangover.

Irwin Shaw, interviewed in 1976, described how he got up very early in the morning, worked for four or five hours, played tennis or took some other physical exercise in the afternoon and went back to his desk at 4 p.m. or 5 p.m. to go over his morning's work.

Kingsley Amis, for his part, displayed a less Spartan attitude. Apparently, he lingers over breakfast, reading the newspapers and pottering around, 'still in pyjamas and dressing gown', putting off the dreaded moment as long as possible. He usually starts typing at about 10.30 a.m., stops around 1–1.15 p.m. for a shave, a shower and to get dressed, then works on till 2–2.15 when he breaks for lunch. If the work is urgent, he will continue – unwillingly – in the afternoon. He takes a break around 6 p.m. and then will work on till about 8.30 – 'and I always hate stopping'.

He admitted under questioning that some external stimulus is occasionally useful.

> . . . quaking, you sit down at the typewriter. And that's when a glass of Scotch can be very useful as an ice-breaker . . . artificial infusion of a little bit of confidence which is necessary to begin at all.

He added, 'A page takes me quite a long time. Two pages a day is good. Three pages is splendid.' Three pages would work out at approximately 1,000 words a day; he revises as he goes along.

Wilbur Smith is a very model of consistent output. Living in South Africa, he reckons to start a new novel in February, when the local winter is approaching, and to deliver the complete script in October the same year. During the writing, he works from 8.30 a.m. to mid-afternoon every day and goes to bed at 8.30 p.m. His novels are usually about 180,000 words in length and so, allowing time for revision and clean typing, he writes about 30,000 words every month during his stint, or an average of 1,000 words a day throughout. Now in his mid-fifties, he has published twenty long novels in twenty-four years. His sales are over 40 million; indeed, Pan Books alone have sold 19 million copies of nineteen of his novels.

Joseph Heller says:

> I ordinarily write three or four handwritten pages and then rework them for two hours. I can work for four hours, or forty-five minutes. It's not a matter of time. I set a realistic objective: How can I inch along to the next paragraph?

And Gore Vidal strikes a realistic note – how much an author depends on the state of his digestion:

> First coffee. Then a bowel movement. Then the muse joins me . . . The first sentence is all-important.
>   Whenever I get up in the morning, I write for about three hours. I write novels in longhand on yellow legal pads . . . For some reason I write plays and essays on the typewriter. The first draft usually comes rather fast . . . I never re-read a text until I have finished the first draft. Otherwise, it's too discouraging . . . For me the main pleasure of having money is being able to afford as many completely retyped drafts as I like . . . I get through four, five, six. The more the better, since my style is very much one of afterthought.

At the end of each workday I do make notes on what the next day's work will be.

It is perhaps surprising – and would no doubt have been especially pleasing to Evelyn Waugh – to note how many established novelists retain the eighteenth-century method of writing books in their own hand or by the typewriter, which was invented nearly a hundred years ago. Novelists have often told me that they like to *see* the words emerging on to the paper; they feel more in control and they have a sense of achievement as one line follows another, gradually working their way down the page. Some prefer the fountain pen or the ballpoint or the felt-tip pen because it keeps them in direct contact with their medium. As one writer put it:

> This may sound mystical but I do believe it's essential – at least for me – to feel that something's flowing straight from here [he tapped his head] through my right arm, my hand, my forefinger and thumb, into the pen and right on to the paper without a break. When the words are coming fast; nothing must break that circuit.

Something of a pattern is discernible even from these random examples. Authors, at least, look on their writing as 'real work'. They spend a regular amount of time each day at their desks (or the dining-room table) getting some words on to paper. On average, the output seems to run around 1,000 words during the working day. There are great exceptions: Macmillan announced in the late 1970s that Jane Duncan, who wrote the *My Friend* series, would often, when in full flight, achieve up to 12,000 words a day. Barbara Cartland, of course, has always worked prodigiously. Allowing for interviews, many of which she records in some detail in her *Who's Who* entry, correspondence, holidays and some attendance on the prolific business side of her writing, she must have averaged on working days an outflow of anything from 6,000 to 10,000 words, day after day

Flaubert might have been appalled, but professional novelists write at the speed that suits them best. The one thing they have in common, when 'on the job', is to regard themselves as honest toilers, working a set number of hours per day for four, five or even seven days a week.

In discussing the working habits of novelists, it is worth studying in some detail the career and output of one such dedicated professional who has been earning his living – and a good living – ever since the end of the Second World War. Jon Cleary, an Australian, saw active service in the Middle East and New Guinea. In the early peacetime period, he and his family lived for lengthy spells in London, New York and the Italian Riviera but for many years now he has stayed permanently in his native Sydney, apart from regular trips abroad for research and an annual round-the-world journey to visit his main publishers and agents.

His first novel, *You Can't See Round Corners*, won the *Sydney Morning Herald* fiction prize of £1,000. Translated into post-inflation money, that would be the equivalent of nearly £15,000 today. It was published in Britain in 1947 by Eyre & Spottiswoode and was favourably received. Graham Greene, who was then editorial director, invited Cleary to call on him. It was a memorable meeting for the tyro, who looked on Greene as his hero among current novelists. As he put it to me during our interview, 'In those days I was influenced by certain writers, particularly by Graham Greene because he can say more in a page than the rest of us can say in a chapter. He's one of the most economical authors I know. I was a great admirer of H. E. Bates, who had a sensual feel for the countryside and for his women characters. Since then, I've developed my own style but that influence was there. The dialogue influence was through John O'Hara, who had an absolutely flawless ear.

'At the meeting, Greene said to me, "Now you're going to write your second book." The analogy he used was of a paratrooper. He said, "You're scared when you jump out the first time but you don't really know what's going on. The second time you jump out, you know what it's all about and so it's much tougher." He went on to say, "I wrote my first novel and I was feeling my way, so then I wrote a thriller to learn about construction. It's the best format of the lot if you want to know how to construct a novel." That's one of the best pieces of advice I've ever been given about writing.'

Eyre & Spottiswoode changed its fiction policy soon afterwards and Mr Cleary moved to Werner Laurie, where he wrote three novels including *The Sundowners*, which was highly praised. He was then living near London and, as a keen cricketer, was invited to play in the Authors v. Publishers match at Vincent Square. Billy Collins, head of the firm of Collins, was captain of the Publishers.

'As he crossed over at the end of an over, he would say, "Happy where you are?" I thought he meant, was I happy to be scoring runs and so I said, "Yes, why not?" After I'd been batting for half an hour and he'd repeated the question three or four times, the penny dropped! After lunch, he asked, "Would you care to play next Wednesday for the Collins authors against the house?" . . . In those days, gentlemen publishers didn't pirate other authors – but Billy was the last of the Calvinist pirates! I talked it over with my agent who said I might as well leave Werner Laurie as my editor there was about to leave anyway. I had no particular loyalty to the others at Werner Laurie and so I joined Collins in 1953 and have been with them ever since.

'I belong to the lucky generation. When I first started to write, it didn't matter if your first or second novel didn't sell because there was a market for short stories. In America, there were at least eight magazines that would pay $750 for your first story, $1,000 for your second one and so on. When I wrote my last story for the *Saturday Evening Post* in 1952, I was getting $2,500 a story. If you didn't sell to the top magazines, you could work down to *Argosy*, whose top price was $750 but who would usually pay $500. In England, there were *Britannia and Eve*, *John Bull*, *Argosy*, *Strand Magazine* and *Everybody's*. In England, I would get between £50 and £75 for a story that had already been sold in the States. Then there was the Australian market, there was *Outspan* in South Africa. I always made enough to pay the grocer and the rent out of short stories . . . There was no inflation in those days: inflation was something that had happened to the Germans after the Great War!

'A young writer today doesn't have that backstop. If he writes a novel that doesn't click, he says, "The hell with it" and he turns to television and says he will make his money there – if he can get in. "When I've got my stake, I'll go back and write another novel." And it never happens. If he's successful at television, it's writing to a formula and he gets used to the mink-lined set-up . . . The only man who's successfully changed from that highly paid medium to another where he's equally highly paid is Sidney Sheldon. Sidney started as a screenwriter – he was an apprentice screenwriter at MGM when he was eighteen – and later he had three hits at once on Broadway for which he'd written the "book" . . . William Goldman was a novelist who became a screenwriter. He goes on writing novels but they haven't lived up to his early promise. That's the trap for the young writer today.

'There isn't the same relationship between publisher and author as there was when I started . . . I've been with Collins since 1953 and with Morrow in the States since 1954. That was the day of the old-fashioned publisher: you were part of a family. I'm still looked on as "family" but that's because I'm one of the oldest inhabitants. There is not the same approach to authors . . . with money men running the place. I don't think they can nurture authors that way.'

I asked Jon Cleary to describe in some detail how he sets out to write a new novel. He answered, 'I usually start with a character and an idea. Sometimes I get it from a headline in a newspaper but I'll give you a definite example – *The High Commissioner*. It was one of my better selling novels, was made into a movie and goes on being reprinted. I was living in London at the time and was on my way to Australia House, when I bumped into a detective sergeant I'd known in Australia some years before. While I was waiting for the lift, the thought came into my mind, "What if he were here to arrest the High Commissioner for murder?" I thought some more – and that was more or less the opening sentence of the book. *"We want you to go to London," said the Premier, "and arrest the High Commissioner for murder."*

'I pride myself on my research. I don't think I've written a book where I haven't visited part of the location at least . . . Any writer will say that you only use 10 per cent of the research but having the other 90 per cent in the back of your mind gives you some authority. I did a book called *Pulse of Danger* set in the Himalayas. There's a small apple up there called a *lachen*, like a Christmas apple in England, and I had my characters stay overnight in a Buddhist *lamaserai*. They were fed tea with yak butter in it – one of the most vile-tasting concoctions ever – and were given *lachen* apples. I got no less than seven or eight letters from all round the world asking where they could get cuttings to grow *lachen* apples. It's gratifying to see that someone reads every line!

'Having got my idea, I then sit down and do "character blocks", which usually each run to a foolscap page single-spaced – where the man was born, where he was educated, his idiosyncrasies, what habits he's got, his medical history, his relationships, what music he likes. It was a scheme that Scott Fitzgerald used.

'Then I do "chapter blocks". I do only the first four chapters in "blocks"; I might describe the weather on a particular day, I choose the location for whatever sequence I want. I do all this by hand, writing on American yellow legal pads with a ballpoint pen. My first twenty-five novels were all written in longhand but, as I got older, I found that tiring and now work straight on to the typewriter. I *don't* use a word processor. I started writing in 1940 when I joined the army and up to last year I'd only had two typewriters in the whole of that forty-seven years. I had an old Royal portable and, when that finally wore out, I bought myself an Olympia portable. Last year, my elder daughter persuaded me to come into the twentieth century and I paid $1,000 [Australian] for an electronic with bells on it – and it slowed down my output 50 per cent! I suffered it for three weeks and then I put it away and went out and paid $90 for an old ironframe Olympia, which must be at least thirty years old. It sounds like a threshing machine – and I'm happy as Larry. My wife is happy, too; she knows I'm working because she can hear it, whereas with the electronic one there was no noise at all. For a novelist like myself, I can't see the use of a word processor . . . I like to see the words going on to the page.

'Once I've done my four chapter blocks, I've got an idea where I'm going – and then I start. The chapter blocks are fairly detailed; they're really treatments of the chapters. If the characters haven't taken over the story by then, all I've got are cardboard cut-outs. So I don't do any more chapter blocks until I get within two chapters of the end. By then, I know where I'm going but I need to tie up the ribbons, if you like. I don't do an awful lot of note-taking but when I finish working each day, I just jot down where I will be going tomorrow.

'I usually do between 1,500 and 2,000 words a day – five foolscap typed pages, triple-spaced. If there's a lot of dialogue – I like writing dialogue – that might be only 1,500 words that day. But when I finish those five pages, even if it's going well, I knock off. It's better to go to bed knowing what I'm going to write tomorrow than to go to bed with an empty skull and lie awake all night wondering what I'm going to write. You get up next day and you're too tired. I believe, again, that was a working habit of Scott Fitzgerald. Everybody thinks of him as a drunk who caroused all the time but he was a most disciplined writer. I'm a naturally disciplined person, so I didn't have to learn that sort of thing.

'I can write anywhere because I learned to write in an army tent with five other fellows [in it] during the war . . . There's a big picture window in my study but I sit with my back to it. I'm always at my desk by nine in the morning, almost as if I'm working for a public service. I usually work until about eleven thirty and sometimes, if it's coming well, I've got my quota finished by then . . . I know when I get up at the end of my morning session whether I've done a good day's work or not.

'When I go back after lunch, I read those 1,500 words or whatever, which have taken me two and a half hours to write: now they take me three minutes to read. That fits into perspective because the reader will only take three minutes to read it . . . Sometimes, it's necessary for me to go back in the afternoon to finish my quota. I never work at night – I just find that's tiring. I get my quota done each day and I keep working on until my first draft is done. I work Mondays to Fridays – no weekends. I'm strictly a union man!

'I never send anything off to my agent or my publisher until I've finished. A lot of writers will do 30,000 words and send them off. I've done that once or twice but it's not a system that works for me. I never know how a book of mine is going to end and if I send off 30,000 words to an editor and he or she starts writing back, saying "I think this should be changed or that should be changed", all it does is deaden my enthusiasm. So I go through and finish my first draft, which is also my fair copy. I don't send it out to a typist: I'm a very clean typist myself. Then I have so many copies xeroxed locally.

'I'm fortunate in that I very rarely have to rewrite. I don't think I've ever had to restructure a book . . . but the agent or the editor may write back and . . . come up with a few valid points. With my latest book, my new editor in London came up with three very valid points that meant my rewriting three pages in each case – nine pages of rewriting in a 350-page manuscript. But she'd improved it because she'd picked various things I'd overlooked.'

Few novelists have the stamina and level of professional skill to continue publishing with success for such a long continuous period. Perhaps Jon Cleary revealed something of his secret when he said, 'If people say writing's a lonely chore, they're not creating characters they're interested in . . . I've been writing for forty-seven years now and I enjoy my writing just as much as when I started. More – because I know my craft.'

CHAPTER II

# Bestsellers – Born or Made?

Literary success liberates the tensions generated by a
hostile environment by removing the environment and
so prepares the way for literary failure.
Cyril Connolly's Second Law (1960)

Dust hath closéd Helen's eye,
Worms feed on Hector brave.
Thomas Nashe

To adapt the government anti-smoking warnings, writing novels can
seriously injure your health. Let us regard soberly the roll of honour
over the past fifty years, bearing in mind recent statistics which show
that, on average, men are expected to live until their mid-seventies
and women a few years longer.

F. Scott Fitzgerald – died aged 44; Albert Camus (road accident) – 46;
Jacqueline Susann – 53; Peter Cheyney – 55; Ian Fleming – 56; Paul
Scott – 57; Virginia Woolf (suicide) – 58; Desmond Bagley – 59; Nevil
Shute – 60; R. F. Delderfield – 60; Nigel Balchin – 61; Ernest
Hemingway (suicide) – 62; James Baldwin – 63; John Braine – 63;
Dashiell Hammett – 63; Evelyn Waugh – 63; Alistair MacLean – 64;
John Creasey – 64; Charles Morgan – 64; C. S. Lewis – 64; John
O'Hara – 65; John P. Marquand – 66; John Steinbeck – 66; C. S.
Forester – 66; Jane Duncan – 66.

To balance this sombre roll-call, one can point to J. B. Priestley
who died in his ninetieth year, to Somerset Maugham and P. G.
Wodehouse who lived on into their nineties and Graham Greene
who is still going strong in his eighties. Eden Philpotts, as already
mentioned, wrote his last novel at ninety-five and Frank Swinnerton
died at ninety-eight, still writing. But in the main, novelists, who
like spiders spin their works out of their own entrails, are subject to
unusual stresses. Theirs tends to be a sedentary life, hunched over a

desk, whether it be writing by longhand or typing or tapping the keys of a word processor. Some of them – the men, perhaps, more than the women – smoke heavily, some drink heavily and some do both heavily. And as Ted Allbeury remarked after finishing his twelfth novel, 'It doesn't get easier, it gets harder'.

The beginner, who may have the good luck to be a natural story-teller, starts on page one and in blissful ignorance presses on to the end. Quite often, the instinctive recipe works first time. But, as he gains experience with each successive novel and begins to learn about 'pace' and 'construction' and 'conflict' and 'mini-climaxes' and 'the end climax', he gradually realises how difficult it is. Like Monsieur Jourdain, he began by speaking (or writing) prose without realising it. Now the intricacies of technique start to rear up like barriers between him and his story.

In our 'ever upwards' society where there are salary rises but seldom salary decreases, he is taught to expect that every new book will attract a higher advance than the previous book, he sees his contemporaries, certainly no worthier and often less worthy, attracting outrageously high (in his terms) advances – and always he has to come back and work his magic on the next blank page, and then the next blank page after that; and on and on. His agent will be a sympathetic friend and his editor, if he has not moved on to another house, will help him with constructive advice, but when he is confronting that clean white page first thing every morning, he is on his own. It is little wonder, perhaps, that many novelists die untimely through cancer or heart disease, both stress-related illnesses.

Many years ago, Evelyn Waugh wrote an essay in the *Cornhill*. His main contention was that the writing instrument largely dictated the author's style and output. For example, the quill pens used in the eighteenth century – with their continual need to be dipped into the inkwell and to be sharpened – led to a leisurely balanced prose style with antithetical sentences. Novel-writing then took much longer and so Richardson, Fielding, Walpole and Smollett each wrote half a dozen novels or fewer in a lifetime. By the middle of the nineteenth century, the fountain pen had been invented. Now an author could write for several hours without having to replenish the instrument. Hence the discursive and ongoing style of a Dickens or a Thackeray and their considerable output. Seventy years later, the typewriter had long arrived – and with it the staccato prose of novelists who had also been journalists like Ernest Hemingway.

The breakdown of prose style, according to Waugh, came with the dictating machine. Novelists could ramble away at high speed in a conversational but prolix way. He did not live long enough to see the increasing use of the word processor but one imagines that he would have been equally scathing about its effect on new writers.

There are many other factors that influence novelists to write in their particular style – their own personalities, for a start, their education, the influence of established novelists during their formative reading years, the possibly subconscious influence of films and television on the way they construct their stories. For example, the advent of 'rolling credits' thirty-five years ago in the movies – where the action and atmosphere were established as, or even before, the title and the production screen credits were shown – may well have encouraged novelists, almost without conscious knowledge, to opt for a dramatic opening with no immediate attempt to describe and develop the leading characters. Graham Greene, highly experienced in writing screenplays, has always been a master at this kind of 'button-holing' start to a novel. On the other hand, many bestselling modern novelists – Irving Wallace and Barbara Taylor Bradford are two examples – have usually stuck to the Victorian leisurely approach, where a character's antecedents from the cradle to the moment of the novel's action are recounted in detail and the physical appearance of the characters, the clothes he or she wears and the places where they live, with each item of furniture and furnishings, lovingly described. At any one time, the novel exists, indeed flourishes, on several different cultural levels: Angela Carter and Barbara Cartland, Ian McEwan and Alistair MacLean, have their contemporary and not always mutually exclusive admirers.

If commercial influences have had a marked effect on the writing of post-war full-length fiction, that effect should be most noticeable among the major bestsellers. Here we come up against two radically opposed theories. The first, explored at length in J. A. Sutherland's *Bestsellers*, published in 1981, propounds the view that bestsellers are made, not born. As Sutherland puts it:

Nor are bestsellers entirely made by their 'authors'; a whole string of agents, editors and salesmen could – if copyright law and literary convention allowed – claim 'credits' in an essentially corporate venture.

Anyone with inside knowledge of the publishing trade will know at once that this claim is either totally inaccurate or at the best applicable to the tiniest minority of bestselling novelists. Some agents and some editors work very closely with their authors, both in discussing plot ideas and in helping to develop the text by constructive criticism of each draft. But woe betide any agent or editor who tried to foist his own ideas on one of the five biggest-selling contemporary novelists – Jeffrey Archer, Frederick Forsyth, Dick Francis, John le Carré and Wilbur Smith – or who tried to shape the delivered text according to his own criteria.

Mr Sutherland appears to be on safer ground when he states:

Bestsellers and big publishers make natural partners

or

Rarely in MacLean's novels is it directly indicated that men and women have genitals, or that one sex's set is different from the other's

or

The bestseller . . . has an intimate connection with the news. Frequently, it presents itself as 'tomorrow's headlines'.

The summary of his theory occurs in the following passages:

Very largely speaking, the bestseller has two functions. The first is economic. It exists to sell the best and make money for its producers and merchandisers. The second more flexible function is ideological. The bestseller expresses and feeds certain needs in the reading public. It consolidates prejudice, provides comfort, is therapy, offers vicarious reward or stimulus . . .

Fiction is therefore constantly testing response and itself responding to the market. Its supply-demand-supply cycle is rapid, pulsating, constantly adapting.

Mr Sutherland appears to overrate bestselling novelists in some areas and underrate them in others. As a publisher and, later, as a literary agent, I have worked with several hundred novelists since the Second World War, some of them household names. I do not know of a single one who tried to analyse his or her readership or who redesigned the techniques, the integral approach and even the kind of novel he or she writes in direct response to market conditions. Indeed, most novelists are incapable of such changes. Whatever artistic level his books attain, the novelist has to *believe* in his abilities, be deeply serious about what he is doing. Writing a novel is not like applying make-up when entering a fancy dress competition. It involves at the least several weeks and months of unremitting slogging away. Just as clever journalists with a gift for parody sometimes try to knock off, tongue-in-cheek, a short story for a woman's magazine – and always fail – so Mills & Boon would inevitably spot as insincere and self-conscious a novel deliberately aimed at them by a clever young man or woman who was indulging in what he or she thought was a spot of intellectual slumming. In my experience, a novelist writes what is in him to be written. If a certain series of novels fails or shows steadily diminishing sales, the writer might well discontinue that series and try to shift to different ground – by, for example, breaking away from historical novels into modern adventure stories – but generally his style of writing and his technique of plot construction will remain as before, directed at a new target. The essential *him* remains.

Bestselling novels arise in one of three different ways. There is the 'thunderclap' way – the book that makes a loud bang out of a clear blue sky. It is usually a first novel or a second or third novel by a virtually unknown author. Examples are *The Naked and the Dead* by Norman Mailer, *Lucky Jim* by Kingsley Amis, *HMS Ulysses* by Alistair MacLean, James Jones's *From Here to Eternity*, Frederick Forsyth's *The Day of the Jackal* and John le Carré's *The Spy Who Came in from the Cold*. Almost without exception, novelists who take the public fancy by storm in this way continue throughout their careers – or at least for a considerable time – to attract a large band of loyal readers.

The second way is the gradual approach. The author in question usually starts more than moderately well and turns out to have a steady, sometimes prolific, output where each succeeding novel fares that much better than its predecessors. Examples would include Paul Scott, Dick Francis, P. D. James, Ruth Rendell and Wilbur Smith. In each case, it took perhaps ten to twenty novels, often published at yearly intervals, for the respective author to break into the charmed circle of top-selling novelists, although Heinemann did print and sell 20,000 copies of Wilbur Smith's very first novel. Both Dick Francis and P. D. James benefited through a latish breakthrough in the United States, which reflected back favourably on their British status. In all the popular arts – films, television, the novel – America since the war has had a far greater influence on European sales than we often care to admit. Unless the subject-matter is highly arcane, a bestselling American novel will almost certainly hit the British bestseller lists, whereas many bestselling British novels will get nowhere in the States.

Which brings us on to the third way in which a novel may become a bestseller – by 'hype'. In a later chapter 'The Crunch', I suggest that the British agent who felt he had a big bestseller in the making would probably take the script, or a detailed treatment and a few specimen chapters, to auction in New York before repeating the process in London. Arthur Hugh Clough was a prophet as well as a poet when he wrote, 'But westward look, the land is bright!'

The 'hypable' novel is usually by a newcomer (or an experienced author working under a pen-name). The reason is simple. Publishing nowadays deals in 'futures', rather like the Stock Exchange. The new is exciting; it has no track record to quantify hope. Publishers know from long and hard experience that it is virtually impossible to shift a novelist who has brought out six or more novels above the sales record he has established in the trade. However much advertising or publicity is devoted to his new book, the sharp edge of the battle is at the point where the representative goes into a bookshop soliciting orders. He may well say – and indeed believe – that 'this is X's best novel by far' but the seasoned bookseller will usually shrug and reply, 'I've heard that one before. Let's see, I took half a dozen of the last one – put me down for another six this time.' It is so much easier to wax lyrical when there are no previous results to measure the book against.

The novel to be hyped often turns out to be aimed at women readers, who provide some 60 per cent of the general readership. It may be a family saga spread over three generations or a modern novel with a background where women are likely to be dominant – high fashion, the distaff side of Hollywood, jewellery, the perfume industry. It usually includes some esoteric (more than erotic) sex passages. Recent examples are *Destiny* by Sally Beauman and Shirley Conran's *Lace*.

This third method of entry into bestsellerdom is the only one that supports Mr Sutherland's contention that bestsellers are 'made', not 'born'. Claud Cockburn, who in 1972 published a book with an almost identical title, *Bestseller*, took the opposite view. His book concentrated on novels published between the turn of the century and the outbreak of war in 1939. A *Bookseller* report of his speech in June 1972 to the Publishers' Publicity Circle said,

> Mr Cockburn added that the idea of bestsellers being made rather than born downgraded the author and his craft. He believed it was true in the past and true now, that there was a born element in bestsellers.

It has to be added that the 'born element' often sadly proved to be a short-lived one. Nearly all the authors discussed in *Bestseller* were out of print by 1972. In the 1930s Cassell had kept forty-seven Warwick Deeping titles in print; three decades later, there was only one – *Sorrell and Son*. There was only one Michael Arlen title in print – *The Green Hat*. Of thirteen A. S. M. Hutchinson titles, only one was extant – and that was not, as might be expected, *If Winter Comes* but *Once Aboard the Lugger*. Twenty P. C. Wren titles had been reduced to three; thirty-five W. J. Locke titles were down to five.

Britain in particular and the world in general probably changed more in the third of a century after 1939 than at any other comparable period in history. The invention of antibiotics, man-made fibres, nuclear weapons, the contraceptive pill, the universal spread of television, the jet engine, the loss of empire, the welfare state – these did much to change the way of life and the expectations of succeeding generations. So it is not surprising that stories appealing to what I. A. Richards termed 'stock responses' would be swept into oblivion as the brave new world rolled on.

Yet the special vision, allied to a special skill with words, usually endures. Leonard Woolf in the final volume of his memoirs, *Downhill all the Way*, published in 1967, mentions that in the six years up to 1924, Virginia Woolf, a contemporary of Deeping, Arlen, Hutchinson, Wren and Locke, earned just £229 in Britain and America for her three novels, *The Voyage Out*, *Night and Day* and *Jacob's Room*, an annual stipend less than Oliver Goldsmith's vicar of Auburn in *The Deserted Village* enjoyed over 150 years earlier. But, forty years and more since her death, Virginia Woolf has remained steadily and increasingly in print. If her English language sales today – including all the trade paperback, school and campus editions – were totted up, they would show her as a bestseller to match her more ephemeral contemporaries.

'Paperback' is the operative word for present-day bestsellers. Cassell published Nicholas Monsarrat's *The Cruel Sea* in 1951 and by the end of 1953 had sold over 750,000 copies in hard covers at the original net price of 12s 6d (62½p). By the tenth anniversary after first publication the full-price sales were 1.2 million, easily a post-war British record for a novel. But Cassell deliberately held off a paperback edition while the hardbound one sold well. Alistair MacLean's first novel *HMS Ulysses* sold over 300,000 in 1956 in the Collins hardcover editions. Nevil Shute and Daphne du Maurier would have first hardcover printings of over 150,000 copies – for sale in the trade, not through book clubs. But in the first decade after 1945 the full paperback revolution had yet to arise. In the succeeding thirty years, probably fewer than five novels in any one year would sell more than 100,000 copies in their hardcover editions through the trade, and of those sales between 25 per cent and 35 per cent would be for export.

For sheer aggregate sales, book for book the highest-selling British novelist alive today must be Catherine Cookson. The worldwide sales of her sixty-five novels exceed 85 million copies. And yet she was forty-three before her first book was published. For nearly ten years Macdonald built her hardcover sales slowly and steadily until in 1958 Corgi bought paperback rights in *Rooney* for an advance of £150 on account of a home royalty of 1⅞d per copy and an export royalty of ¼d per copy. It took another ten years before her paperback sales broke through but since 1969 Corgi has sold over 32 million copies of fifty-two novels. Catherine Cookson moved from Macdonald to Heinemann in 1973 with *The Mallen Streak* and has recently moved her hardcover rights again to Bantam Press. Without a flourishing paperback industry, she would always have had a solid band of (mainly library) readers but it is the wide spread of cheap paperback editions that has reinforced and widened her appeal.

What are the prospects for new novelists as we approach the last decade of the century? Statistics provide some comfort but, as Arthur Koestler observed, 'Statistics don't bleed'. In the fifty years to 1980, allowing for the exigences of the wartime period and the aftermath of paper rationing, the annual total of published full-length fiction, including reprints and works translated from other languages, remained for a long time in the fairly narrow band of 3,500 to 4,500 annual titles. For example, in 1939 it was 4,222 and only in 1956 did it drop as low as 3,443. In the seven years to 1987, it has shown a small but steady increase from year to year – from 4,747 in 1981 to 4,879 to 5,265 to 5,537 to 5,846 to 6,002 and finally to 6,389 in 1987. Throughout all this period, the American output of novels, in spite of the vast geographical and population differences, has run at around 50 per cent to 70 per cent of the British totals.

One main reason for the steady publication graph in the United Kingdom and its greater number of annual titles must be the presence here of a universal and well-organised public library system with over 600 million lendings a year. The existence of many more serious national daily and Sunday newspapers with their comparatively large space devoted to fiction reviews has also encouraged publishers to take a chance on unknown novels in the hope that sympathetic reviews will aid their sales. And until recently British publishers – or the majority of them – were sufficiently independent to publish a book for the hell of it without keeping both eyes fixed on 'the bottom line'; their overheads were low enough to give them the luxury of taking a modest chance several times a year.

But the perspective changes sharply when one contrasts the slowly increasing annual fiction output with the rocketing overall growth of British publications each year. In 1946 – admittedly an unrepresentative year when publishing was still struggling with the hangover of wartime shortages – there were 1,995 new and reprinted fiction titles out of a grand total of 11,411: 17.5 per cent. In 1966, the fiction total was 4,263, the overall total 27,424: 15.5 per cent. In 1986, 6,002 as compared with 57,845: 10.4 per cent. So the proportion of fiction in the post-war period has declined by just over 40 per cent. In 1987 there were 6,389 fiction titles out of 59,837 titles in all – the proportion was virtually the same: 10.6 per cent.

The decline is even greater when one looks at the turnover figures. In 1985, British publishing turned over a (then) record amount of £1.934 billion. Hardback fiction sales accounted for £73.43 million and paperback fiction sales for £80.57 million – £154 million for the two together. That works out at 7.86 per cent of the total turnover. A large part of the decline in value is due to the increased impact of paperback sales at well under half the published price of hardcover titles. But the figures must mean that, apart from the relatively few bestselling novels, the majority is being elbowed out of the available

28

display space in bookshops by the dictionaries, reference books, royalty books and gimmick books that more and more monopolise the non-fiction bestseller lists.

How does a new novelist get published today? Forty years ago, he might have cut his teeth – and been spotted by perceptive editors – through writing short stories for one or other of the numerous general magazines then prospering: *Argosy, John Bull, Everybody's*, the *Cornhill, Illustrated, John O'London's Weekly, Picture Post*, the *Strand Magazine* – all of them killed first by the spread of television and then by the 'give-away' colour magazines published with national Sunday newspapers, none of which (with the exception of the *Telegraph* magazine) has encouraged short-story writing. It has been said that Graham Greene was first spotted as a likely author by a piece he wrote for the *Cambridge Review* in his youth. In the 1950s Ian Chapman, then working in Collins' Bible department, and his wife Marjory were moved by a short story they read that had won a competition in the *Glasgow Herald*. He met the author, a schoolmaster named Alistair MacLean, and without reference to anyone else in Collins persuaded him to write a novel. The result was *HMS Ulysses*, the first of a long string of bestselling novels. It is a matter for wonder whether that piece of history could repeat itself now, for today only Bill Buford's *Granta*, also of Cambridge origin but now backed by Penguin, could claim to discover and encourage new fiction writers.

A large London publisher may receive in any one year 2,000 or more unsolicited manuscripts. Many literary agencies would expect to get at least 500 thudding on to their reception desks. The agent's tastes would be more catholic: the book that Publisher A would not touch might well be one for Publisher B. Even so, it is doubtful whether more than 5 per cent of those unsolicited scripts would be taken on by an agent – and probably not much more than 1 per cent would eventually be accepted by a publisher. At any given time, there may well be up to 10,000 scripts circulating in a Dante-like progress through one or other of the circles of publishing hell, perhaps 60 per cent of them – 6,000 indeed – being fiction. And of that vast number perhaps fifty may end up with a publishing contract.

This sad fact is borne out by a significant note in the *Bookseller*'s issue of 11 September 1987. It was announced that Hodder & Stoughton had high hopes of a first novel entitled *Chekago* by Natalya Lowndes (a pen-name), which they were to publish in January 1988. It happened to be an unsolicited script and the note went on to say: 'This is a rare publishing event. A spokesman goes so far as to say he cannot remember the last occasion on which a novel from the slush pile was published.'

As Kipling might have put it, 'High hopes faint on a warm slush pile'. We may be getting perilously close to the point, already long reached in the film world, where studios and producers will only pay attention to scripts submitted by recognised agents. In their turn, agents are always looking out for important new writing talent which will eventually replace their elderly existing clients, but an agent can only handle so many clients to his and their satisfaction and, if he spreads himself too thinly, all his clients may suffer. So, perhaps for the first time since the age of Dickens, there is a real and growing risk that genuine talent may go begging.

The prospects, however dim, are unlikely to deter those thousands of would-be novelists. As with pools winners, the lightning of luck strikes just often enough to inspire the dreamers of dreams to keep their eyes tight shut. Maeve Binchy did it and Sarah Harrison and Shirley Conran and Sally Beauman and, way back, Kingsley Amis and Frederick Forsyth and Jeffrey Archer – so why shouldn't I? is the secret hope that fuels them. One could answer them with a quotation from that clear-eyed exponent, Aldous Huxley:

A bad book is as much of a labour to write as a good one; it comes as sincerely from the author's soul. But the bad author's soul being, artistically at any rate, of inferior quality, its sincerities will be, if not always intrinsically uninteresting, at any rate uninterestingly expressed, and the labour expended on the expression will be wasted.

Nature is monstrously unjust. There is no substitute for talent. Industry and all the virtues are of no avail.

As an antidote to that depressing picture, here is a brief anthology of comments from leading writers on a subject they care deeply about and must have pondered over their working careers – the writing of full-length fiction.

The novelist should, I think, always settle when he starts what is going to happen, what his major event is to be. He may alter this event as he approaches it, indeed he probably will, indeed he probably had better, or the novel becomes tied up and tight.

E. M. Forster

The important thing is that you make sure that neither the favourable nor the unfavourable critics move into your head and take part in the composition of your next work.

A dramatist is one who believes that the pure event, an action involving human beings, is more arresting than any comment that can be made upon it. On the stage it is always *now*; the personages are standing on that razor-edge, between the past and the future, which is the essential character of conscious being; the words are rising to their lips in immediate spontaneity. A novel is what *took place*; no self-effacement on the part of the narrator can hide the fact that we hear his voice recounting events that are past and over, and which he has selected – from uncountable others – to lay before us from his presiding intelligence.

Thornton Wilder

I've never known anything good in writing to come from having accepted any free gift of money. The good writer never applies to a foundation. He's too busy writing something.

In my opinion it's a shame that there is so much work in the world. One of the saddest things is that the only thing a man can do for eight hours a day, day after day, is work. You can't eat eight hours a day nor drink for eight hours a day nor make love for eight hours – all you can do for eight hours is work.

William Faulkner

In one way, of course, all writing that is any good *is* experimental; that is, it's a way of seeing what is possible – what poem, what novel, is possible.

Robert Penn Warren

I've always felt strongly that a writer shouldn't get involved with other writers, or with people who make books, or even with people who read them. I think the farther away you get from the literary traffic, the closer you are to sources. I mean, a writer doesn't really *live*, he observes.

Nelson Algren

31

So many people have talked out to me books they would otherwise have written. Once you have talked, the act of communication has been made.

Angus Wilson

American writers, more than any others, are haunted by the fear of failure, because it's such a common pattern in America. The ghost of Fitzgerald, dying in Hollywood, with his comeback novel unfinished, and his best book, *Tender is the Night*, scorned – his ghost hangs over every American typewriter.

Writing is finally play, and there's no reason why you should get paid for playing. If you're a real writer, you write no matter what. No writer needs feel sorry for himself if he writes and enjoys the writing, even if he doesn't get paid for it.

Irwin Shaw

A novelist is a sort of mimic by definition.

Writing for me is to a large extent self-entertainment and the only child is driven to do that.

The only requirement, I think, is a room to oneself, however small.

When starting to think about any novel, part of the motive is: I'm going to show them, this time. Without that, a lot of what passes under the name of creative energy would be lost.

Kingsley Amis

The most important ingredient in writing fiction is that *choice* is always available.

Joseph Heller

It is not wise to solicit the opinions of publishers – they become proud if you do.

It is not the novel that is declining, but the audience for it . . . Eventually the novel will simply be an academic exercise, written by academics to be used in classrooms in order to test the ingenuity of students. A combination of Rorschach test and anagram. Hence the popularity of John Barth, a perfect U-novelist whose books are written to be taught, not to be read.

32

## Bestsellers – Born or Made?

Strange business, all in all. One never gets to the end of it. That's why I go on, I suppose. To see what the next sentences I write will be.

Gore Vidal

And what is writing about if it's not fulfilling your own dreams?

Michael Korda

Lord love you, being a writer isn't a profession, it's a condition.

John Wain

The lyfe so short, the craft so long to lerne.

Geoffrey Chaucer

CHAPTER III

# Still at Work

Experts ranked in serried rows
Fill the enormous plaza full
But only one is there who knows
And he's the man who fights the bull.

Robert Graves

In his presidential address to the Classical Association in 1960, Professor T. B. L. Webster said,

> Books about books, selected by assiduously reading books about books about books, may take up so much of our time that we abandon reading the classics themselves.

When I was well on with the research for the present study, I began to realise the considerable temptation of concentrating on secondary and tertiary sources and ignoring 'the horse's mouth'. Without having the time or the scope to emulate even in a modest way *The Paris Review*, I felt it essential to approach a few carefully selected novelists and try to find out how they set to work, what they considered to be their major problems and how they tackled them. It would be a bonus if they could throw any light on that mysterious shadowy area between the concept and the execution.

To give reasonable space to the results of each interview, it soon became apparent that only three or four novelists could be included out of the several dozen potential candidates. Just as savages in the Brazilian jungle resent having their photographs taken because they believe that the camera steals away their spirits, so some 'important' novelists today consider that they give something of themselves away each time they are interviewed. (To judge by certain interviews I have read, they have reason to feel thus.) Others were too busy working on a novel or publicising their latest offering or unwinding after the promotional tour was over.

From the many still available, I decided to get as wide a range of opinions as possible by approaching an acknowledged international bestseller, a 'quality' woman novelist and a long-term professional author to provide my ABC. Which indeed they did, as it fortuitously turned out – Jeffrey Archer, A. S. Byatt and Jon Cleary. I have quoted in Chapter I a substantial part of the Jon Cleary interview. What follows are the other two interviews in alphabetical order.


## Jeffrey Archer

The structure of a realistic novel requires an inherent sense of logic, a feeling of credibility, that real life so often lacks. Those strange coincidences we all experience, the apparently telepathic messages, the hundred-to-one shots that occasionally succeed – you can't, as they say, get away with them in a novel. If Mr Archer were to recreate his life story in fiction form and submit it under a pen-name, almost every publisher would reject it smartly on the grounds of incredibility.

A double Blue at Oxford for athletics and gymnastics, President of the Oxford University Athletics Club, representing Great Britain as a sprinter, holder of the university record for the hundred yards, a GLC member at twenty-six, Conservative MP for Louth at twenty-nine, a backbencher tipped for a ministerial post – then the crash into near-bankruptcy through unwise investments, resigning his seat after close on five years and the vow to pay off his creditors and rise again to affluence through writing novels. Through writing novels? At this point, the shrewd editor would close the script and toss it on to the reject heap with a laugh.

But, as the world knows, it happened. *Not a Penny More, Not a Penny Less* was published in 1975. Two years later came *Shall We Tell the President?* with the wide publicity caused through Mrs Jacqueline Kennedy's resignation from Viking, its American publisher. Another two years saw *Kane and Abel* published. By now, Jeffrey Archer was a rich man, having paid off his debts; with the publication of *The Prodigal Daughter* in 1982 he was a millionaire. By the time *First Among Equals* appeared in 1984 and *A Matter of Honour* in 1986 he was a multi-millionaire. It had only taken four or five years to achieve his vow. As if that was not enough to make his story almost ridiculously unbelievable, he decided to try his hand at a stage play and wrote *Beyond Reasonable Doubt*, which quickly became one of the biggest West End successes of 1987.

Our interview took place in November 1987. I knew him to be a keen cricketer and my first question was a gentle full toss outside the leg stump: '*How do ideas for novels come to you?*'

He dispatched it firmly to the boundary. 'I get asked that question more than any other question – by newspapermen, by journalists and by fans; almost as if you can go down to Marks & Spencer and buy ideas in packets. Ideas are the one God-given gift – the rest is hard work . . . For me, they come every single day of my life . . . That is the one gift that is necessary for a *story-teller* to succeed. A writer doesn't need it. A writer can survive on a tremendous amount of Greek, Latin, the classics, knowledge of literature and produce great work.'

My next question was: '*Do you tend to think of situations first or characters?*' He replied: 'Situations – in the sense that *Kane and Abel* is the story of two men born on the same day, one born with everything and the other born with nothing. I develop the characters afterwards . . . I want to write the story of the first woman President of the United States. I don't know what she looks like or what she does; that all comes later. The idea is the first thing. *First Among Equals* – four men want to be Prime Minister. I don't know anything about the four men – I just know I want to write a story about their trying to be Prime Minister.'

'*Do you bounce ideas off your editor or your agent before you start?*'

'Never. Otherwise, they'd be writing the novels and not me. Most editors and agents, when it actually comes to ideas, are moronic. Their judgment is much better later when they see the final work. Cortland (Cork) Smith (then at Viking Press), arguably one of the great and legendary living editors . . . once said the difference between an author and an editor is the first draft.'

'*How long do you take on average in researching a new novel?*'

'It's hard to answer in the sense that one does a lot of research before, a lot of research during and even a lot of research after one's finished the script. For example, if I'm writing a book – *A Matter of Honour* – about a man travelling across Europe and getting back to England and being chased the whole time, I have to do the whole job. I went to Switzerland, saw the Swiss banks, stayed in Swiss hotels, moved across Germany, moved across France, escaped in and out, got back. That was fine – a bonus before I sat down and wrote the book. But if you suddenly discover when you're writing the book, it actually doesn't work to go to Germany – what you really want to do is to go to Sardinia because you discover there's a monastery there that has got an icon in it, you have to start again. You can't say, "Ah, but the research I've done!"

'The brain and the mind and the imagination must go anywhere and I'll find halfway through a book, "Oh, I didn't research that, so I'll invent it." I know I'll pick it up afterwards but I mustn't stop the writing to go and do research on that because I'd then lose the whole flow . . . With the first draft, I'll go right through without a stop. It doesn't matter how bad the research is or what is going wrong with the research, I mustn't, mustn't, mustn't, stop. But I suppose every author does it a different way.

'The best example I can give you is *The Prodigal Daughter*. I have the girl growing up. (In a Jeffrey Archer story you get everything in the first page. You don't have to read the rest of the book. You know the whole story on page one. My secret is to try and hold you there for the next four hundred pages.) . . . On the third page of *The Prodigal Daughter*, there is a discussion between this girl and her father on whether he will supply the money to back her to be President of the United States. He says, "I'll go as far as New Hampshire with you" – which is the first primary. "But if you don't get 30 per cent [of the vote] in New Hampshire or come in the first three places, I won't give you any more money." And she agrees. And then you have the sentence: "The eleven-year-old girl turned and walked down the stairs." Every reader across the world has got the picture. "This is the kid who's going to be President and we're going to follow her." At that point, you could put the book down. All you've got to do is turn to the last page and see if she makes it. Thank God they read in between!

'Now this is the point I'm trying to make. On page 30 or 40, I think I'll have her tutored by an English governess, a Cheltenham Ladies College spinster, who will never have any children. In my mind, I had said we'll give her three pages and then kick her out. She lasted 200 pages and her death scene in my view is the best piece of writing in the book. It's because she took over.

'Now you can't research and anticipate that because the excitement happens while you're writing. In another scene, I suddenly decided I wanted her to cross the road and to give the effect that she'd been killed when it was in fact her dog that had been killed . . . She hadn't got a dog! So here I was on page 70 and I gave her a dog. When I did the rewrite, the dog had to be introduced on pages 12, 19, 23, 37, so that the dog fitted in and the death scene worked. But [in the first draft] I didn't stop and go back to work the dog in. I went on through, making a note that this had happened and it would have to be sorted out. You must keep the flow going, otherwise the reader will be jumping up and down. Again, it was Cork Smith who said, "Reading a Jeffrey Archer book is like being on an express train and there's one thing he hates – stations!"'

*'Do you lock yourself away to write a novel?'*

'I will allocate eight weeks and go away – somewhere like the Bahamas – in a house where no one could get me, no telephone, no contact, and sit down and write for eight weeks. Fifty-six days in a row – non-stop. I have an absolutely disciplined regime, I can't work in any other way. I don't have the ability to be casual. I don't have the ability to do it when the muse comes. There's no muse with me – I *work*. I get up at six, I will walk for an hour round the golf course, about two miles . . . I get back at seven, have a light breakfast and start writing at eight. I'll write from eight to ten, take a one-hour break, then write for another two hours. Then take a two-hour break. Then write from three till five. Take a one-hour break. Then six to eight. Then supper and bed. The first two hours are original writing – the only time (in the day) I do original writing. Between eleven and one I will rewrite what I wrote earlier in the morning. Between three and five I will continue the rewrite and so there will be the script I wrote in the first two hours expanded in two further sessions. That will be typed for me in the hour I take off. I go over it with a pencil between six and eight [in the evening], then bed and get up again at six the next morning.

'When it's finished – which in the case of *Kane and Abel* was nine weeks – I take a three-month break and do it again. The second time round it will take four weeks . . . The only draft that matters is the first draft . . . If your wife or child come in and interrupt you on the second draft, you can turn the page over and stop – it doesn't matter. While the ideas are coming out, while the ideas are flowing, it's a disaster to have an interruption.

'I write with a felt-tip pen all the time. I can't type, I don't know how to, dictating is for me lazy and disastrous. I handwrite every word – it's very tiring, it's very "work-ethic Somerset boy" but it's what I like. I feel good at the end of it, I feel I've done it, I've handled it – and it's me.

'I try to write ten handwritten pages every day, which works out at about 2,500 words. I conk out just before the two-hour mark. The originality stops. I'm tired and I put the pen down. You mustn't write another word when you're tired . . . I can do two hours of physical and mental concentration – I can't do more.'

*'How much are you influenced in the editing process by your editor or your agent?'*

'A tremendous amount . . . Richard Cohen is, I think, quite the most exceptional editor in the world today. The tradition is that there are no English editors – the great editors are in America. I've been told that for years. This may well be true overall but in the case of Richard Cohen, he's as good as Cork Smith. He's as demanding, as agonising, as annoying. He never gives in if he thinks you're wrong on something, he'll go on and on nagging you. His genius is not to say, "You should write a story about the first woman President" . . . it is to see that chapter three should be at chapter seven and chapter six should be chapter four and that you should do rewrites – even on sentences. He never actually writes a sentence or indeed a word – that would be insulting . . . His ability is to see where you'd written too much or written too little, that it needs an extra paragraph or that a paragraph should come out: in that, he's unequalled. I need him but in a sense Richard requires me. He's a frightful literary snob: he'd love to have a Booker Prize winner, a Nobel Prize winner – and die! . . . In fact, he gets a great kick out of having one author he considers an illiterate toad but who actually sells more than all his other authors put together.'

*'Is there a difference in principle between writing a novel and writing a play and how do you find the techniques differing?'*

'For me, there is one underlying importance – and that is the story. People go to see *Beyond Reasonable Doubt* every night – God bless 'em! – and pack it out because there's a story there. They're not going to get clever wordplay and come out thinking they've had "a literary experience", either with my books or with my play. If you go to *Beyond Reasonable Doubt*, you get a story from beginning to end and, if you like stories, that's all I pretend to do. I'm an entertainer – I'm not a literary genius.

'With a play there are many new techniques to learn . . . Dialogue has always been my strength because that is what moves a book along. This is a bit of a cliché but the great story-tellers are good at dialogue, the great writers are good at description. So I had a slight start in the sense that dialogue was my strength. Second was that I lived in the theatre. Before I became deputy chairman [of the Conservative Party], I used to go two or three times a week. I *love* the theatre. So I was an "amateur professional" but I still made a lot of mistakes. A good director, David Gilmore, guided me and helped me in the way an editor would, saying, "Look, you've got this girl going off in an evening dress and we need her back in a nightie. You've done it in three lines. What do you want the audience to do – sit and wait while she changes?" It never crossed my mind while I was writing it. In a book, she can change into a nightie in three lines. But in a play, you've got to get her offstage sixty seconds earlier and back on stage sixty seconds later, so that she's got another two minutes to get out of the evening dress and into the nightie. When I come to write my second play, I'll have learned all that. I'll know what I can and cannot do. That's called experience.'

Jeffrey Archer earns £2 million a year from his writing. After charging his duly incurred expenses and paying tax, he is probably left with about half that sum. He has never considered living permanently abroad in a tax haven and says, 'I was very lucky. My rise from penury to being one of the richest authors in the world . . . has been through eight years of Margaret Thatcher. I pay 60 per cent tax* – but I don't mind paying. It's a large sum of money but that's the privilege of staying in the country you want to be in.'

He gets a straight $17\frac{1}{2}$ per cent royalty on his hardcover sales in the United Kingdom and a straight 15 per cent on his paperback sales in the same territory. In the USA, the respective royalties are 15 per cent and $12\frac{1}{2}$ per cent. In both countries, the scales are, as one would expect, 'tops'. In Britain, however, the only advance he demands is a nominal £1. This is on the sensible grounds that (a) he does not need the money and (b) he trusts Hodder & Stoughton to do a good job for him and (c) if they succeed in doing so, the money will eventually arrive in the shape of very large post-publication royalty cheques. Very few novelists are in the same earnings bracket as Mr Archer but there are at least several dozen to whom a large advance is mainly a status symbol. It seems a pity that more of them do not share his attitude but are prepared to let themselves be bought and sold 'for a few dollars more'.

He put it thus: 'It's the human relationships that matter. I *need*

---

* In the 1988 Budget, the top rate of income tax was reduced to 40 per cent.

my agent, I *need* my editors – and I *need* to work with them. If you came to me and said, "Random House plus Collins will offer you five million" – it wouldn't mean a thing . . . The publisher who realises that the author is a human being and treats him as such is a very clever publisher. The publisher who thinks the only thing the author is interested in is money – in some cases it will be true but basically it's a stupid approach.'

'*Do you foresee many changes between now and the end of the century in the way successful novels are written, produced, sold?*'

'My books are incredibly simple story-telling. They would have worked a hundred years ago and they'll work in a hundred years' time . . . The video techniques will be important [to some novelists] – not to me, because I only want to write an original book . . . It's getting harder and harder for the first author to be launched and harder and harder for anyone to get into the top category. There are many more people right in the bottom category, very few now in the middle category and just a few of us on top of the mountain. When I first started, publishers told me stories of how "we produce four or five new authors a year".

'Bookshops and the public seem to be going for bestsellers and top names. Booksellers tell me it wasn't unusual for someone to come in and buy four or five paperbacks, two of which they knew they weren't going to like. Now they go in and buy one of mine or whoever it is they want. That's jolly rough on the new author . . . There used to be twenty authors doing quite well over Christmas – now there are three authors doing quite well over Christmas. At the end of the day, all that will really matter is the talent to tell a good story . . . It doesn't matter what changes happen in the rest of the century, what direction the world goes, the story-teller will win, the gimmick-people will lose, the great writers will survive. But the story-tellers will win.'

'*Finally, how do you see your own future as a novelist?*'

'When I read John le Carré, whom I greatly admire, as you know, and when I read even Dickens, after about eight of their books, I find it's a repetition – not of the same formula, that would be rude – but of the same general ideas all put down on paper and well written. I would rather write one more major novel and one more set of short stories and say, "That's it – that's all you're going to get." . . . Writing a book is like marathon running. It's wonderful when you've never done it before but once you've run a marathon and you know it aches for the next three weeks, it's not fun going

41

back and doing it the year after. The first one was easy in that way because you never know what the pain will be like. Now I *know* what writing a new *Kane and Abel* would cost me in time and energy. I'm going to do it once more and I'm going to write the best book I've ever written in my life. And I would like to do one more set of short stories. But I then want to say, "That's it."

'I don't want to write eight more novels because that will make me twenty more million pounds . . . I don't ever want to see my sales fall and I don't want anyone to say, "That's not as good as the last one." I think I could put my energies and my enthusiasm into that last set of short stories and that last novel – and put in every last ounce I've got.'


## A. S. Byatt

Antonia Byatt must be one of the most intelligent novelists writing today. After a brilliant academic career at Cambridge, she did further researches in English and American literature at Bryn Mawr College in the USA and at Somerville College, Oxford. She was for nine years an extra-mural lecturer at London University and also taught at the Central School of Art and Design; for a further nine years she was a lecturer in English at University College, London, before taking up full-time writing and reviewing. Her public duties include membership of a BBC advisory group from 1974 to 1977, the Kingman Committee on English Language and the Management Committee of the Society of Authors, where she is at present chairman. She has acted as a judge for the Booker Prize, the Hawthornden Prize, the David Higham Award and the Betty Trask Prize. She is a Fellow of the Royal Society of Literature.

I had sent her in advance a list of questions for our interview, which took place in mid-April 1988. The first question was: *'With your public duties and frequent reviewing, do you (a) find it difficult to set up a regular daily routine when writing a novel and (b) if so, how do you cope with the problem?'*

'I do the public duties not so much out of a sense of public duty as out of a curiosity about human beings. I actually like watching people on committees behaving like people on committees . . . Most novelists have no idea how people work in groups or corporate bodies; they over-emphasise personal relationships. Any novelist ought to know about all the manoeuvring that people do when they are working

together. Most women novelists don't – and it's a great limitation
. . . One ought to try to observe the world in which one finds oneself
living. Not all of it – I've no sense of myself as a recorder of the
whole of twentieth-century life. But if you don't observe some of it,
you can't pick up its voices and you start writing in the 1930s when
you're actually living in the 1980s.

'I had a marvellous conversation with the Japanese ambassador
about the cunning of men in public life, which I would never have
had if I hadn't been chairman of the Society of Authors. I actually
learned something, watching him talk about Mrs Thatcher and the
difference from the way men conducted public affairs. I do have an
insatiable greed about people. Slightly more boring people interest
me more than slightly more interesting people.'

'*Do you consider your expert knowledge of Eng. Lit. and critical theory has
had in any way an inhibiting effect on your own writing?*'

'I remember thinking it out, even at Cambridge, that there were
two ways to deal with this. One was simply to stop doing the criticism
and the other was to do so much that you weren't trapped by it; you
came out the other side with the desire to write . . . It's the most
theoretical aspects of literary criticism that make me want to write,
whereas, when I was teaching a class on the modern English novel,
it began slightly to nauseate me and I didn't want to write. If I get
on to really high-powered literary theory and the nature of aesthetics
and what is the nature of art, it jumps me off into feeling that writing is
the most important thing you can do and that it must be complicated
and beautiful.

'Technique . . . becomes easier as it becomes more difficult because
the problems become more interesting and therefore you take a harder
run at them . . . My first novel I wrote over and over again at
Cambridge. Of the writers that were around, the person I wanted
to write like was Elizabeth Bowen. I knew she wasn't really the
model but she was the only one I had in mind and so there was far
too much "sensibility" in that book. And there was D. H. Lawrence
who haunted it against my will . . . I had terrible problems with the
first novel over things like pace; I didn't know when to stop telling
any particular bit. As I get older, I find selection easier, I find the
jumps easier.

'If I don't know everything that happened to my characters, I
haven't invented that world. If they go out of the door, *I* know
what happened to them when they got the other side. It's very

43

hard not to tell it. In fact, you ought to jump two weeks and go into another place.

'I'm trying to learn to write faster. I wrote short stories in order to write them more spontaneously and faster – with some degree of success – in order to break this very tight critical grip I had on my work, which was also owing to writing it in little bits between earning money by teaching and looking after children and trying to hold the whole continuity of it in my head. I had a very strict formal shape that kept it going.

'Most days in the school term, I could write from ten to five – reading as well as writing. I would probably write flat out for two or three hours but I would read towards it, fiddle around in the notebook for another hour or so and perhaps reading for reviewing. I work up to it in the day. I start by reading something fairly easy until I've woken up, then I read something very, very difficult which starts my mind sparking and then I read what I've already written and what's in the notebook and then I start writing. That's the ideal pattern. Then I do a lot of writing. Then I take the dog out and think out the next bit. But it never quite works out because there's the telephone and the children and the Society of Authors and . . .

'While I'm writing a novel, I'd rather not review novels. I don't like to be thrown by thinking, "This is terribly good and it's not what I'm doing," or, if it's terribly bad, thinking, "Why am I bothering with this?" '

'*Why do you write novels?*'

'All my childhood, I lived inside a story I was telling myself, which was more interesting than what was happening. That was to do with reading. I kept saying to myself, "This world is better than that world." The reading and telling world was infinitely more interesting. If you write [a story], you put yourself in the reading and telling world. I've never written novels to make a social, didactic point or reform the world or, as some people do, to justify myself. And certainly not to make money. Increasingly now, I write them out of aesthetic pleasure. I get this intense, very pure pleasure from the shapes of putting things together, knowing that they fit. In the beginning, I didn't feel that because I was too scared. And it's out of an obsession with language.

'*When you decide on the idea to tackle next, can you say how you plan its development? For example, do situations or does a particular character (or set of characters) strike you first? Or both together? Or what? Do you tend to*

44

*use backgrounds you already know well or do you research closely some new*
*background? When you are writing the opening chapter, is the complete story*
*clear in your mind – and, if so, do you stick closely to it?"*

'I always research, even with backgrounds I know well. The novel
I'm writing actually began with a word and an idea. I suddenly
thought you could write a novel called *Possession* and the idea was
about Kathleen Coburn and Coleridge. She spent the whole of her
life on editing his work and it's a question of – does she possess him
or does he possess her? And then it spread out and a lot of people got
attached to this phrase and then several plots appeared and then I
started inventing poets and poetry and scholars and scholarship and
it grew from there. Neither Kathleen Coburn nor Coleridge comes
in at all, so in a sense it began with the word.

'On the whole, the story moves along in the way it's been planned
to move from the beginning to the middle to the end. Sometimes,
things that you thought were part of it can't happen when you get
there because you see that they were implausible or unnecessary.
Quite often, the set-piece you thought was coming turns out to be
unnecessary. But, in general, I stick to my overall plan.'

She then showed me two or three of her working notebooks, large
stiff-covered exercise books. A sample page might include in her
small, precise handwriting a note on one of the characters, reminders
to herself on various plot points, quotations and, in the case of the
novel she was then working on, many lines of poetry that she had
herself created for inclusion in the story. Here was the 'anatomy of a
novel', an author's dissection of her own thoughts and the gleanings
of wide and deep reading that in the end the mysterious creative
process would turn into a full-length imagined story.

'I started the notebooks in the early days of my first marriage
because I saw that I had to create a continuity of thinking if I was
going to have to work in tiny little snatched bits. And so I wrote
everything down. You could always start again by reading what you'd
written down because it all came back into a form. Also, the act of
moving the pen over the paper would start you. All this planning
gives me great pleasure.'

We then discussed an episode in her novel *Still Life*, where Stephanie,
one of the major characters, is killed through accidentally electrocuting
herself by touching the socket of a power plug in the kitchen, just at
the moment when her life is secure with a devoted husband, and two
young children.

Her comment was, 'Most deaths in novels are there for a reason, so that the death will point up the meaning of the whole story or – in a tragedy – you deserve your death because like Oedipus you've done something wrong. I wanted to say that death isn't like that. It just happens – not necessarily to the person who deserves to be dead.'

*'Arthur Koestler was quoted as saying that he would swap a hundred readers today for ten readers in ten years' time and one reader in a hundred years' time. Do you agree?'*

'I partly agree – in the sense that I'm not writing for immediate popular success, I'm writing to construct something that somebody will notice how beautifully it's been constructed and perhaps that it's accurate. That always takes time because people have to learn how to read anything complicated. On the other hand, I do believe that our cultural values are shifting so violently and so wildly and that the international boundaries are shifting by the minute, so that in a sense you've got to be writing world literature. Writing English literature won't do. There may well be very good books that would have had a reader in a hundred years' time if England had gone on being England and small – but are not going to, simply because the rest of the world won't be interested in England.

'If you meet the upsurge of Marxist theory in the polytechnics, you suddenly see that you may not have a reader in a hundred years' time because the theory will be against what you've done without anyone trying to see what you've done. So in a sense it becomes more important to care about readers now in order to make sure you protect the readers of the future. Writing for posterity is something you could safely do in the nineteenth century; if you can't create your readership while you're writing in the twentieth century, you've not got much chance. The culture is all fraying at the edges; a lot of powerful people in positions in teaching are saying that the canon of English literature must go and, anyway, literature doesn't matter: any piece of writing is as good as any other. The sense of writing to last is a much more fragile thing than I think it was for Koestler. But I still would hope to write something that would last.

'It's the Marxist end of the teaching profession that really frightens me. It actually believes that what has been thought to be valuable in our literature was determined by class ideology and should therefore be knocked down and got rid of and expunged. You can do that very easily in a generation. If you just don't teach Shakespeare to anybody for two generations, it will be like the Bible, it will have gone. It will

46

be got back by the academics but that's not the same as its being alive in people being able to quote the odd line in the grocery shop. What they are putting in its place – a kind of literary "voice of the people", of insistence on "popular culture" – has its interest but isn't the *same* as a highly self-conscious worked-out cultural tradition. I partly see what they're talking about. The country house poem in the seventeenth century that was a compliment to a great lord doesn't interest me greatly – I'm not interested in great lords – but the actual flow of those sentences I would never lose.'

*'It has been argued that in male novelists creative ability and sexual virility are somehow linked. Do pregnancy and childbirth affect a woman novelist's creative writing ability at the time and for some time afterwards?'*

'There are two different answers here. One is about hormones. My sister Maggie [Drabble] wrote novels very fast when pregnant whereas I had a phenomenon that a lot of women have – which is that I couldn't be bothered to finish a sentence. I went very lethargic. Susan Hill ceased to write novels when she became happy; she wrote them in her solitary state and then, when she had a husband and a child, they seemed not to matter to her. The urgency went out of it. I always knew I wasn't going to be one of those. Children or no children, I had to write a good book.

'The most terrible thing about children and writing is the total uncertainty of being able to plan ahead. Because the moment you sit down, they fall off a wall, they get measles . . . You plan to go to the library and finish a track of thought but the phone will ring and the teacher will say, "I'm sending Miranda home, she's not very well today." You feel terrible in all directions all the time. You're totally dependent on people you don't feel it easy to get on with – like childminders and au pair girls and nannies. You feel guilty about leaving your children to them but, if you don't, you can't write. Then you do what my own mother did – which is scream at your children all the time. You have to plan every minute of every day and you have to be infinitely flexible because none of those minutes is actually predictable. Somebody may snatch it from you at any time. If you survive, then you're tough. But what you often don't have is panache and dash and just tossing things off.

'I don't know that women write as men do out of any sexual urgency. The whole thing is connected up with hormones. Another thing about a woman writer is that she probably writes around her menstrual cycle. It's part of the planning that you have to work in with the children and the cooking and the school term and everything else. You know you're going to get your good week and you know you're going to get your very bad week. I used to plan it so that in my very bad week I doggedly did all the background reading for my teaching and in my good week I would try to write.

'One of the advantages of getting older is that you don't have all those things and can go ahead full speed all the time. Rebecca West said a marvellous thing: "All women over fifty become men but they don't let anyone know." I used to be afraid of being fifty because I was used to dealing with swings of mood that I thought were necessary for my writing, whereas I now have, as long as I don't lose touch with the thread of the book, this perpetual high, and can just go on. Being fifty is the first time in my life I've been a primarily intellectual being.

'Almost no women have anybody thinking they're a genius and trying to help them, whereas quite a lot of men writers do have somebody who brings them the cup of coffee. I can count on one hand the number of times anyone has brought me a cup of coffee when I was writing! One of my daughters did – once. I remember that because I was so staggered.

'I'm very interested in the difference between men and women . . . I'm very interested in the limitations on human thought that are imposed by people seeing themselves so primarily as sexual beings. Feminism has been very good for a lot of women but it has had more ambivalent effects on those women who would have achieved something, anyway. Because we were liberated by George Eliot and Doris Lessing and Iris Murdoch – they proved that they were writing better novels than the men around them – women novelists didn't actually need women's lib *as novelists*. If you look at the novel now, where are they – the successors to Doris Lessing and Iris Murdoch? All the up-and-coming novelists are men. Julian Barnes, William Boyd, Martin Amis, Nigel Williams – they're macho men.

'The feminists feel we should write about women being trapped, which men don't want to read about, and they've got the readership because most novel-readers are women, anyway, but they're not writing the big novels. They've betrayed us in one way. They've invented a subject-matter that was peculiarly female and they said that women must write in a particularly female style, whereas those of my generation who knew that we were trying to be serious writers, were on the aggressive – we had to prove more than any man. We just set out and took a run and tried to prove it . . . No writer is really part of a group sensibility. You can record one and sympathise with it but, when you're writing, you're on your own.'

CHAPTER IV

# Enter the Literary Agent

'A well known journalist had written the life of Christ
and took the manuscript to the late J. M. Dent, saying
that he would have to negotiate with his new agent. The
publisher spluttered, "And to think, Mr Gardner, that
with the life of Our Saviour you saw fit to employ an
agent! It is more than I can bear."'

Cass Canfield,
chairman of Harper & Row, New York, 1972

'With a few notable exceptions I would suggest that
authors have always been shabbily treated by publishers
and still are. That is why they have to employ literary
agents to negotiate with publishers on their behalf.'

Sir Brian Batsford in a letter to
*The Times*, January 1975

In 1812, John Murray published a book entitled *Calamities of Authors*
by Isaac D'Israeli. It contained the plaintive passage:

What affectionate parent would consent to see his son devote himself
to his pen as a profession? . . . Most authors close their lives in apathy
or despair, and too many live by means which few of them would
not blush to describe.

He could hardly foresee that his son Benjamin, later Prime Minister,
would be paid £10,000 for *Endymion*, apparently a record sum for a
novel up to that time. Almost ninety years later, William Heinemann,
the publisher, writing in the *Author*, remarked, 'The author's agent
fosters in authors the greed for an immediate money return . . . at
the cost of all dignity and repose.'

How the change in some authors' fortunes came about, at whatever
loss of dignity, and to what extent the rise of the literary agent – who

is the author's business manager and general adviser – has influenced and is still influencing that change is the subject of this chapter.

A glance at the history of copyright in England shows that the man without whom book printers, book publishers, booksellers and indeed literary agents would not exist was treated like a serf for over 300 years. In 1557 the Stationers' Company was granted a Royal Charter, which with negligible exceptions vested all copyrights in the company. That situation remained intact for over 150 years – until the Copyright Statute of 1709 – the first such statute, it seems, enacted by any country. Even though it established that an author could hold copyright in his work for fourteen years, renewable for a further fourteen, it still permitted publisher/booksellers to buy that right permanently from the author for a lump sum. It was not until 1842 that a new copyright law came into being, which was more advantageous to the author. Now he could retain his copyright throughout his lifetime and for seven years after his death or for forty-two years from first publication, whichever proved to be the longer period.*

Up to the 1860s there were four main methods by which authors could receive payment for the exploitation of their copyrights. They were:

(a)   Commission publishing. The author paid all the production costs of the book and received all the profits (if any) after the printer-publisher had deducted a commission for each copy sold. This is the method by which 'vanity publishers' still conduct their business today.

(b)   Profit-sharing. The publisher was responsible for paying production and selling costs plus a share of his overheads. All these costs were a first charge against the sales of the book. Any resulting profit was shared between the publisher and the author, usually on a 50/50 basis.

(c)   The publisher bought the copyright for a fixed sum.

(d)   The publisher bought the copyright for a set number of years and for an agreed number of editions, after which it reverted to the author.

---

* This law largely helped the rise of cheap illustrated editions around the turn of the nineteenth century. In 1903 Collins put out its Illustrated Pocket Classics with such recently out-of-copyright authors as Scott, Dickens, George Eliot and Thackeray. *David Copperfield*, with 867 pages, 16 illustrations and bound with 'full gold back', cost one shilling. Three years later, Collins had sold 400,000 copies of the Pocket Classics and by 1929, 25 million. The published price rose to two shillings in 1922 and remained at that price until 1939.

In 1875, the Society of Authors came into being, with Tennyson as its first president and Matthew Arnold, T. H. Huxley, Charles Reade and Wilkie Collins as vice-presidents. It has a threefold aim: the maintenance, definition and defence of literary property; the consolidation and amendment of the laws of domestic copyright; and the promotion of international copyright. In the words of James Hepburn's *The Author's Empty Purse and The Rise of the Literary Agent* (1963):*

> As late as 1890 the Society of Authors recommended commission publishing as the best system for the author, but they had to admit that the author needed to be famous or of independent means for it to work. Mark Twain employed it to his enormous advantage with the sale of *Innocents Abroad*.

It could be added that George Bernard Shaw shrewdly used the same system in his dealings with Constable, his publishers. The rich and famous author could afford to pay for the production costs before the book began to earn its keep; the publisher had to put forward accurate – or reasonably accurate – accounts of sales in order to claim his commission. And the author as the outright owner of the unsold stocks had a perfect means of checking the publisher's claims for sales. In any case, with a certainty of risk-free profit, the publisher was unlikely to cheat the famous author by 'loading' the production costs or adding a share of overheads to the number he first thought of.

With a few honourable exceptions, the same claim could not be made for vanity publishers catering for the innocent beginner. Many of them have grossly overcharged the author for production standards that at the best are just adequate and at the worst appalling. Most of them have not employed efficient salesmen and have no visible means of distributing their stocks. The sad result is that the author pays out money he can probably ill afford to a so-called publisher who makes a large slice of profit by skimping on the quality of paper, print and binding. The shoddy book copies, when ready, are largely left to gather dust in the publisher's warehouse for a few months. The unwitting author will find in the small print of the contract he signed a proviso whereby after a fairly brief period he either has to take over the unsold stocks or pay an excessive rent to the publisher for retaining them.

* Many of the historical facts in this chapter were gleaned from Mr Hepburn's valuable monograph.

The profit-sharing method would appear to be the fairest one where the average author was concerned but it depended almost entirely on the honesty of the publisher and his staff. Not every nineteenth- and twentieth-century publisher qualifies for Lord Byron's epithet – 'Barabbas was a publisher' – but many of them would have agreed with W. C. Fields's remark, 'Never give a sucker an even break'. Publishers one hundred years ago – and even today – did not as a matter of course divulge the details of their printings or the number of copies left in stock. Nor have they ever itemised their selling costs or their expenditure on advertising. Far from treating the author as an equal partner in the enterprise, they have usually looked on him as the purveyor of the words which their skill and experience have turned into a saleable commodity. Thus, as James Spedding pointed out in his book *Publishers and Authors*, published in 1867, there was the case of a book whose publishing costs were £600 which sold 1,000 copies at £1.16s. There should have been a profit margin of £1,200, from which the author would have received his 50 per cent share, i.e. £600. His actual receipts were £50, the publisher's 'costs' having consumed £1,700 out of the £1,800 gross profit. Nineteenth-century publishers were adept at slipping in surcharges for their time, trouble and skill in negotiating with printers, binders and stationers.

The third method – the purchase of the copyright for a fixed sum by the publisher – has nothing to recommend it. The author is selling his work into a form of bondage and the price obtained usually bears no relation to the real value of the copyright. Many years ago, I appeared as an 'expert' witness in the High Court in a case where a journalist was suing the then Mahdi of the Sudan for breach of contract and the loss of earnings and enhanced prestige that would have accrued to the writer had the official biography of the Mahdi gone ahead. Various large sums were bandied about by plaintiff's counsel as the likely revenue from serial, translation and book club rights had the book proceeded to publication. The judge in a rueful aside remarked that the figures astounded him; he had been under the impression that authors sold their copyrights for a pittance. There was a knowing ripple of laughter from the lawyers in court. When he was a young and struggling barrister, the judge had written a standard legal work which thirty years later was still much in demand in its revised editions. A well-known firm of legal publishers had paid him £50 for the entire copyright and had made substantial profits from the book ever since. The practice is still prevalent among certain medical and legal publishers – and one big group that spreads its tentacles among cookery, gardening, crafts, and other works of reference. The argument put forward is always that if Author A will not accept the lump sum offer, Authors B, C or D are in the wings, holding out their eager arms to grasp the opportunity.

The fourth method, whereby the copyright reverts to the author after a number of years and an agreed number of editions, was (and is) slightly less onerous in that it does give the writer a second chance of making money from his copyright. But one can be sure that the shrewd publisher, when conducting the original negotiations, would have set the terms to the point where most of the 'juice' had been squeezed out of the 'orange' before the rights again became available.

Throughout the first half of the nineteenth century and after, there were many publishers who treated their authors fairly and generously; in some cases, over-generously. John Murray made quite frequent loans to Lord Byron and continued to increase his copyright payments when *Childe Harold* and later *Don Juan* set London alight. Sir Walter Scott occasionally earned £20,000 a year and on one occasion received the sum of £18,000 for his biography of Napoleon. (The present-day equivalent would be well over £500,000.) When Benjamin Disraeli was paid £10,000 for *Endymion*, his publisher probably lost on the deal. Anthony Trollope, a comparatively late starter who published his first book at the age of thirty-two, earned £70,000 in all from his writings. Publishers have always been ready to make allowances for successful writers but, certainly as late as 1950, they tended to look on the general breed – and, it has to be added, with some reason – as insecure, irresponsible and unreliable. In an increasingly complex industrial society, the rise of the literary agent was probably inevitable. But there is a cogent argument to be made that the overall attitude of publishers towards authors and the subsequent treatment they meted out not only did much to accelerate the agent's influence, but virtually created him.

One event in particular opened the way for the agent. In the mid-1860s, the Hurd and Houghton Company, a New York publisher, began to pay royalties. It is the fairest method – fair to both parties – that has been devised to settle the problem of how and how much an author should be paid in return for licensing his copyright exclusively to one publisher in a given territory, which has been proved by the fact that 120 years later it is still the system employed in the vast majority of publishing contracts. It meant that the publisher has had to disclose some of his previous secrets – the exact number of copies sold at home and for export, as different royalty rates usually apply, and the amounts and sources of sales from subsidiary rights assigned to the publisher, which would include book club, large print and paperback reprint rights. Even today, many publishing houses refuse to disclose how many copies they originally printed and how many remain in stock but the author does at least escape having to pay invisible charges incurred by the publisher and is able to tell just how well (or ill) his book has sold.

Payment by royalties has the additional merit of establishing publicly the author's sales pattern and his potential worth in the marketplace. This can be beneficial to the publisher as well as the author. Although the publisher may make an overall manufacturing profit, even though the advance paid to the author of a particular book has not been earned back in royalties, that publisher is unlikely to continue for a long time paying that author advances far in excess of the royalty earnings. As Evelyn Waugh said in 1961, 'A writer is worth no more to anyone than what he himself earns'. There is thus far more common ground for bargaining within the royalty system than when the publisher proposes an arbitrary lump sum that has to be taken on trust.

For historical reasons, the author's royalty has always been paid as a percentage of the published price of his book. This has throughout appeared to be an illogical process. Very few copies of any one edition – probably well under 10 per cent of the whole – are sold by the publisher at the full price. The vast bulk of the sales are made through wholesale and retail outlets at varying discounts. Nevertheless, at each accounting period, the publisher's accounts department, whether working manually or through a computer, has to undergo an extra (and unnecessary) function in reckoning up the number of copies sold in the home market or for export and paying out royalties on a pricing figure that probably only a few dozen copies at the most had achieved. It would be far simpler and quicker to pay an adjusted and increased royalty rate on the actual turnover achieved; that is, after all, in aggregate the publisher's key figure to set against his overheads and, he hopes, show a profitable surplus. Almost twenty years ago, before most publishing accounts departments had been computerised, Maurice Temple Smith, a young and astute publisher, forcefully proposed that royalty accounting should be based on the actual turnover figures and not on a notional published price but, as with so much else in the book trade, the traditional methods still prevail.

There is no definitive identity for the first official literary agent. Throughout the nineteenth century, authors had unofficial advisers who were usually personal friends. For example, the Ballantyne brothers, John and James, who were printers-cum-publishers, assisted Walter Scott after 1813. James, it seems, was his literary adviser and what we would now call his copy-editor; John would negotiate terms on his behalf as his business manager. After the 1826 crash, when the Ballantynes went into liquidation owing £250,000 and Scott was declared bankrupt, his 'law agent' on behalf of the Bank of Scotland, the chief creditor, conducted and controlled all the negotiations with publishers.

John Forster acted behind the scenes for Thackeray, Tennyson, Landor, Carlyle and Dickens. On Dickens's behalf, he worked out contracts with Richard Bentley and later with Chapman & Hall. He advised Dickens over the break-up of his marriage and held his power of attorney during his second American lecture tour. But he appears to have acted purely out of friendship, without receiving any payments for his advice and help.

The same status applied to Theodore Watts-Dunton, Swinburne's close friend. He had been trained as a lawyer and helped to place the articles that Swinburne wrote. Later, he moved the poet's work from Chatto & Windus to Chapman & Hall. Living with Swinburne at The Pines in Putney, he must have had a close influence on the writings – but again it was as a friend and not a paid business adviser.

The first known use of the term 'literary agency' occurs in an advertisement placed in the third edition of *Guide for the Writing Desk; or, Young Author's and Secretary's Friend*. The date was 1851. Even so, there are no traceable agencies dating back to that point. There were theatrical agents like John Lee, who acted for Edmund Kean, and lecture agents like George Dolby, who organised Dickens's readings during the period 1866–70 and earned £3,000 thereby. There were also newspaper agents, who not only helped potential writers over matters of subject, style and punctuation but also placed their work with provincial newspapers and magazines. (When in 1861 the paper tax was repealed, *The Times* reduced its price from 4d to 3d and its circulation swiftly rose by 30 per cent to match almost exactly the drop in revenue. The result was that fiction, which previously would have attracted the paper tax, was much in demand and gave rise to the part-issue novel and the shilling magazine.)

One leading newspaper agency, the Tillotson Syndicate, started around 1873. Its main job was to supply fiction to provincial newspapers. It paid authors so much per 1,000 words and took the responsibility of reselling its wares to the press. In the early 1890s Tillotson paid Conan Doyle £5 per 1,000 words, which by 1896 had become £40 per 1,000 words – £2,500 for a 60,000-word book. The present-day equivalent would be between £75,000 and £100,000. Tillotson paid Arnold Bennett £75 for his first serial, *Love and Life*, the initial offer having been £60. But, as its name suggests, the Tillotson Syndicate concentrated on selling serials and individual articles to the press and so could not be classed as a literary agency.

The first real claimant would be Alexander Paterson Watt, born in Glasgow in 1834. Some time after 1862, he joined his brother-in-law, the publisher Alexander Strahan, in London, where he acted as secretary, read manuscripts and handled the advertising. He became a partner in 1876 but the firm was already running into difficulties and for a brief time he was an advertising agent. The actual date when he became a full-time literary agent is in doubt. The present firm of A. P. Watt, flourishing well over a hundred years later, claims 1875 as the starting year. Some evidence suggests that 1878 is the more likely date. Watt appears to have begun acting for Wilkie Collins as early as 1875 – but possibly in an unofficial capacity while he was either a partner of Strahan's or working as an advertising agent.

Whatever the exact date, there is no doubt that all modern literary agencies derive from the activities of Mr A. P. Watt. It was he who introduced the fixed commission basis of 10 per cent, based on the charges made by advertising agents. He was also the one who instituted the process whereby the publisher paid the agent in the first place the sums that were due to the author; the agent, having first deducted his commission, then paid the author the balance owing to him. Whether Watt was merely a canny Scot or whether he privately shared publishers' views on the unreliability of authors is unknown. All the same, the method of payment is still in force. It is true that Watt undertook tasks that modern agents might consider beyond their scope – or even unethical. He represented publishers for rights that they were unable to sell through their own efforts and he sometimes touted for business by writing to established authors and sending them his brochure of testimonials from satisfied clients. When Joseph Conrad received the brochure, he told J. B. Pinker, his own agent, that it reminded him of the credentials of his Malayan laundry-woman. As James Hepburn describes the developing process:

> . . . the publishers were an evolutionary phenomenon in a progress-ive division of commercial labour, and the literary agents were the inevitable next phenomenon, hard on their heels, taking away some of the publishers' function just as the publishers took away some of the booksellers' and patrons'.

Nevertheless, A. P. Watt was a progressive pioneer who set out the functional pattern for agencies for the next century and more. His clients included Kipling, Yeats, Somerset Maugham, Galsworthy and many other outstanding names.

The next important figure was James Brand Pinker, Conrad's agent, who started his firm in 1896. Where Watt tended to concentrate on acquiring clients who had already made their mark in the writing world, Pinker helped to encourage the young and the new. In an advertisement – it is interesting that in those days literary agents advertised extensively whereas today they usually rely on word-of-mouth recommendation – he wrote:

> Mr Pinker has always made a special point of helping young authors in the early stage of their career, when they need most the aid of an adviser with a thorough knowledge of the literary world and the publishing trade.

H. G. Wells, Oscar Wilde and Stephen Crane were among his first clients and by 1901 he was acting for Henry James and Arnold Bennett as well as Conrad. He appears to have been a warm-hearted man of great social charm. At one time or another, he advanced £1,600, a very large sum in those days, to Conrad, who must have placed enormous reliance on him. As Conrad ruefully admitted in a letter to Pinker:

> I generally sell a work before it is begun, get paid when it is half done and don't do the other half until the spirit moves me. I must add that I have no control over the spirit – neither has the man who paid the money.

Many modern agents have similar, if less distinguished, clients. Unlike the present practice, Pinker insisted on having formal contracts with his authors but most of them would have stayed with him regardless, it seems, for his friendship and his shrewd powers of negotiation. Arnold Bennett wrote to a nephew, 'There is *no* other really good agent in England. The difference between a good and a bad agent might mean a difference of thousands a year to me.'

But Pinker did have occasional differences of opinion with Bennett. One letter he wrote will strike a sympathetic chord in the breasts of all present-day agents. Bennett, at the height of his fame, had sold some articles direct to a newspaper and was unwilling to pay Pinker his commission. Pinker replied in these terms:

> You would, I know, be the first to admit that you were able to sell those articles on those terms because of my work in building up your market. If when the market is worked up an author is going to take pieces of business into his own hands he will naturally take all the easy pieces and leave the agent the difficult ones. That would be most unfair to the agent, and it would end in changing the whole relationship. As you know, it frequently happens that there is work to do for an author which involves no commission for the agent or a commission so insignificant as to be negligible, but at the same time it is work the author particularly wishes done. One does it with the good will and energy that one applies to the more profitable business but only because one has toward the author the feeling of complete service.

J. B. Pinker died comparatively young in 1922 and his son took over the flourishing business. Unfortunately, he must have had a criminal streak: he defrauded several of the clients, was convicted and sent to prison and the agency collapsed around 1930.

The third outstanding figure among the early agents was Albert Curtis Brown. An American, he was born in 1866 and came to London at the age of twenty-two as the representative of the *New York Press*. Part of his job was to place British rights in articles published in the *Press* and hence he came to know London newspaper editors and book publishers. By 1899, he was head of the International Publishing Bureau in Henrietta Street and six years later was operating at the same address under his own name. The firm remained in Covent Garden until well after the Second World War.

Whereas A. P. Watt stayed strictly a family firm until the 1960s, Curtis Brown expanded steadily until it became – and has remained – the largest of all London agencies, in spite of the fact that over the years many of its leading figures have broken away to form their own firms. In 1919, John Farquharson, who had been the English Books Manager at Curtis Brown before going off to the wars, set up an agency under his own name. In 1935, a more serious defection occurred when Nancy Pearn and Laurence Pollinger, to be followed two years later by David Higham, three of the senior managers, broke away to form a large rival agency. That in turn split up again some years after Nancy Pearn's death in 1950 when David Higham and the Pollingers went their separate ways. Laurence's younger son Murray went solo in 1969 and thus in a generation and a half three individual and sturdy offshoots had emerged from the Curtis Brown 'tree'.

Other early agencies still going strong today are Hughes Massie (1912) now merged with Aitken & Stone, A. M. Heath (1919) and A. D. Peters (1924). If J. B. Pinker had the best claim to being considered the outstanding individual agent of the first two decades of this century, A. D. Peters must be reckoned as his successor over the next forty years and more. His clients included Norman Collins, C. S. Forester, Arthur Koestler, V. S. Pritchett, Evelyn Waugh and Rebecca West – and Terence Rattigan on the theatrical side. Astute, tough and straight, Peters was still active at eighty, not long before his death in 1973. Michael Sissons had already taken over the management of the firm and has expanded it still further.

In 1935, Cassell published a pleasantly rambling memoir by Albert Curtis Brown under the apt title of *Contacts*. Although it reveals a few of the *coups* he enjoyed, it gives little idea of the real secrets behind his success or any intimate glimpses of his best clients at their most vulnerable. Agents should perhaps be advised – but by whom? – against trying to write their memoirs. If they do show any literary talent, they are usually inhibited by the fact that their best anecdotes derive from their confidential relationship with their authors. Curtis Brown did, however, put down some pithy maxims based on his long experience of negotiating:

> The horrid truth is that advertising can do no more at first than launch a book. Whether that book floats or not depends on the book itself.

Great deals from little amenities grow. Great disasters from little insults grow.

A bargain is better led than driven.

One drop of condescension spoils a gallon of negotiation.

Watch out for the people whose motto is: 'We will do your best for us'.

The references to 'condescension' and 'insults' are interesting. Many publishers of note during the first third of this century, and for even longer – men like Sir Stanley Unwin, William Heinemann, Thomas Werner Laurie, Walter Hutchinson, either actively disliked agents for coming between them and their natural 'prey' or echoed George Bernard Shaw's remark in an article for the *Author*, published in 1911: 'The literary agency is a . . . favourite resort of persons who have not ability enough for ordinary business pursuits or for literature'. And yet Alec Waugh, writing in the same periodical a quarter of a century later, gave proof of what agents had achieved for their clients. Up to about 1920, virtually all publishers had indulged in the 'baker's dozen' when accounting for royalties. In earlier days, it had been a common practice to encourage booksellers to increase their orders by throwing in one free copy for every twelve ordered. The publisher did not pay a royalty to the author on that thirteenth copy. Even though by the First World War the practice of supplying booksellers thus had ceased, most publishers continued to penalise the author unjustly by not paying a royalty on every thirteenth copy – an overall loss to the author of 7.7 per cent of his due earnings. A concerted effort on the part of the major agents during 1919 and 1920 managed to put a stop to the iniquitous practice; thereby in one blow, as Alec Waugh pointed out in his article, they virtually earned their commission charges per author.

The agent has a twofold function: to discover new talent and find a good home for it and to provide a worldwide service for established authors. Despite many wise remarks in his monograph, James Hepburn misses the target when he says: 'It is certain that the agents are not in the forefront of efforts to encourage new writers or to assist the profession as a whole'. Authors run out of inspiration, they grow old, they die; if only as a means of self-preservation, agents have to keep nurturing new talent which will eventually replace the old. Most literary agents today, indeed, are educated men and women with university degrees and quite often ex-publishers themselves.

Their taste and literary judgment are usually on a par with their business sense and negotiating skills.

A successful novelist in the post-war period might confidently expect to place half a dozen or more translation rights as well as British and American hardcover and paperback rights in every book he publishes. There is also the possibility of placing film or television or dramatic rights, audio-cassette rights and occasionally serial rights. In addition, he may from time to time wish to write articles or short stories and appear on television and radio programmes. Even if that novelist were a shrewd businessman who had spent years studying the available markets and the 'going rates' in each, by the time he had fully exploited each of the many markets, there would be little opportunity left for writing the next novel.

Publishers would argue that they have efficient subsidiary rights departments which can sell serial and translation rights as well as – or better than – the agent can. With a few exceptions, it just is not so. And, for example, when it comes to the publisher selling American rights, there could be a conflict of interest if he is sitting on large unsaleable stocks of the title in question. It could pay him better to sell copies of his edition to an American publisher than the rights for the American publisher to set up his own edition. In essence, a publisher's job is to sell books; selling rights as well is jam on the bread and butter. The agent's sole function is to sell rights. The good agent *has* to be better at that than the good publisher.

The agent offers two other advantages to the client. Unlike doctors and lawyers, he only charges when he actually 'wins a case'. When acting for a tyro, an agent may – and often does – approach a dozen or more publishers before finding one to accept the proffered script. Sometimes, his efforts fail and he has to return the script with regret. In that case, the author has had the free benefit of his efforts. Even when the agent does finally place a marginal script, his commission on the modest advance will not cover the amount of his overheads and the time involved. His reward will only come if that author stays with him and prospers before long.

Writing of Pinker's dealings on behalf of Conrad and Bennett, James Hepburn says that they 'offer evidence of what publishers often complained of; that the agent destroys the personal relationship between publisher and author'. Without knowing exactly how Pinker functioned, one can only reply that the complaint is surprising. It could be argued with equal or greater strength that the advent of

the agent freed both publisher and author to develop a personal relationship devoid of embarrassing haggling over terms. Authors have
been known to confess to their publishers, usually tongue-in-cheek,
that left to themselves they would have settled for far more modest
terms had it not been for their grasping agent who forced up the
terms. And publishers have been known to converse *sub rosa* with
an agent and complain bitterly about the latest goings-on of 'your
prima donna client'. It is not necessarily an ignoble function to act
as a safety-valve or 'pig-in-the-middle'.

The 1946 edition of *The Writers' & Artists' Yearbook*, that invaluable
reference work, lists thirty-nine British literary agencies of which four
were not strictly 'literary'. The 1966 edition listed sixty-four British
agencies of which again nine concentrated on film/TV/theatre or on
syndication or translation. The 1986 edition listed 106 agencies of
which twenty-two were mainly on the performing arts or translations
or non-fiction. Thus, if those other agencies are extracted, the literary
agencies increased from thirty-five to fifty-five in twenty years and then
by a further twenty-nine in the next twenty years – an increase of 57 per
cent in the first period and a further increase of just under 53 per cent
in the second. In 1968, James Hepburn claimed that 90 per cent of all
agency work in London was carried out by the 'Big Five' – whoever
they might be (he does not specify) but presumably including Curtis
Brown, A. P. Watt, A. D. Peters and Pollinger/Higham. It is a highly
doubtful claim as it would leave fifty other agencies sharing only 10
per cent of the market. Hughes Massie, representing Agatha Christie,
and John Farquharson with bestselling authors like Enid Blyton, Sir
Francis Chichester, Sir Edmund Hillary and James Hilton, would
easily have made up the remaining 10 per cent by themselves.

Apart from the increase in the number of agents, the business
methods of agency work in handling fiction have changed to a
considerable degree over the past twenty years, and more so in the
last ten years. Agents have often gone looking for the big 'one-off'
non-fiction book – for example, a politician's memoirs or the official
account of an important expedition. In the past, however, they mainly
sat back and waited for the typescripts of novels to reach them, either
unsolicited or through the recommendation of an existing satisfied
client or even sometimes a publisher. The belief was that, 'You can't
make a novelist.' The inherent talent could be improved by advice
and practice but the author was the only person who could determine
what novels he would write and when he would write them.

In the last ten years or so, that outlook has changed. Agents have become more entrepreneurial in their approach to fiction as well as non-fiction. This may partly be due to the appearance of new and hungry agents who, lacking the established authors, have had to find or make their own bestsellers, and partly to the growth of the large conglomerates. Publishing has always dealt in 'futures'. The unwritten work will have a fascination, a potential, which may be circumscribed when it comes to the actual words on the page.

Most agents look after a general list of clients but some either specialise in one area or over the years have developed a close interest in one field, as well as the wider-ranging aspects. For example, the Carnell Literary Agency concentrates on science fiction; Deborah Rogers is known for the care with which she nurtures new writers of literary fiction; and John Farquharson has for many years made a virtual 'corner' in important books of adventurous travel and exploration – with such clients as Chris Bonington, Sir Francis Chichester, Sir Ranulph Fiennes, Sir Vivian Fuchs, Dougal Haston, Sir Edmund Hillary and Robin Knox-Johnston. Thus, even though *The Writers' and Artists' Yearbook* includes notes on each agency's general areas of operation, it is not easy for the new author to decide which one of so many would be just right for him. Word-of-mouth recommendation from an established author – assuming he knows one – is perhaps the answer. Trial and error is the only alternative.

The rest of this chapter offers the views of five leading agents on the current state of the book trade and the advantages and problems that confront novelists. As an *aide-mémoire*, I gave a list of questions to each of them before they were interviewed and tape-recorded. The questions were:

1  When, how and why did you become an agent?
2  Approximately how many full-time novelists do you personally represent?
3  What percentage of them actively seek your advice before they embark on a new novel?
4  After reading the typescript of a novel from an important client (before it is delivered to the publisher), do you often/ever offer critical advice on it?
5  It has been said that a literary agent should be 'a marriage-broker, not a divorce lawyer'. What are your views?

6   In what circumstances would you auction a new novel?

7   When drawing up a contract for a new novel, would you normally include an option clause?

8   What do you think of the Minimum Terms Agreement?

9   Do any of your clients ever consult you over what kind of novel he/she should write next? Conversely, if a brilliant idea for a novel struck you, would you offer it to a client who happened to be 'between books'?

10   With the fairly recent trend towards conglomerates in publishing, do you think it has become more difficult to launch a promising new novelist?

11   Are you generally optimistic – or pessimistic – over the future of the novel (in particular, the 'literary' novel) in England? And are there any special trends you foresee?

The five agents consulted were chosen to furnish a wide spread of experience. In alphabetical order, they were Giles Gordon of Anthony Sheil Associates; Deborah Rogers, who runs her own agency; Michael Shaw, managing director of Curtis Brown; and Carol Smith and Ed Victor, each of whom heads her or his own firm. The interviews took place in the early summer of 1987.

All but one of them, Deborah Rogers, had had considerable first-hand knowledge of publishing before becoming agents. Giles Gordon had worked at Oliver & Boyd, Secker & Warburg, Hutchinson, Penguin (under the late Tony Godwin) and Victor Gollancz; after Oxford and research, Michael Shaw had worked at Macmillan for seven years before starting his own agency which another seven years later was acquired by Curtis Brown; Carol Smith had spent two years at Thames & Hudson, then two years with Basic Books in New York and a further year back in London at Heinemann, followed by eight at the A. P. Watt agency; Ed Victor, who is American, took a M.Litt. at Pembroke College, Cambridge, then went to Weidenfeld & Nicolson, and after three years to Jonathan Cape, where he stayed for a further three to four years. After a brief spell back in New York with Alfred A. Knopf, he returned to England and spent four years with the John Farquharson agency before setting up on his own.

Deborah Rogers stumbled on to the agency world by accident through answering an advertisement when she was living in New York and finding herself the flatmate of Lynn Nesbit, a noted literary agent there. She also acted as secretary to the wife of Sterling Lord, another successful New York agent with whom Lynn Nesbit had once worked. Attracted by the agency life, Deborah Rogers on her return to London wrote to several agents, three of whom at once offered her a job. She chose Peter Janson-Smith; after several years she left to set up her own firm which, in 1988, was expanded to become Rogers, Coleridge & White.

The agents' answers to questions three and four in my list varied widely, as might be expected. Established novelists rarely sought advice before embarking on a new novel, occasionally to their detriment, as Ed Victor pointed out over one bestselling American client, who telephoned him and said he had 'this great idea for a novel – very different'. Mr Victor said, 'Be careful' but the author went ahead without further consultation and wrote the novel, which turned out to lack pace and suspense; it was a straight, old-fashioned story. The author's regular American publisher, who had paid well over $1 million for the previous novel, was disappointed with the new one and halved his previous offer. The book then went out to auction but the highest bid was far below $1 million. As Ed Victor put it, 'The book hasn't worked and now he's going to pay a double price because it's going to be very hard for me to get him back to that $1 million level which he psychologically needs . . . There's that wonderful title by Jimmy Baldwin, *The Fire Next Time* . . . if you write a bad book, an off book, quite often people go out and buy it because they're fans. You pay for it the next time out.'

Michael Shaw gave two instances of whether his novelists do or do not discuss their work in advance of the writing. 'Angus Wilson never does, whereas Malcolm Bradbury might just want to talk about one or two ideas he has – and all you're really doing is to reassure him that he's made up his mind in the right direction; that what he was going to do anyway is the right thing to do. It's really more a psychological thing than any intellectual input that you can provide.'

Deborah Rogers's response was similar. Speaking of her client, Kazuo Ishiguro, she said, 'Everything he does has a kind of purity and a kind of simplicity . . . The only thing you can do with a writer like that is to listen and wait and act on the direction their own impulse takes them.' If after reading the script of a novel by one of her clients she has any critical comments to make, she is 'always careful if it's an instance when the publisher and I are reading it simultaneously that we aren't going to say things that conflict totally . . . If it's something that I feel really strongly about – and the publisher doesn't – I might still say something to the author. But I feel terribly strongly that no author should do anything that they feel is wrong or that somehow doesn't feel right to them.'

Both Giles Gordon and Carol Smith take a very different view. After reading the first draft of *Hawksmoor*, Mr Gordon advised his client, Peter Ackroyd, that it needed a short opening chapter to set the scene and establish the main characters. The original opening was 'totally hermetic and rather academic'. The author at once saw the point, rewrote the opening and, to show his gratitude, dedicated the book to his agent. Again, 'I suggested *Falstaff* to Robert Nye because I'd always thought that someone should write a big book about Shakespeare's Falstaff. There are only a few hundred lines about Falstaff [in the *Henry IV* and *Henry V* plays] and yet Falstaff is as big as John Bull. I'd been reading a novel by Robert Nye, whom I didn't know, and I just wrote to him out of the blue. He's become one of my closest friends and dedicated the novel to me. I also suggested Peter Ackroyd's book on Oscar Wilde to him. I love doing that, particularly since I stopped writing novels myself.'

Carol Smith is in the modern jargon a very 'hands-on' kind of agent. Her task at A. P. Watt was to seek out new writers and she has continued in the same way since setting up her own agency. As she put it, 'It seemed to me as a natural progress . . . that, although short-story writing and novel-writing are two different art forms, most potential novelists start off with shorter pieces. It seemed quite obvious that after an author had sold two or three stories to magazines, the next step was to write something longer, aiming towards the full-length novel.'

With this in view, Carol Smith coaches new writers on the themes and techniques for writing successful short stories and serials, ensuring that with the latter the tyro plans the number of instalments required, keeps to the defined lengths and incorporates 'cliff-hangers' at the end of each episode. She instanced Rosalind Ashe, who happened to remark that she was going on a skiing holiday for the first time. Miss Smith instructed her to tackle a serial – 16,000 words in all, split into four parts, working in those 'cliff-hangers' at the end of the first three parts – and the final instruction to 'set it in Zermatt. You'll see it with new eyes.' The author followed her instructions and Carol Smith sold the resulting serial for a substantial sum within twenty-four hours of receiving the script.

On another occasion she was lunching with an American academic writer who bewailed the fact that he had made virtually nothing out of his learned non-fiction writings. 'If you want to make money,' she said, 'write a Gothic novel.' He replied, 'What's a Gothic novel?' She explained so convincingly that she eventually sold his first effort to Jonathan Cape for £10,000 advance and after a few more books managed to establish him as one of the pre-eminent novelists dealing with the supernatural. Almost all her clients actively seek her advice both before and during the writing of their novels. In her words, 'It's what literary agents are all about – encouraging talent and fostering the new crop . . . I write long editorial letters to my authors . . . My reputation as an agent matters to me as much as their reputations matter to them . . . I will not send out a book if I don't think it's good.'

All the five agents took the view that their role was essentially that of a marriage-broker, not a divorce lawyer. Michael Shaw put it well: 'An author and publisher are best if it's for ever through good and ill. The publisher must take the rough with the smooth . . . The author's previous novels are rather like children – you have to consider them as well if it comes to a divorce.' He went on to say, 'Publishers nowadays seem to be less prepared to publish an author – they're much more interested in whether or not this is a big-selling book and they like to typecast their authors more, fit them into slots.'

Ed Victor put forward an interesting variation on the same theme: 'There is a tendency now to sell top-end-of-the-market authors in multiple book contracts . . . There are major advantages on both sides. The effect of "house hopping" is sometimes to inhibit the publisher's will to promote . . . Both sides are feeling the need for security.'

Deborah Rogers pointed out one fairly new problem that can confront the agent's choice of a publisher as being the right one for a particular novelist – the fact that nowadays editors tend to move from one house to another far more than in the past. 'An editor will go somewhere else as a step up [and find] it's an instrument they don't understand and it doesn't work for them.' She instanced a youngish editor in 'an antiquated house' who managed to 'pull out performances that were stunning – original, quirky, offbeat. He knew he wasn't in the running for the big books and so he wasn't even trying for them. He was trying to make things that he loved work . . . When he got to [the big publishing house], there was this huge machine waiting, desperately hungry to be fed with the big books . . . Some of the books he bought did well but he lost that special quality.'

The summing-up comes from Carol Smith. 'There's no point in being too aggressive towards a publisher unless they're doing wrong . . . We all want to make it work together . . . If the author is known to change too often . . . then the author doesn't have any loyalty from the publisher either.'

The five agents had divergent views about auctioning a new novel to several publishers at once. Ed Victor was much in favour while at the other extreme Giles Gordon put it thus: 'I think an agent's auctioning a book is a cop-out when the agent doesn't know what to do with the book and can't make up his mind.' The other three felt that they would only set up an auction when the book in question was of American origin, the author had no regular British publisher and there was a queue forming up for the rights. As Carol Smith put it: 'If you auction, you don't necessarily end up with the best editor and the best publisher. You may get the second-rate publisher who needs the book. One of the reasons you give 10 per cent to the agent is because the agent has market knowledge . . . Auctioning is the lazy way out.'

Deborah Rogers pointed to one bad effect of excessive auctioning. 'Publishing time is extremely valuable. I cherish the time that people spend publishing properly. More and more, each time you put a book out on auction, you've got an editor, you've got the marketing department, you've got the publicity department, you've got the rights people, all putting together their offer. So you've got, say, half a dozen people taking up how many hours – and that's happening over four, five or six or whatever number of publishers. And all but one of them won't get the book. You then have another author of yours who is published by one of those publishers; you can't get people there to do this or that because of the big acquisition, if it comes off.'

The response was also varied over whether or not to include an option clause on the author's next book in publishing contracts. Michael Shaw never includes an option clause and nor would Giles Gordon by preference: 'I don't think an option means anything and often wish it weren't there.' Ed Victor said, 'I will not let publishers have any option other than a first-look option – none of these first refusals or matching offers.' But he is still concerned to maintain continuity, if possible. As he put it, 'Back list sales are very stimulated by front list sales . . . If you have a guy who's been with one house and they've got a nice back list [of his books], if he leaves, there's a kind of tendency for the foot to come off the accelerator. If they don't have the stimulus of a new book from that author on the front list, they just tend to let the back list go.'

Carol Smith summed up her own thinking in one sentence: 'I always give an option on fiction because of the build-up of loyalty.'

The five agents broadly held the view that the Minimum Terms Agreement – in the words of *1066 and All That* – was 'a good thing'. Carol Smith did remark that 'the MTA Agreement is an irrelevance to any author who has an agent' but Giles Gordon felt it struck a blow for the agentless author: 'The short answer is that if one could rely on publishers to treat the rawest, most innocent novelist decently, there'd be no need for the MTA. Given that all authors can't get agents because there are far more authors than there are available agencies, as a generalisation, the MTA is a good thing. But when publishers start wielding it as a maximum or an optimum, then it's counter-productive.'

Deborah Rogers made one useful point that could easily be over-looked if opposing parties get too entrenched. 'The MTA is a good way of protecting those authors who can't protect themselves . . . There can occasionally be good reason to sell a book below the Minimum Terms Agreement – say, a first novel of over 600 pages – without setting a precedent and where it's in everybody's best interests.'

Opinions were far more varied when it came to discussing the last two points on the list – whether it has become more difficult under present-day conditions to launch a promising new novelist and whether the agents were generally optimistic or pessimistic over the future of the novel, especially the 'literary' novel, in England.

Giles Gordon was perhaps the most pessimistic. He said, 'We're not finding, because I don't believe they exist . . . many good first novels . . . The reasons are twofold, complementary yet different – one, because there's so little money in it, and, two, because they can get more instant money writing for television or film . . . It's so much more difficult to write 60,000 or 80,000 sustained words of a novel.

'I think it's become a bit of a myth that it's more difficult to publish a new novel. Given that there are so many publishing houses looking for new novelists, it's actually easier than it's ever been. There's a lack of authors of real quality. Some years ago, they would have had to work much harder to get their first novels published . . . There are very few authors today who are prepared to work in the way authors did early in the century and in the late nineteenth century.'

Talking of the current tendency towards larger and larger groupings of publishing houses, Ed Victor said: 'I don't worry about these agglomerations . . . While the competition shrinks in terms of numbers, it intensifies as a direct corollary of its shrinkage . . . I used to rub two sticks together and get friction – say, Christopher Sinclair-Stevenson [of Hamish Hamilton] and Peter Mayer [of Penguin]. Perfect people to go to and get them hot and bothered. Now you can't do that. But one of them is going to have that much more appetite because he's got to go up against the Collins group, he's got to go up against the Hodder group and so on.'

Michael Shaw was more doubtful. 'The old-fashioned editor was a broad-ranging figure. He felt that he was *the* publisher – he was determined to deliver the firm in all its different departments and different expertise behind a novel. The editor now seems to see his job sometimes stopping as soon as he's signed the contract – he's merely an acquiring editor – or when he's finished the editorial work . . . The very close personal bonds with a publisher have been weakened not just by the editor moving but by the structural organisations in the way publishing has changed . . . The chairman figure has often become more interested in international acquisition than seeing that the author is properly looked after.'

Deborah Rogers inveighed against the present emphasis on prices obtained instead of on the literary merits of the novel in question. 'If I could abolish one thing in life, it would be the Paul Nathan and the Maggie Pringle columns.* They do more damage and cause more pain . . . You haven't heard one person say, "You must read the new Graham Swift, it's wonderful," nobody says that. All they say is, "Have you heard what Graham Swift has made?" '

And how do these agents view the future of the novel? Giles Gordon again struck the most sombre note: 'In commercial terms, successful writers have done exceedingly well for the first three-quarters of this century but possibly . . . the novel has had its day. When you get people like some of the European writers and avant-garde novelists

* Paul S. Nathan writes a weekly column in the *Publishers Weekly* and Maggie Pringle writes a regular column, 'First Report' in the *Bookseller*. Both deal with up-to-date sales of various rights in the respective territories – USA and UK. See Appendix B.

breaking up the form and fragmenting it and not being concerned with "story", has it – except as entertainment – had its day as an art form?'

Ed Victor uttered a cautionary note. 'There is a kind of brand name-ism which is very disturbing in that people now buy novels the way they buy magazines . . . A young man writes a novel named *The Day of the Jackal*. What's his next novel called? The new Forsyth.' But he went on to say, 'It's an entertainment-glamour industry. Why are people so interested? . . . Would anyone care if a toilet seat manufacturer had taken over an alarm clock manufacturer? No. But publishing is a form of showbiz now and all these large institutions start to resemble the movie studios . . . The way a publishing house gets things is through its editors. The editors are like the facets of a crystal – to catch light . . . Some of the taste is still going to be for the interesting new novel.'

Michael Shaw also felt cautious. 'The conglomerate has not really got a firm grip as yet; perhaps we ought to wait a couple of years. For example, Christopher Sinclair-Stevenson will still take a first novel now that Hamish Hamilton is part of the Penguin group much in the same way as when he was an independent. But whether Christopher will continue to do that when the next turn of the screw happens in the conglomerate structure or whether his successor who was born within the conglomerate structure will have the same view, I have no idea. It's how the next generation is going to operate that will be very interesting . . . So far I don't find getting a brand-new novelist off the ground particularly difficult. You may not get the publisher you would ideally have chosen but you are getting him published by someone who is competent – not a fly-by-night publisher or someone who's got more money than sense.'

Carol Smith was reasonably optimistic. 'However much videos and cassettes and television develop, I don't think they'll ever kill the book as a pleasure . . . There'll have to be fewer novels published, which will be a good thing.' She did, however, add, 'I'm concerned about the mid-list book.'

Deborah Rogers put it thus: 'It is not as hard to launch a promising new novelist here as it is in America . . . With a conglomerate, the emphasis must be on making money . . . The cultural importance of the novel is such that I can't feel that there won't always be room for it . . . To have the writers that I really care about is a far better long-term investment than a lot of those who are merely today's flavour.'

As an ex-publisher and, latterly, as an ex-agent, I have to say that I came away from these individual interviews refreshed and appreciative of the capacities of those who were once friendly rivals. The old joke, quoted by William Goldman in his memoirs *Adventures in the Screen Trade*, of the man who, needing a heart transplant and offered by the surgeon a choice of two – the heart of a twenty-five-year-old marathon runner and the heart of a sixty-five-year-old agent – chose the latter on the grounds that he wanted 'a heart that had never been used', has not been relevant for many years, if ever. Good agents today – and there appear to be few, if any, indifferent agents – possess a literary acumen and a concern for their clients that could be very necessary in the interesting but difficult times ahead. But I leave summing-up to the agents themselves:

Carol Smith: 'What I want all my writers to do is to be good writers but write for a wider readership.'

Giles Gordon: 'I get phoned up at home more by authors I represent in the evenings and at weekends than I do in the office almost . . . Very few authors treat their publishers that way – there's something significant in that.'

Michael Shaw: 'The agent by always being there becomes a familiar landmark.'

Ed Victor mentioned Arthur Koestler's remark: 'I would trade a hundred readers today for ten readers ten years from now and one reader a hundred years from now.'

The last word has to go to Deborah Rogers, who encapsulated the agent's vade-mecum in one short sentence: 'The only clients you should take on are the ones who make your own heart beat faster.'

CHAPTER V

# The Way It Was

*The Author's Epitaph*
I suffered so much from printer's errors
That death for me can hold no terrors;
I'll bet this stone has been misdated,
I wish to God I'd been cremated.

Anon

Until some years after the Second World War, there were few, if any, publishing editors in Britain in the terms in which we know them today. There were newspaper and magazine editors, indeed, and editors of distinguished journals, reference works and dictionaries. Publishing houses had employees who were copy-editors, checking the typescript of a book for punctuation, grammar and facts before it was sent off to the printer. Even then, the better printing firms, R. & R. Clark, Jarrolds, Maclehose, Northumberland Press and others, employed readers of their own with the breadth of knowledge to query a Greek quotation or firmly amend a mistake over the mechanics of the hero's Hispano-Suiza. But 'acquiring editors' were both unknown and unnecessary.

There were several interlocking reasons. In those days most publishing houses were run by one man who was likely to publish those books that appealed to him personally. He might well make use of cultured helpers, as Jonathan Cape did, first with Edward Garnett and then with William Plomer and Daniel George Bunting, and as Macmillan did with Sir John Squire in his latter days – but they were advisers and not by themselves formal acquirers of books. Before air traffic was available, except to the extremely rich, and the motor car was still something of a novelty, London was a far more cohesive centre, both socially, culturally and geographically, than it has ever been since. Many novelists and most publishers

74

were of the educated middle and upper-middle classes, belonged to the same clubs and met at the same social gatherings. The novels of Aldous Huxley, Anthony Powell and Evelyn Waugh often portray a society whose northern border was Bloomsbury* and its southern border Pall Mall or Carlton House Terrace where lion-hunting titled ladies lay in wait. It was not until the raising of the school-leaving age and the spread of provincial universities in the post-war years that the role of 'the novelist as outsider' became established with the newly educated lower-middle-class writers like Stan Barstow, John Braine and Alan Sillitoe.

At the end of 1949, the Manchester City Librarian analysed the fiction preferences of the Mancunian borrowers. In descending order, the most popular novelists of the day were Dorothy L. Sayers, Hugh Walpole, Jeffrey Farnol, John Buchan, Agatha Christie, John Galsworthy, A. E. W. Mason, Mazo de la Roche, Howard Spring, J. B. Priestley, Leslie Charteris, A. J. Cronin, Naomi Jacob, Charles Dickens, Francis Brett Young, W. Somerset Maugham, Sir Philip Gibbs, Pearl Buck, E. Phillips Oppenheim, Daphne du Maurier, Cecil Roberts, Upton Sinclair, Frances Parkinson Keyes, Angela Thirkell, Neil Bell, John Brophy, Georges Simenon and Taylor Caldwell. In that list of twenty-eight, there are one Canadian (Mazo de la Roche), four Americans (Pearl Buck, Upton Sinclair, Frances Parkinson Keyes and Taylor Caldwell) and one Belgian (Simenon). The other twenty-two are solidly middle/upper-middle-class British citizens.

In *Jonathan Cape, Publisher*, brought out to celebrate the fiftieth anniversary of the firm, Michael Howard quotes Dame Veronica Wedgwood's verdict on the founder:

> He had a great respect for literature rather than a familiarity and feeling for it. He thought he knew about books, but he knew about them from the point of view of the traveller on the road, not that of the bookman. He liked the outside of books, he was interested in the standard of production, but I don't think he cared for the inside very much.

Much the same could have been said of the Harrap brothers or Sir Stanley Unwin or Sir William Collins; and certainly of Walter Hutchinson, who never appeared very interested in the outside of a book either, except for the dust-jacket which he always insisted on

* 'The triangles who lived in squares,' (Judith Burnley).

approving. Sir Stanley Unwin's *The Truth about Publishing* says much about production costs and standards but virtually nothing of the merits of the words that keep the covers apart.

All the same, each of them knew that there were literary standards to be maintained and they looked to expert readers to advise them. One of the very first letters Jonathan Cape wrote after starting his firm in January 1921 was to Edward Garnett, inviting him to act as professional reader and 'contact man', although he did not phrase it thus, for a salary of £200 a year. And four years later, when the two of them were in dispute, Jonathan wrote to Garnett again in these terms:

> Our position is that we should like you to be in reality what you believe yourself to be, i.e. the literary adviser and conscience of the firm – one directly and indirectly responsible for what we publish – one to whom we could without question assign the credit for what was successful and noteworthy on the list.

The presence then of literary magazines like the *London Mercury*, the *Adelphi* or T. S. Eliot's *Criterion* and general magazines like the *Cornhill* and the *Strand* helped promising young writers to emerge by providing an opening for their shorter work. Literary editors such as John Middleton Murry, caricatured by Aldous Huxley in *Point Counter Point* as a toady to the wealthy upper classes, and John Squire with his eccentric cricket team so wittily described in A. G. Macdonell's *England, Their England*, served the small literary/social circle by passing the word on when a bright newcomer had arrived. Huxley himself worked as a 'sifter' of articles for Middleton Murry's periodical even after Chatto & Windus offered him a far-sighted arrangement – consecutive three-year contracts in which the publisher agreed to make annual payments and Huxley agreed to deliver so many novels or non-fiction works in the period.

Nevertheless, the figure of the literary adviser was ever-present. As Michael Howard pointed out, 'Even so literary a publisher as Geoffrey Faber, when he began in business, would look around for an adviser: and choose T. S. Eliot'. Edward Garnett, who had been Duckworth's reader from the turn of the century to the outbreak of the First World War and who had nursed Conrad and W. H. Hudson, discovered D. H. Lawrence and was one of the few to commend Virginia Woolf's first novel *The Voyage Out* (1915), was probably the epitome of the reader/consultant until his death in 1935. It was he who prompted

Jonathan Cape to look for talent across the Atlantic as well as at home. Until the Second World War, British publishers tended to regard their American counterparts as 'wild colonial boys'. London was, they thought, the centre and if the Americans wanted to find out how things were done properly, all they had to do was travel to London. But Cape, urged on by Garnett, visited New York at least once a year from the very year his firm began – with occasional visits as well to Boston and Toronto. Among the early authors he acquired in that way were Louis Bromfield, Ernest Hemingway, Hugh Lofting (*The Story of Doctor Doolittle*), Sherwood Anderson, Sinclair Lewis and Eugene O'Neill.

Another distinguished adviser whose career spanned the inter-war period and who continued well into the 1950s was the American, Frank Morley. In the mid-1920s, he was London manager for an American publishing house, the Century Company. He was later to be a founding director of Faber & Faber and later still, after the Second World War, a director of Eyre & Spottiswoode under Douglas Jerrold's 'command'. He had been a disciple of Edward Garnett, as had Hamish Hamilton in his trainee days, and he did much to foster yet closer links between London and New York. In a *Bookseller* article in 1958, he pointed out that in New York a publishing house which issued fifty to sixty titles a year would employ not less than five editors to prepare those books for production. In London, he claimed, the publisher would employ *one* editor and an associate to edit that number of titles. Since Morley had also worked for Harcourt Brace in the United States he had first-hand knowledge of both markets.

For perhaps ten or fifteen years after 1945, the situation did not change greatly, except that the literary adviser was now more likely to be employed *inside* the publishing house as an active director on the staff – but not as yet under the term 'editorial director'. For example, *The Writers' and Artists' Yearbook* of 1951 lists numerous chairmen, managing directors and even publishers but not a single director nominated for purely editorial skills. The final choice of what books would appear under the imprint fell to the Warburgs, the Hamish Hamiltons, the Michael Josephs and the Collinses, the men whose name was over the door, whereas David Farrer of Secker, Roger Machell of Hamish Hamilton, Roland Gant of Michael Joseph and Fred Smith of Collins were largely and often invaluably 'backroom boys'. They looked after the influx of typescripts, read the more promising ones, kept in close touch with the firm's authors and through clubs like the Garrick and the Savile kept abreast of rumours and hints of promising talent.

Sometimes, they did more. David Farrer, one of the best post-war editors, used to tell a story of how he managed to save Alberto Moravia for the Secker & Warburg list. The firm was then in John Street and David occupied a tiny room, basically a broom cupboard, under the stairs while the ineffable Fred had a large, high-ceilinged room on the first floor. Moravia had come specially from Italy to see Fred Warburg and discuss his next novel. Fred had just published – or was just about to publish – with Hutchinson the first volume of his memoirs, *An Occupation for Gentlemen*. ('How would Fred know?' was one comment in the trade.)

David Farrer was going through a script when he heard thunderous footsteps on the stairs above his head. He rushed out to encounter an enraged Moravia, who said, 'I go – and I no come back. I come all ze way from Rome to talk about *my* book. That Mr Warburg, he spend all ze time talking about *his* book! I no come back.' The ever-genial Farrer hastily bundled Moravia into a cab that fortunately happened to be cruising down John Street, took him to the Garrick Club and plied him with wine and genuine admiration in equal measure until at length Moravia relented.

Smallish publishers like Secker & Warburg in those days were often short of money: in the modern jargon, they had a 'cash flow problem'. So they would often discreetly take in an Oxford or Cambridge graduate, who (usually through a doting parent) could afford to buy shares in the firm and thus put more capital into the business. David Farrer had been the private secretary of Lord Beaverbrook, the owner of the *Express* newspapers and the man who turned irresponsibility into the eighth deadly sin. Beaverbrook was all in favour of Farrer's joining Secker & Warburg and offered to stake him to the subscription fee of £5,000. David Farrer, honest if rash, said that he had £5,000 of his own to put up. Whereupon Beaverbrook summoned the *Daily Express* in-house lawyer and, keeping the door between his office and Farrer's wide open, ostentatiously arranged to cut him out of his will.

There was very little 'cheque-book' publishing in those early post-war years. The one big example occurred in the late 1940s when Lovat Dickson – who once said to me, 'At Macmillan, we don't bother to *discover* authors. We let other publishers find them and then, when they've got established, they usually come to us' – himself 'discovered' that Thomas Hardy, Kipling and Hugh Walpole were dead and that

Charles Morgan, Macmillan's leading live novelist, was unlikely to write much more. The directors of Macmillan in those days lived a sheltered life; they had heard about literary agents but had hardly met any of the breed.

Around 1954, they decided to risk the arena once again and set up a series of boardroom lunches with agents. My partner, Innes Rose, and I were the first two to be formally invited (as I later learned, because we had both been to Cambridge and had served in respectable infantry regiments during the war and so were likely to know which knife and fork to use).

Lovat Dickson on the earlier occasion, having heard about Curtis Brown, went to see Spencer Curtis Brown with an open cheque-book and came away having acquired for Macmillan such novelists as C. P. Snow, Pamela Hansford Johnson, Rumer Godden, Storm Jameson, and less prominent authors like Rupert Croft-Cooke and James Wellard.*

There were several other attempts by publishers at 'buying a list' but on the whole they did not succeed. Wilfred Harvey, the driving force at Purnell (later the British Printing Corporation), acquired John Lehmann and poured money into it but the publishing house did not prosper and was eventually put into liquidation. Macdonald, another BPC company, bought lavishly and built up some momentum that survived into the Captain Maxwell days. But, at least until about 1960, a hardcover publisher could not be certain of laying off paperback rights and so was putting his own money at risk when buying an established author away from his regular publisher. And, as Michael Joseph shrewdly pointed out when questioned about the loss of Pamela Hansford Johnson and Rumer Godden to Macmillan, he was prepared to bid up to the limit to keep them – and he was the one who knew their sales figures over several books. Thus, the rival who acquired their future writings would be paying over the odds and, unless his sales force was considerably more effective than the Joseph representatives, he would automatically be losing money.

So the cottage industry went on its quiet way, looking for new talent to build up book by book and occasionally taking on an established author who, usually for some valid reason, was dissatisfied with his present publisher. Chance, as always, played a large part; here are

* C. P. Snow had been with Faber & Faber; Pamela Hansford Johnson and Rumer Godden with Michael Joseph; Storm Jameson with Cassell; Rupert Croft-Cooke and James Wellard with T. Werner Laurie.

two anecdotes to show both sides of that spinning coin – one pre-war and the other post-war.

Forty years ago Mr Gilbey, then the venerable head buyer at Hatchards, told me this first story, which he swore was true. In the early years of this century Mr Sampson and Mr Low arrived at their office one morning. As they went through the post, their faces grew long. There were almost no orders to reduce the stocks that crammed their warehouse but there were numerous bills and letters threatening legal action if certain long-unpaid accounts were not settled at once. To cap everything, there was a letter announcing that their most successful author had just died untimely.

Mr Sampson turned to his partner and said, 'Mr Low, there is only one thing for it. We must go down on our knees and pray to the Almighty. He alone can save us in our hour of need.'

The two elderly gentlemen knelt on the rather threadbare carpet and in an embarrassed silence uttered a fervent prayer. They rose and were in the act of brushing off their striped trousers when there was a hesitant knock on the outer door. Mr Sampson went and opened it in some trepidation in case an angry creditor had arrived in person. A young man stood there, nervously clutching a parcel.

'I wonder if you would care to look at this novel I've written,' he said. 'My name is Jeffrey Farnol.'

The other example – how one man's will (or whim) could affect publishing decisions – is a less happy one. A senior director of Collins told me in the mid-1960s that he was looking for a few choice novels which he could personally oversee. I had just read and greatly enjoyed the script of a novel entitled *The Girl from Petrovka* by George Feifer, a young American living in London. He had previously spent several years in Moscow and spoke Russian fluently. The novel dealt with an unusual aspect of life as we might imagine it lived in Moscow. 'The girl', who came from the provinces, had no authorisation to remain in the capital and so lived off her wits in an anarchic society on the fringe of – and sometimes right in – the black market.

The director read the typescript, admired it as much as I did and by the end of the week we had agreed good terms for its publication. The following Monday, when I was about to draw up the contract, he telephoned me in great embarrassment. It appeared that William Collins, the chairman, having nothing to read that weekend, had taken the *Petrovka* typescript home. He thoroughly disliked it and, when his colleague explained that there was already an oral agreement to publish it, threatened to instruct the salesmen to ignore it. On the telephone, my friend said that he had given his word to publish and would stand by that pledge – but would it not spoil the chance of success for such a good novel if the chairman refused to let it be properly publicised and sold? He was right, of course. We agreed to cancel the deal and the typescript was returned. I sold it within a few days to Macmillan for improved terms: the novel earned excellent reviews and reasonable sales and was later made into a film, starring Goldie Hawn as 'the girl'. So in the end the author did not suffer but I had had a worrying glimpse of how arbitrary power could be wielded in a highly auto-cratic house.

When Jonathan Cape died in January 1960, G. Wren Howard and his son Michael were left in control of the firm. (Jonathan's estate was valued at £120,000 – over £1 million in today's currency.) As the Howards' expertise lay respectively in running the business and in designing and producing the finished books, they needed to find an executive, or acquiring, editor. Michael Howard had become friendly with Tony Godwin, who had proved himself as an imaginative bookseller with Better Books and over the reorganisation of J. & E. Bumpus, the Oxford Street booksellers. Godwin introduced Howard to Tom Maschler, then an assistant fiction editor at Penguin. Apart from the normal task of buying reprint rights from hardcover publishers Maschler had started the Penguin New Dramatists series. He had previously worked with André Deutsch and with MacGibbon & Kee under Howard Samuel.

He joined Cape in June 1960 – and Tony Godwin went to Penguin. But what proved to be a long and in the main successful association for Maschler with Cape almost came to grief in the first eighteen months. It happened thus.

Not long before his untimely death in March 1958 at the age of sixty, Michael Joseph had sold his firm to *Illustrated London News*. In December 1961 Roy Thomson, who was already on the rampage in the media world, having added the *Sunday Times* to the *Scotsman* and his large holding in Scottish Television, bought *Illustrated London News* and along with it Michael Joseph. (On reading the balance sheet, Roy Thomson is alleged to have asked in wonder, 'Who the hell's this guy Joseph – and what does he do?') Robert Lusty had left Michael

Joseph some years earlier to run the Hutchinson group, which meant that Charles Pick, Peter Hebdon and Roland Gant, the surviving Michael Joseph directors – apart from Joseph's widow, Anthea, and Victor Morrison, who was in charge of production – were uncertain what their fate might be under the mercurial Canadian.

Once again, the Good Fairy (or the Demon King) turned out to be from Penguin. In April 1961, Sir Allen Lane sold 750,000 Penguin ordinary shares (out of an issued total of 2.5 million) to the public at three times their face value of 4s (20p). That left him still with a controlling interest and with £450,000 in liquid funds. William Balleny, Jonathan Cape's executor, approached him with the proposal that he should buy Jonathan's holdings, now just under 50 per cent, and approximately 20 per cent of the shares owned by Wren Howard and his son Michael. Sir Allen at first refused but, after lunching with Charles Pick and hearing of the unhappiness of the three Joseph directors, changed his mind. He would now have the nucleus of a strong team to run Cape well. He made it a condition from the outset that Tom Maschler, who was in New York on business when the negotiations began, would not be part of the deal.

From this point, there are two different versions of the story. According to Michael Howard in *Jonathan Cape, Publisher*:

> I spent much anxious time and nervous energy in conference with my father to convince him that we must withstand the opposition and that, if we had to choose, Tom would be worth more to us than The Trinity (Pick, Hebdon and Gant). Although anxious to oblige Balleny my father was, however, disinclined to let a 'sitting tenant', as he put it, be displaced.

Maschler hurried home and there were various meetings with 'The Trinity' and their backers. On the final occasion, they were adamant that there was no place in their plans for Maschler; the Howards were equally adamant that he 'was an inseparable part of Cape'. It was clearly an *impasse* and after a few minutes Wren Howard declared the meeting closed. The deal was off.

According to Charles Pick, Wren Howard's performance was less heroic and loyal. When negotiations began, he agreed that Maschler, then absent in New York, must go. Without such a preliminary step, Pick and the others, realising Sir Allen Lane's strong feelings against

Maschler, knew that further discussions would be fruitless. Several weeks passed before Wren Howard, egged on by his son, as revealed in the above quotation, 'said that he *had to go back on his word* (my italics) and reintroduce the subject of Maschler.' Sir Allen and the three ex-Michael Joseph directors saw no point in continuing and walked out.

What might have happened to the house of Cape if the Howards had jettisoned Tom Maschler is a fascinating but ultimately pointless study. No doubt Pick and Hebdon between them would have stream-lined the overheads, vastly improved the sales force and have made the back list highly profitable. And Roland Gant would have brought all his editorial flair to bear on the front list. Twenty-five years later, the company might well have remained a sturdily independent house and 'The Trinity' on their respective retirements would have sold on their shares locally for a well-earned but realistic profit.

The actual outcome was more ironic. By then, Cape had become a group, embodying the Bodley Head, Chatto & Windus and, for a briefer period, Virago. After the group had reached the verge of insolvency in 1987, Graham C. Greene and Tom Maschler, who had acquired most of the shares, fell into the arms of Random House of New York and sold out at a price that seemed to bear no relation to reality. They had managed their personal affairs with considerable skill and had ended up as rich men.

In publishing as in other business enterprises, happy endings are all too rare. But in this case everyone concerned came out of it well. Charles Pick became managing director of Heinemann, which he ran with real success for twenty-three years until retirement; Peter Hebdon went back to Michael Joseph as managing director and eventually chairman of the Thomson book publishing group until his premature death at fifty-three; and Roland Gant became editorial director first of Secker & Warburg and later of Heinemann. As for Maschler, it was a matter of 'onwards and upwards'. Within a few years, he had attracted to the Cape list Edna O'Brien, John Fowles, Len Deighton and one of Cape's biggest successes, *John Lennon In His Own Write*. Significantly perhaps, neither Deighton nor Edna O'Brien remained with Cape for many years.

The reason why acquiring editors were now coming into their own was because the old order was literally passing away. Jonathan Cape in his prime would never have tolerated someone else buying the rights. On his decline and later death, the Howards, with their forte on the business and production sides, had had to bring in a substantial editor. Similarly, a few years later, when Ralph Hodder-Williams retired from Hodder & Stoughton, his successors, Paul Hodder-Williams and John Attenborough, soon decided that the company must have a more public editorial image. Previously, Elsie Herron had been the managing editor but she was not encouraged to go out and meet agents. That was the task of 'Mr John' and many middle-aged to elderly agents will recall those stiff luncheons at the Athenaeum. But then, in a master stroke, Hodder-Williams and Attenborough invited Robin Denniston to join them from Collins and the Faith Press. It was Denniston, with the complete confidence and backing of the family, who was largely instrumental in acquiring many of the important authors still with Hodder today. Two of his publishing coups were to obtain, against competition, Sir Francis Chichester and John le Carré.

In the early 1970s Denniston moved briefly to Weidenfeld & Nicolson and then became in charge of all the Thomson group publishing houses, which was, sadly, a perfect example of the 'Peter Principle' in action. Robin Denniston's forte was and is his ability to think on his feet, to deal with individual authors and colleagues when his warmth and personality can be given full rein. As an administrator with the task of hiring and firing and scrutinising the weaknesses of balance sheets, he must have found little inspiration to exercise those very qualities that had led him to be widely noticed.

Late in 1978, he was offered and accepted a leading editorial role at Oxford University Press, where he has since flourished. He wrote a valedictory article in the *Bookseller* on 28 October that year. For its grasp of the twenty-five years and more he had then spent in publishing and for its shrewd insights, the complete article would bear reprinting. One extract that endorses my present argument is:

London in the 1950s had yet to see the rise of the post-war fiction editor. At St James's Place [then the Collins London office] novelists like Margery Sharp, Noel Streatfeild, Rosamond Lehmann and Rose Macaulay, Taylor Caldwell and Thomas Armstrong, Marguerite Steen and Howard Spring, stood in no need of editorial midwifery.

And in 1982, when she was about to retire after a lifetime of service with Chatto & Windus, Norah Smallwood, looking back further, said much the same: 'Editor was not a word much used when I started in 1939. You didn't need to edit Aldous Huxley. But there was a call for a good publisher – and there's a great difference.'

During the 1960s, take-overs by large media groups became fashionable. After acquiring Michael Joseph with the *Illustrated London News*, Roy Thomson added Hamish Hamilton, Thomas Nelson, George Rainbird and Sphere Books to the group. Granada under Sidney Bernstein took a 40 per cent interest in Jonathan Cape but remained a largely silent bedfellow, perhaps because it had already bought Hart-Davis, MacGibbon & Kee and Panther Books. As control receded from its 'in-house' status, managers had to be brought in, accountants, business system experts and here and there a real live editor to ensure a supply of the one essential commodity – saleable, preferably good, books. The day of the acquiring editor had come. One such was Tony Godwin.

Godwin had first became noticed in the mid-1950s as the proprietor of Better Books in the Charing Cross Road. He was one of the early booksellers to realise that the wartime and early post-war boom in books was over. No longer would eager buyers seek out the shop; it was up to the owner or manager of the shop to attract them in. So Tony Godwin advertised his shop in the Underground, in the *New Statesman*, then at its highest circulation, and in the programmes of the Arts Theatre, which was not far from his shop. He arranged for artists like Ronald Searle to design posters for him. Better Books became almost a literary salon where novelists and poets could congregate – and not only when the French pub was closed.

He went on to further bookselling successes in buying the small chain of Alfred Wilson bookshops which had gone into liquidation and, a little later, Bumpus in Oxford Street, a fine old shop that had become run-down as J. G. Wilson (no relation to Alfred) worked on into his eighties. In that connection, the *Bookseller* obituary of Godwin says, 'He was ruthless in drastically cutting his staff and in closing credit accounts' and goes on to mention his 'rebuffs and rudeness'.

In 1960 Allen Lane invited him to join Penguin, Tom Maschler having left to go to Cape. Now twenty-five years old, Penguin had become both complacent and arrogant. Years of success had dulled the hunger to acquire more success and thrusting younger competitors like Pan, Corgi, Four Square, Panther and Fontana were narrowing the lead. To Godwin's credit, he transformed the list in seven years.

He launched several new series such as Penguin Modern Classics, Penguin Modern Poets, Peregrines and a serious new hardcover list (then) entitled Allen Lane the Penguin Press. Penguin reinforced its place as the paperback market leader.

Allen Lane was a complex man and Tony Godwin was often very prickly – with lightning changes from cold rudeness to a warm blue-eyed smile. And he was almost always as taut as a violin string. It must be hard for the 'onlie begetter' of a brilliant publishing concept to find a subordinate making it over in his own image, even though the profits were flowing to the originator in the main. The two of them fell out, ostensibly over a choice of picture covers, and in 1967 Tony Godwin was fired. The *Bookseller* obituary by three of his colleagues paints a sad picture:

> the hostages he had given by accumulated slights and cheerful prodigality with others' money, and his first, nearly fatal illness, left him isolated and defenceless.

In fact, during a dramatic session at the Garrick Club where Allen Lane was immured in one room and Godwin in another, with an emissary scuttling to and fro with proposals and counter-proposals, Tony Godwin's severance pay was agreed at £18,000, which in today's terms would be about £130,000.

He soon joined Weidenfeld & Nicolson but the eight years he spent there were by no means as productive as the Penguin days. In 1975, William Jovanovitch offered him the opportunity to work in New York and develop a personal list of books under the 'umbrella' of Harcourt Brace Jovanovitch. It was a developing trend in New York publishing with Linden Press, Summit Books and a little later Richard Marek Books. Godwin gladly accepted but after only about a year died suddenly from a heart attack. Yet during that brief period he appeared more happy and at peace with himself than ever before. Soon after his death, the Tony Godwin Memorial Scholarship was created whereby each year in turn a young British or a young American editor spends several weeks in New York or London respectively, learning something of how publishing is conducted 'across the water'.

Looking back over more than a decade, it is hard to assess exactly what Tony Godwin *achieved* as a hardcover editor in his comparatively short and often stormy career. *The Times* in a particularly ill-judged obituary spoke of him as 'arguably [*sic*] the greatest post-war editor'.

He was nothing of the sort, probably not in the first ten if a ranking list were to be drawn up for the first thirty years since 1945. All editors have their limitations and Tony's were narrow; within those limits, as David Farrer pointed out in a *Bookseller* obituary, he had fine judgment and a warmth of imagination for authors who appealed to him. He was a man of impulse and a man who could be an inspired leader or a bitter enemy. Few who knew him at all closely could be neutral judges. As his three Penguin colleagues wrote:

It was Tony's role to galvanise Penguin; to bring back the editorial zest and daring of the 1930s . . . He believed passionately that in post-war Britain culture could no longer be handed down to the people; it was theirs as of right and Penguin existed to serve them.
. . . Tony's fundamental principle [was] that it is appetite – for writers, for ideas, for communication, for quality – which makes for good publishing.

On the other hand, Jim Reynolds, who knew him well through their association at Weidenfeld & Nicolson, had this to say in his memoirs, *A Kind of Living*:

The year before I left, George's [Weidenfeld's] appointment of Tony Godwin, who subsequently became deputy chairman, was little short of disastrous.
. . . Adored by authoresses, disliked by junior editors who worked for him, he was viewed with some scepticism by the publishing trade as predominantly a stealer of other publishers' authors and as a very extravagant spender of the slender Weidenfeld resources.

The Tony Godwin Memorial Scholarship is an imaginative idea precisely because of the different approaches that used to obtain – and still do to quite a large extent – both between British and American publishers and between their respective novelists. For a multitude of reasons – since 1945 writing in the States has been 'big business' whereas in Britain it is still more of a cottage industry; Americans want to appear professional while Englishmen often prefer to appear as successful amateurs – the American novelist has usually tended to look on the script he submits as a *draft*: the British novelist looks on his as the final version, subject to checking grammar, punctuation and minor errors.

In his memoirs *Contacts*, Albert Curtis Brown, the American founder of the international agency, had said:

> One becomes a little doubtful of authors who can make really radical changes in their plots and characters at editorial and managerial suggestion . . . Of course the great ones are those who plough too deeply in what proves to be the right furrow to be diverted by any advice.

Again, Alfred A. Knopf, giving the R. R. Bowker Memorial Lecture in 1964, said, 'In the olden days, I think, the serious novelist believed more strongly in his own competence'.

One thinks, indeed, of Maxwell Perkins, hacking scores of thousands of words out of Thomas Wolfe's manuscripts, very probably to their advantage. And then one wonders why Wolfe lacked either the confidence in his own talent or the critical faculty to view what he had written objectively, which made him rely on someone else – no matter how talented a critic – to finish off the job for him. It is as if an architect should thrust his plans into the builder's hands and say, 'This is roughly what I envisage. Now I want you to make sure it stands up.'

Harold Harris, an experienced editor and one of the interviewees in Chapter XI, pointed out to me an extraordinary letter written by Maxwell Perkins to Ernest Hemingway on 22 July 1932. The letter starts off:

> Dear Ernest,
> Everything seems now to be right with the book. And you will see, when we send you the page proof, what we have done about the words . . .

The book in question was *Death in the Afternoon* and, to be fair to Perkins, he might have been referring to four-letter words. But what condescension to someone who was already a major novelist and short-story writer! Scribner's could not be bothered to send the man who had actually written the words their proposals for changes: he would be shown the *fait accompli* at the proof stage.

Maxwell Perkins was undoubtedly a great editor. His letters to and from Hemingway, Scott Fitzgerald and Thomas Wolfe, and Roger Burlingame's *Of Making Many Books* prove how much he cared about his authors, how he commiserated with their misfortunes (and in the case of Scott Fitzgerald lent money he could ill afford) and rejoiced in their successes. He was indeed guide, philosopher and friend to them. How much he 'improved' the texts beyond the original version submitted could only be tested by a textual study of the submitted and published versions. But at least the authors must have felt that he made improvements or else they would not have stayed at 597 Fifth Avenue.

Perkins died in 1947, worn out at the age of sixty-two, but his beliefs were not interred with him. In November 1980, *Publishers Weekly* included an article by Harriet Rubin entitled 'Working Both Sides of the Desk'. The interesting concept was to interview editors who were themselves successful novelists – people like Sol Stein, Carol Hill and Michael Korda. Carol Hill was then a senior editor at Harcourt Brace Jovanovitch. Two quotations in particular stand out from the interview she gave.

When you're really trying to work with a writer to develop a novel, you spend an awful lot of your conscious life trying to solve the dilemmas that novel presents.

Why didn't the author develop the novel himself? Did he anticipate those 'dilemmas' when envisaging the novel? And if not, why not? Who's in charge here?

The second quotation is:

An editor's impulse has to be to take apart, to analyse, to criticise, to see why it doesn't come together. A writer's impulse is never to stand that far outside the material; a writer's impulse is to get it all out and then see what you've got.

Most British editors would probably agree with the first sentence and even the first half of the second sentence. It is the second half that makes the eyebrows twitch. Without delving into theories of aesthetics and an analysis of the creative processes, one can say that 'to get it all out and then see what you've got' sounds more like a physical function than the act of writing a well constructed novel. The writer must surely develop his appraising faculties alongside his imagination so that as the words and the sentences come together in his mind, they are being almost subconsciously refined and regulated. To regurgitate a mass of undigested words on to paper and then humbly beg the editor to put them in order appears to abrogate the responsibilities of the author.

In his R. R. Bowker Memorial Lecture, Alfred A. Knopf made some further sharp comments:

> Today a writer who publishes a short story in the *New Yorker* has within the week offers of a substantial advance payment from three or four publishers for a novel. No one – including the author much of the time – even knows whether he *could* write a novel. The prevailing view seems to be that everyone has at least one novel in him.

We sometimes forget that the word 'novel' means 'new'. As publishing has become more commercialised, there is an increasing tendency to pursue the two extremes – the established success and the completely new. To quote Alfred Knopf yet again,

> I suspect that most publishers today lack the ability to smell out a budding talent and prefer to buy away a property that has been discovered and built up by someone else.

The 'discovered property' may or may not be open to editorial suggestion. As a very rough guide, the more 'literary' the novelist, the less open he or she is to radical editing. But the new novelist is understandably more susceptible. When taken to the top of a high mountain and shown what could accrue, few newcomers would refuse to let the editor have the upper hand.

The editor's role has changed substantially over the past twenty years in those publishing houses that have merged or been taken over. There are still several privately owned firms – André Deutsch, Victor Gollancz, Hodder & Stoughton, John Murray and Souvenir Press are prime examples – where large or controlling shareholders exercise personal supervision. But more and more the bosses of the conglomerates and the large houses are men of business, policy makers, cash flow experts, men with City influence. Sir William Collins had an extraordinary publishing flair but Ian Chapman today is almost certainly a shrewder overall judge of a book. But – and it may be doing him a serious injustice – one cannot see Ian Chapman, having nothing to read over the weekend, walking into an office and grabbing a script to take home, as Billy Collins did with *The*

*Girl from Petrovka*. The Collins group is now so much bigger, more international with its large shareholding in Harper & Row of New York, more 'big business' in every way. Men like Ian Chapman, Peter Mayer of Penguin, the Attenborough brothers of Hodder & Stoughton, though they no doubt conscientiously read the books of their major authors and as much else as they can, have to rely on editors to sift and select the dozens of novels published annually by their respective houses.

But those editors today are preserved from one previous danger in selecting novels for publication. That was the risk of landing in the dock of the Old Bailey, charged with publishing an obscene work.

# Chapter IV

# Censorship and the Novel

This business of denying people what we feel they
shouldn't want.

C. H. Rolph

Is it a book you would even wish your wife or your
servant to read?

Mervyn Griffith-Jones

The schoolboy's essay on 'The Elephant' that began: 'It is difficult
to describe an elephant but you know one when you see it' would
as well apply to the definition of an obscene publication. Most
adults with a modicum of common sense would agree that certain
illustrated magazines and books containing photographs of bestiality,
other unnatural acts, child pornography and sadistic practices should
not be readily available for sale to the young and impressionable.
When it comes to the printed word, which lacks the visual impact
of the photograph and which can comment on as well as describe
the actions of the characters, an adequate definition of obscenity
becomes more difficult, particularly one that will be acceptable to
all ages and classes of society. Lord Chief Justice Goddard, who
was over seventy years of age in the 1950s, was born and reared in
the Victorian era. His attitude towards what might or might not be
obscene – and he was in a position to enforce that attitude – would
be likely to differ considerably from that of the young man or woman
who had experienced the upheaval of a major war and the consequent
change in morals, the greater frankness of language and the crumbling
of social customs.

In 1953, the prevailing definition of an obscene libel dated back to
the Hicklin judgment of eighty-five years earlier, pronounced by Lord
Justice Cockburn. Any work liable to deprave and corrupt anyone
open to such depravity and corruption was *ipso facto* obscene; the

author who wrote it, the printer who printed it, the publisher who published it and the bookseller who offered it for sale, were all equally liable to prosecution. The procedure was that, acting under the instructions of the Director of Public Prosecutions, an officer of the Metropolitan Police (if in the London area) would buy a copy of the offending publication from a bookshop – as evidence that the book was readily available to the public – and, when the matter came up for trial, the same police officer, having read the book, would give evidence on oath that he had been an innocent, unspoilt character up to the point when he opened the offending volume but that, as a direct result of his close perusal, he was now a lost soul, wholly depraved and corrupted.

(One such officer had a drink with a defendant at the conclusion of an obscene publication case, when he described with relish some of the more *outré* instruments in Scotland Yard's Black Museum and invited the publisher involved to inspect the Black Museum for himself. The publisher was reminded of the old story about an earnest undergraduate at Oxford, a Moral Rearmer, who asked the Master of his college whether he suffered from indecent thoughts. 'No, my boy,' the Master replied, 'I rather enjoy them.')

For at least a quarter of a century, it had been an axiom in publishing circles that only 'filthy' books and magazines, either imported from the Continent or issued by back-street publishers, were liable to be prosecuted for obscenity. A reputable and well-established hardcover publisher, it was held, would be immune. It was true that in 1926 the Home Secretary, Sir William Joynson-Hicks, spurred on by the dour Scottish editor of the *Sunday Express*, James Douglas, had set up the successful prosecution of Radclyffe Hall's *The Well of Loneliness* but by 1953 that was in the distant past and 'Besides, the wench is dead'. But hardcover publishers were about to be woken from their complacent doze, again by a morally crusading *Sunday Express* editor, John Gordon. He wrote a weekly commentary in his newspaper and, shrewdly combining the knowledge of what helps to sell newspapers with the rectitude of an elder of the Kirk, in July 1953 he inveighed against two recent hardcover novels, *The Philanderer* by Stanley Kaufman, published by Secker & Warburg, and *Julia* by Margot Bland, published by T. Werner Laurie. Any adult reader of those two novels today would wonder what all the fuss was about. Indeed, it could well be argued that *The Philanderer* is a highly moral work, in that the main character through his promiscuity brings unhappiness upon his family and himself.

93

Nevertheless, as a result of John Gordon's original article and follow-up remarks in his column, wondering why no official action had been taken against the offending (in his opinion) books, the police issued a summons against Boots Library in the Isle of Man for handling obscene publications. Boots pleaded guilty at the magistrates' court and received nominal fines – but Gordon's first shots had hit the target.

The book trade was both disturbed and incensed. It was obvious that the average bookseller with a stock of several thousand titles could not possibly be aware of the contents of each book. In September that year, under the title of 'The Bookseller's Dilemma', one of them wrote to the *Bookseller* about Vicki Baum's *The Mustard Seed*: 'Quite frankly, I am horrified to find that I have unwittingly been selling 400 pages of detailed and unrelieved descriptions of sex and lust.'

There were further rumblings in the trade throughout the rest of 1953. In December, Sir David Maxwell-Fyfe, formerly Chief Prosecutor at Nuremberg and by then Home Secretary, in reply to a parliamentary question proclaimed that the penalties for publishing obscene books were a fine of £100 or six months' imprisonment – or both. That same month, an article in the *Bookseller* pointed out that publishers would be put in an extraordinarily weak position if booksellers automatically pleaded guilty when charged with selling an obscene book.

In January 1954, two 'back-street' publishers were found guilty at the Old Bailey, fined £6,000 and sent to prison for six months for publishing 'obscene libels' in the shape of various paperback novels by the prolific Hank Janson. The author himself, living in Spain, was beyond the jurisdiction of the court. They appealed but two months later Lord Chief Justice Goddard, who was a great devotee of hanging and flogging, dismissed their appeal with the words, 'Could anyone really argue that these books were not obscene? They're filthy.' In April, 15,735 books were destroyed in a police raid on the Atlantic Book Company of Leigh Street, London, WC1, by order of the Clerkenwell magistrate. And still the trade believed that reputable hardcover publishers would not be caught in the spreading net.

They were wrong. In May, thanks to John Gordon's thunderings, Secker & Warburg and T. Werner Laurie were summonsed for the respective titles found guilty in the Isle of Man proceedings. A third victim was charged – Hutchinson for publishing *September in Quinze* by Vivian Connell. The three publishers had the choice of being dealt with summarily at magistrates' court level or electing to go for trial at the Central Criminal Courts. Werner Laurie was not sufficiently prosperous at that stage to risk expensive legal fees at the higher level and so opted for summary trial. On 29 May at Clerkenwell magistrates' court, it and the book's printers were fined a total of 75 guineas with an extra 25 guineas in costs. The author, Margot Bland, was fined £25 with 5 guineas' costs.

In June, Hutchinson appeared at the Marlborough Street magistrates' court but the presiding magistrate refused to deal with the case on the grounds that it would better be heard in front of a jury at the Old Bailey.

Secker & Warburg had already opted for trial at the Old Bailey. In July, the case came up for trial before Mr Justice Stable and for the first time a breeze of moderation blew across the perfervid atmosphere. The learned judge began the proceedings by saying that he did not wish to see a distinguished publisher in Mr Frederic Warburg standing in the dock like a common criminal. He requested Warburg to leave the dock forthwith and sit with his solicitor in the body of the court. Students of the subject should read carefully Mr Justice Stable's complete summing-up for the jury – a model of wise tolerance – for one of his key sentences, in response to the prosecution claims pressed by that strange archaic figure, Mervyn Griffith-Jones, was this:

Are we going to say in England that our contemporary literature is to be judged by what is suitable for a fourteen-year-old schoolgirl to read?

Secker & Warburg were found not guilty.

But any prolonged cheering was premature. Two months later, the Hutchinson case came up at the Old Bailey under the Public Recorder, Sir Gerald Dodson. Many years earlier, he had written the insipid libretto of *The Rebel Maid*, which presumably made him an authority on modern literature. His summing-up on *September in Quinze* was generally hostile and in his remarks to Mrs K. Webb, the Hutchinson director charged, he said:

I should have thought that any reader, however inexperienced, would have been repelled by a book of this sort, which is repugnant to every emotion which ever stirred in man or woman.

Hutchinson was found guilty and fined a total of £1,500 – close on £15,000 in modern terms.

There was some light relief that same month when the Swindon magistrates allowed an appeal with costs against their previous decision to destroy stocks of Boccaccio's *The Decameron*. Counsel for the Director of Public Prosecutions had put forward a novel theory – in his words, 'A book can be obscene in one place and not in another.' He claimed that as Swindon was a borough of great respectability, its good citizens might be disturbed by a frankly written classic that more sophisticated towns would regard as harmless. In October, Heinemann was hauled into the Old Bailey for publishing Walter Baxter's *The Image and the Search*, a seriously intended novel about homosexual love. A. S. Frere, the director concerned and one of the most distinguished figures in London publishing, was granted bail in the amount of £100! And at the very end of the same month, Arthur Barker Ltd was prosecuted for *The Man in Control* by Hugh McGraw, a book it had published many months previously and which was out of print.

By now, the defence was forming up. On 27 October 1954, a letter appeared in *The Times* under the heading, 'Censorship by Prosecution'; it was signed by Lord Russell of Killowan, Sir Compton Mackenzie, J. B. Priestley, H. E. Bates, W. Somerset Maugham and Sir Philip Gibbs. Major Gwilym Lloyd George, the son of the goat-footed earl who had himself danced many an antic hay in his time, was now Home Secretary and, when faced with a barrage of questions in the House of Commons, promised to 'look into' the law on obscene libel. That December, an Old Bailey jury could not reach a verdict in the case of *The Image and the Search*; Mr Justice Lynskey abandoned the case. Also in December, again at the Old Bailey, Arthur Barker were found not guilty of the charges against them. Early in 1955, Hank Janson, who had returned to England to face charges, was acquitted on all the seven counts against him – poor consolation to his publishers who had by then served their sentences.

But, not for the first time, the laws of England on the statute books lagged a long way behind the interpretations put on them by liberal-minded judges and public figures. In March 1955 Roy Jenkins introduced a new Obscene Publications Bill in the House of Commons. It proposed that a judge and jury would have to take into account the author's intention when writing his book and they would also have to study the dominant effect of the publication, not look at isolated passages picked out by the prosecution. The type of person likely to read the book was also to be considered – and the defence could have witnesses called to testify to the work's literary or other merits. The bill, not surprisingly perhaps, was talked out by right-wing Conservative members.

Fourteen months later, Mr Jenkins and Sir Alan Herbert proposed the bill again but Major Lloyd George, still Home Secretary, said that the government would not back it. And there the matter rested until March 1958 when a Select Committee of the Commons put forward recommendations for changes in the law on obscene libel. These included several of the 1955 proposals, in particular that a defence of literary and artistic merit could be argued, that the author had the right to be heard in his own defence, that expert evidence would be admitted and that any bookseller charged with issuing an obscene libel could plead 'innocent dissemination'. Once more, in November, the Macmillan government – it was not one of that ex-publisher's few 'finest hours' – killed off the embryo bill but Mr Jenkins did make a moving appeal on 18 November in the House under the 'ten-minute rule'.

Gradually, parliament was beginning to reflect the growing opinion of the public outside – that literature should reflect the realities of modern life and that men and women who not much more than a decade earlier had experienced the full force of war should not be treated as a nanny treats small children. At the end of January 1959, the Obscene Publications Bill passed its second reading unopposed. Even so, the Solicitor-General, Sir Harry Hylton-Foster, speaking on the test of obscenity, proclaimed – shades of Swindon! – two months later, 'A book may be wrong in one place and right in another.'

Nevertheless, the Obscene Publications Bill became law on 1 August 1959 and the stage was now set for the final act in the farce: the prosecution of *Lady Chatterley's Lover* in its unexpurgated version. In January 1960 Penguin announced that, to celebrate the thirtieth anniversary of D. H. Lawrence's death in June, it intended to publish seven of his novels including the complete edition of *Lady Chatterley's Lover*.

Not even his friends and admirers would ever have claimed that Allen Lane was a crusader, prepared to tilt at the windmills of outworn beliefs in the names of Progress and Culture. He was a shrewd, tough publisher of the old school, who had had one brilliant innovative idea and who had pursued it with remarkable success and zeal. He had proved himself a gambler in 1935 and now, twenty-five years later, he was ready to undertake another expensive gamble, presumably suspecting that there could well be a brush with the law but certain that if he won, the resulting public controversy would lead to a huge bestseller. Irrespective of their literary qualities, to modern tastes those previous novels that had been charged as obscene would appear innocuous, mildly titillating at the most. But *Lady Chatterley's Lover* was a different case. The continual use of short Anglo-Saxon words to describe the sexual organs and the explicit sex scenes made it appear that Lawrence had deliberately intended to startle the bourgeois; the general silliness of the novel also made it more difficult to defend on the grounds of literary merit. If it had not been one of the few bad novels by an admittedly great writer, one doubts whether any publisher would have fought for the reading public's right to read it in the unexpurgated version.

On 13 February, a deliberate question was put to the Attorney-General in the House of Commons. Would the Right Honourable gentleman give an assurance that *Lady Chatterley's Lover* would not be prosecuted? The one-word written answer was 'No'. Two months later, he was again asked for an assurance that Hazell, Watson & Viney, the printers designate of the book, would not be prosecuted. Again, the one-word answer was 'No'. No one can blame Messrs Hazell, Watson & Viney for deciding to take the path of discretion. However, Western Press proved braver and Penguin announced publication for late July or early August. The company was feeling bullish. A week later, it announced that its profits for the first quarter of 1960 were 25 per cent up on the same period in 1959, which had been 12 per cent up on the same period in 1958. Perhaps the announcement, made at that crucial moment, was to let the Director of Public Prosecutions realise that it could afford to fight a costly action.

But general publication did not take place on or near the thirtieth anniversary of Lawrence's death. A tentative date was set for 25 August but, when five days earlier the police demanded and received an advance copy of the book, publication was postponed 'until further notice'. The press had a field day. Sex, four-letter words, a notorious dead author, a famous publishing house bearding the authorities – what spicy ingredients for a tasty dish to set before the hungry public! The more serious newspapers pointed out that under the 1959 Act the penalties if found guilty were (on summary conviction) a fine of £100 or imprisonment for six months; on conviction in the higher court, an unspecified fine or imprisonment up to three years – or both. The stakes were high.

On 3 September, summons were issued against Penguin and a preliminary hearing took place. It was adjourned for a week when the trial was set for the Old Bailey for 11 October. Sir David Cairns, QC, (later replaced by Gerald Gardiner, QC,) was to lead for the defence, with Jeremy Hutchinson and Richard du Cann as his juniors. Mervyn Griffith-Jones, Senior Crown Counsel, was to lead the prosecution. The trial opened on 20 October under Mr Justice Byrne.

He adjourned the case for eight days so that the jury (nine men and three women) could read the book for themselves. The case re-opened on 28 October. The defence had assembled a formidable list of expert witnesses including Dame Rebecca West, three Cambridge dons in Graham Hough, Joan Bennett and Raymond Williams, Helen Gardner, Professor V. de S. Pinto, Richard Hoggart, E. M. Forster, Roy Jenkins, Walter Allen, Norman St John-Stevas, Sir Stanley Unwin and Cecil Day Lewis. And the Bishop of Woolwich, Dr John Robinson, who found no problem, apparently, in reconciling a bishopric with what appeared at times to be a lack of belief in the tenets of the Anglican faith. Not all of them were called into the witness-box but the good bishop had no trouble in making a fool of himself and bemusing prosecution and defence alike with his evidence.

Throughout his cross-examinations and in his address to the jury Mr Mervyn Griffith-Jones maintained a tone of priggish outrage. His closing speech included the following remarks about the book on trial:

> It sets on a pedestal promiscuous intercourse and it commends and sets out to commend sensuality almost as a virtue, and encourages and even advocates coarseness and vulgarity of thought and language . . . Would you approve of your own sons and daughters reading this book? Is it a book you would even wish your wife or your servant to read?

In his final speech for the defence, Mr Gardiner introduced a note of amused tolerance when he gently remarked:

> I don't want to upset the prosecution by suggesting there are a certain number of people who do not have servants. This whole

attitude was one that Penguin Books was formed to fight against, i.e. 'It would never do to let the members of the working class read this.'

The jury unanimously found Penguin Books not guilty but, when asked for costs by Mr Gardiner, the judge refused, commenting darkly that he would know the reason why. When asked afterwards, amid congratulations, what he reckoned the costs would amount to, Allen Lane remarked that there would be only enough for a drink or two left out of £10,000.

He need not have worried – and Mr Justice Byrne's reason for refusing costs was quickly apparent. The public demand for *Lady Chatterley's Lover* was immediate and impossible to satisfy. The first printing of 200,000 copies disappeared in a day. A further reprint of 250,000 copies went as quickly. In the end, four different printing firms, including Western Press who had bravely taken the initial risk, were turning out copies as fast as their presses would permit. By 17 December, six weeks after the trial ended, Penguin had already despatched 2 million copies. Estimating a gross profit of 10d per copy, Penguin had by then made some £83,000 in profits, allowing Allen Lane to enjoy more than a drink or two. The *Observer* neatly rounded off the controversy with its headline, 'Would you let your gamekeeper read *Lady C?*'

But that was not the end of the affair. Although it was said of Mr Griffith-Jones that he used the jawbone of an ass – his own – to smite his moral enemies, he nevertheless had a streak of low cunning. And the good fortune to serve under a complaisant Director of Public Prosecutions in Sir Theobald Mathew. Sir Theobald, a jolly and lazy man, kept a very loose rein on his subordinates. He died on 29 February 1964; in an *Observer* obituary, Louis Blom-Cooper, the noted lawyer, had this to say:

If Mr Mervyn Griffith-Jones thought a book was obscene and not published for the public good, that was enough for Sir Theo, and a prosecution was launched.

Jones the moral scourge had found a loophole in the 1959 law. It was possible for the Director to prosecute in a case of would-be obscenity not the publisher responsible but a bookseller who displayed the offending book. The case could also be tried by a senior stipendiary magistrate and the defence had no automatic right to demand trial by jury. So when Mayflower Books, then a substantial paperback house, published John Cleland's *Fanny Hill* at the beginning of 1964, a West End bookseller named Gold was charged at Bow Street magistrates' court. On 22 February the case came up for hearing before the Chief Metropolitan Magistrate, Sir Robert Blundell. Jeremy Hutchinson, QC, had been retained for the defence. Mayflower Books was permitted to intervene but its position was that of the boxer's second, who has to sit by in a corner and watch his fighter being knocked all round the ring.

Victor Gollancz, always ready to pronounce on other men's problems, had delivered his verdict on pornography; 'the better sort of which, in a poor second-hand sort of way, is to some degree life-enhancing'. The defence was entitled to call expert witnesses to testify to *Fanny Hill*'s literary qualities and in turn Peter Quennell, Montgomery Hyde, Karl Miller and Marghanita Laski gave their opinion that the book, though not a major classic, was gracefully written and displayed a happy view of sex. It was also interesting as a piece of social history.

Griffith-Jones was having none of that. He read aloud many of the 'juicy bits' and kept asking the witnesses in turn if they thought those passages were great literature, a claim none of them had put forward in the first place. The magistrate readily found the book obscene. Counsel on behalf of Mayflower requested that the publisher should now be prosecuted. Sir Robert refused the request. Mayflower Books was ordered to destroy its stocks, running into many thousands of copies, and the unfortunate bookseller was fined.

There was a public outcry and questions asked in the House of Commons. Three months later, a new Obscene Publications Bill was introduced. It removed various anomalies from the 1959 Act. Prosecution could no longer be selective; the publisher would have to be charged in any action that arose. Experienced police officers would no longer be considered 'corruptible'. Finally, the display of priced articles in a shop could not in itself constitute an offer for sale. (Part of Mr Gold's, the bookseller's, defence had been that he bought his stocks in good faith from reputable publishers and put them on display in his shop without having the time or the inclination to read the contents of each.)

There was yet to be one last prolonged act before the curtain fell. Sir Cyril Black, MP, in the summer of 1966, repeatedly asked the

Home Secretary if he would institute proceedings against a recently published book which Sir Cyril refused to name in public in order to avoid affording it extra publicity. Each time, the answer was no. The indignant MP, having discovered a further loophole in the 1959 Act, thereupon instituted a private prosecution at Bow Street magistrates' court. Sir Robert Blundell, the Chief Magistrate, issued a warrant for the seizure of *Last Exit to Brooklyn* by Hubert Selby Jr, published by Calder & Boyars. That was in August. The following month, the publisher was summoned to appear at Marlborough Street magistrates' court at the end of October. The book had already been on sale for several months but prudent booksellers did not display it in the period before the action began. The farcical result was that Sir Cyril Black was forced to call at the office of Calder & Boyars and ask if he could buy a copy, as the book was unobtainable elsewhere.

The case opened on 5 November, with Michael Havers, QC, appearing for the prosecution. Witnesses for the prosecution included Montgomery Hyde, Robert Pitman (yet again the *Express* group was to provide a judge of morals), David Holloway, Professor George Catlin and, strangely, two publishers – one a publisher/bookseller – in Sir Basil Blackwell and Robert Maxwell, neither of whom was concerned in fiction publishing. One would have thought that a fellow publisher would either have supported a colleague's freedom to publish or at least would have remained silent if he disapproved of the published work.

For the defence, Marion Boyars testified that *Last Exit* had sold 11,000 copies for a turnover of £10,465. When production and overhead costs and payments to the author were deducted, there was a before tax profit of £1,148. That did not take into account the legal costs which would turn the profit into a loss. Calder & Boyars, she maintained, had published the book because of its literary merit and not to make a large profit on pandering to the lower tastes of readers. Various defence witnesses, including Robert Baldick, the Oxford don-cum-book-reviewer, Timothy O'Keefe, the publisher, Bryan Magee, the author and broadcaster, and Edward Lucie-Smith, the art critic, gave evidence to support the literary qualities of *Last Exit* but Mr Leo Gradwell, the stipendiary magistrate, declared the book to be obscene and ordered the three copies that had been seized to be destroyed.

The crazy outcome of Sir Cyril Black's private prosecution was that *Last Exit to Brooklyn* would be considered obscene in the Marlborough

Street area – but nowhere else. An Oxford Street bookseller would be running a grave risk if he stocked and displayed the book. But Truslove & Hanson, Harrods book department and Mr Simmonds of Fleet Street would presumably sell it with impunity. The whole episode was neatly rounded off when, in the week before Christmas, that time of goodwill, several Labour MPs, led by Tom Driberg and Michael Foot, tabled a motion of censure against Sir Cyril.

But the Director of Public Prosecutions kept on with the war. In February 1967 he issued a summons under Section 2 of the Obscene Publications Act 1959 against Calder & Boyars for publishing *Last Exit to Brooklyn*. The case was to be heard on 29 March at Marlborough Street but under a different magistrate. It was small consolation to the harassed publisher to read that in mid-March Mr Roy Jenkins, then Home Secretary, announced in the House that he would be tabling an amendment to the Criminal Justice Bill, prohibiting private actions for forfeiture under Section 3 of the Act. On 3 April Calder & Boyars was committed for trial at the Old Bailey.

The case opened on 13 November with John Mathew appearing for the Crown and Patrick Neill, QC, for the defence. They both agreed that an all-male jury should be selected – a strange step, one might think, on the part of the defence when the book dealt repeatedly with male homosexual practices. Even though, as emerged in the cross-examination, Blackwell's bookshop in Oxford had continued to sell *Last Exit* since the magistrates' court action, Sir Basil presented himself as a major prosecution witness, along with the old team of Professor Catlin and Montgomery Hyde but with an impressive newcomer in the Reverend David Sheppard. Defence witnesses included Professor Frank Kermode, Alfred Alvarez, Eric Mottram, a lecturer in American literature at London University, Michael Scofield, the social psychologist, Quentin Crewe, Kenneth Allsop and Martyn Goff.

The moral fervour of a Mervyn Griffith-Jones was refreshingly absent in the prosecution's approach; John Mathew even spoke of 'the verbally permissive 1960s'. The all-male jury took five and a half hours in its deliberations but found the publisher guilty. Judge Graham Rogers, in fining it £100 and a contribution of £500 towards the prosecution's costs, stressed that it had published the book in good faith.

The modest penalty was almost a vindication of the stand taken by Calder & Boyars but it was heavily overshadowed by its legal costs to date and the very substantial further costs that would be incurred if they were to appeal against the verdict. A supporting fund was opened and at the beginning of August 1968, over two years since Sir Cyril Black had appointed himself the guardian of public morals, the Court of Appeal quashed the conviction. Adjudicating only on matters of law, Lord Justice Salmon gave a reserved judgment. The grounds for quashing the verdict were that Mr Justice Rogers had not guided the jury sufficiently on the implications of Section 4 of the Act, the section that dealt with expert evidence. Calder & Boyars was awarded the costs of its appeal, which amounted to about £15,000.

It was perhaps fitting that the last major case of a trial for obscenity should result in a David and Goliath victory for a small publishing house that had the courage of its convictions to go on fighting for a novel which many readers might find painful and depressing in its descriptions of drug-taking and homosexual acts but which was imbued with an honesty of purpose and a certain literary talent. Almost exactly fifteen years had gone by since the Isle of Man action against *The Philanderer* and *Julia*. The public reading taste had advanced to the point where it could now accept that whatever happens in real life may be a fitting subject for fiction; the judiciary was rapidly catching up with the public. As Lord Annan put it with some wit in a House of Lords debate in 1966,

> . . . the day of the jewelled epigram is passed, and, whether one likes it or not, one is moving into the stern puritanical era of the four-letter word.

What has that fifteen-year battle long ago won for the novelist? It won him the right to introduce realism into his dialogue. Men (and women) under stress do use four-letter words; one forgets that a couple of decades earlier Norman Mailer in *The Naked and the Dead* had had to use the coy bowdlerising of 'fugging' for the fighting soldier's favourite adjective. Other common substitutes before the mid-1960s were 'flicking' or 'effing' or 'f . . ing'. Editors even used to delete the word 'shit' from authors' typescripts as being too vulgar to print and recommended 'crap' instead. 'Bloody' was permitted but slang terms to describe male and female genitals were out – as were 'Jesus Christ' or 'for Christ's sake' when used as expletives. Sexual acts and the emotions they evoked were not to be described except in some symbolic way such as waves surging and crashing on an imaginary beach. The only kind of organ music permitted was that played in churches.

Above all, it afforded the novelist the opportunity to follow through in his work the classical dictum: 'I find nothing human alien to me.' A young barrister in the 1950s, later to become an Old Bailey judge, earned extra income by writing popular legal articles for a large-circulation women's magazine. One of them dealt with changing one's name and whether it was essential to do so by deed poll. He instanced a fictitious case of a woman who had undergone a painful divorce and who decided to make a fresh start by changing her name. The magazine editor liked the article but insisted on his altering the reason for the fresh start. 'My readers,' she claimed, 'do not like to be reminded that such a thing as divorce exists.' It is that ostrich-like attitude that the Act helped to remove.

Today, novelists can deal honestly and sensitively with the human condition in all its manifestations. Some of them have indeed taken too much advantage of that freedom. In recent fiction, the innocent goldfish has been subjected to practices that would offend the Society for the Protection of Aquarium Fishes, should it exist; diamonds have also been displayed in unusual settings. Robin Denniston, commenting in 1978 on his experiences in general publishing in the post-*Lady Chatterley* era, wrote:

> I emerge from editorial experience knowing more of oral and anal sex, paedophilia, coprophilia, bondage, SM, you name it, I've read about it, than I'll ever need in this life or, hopefully, the next. It is salutary for editors to be occasionally reminded that they are in the erotica business.

Over the past ten years, one could pick out dozens of examples of novel-reviews where the presumably broad-minded reviewer gagged on the subject-matter. A flagrant case was the London *Evening Standard* review by Miranda Seymour in February 1987 of Hugh Fleetwood's novel, *The Past*, a 'tale of murder, incest, sodomy and sadism'. After setting the scene, in which the mother is straddling the German gardener, her son is working off 'his filial disgust' by buggering the gardener's son and the father is acting as voyeur to his wife's infidelity, the review goes on to report more of the plot in which the son rapes his mother and the child of that misunion ends up being starved to death in the family dungeon. And so on. The concluding paragraph of the review came up with this verdict:

> *The Past* is stylish, elegant and well-constructed but to recommend it is like saying you really ought to try swimming in a cesspit. Some reviewers have compared it to a Jacobean tragedy. It is true that all the horror is here. What is missing is any sense that spiritual depravity can mean more than a variety of sexual perversions.

It is small wonder that two right-wing Conservative MPs, Winston Churchill and Gerald Howarth, have at different times pressed for changes to the Obscene Publications Act. Mr Howarth in January 1988 introduced a Private Members Bill which promulgated a new test – 'gross offensiveness to a reasonable person'. The definition was too vague and the bill was talked out but not without a commitment from the government that the existing obscenity law would be amended during the lifetime of the present parliament.

Thanks largely to the pioneering efforts of Roy Jenkins and the late Sir Alan Herbert, however, British novelists in the past quarter of a century have enjoyed the freedom of honest realism that would never have been dreamed of in the philosophy of Mervyn Griffith-Jones. Under a pragmatic government, it may pay them to ensure that liberty does not slide into licence.

# Chapter VII

# Early Years and the Rise of the Paperback

There are only four kinds of books. There are good books
that do sell and good books that don't sell; bad books that
do sell and bad books that don't sell.

Sir John Squire, 1948

Publishing is merely a matter of saying Yes and No at
the right time.

Michael Joseph,
speaking at the Foyle's Jubilee Dinner, 1954

The publishing scene in Britain since the end of the Second World War falls roughly into three phases. For the first fifteen years, indeed, as it happened, up until the *Lady Chatterley* trial, the term 'a cottage industry' could well be applied. Many houses were still run by the founder or a direct descendant. The man was the list. One thinks not only of Jonathan Cape or Billy Collins, or Michael Joseph or Frederic Warburg, but also of Peter Davies, Martin Dent, André Deutsch, Noel Evans, Geoffrey Faber, Sir Newman and then Dr Desmond Flower of Cassell, Victor Gollancz, Robert Hale, Hamish Hamilton, George and Walter Harrap, Walter Hutchinson, John Murray, Sir Stanley Unwin, and Lord Weidenfeld. During the period too, a seventh-generation Longman – Mark, whose career was tragically cut short by a fatal illness – created a vibrant general list and Daniel Macmillan kept a fatherly eye on his firm that had been founded over a hundred years earlier.

(It is an interesting side-issue that English publishing this century has largely been run by Scots and Jews. Of the twenty names just listed, only four or five are English. Taking the other nationalities that make up those saloon-bar jokes, the Welsh could claim the Hodder-Williams family, Peter and Nico Davies and those far-off Evans Brothers. With the notable exceptions of Michael Dempsey,

Timothy O'Keefe and Robert Kee in his early days, the Irish have not excelled in this field. Many, relying on a mixture of blarney and verbose broguery, have found it easier to scale the depths of radio and TV talk shows than apply themselves to the rigours of publishing. In any case, most of them have lacked the necessary higher education.)

When the founder happened to be the day-to-day controller of the house, publishing lists tended to be idiosyncratic. The in-house editor would meet or correspond with the author over editorial points but the publisher always made it clear that manna flowed from him in person. If any of his important authors happened to call at 14 St James's Place, Billy Collins was apprised at once and would drop whatever he was doing to go and greet the visitor. The stamp of Victor Gollancz was on every aspect of the books he published – from the yellow jackets to the garish typefaces and the wording of the bold advertisements with their sweeping claims for the number of impressions chasing each other off the presses.

The built-in disadvantage of the personal publisher was that he could at times believe he was doing authors a favour by affording them the special privilege of belonging to his august list. Authors are notoriously unreliable people; they never deliver their books by the contracted date, they either write too much or too little, they are always asking for money; as Walter Harrap once said to me in tones of complete conviction, 'Ours would be a wonderful job if it weren't for authors'. He found it difficult to accept the retort that publishers would not have a job at all were it not for authors. Victor Gollancz lost John le Carré because he tried to patronise him during the enormous success of *The Spy Who Came in from the Cold*, believing that the success was due more to the publisher than the writer himself. The earlier editions of Sir Stanley Unwin's *The Truth About Publishing* were notable for the tone of asperity that crept in when he discussed authors and their fallibilities. The author-publisher relationship is dealt with in more detail elsewhere in this book but at least it can be said that a real relationship usually did exist in the 1950s and 1960s, which is not always the case at present.

On the whole, most novelists probably benefited from the close personal touch. But if it is a truism that writing is 'the lonely art' – the author is on his own when he faces that blank sheet of paper – the knowledge that a powerful individual is interested in him and his work can be beneficial. Now that many of the privately owned firms have been merged into larger corporations, the editor has to a great degree taken the place of the owner but there are very few editors in British publishing today with a comparable degree of power and responsibility and who stay in the same job for ever.

Elderly publishers and booksellers look back on the immediate post-war years with a nostalgic gleam in their eyes. Millions of young men and women, drafted into the forces, had made a dual discovery. They had discovered that war consists of a few short, sharp moments of danger interspersed with long bouts of boredom. They had also discovered that books are easily portable and are a useful means of alleviating that boredom. Demobilisation after May 1945 was carried out through an orderly points system, based on essential occupations, age, length of service and time spent overseas. Thus, up until the end of 1946 and even beyond, there were still hundreds of thousands of service men and women with diminishing military duties and many spare hours of reading time.

The Luftwaffe caused the second Great Fire of London on Sunday, 29 December 1940. I still remember, as a private soldier going home on leave, walking from Liverpool Street to Victoria along the Embankment the following morning – there was no public transport – crunching shards of broken glass from the windows of the Savoy Hotel and Shell-Mex House under my ammunition boots. A pall of thick black smoke hung across the Thames, so that it was impossible to see the south bank. Fifteen hundred fires, caused by incendiary bombs, had ravaged the City and the docks. In and around Paternoster Row, then the home of the publishing trade, the premises of nineteen publishers had been destroyed in that one night; they included William Collins, Hodder & Stoughton, the Hutchinson group, Longmans, Thomas Nelson, Ward Lock and the wholesalers, Simpkin Marshall. Only the Oxford University Press building had remained unscathed.

Stocks of over 20 million books had been reduced to ashes or to sodden pulp. Standard works and stocks of popular fiction had gone up in the blaze. There was an urgent demand for their replacement, a demand that could not be met at once, since all publishers were bound by a paper quota. It was based on each publisher's actual usage in the twelve months preceding the outbreak of war. Those publishers who had had a successful 1938–39, or who by accident had published more than their usual output in that period, were relatively better off than others. Up to October 1945 the quota was 50 per cent, which was raised to 65 per cent in the twentieth licensing period that ran from 28 October 1945 to 2 March 1946. (The Ministry of Supply urged publishers to devote the extra ration to export sales.)

Rationed goods usually attract an extra demand. In those palmy days, sales managers could, and quite often did, sell a complete edition of 3,000 copies of a new novel in three or four telephone calls. Boots Libraries, W. H. Smith libraries and retail, and Gordon & Gotch, one of the largest of book exporters, would plead to be allowed to order 1,000 copies and not to have to accept a ration of 750! *Bookseller* advertisements in the eighteen months from the middle of 1945 harp on the one theme:

> The difficulty of using our paper quota to the best advantage . . . When paper is once again to be had for the asking . . . Subscription orders have been heavy and the scaling of orders has had to be rather drastic [that of Kathleen Winsor's *Forever Amber*] . . . When paper allows Hodder & Stoughton will resume the publication of their world-famous yellow jackets . . .

and so on.

One step publishers did not take was to raise the prices of their much desired commodity. Prices of hardcover novels (bound in cloth, not Linson), running to 256 pages and more and with a three-colour jacket, remained at 7s 6d ($37\frac{1}{2}$p) or 8s 6d ($42\frac{1}{2}$p). Looking back, one can argue that publishers were too timid at a time when they held all the advantages. J. A. Sutherland has calculated that the published price of hardcover novels has been 10 per cent of the average weekly wage throughout the twentieth century. That may well be so – but it is not the average wage-earner who buys novels. Partly held back by the competition of their rivals and partly perhaps by a sense of social responsibility, publishers have usually waited until the rising costs of production or postage or general overheads have forced them into raising their published prices.

One wartime casualty was the decline in the number of new fiction titles published each year. In 1939, 4,222 new novels were published. The following year there were 3,791. Then a sharp decline set in with 2,342 (1941), 1,559 (1942), 1,408 (1943), 1,255 (1944) and 1,179 in 1945. Why this should be so, apart from the rationing of paper, is not entirely clear but one important reason may be that novelists, both actual and potential, of military age were otherwise engaged and at the best could only snatch enough time from their war duties to write

110

short stories. *Penguin New Writing* flourished during the war years by selecting non-fiction articles, short stories and poems of real promise.

The war established one publisher as a major force – Penguin Books. Its only competitor had been Guild Books, created by that great innovator, Alan Bott. Nearly a score of publishers banded together under his aegis to allow paperback publication of titles which they controlled. Among them were Allen & Unwin, Cambridge University Press, Jonathan Cape, Cassell, Chatto & Windus, Constable, Faber & Faber, Robert Hale, Hamish Hamilton, Heinemann, Michael Joseph, John Murray, Oxford University Press and Secker & Warburg. But Guild Books did not long survive the end of hostilities. Penguin celebrated its tenth anniversary in August 1945, by which time it had brought out some 500 titles. In 1935, the early print orders had been 20,000 copies per title, of which half were initially bound up. Allen Lane estimated that his break-even point would be a sale of 17,500 copies. Ten years later, his minimum first printing was 100,000 copies of a title. But Penguin at that stage was not overly interested in the popular novelist as such. Authors had to look to their hardcover publishers with an occasional windfall as a Main Choice or a Recommendation of the Book Society for their remuneration.

In February 1946, the paper quota was raised to 75 per cent, with an additional 10 per cent to be used strictly for export. A year later, the quota was up to 80 per cent plus the same 10 per cent for export. The following week, there were drastic power and electricity cuts throughout the country. The nation, recently assured by the wordy Aneurin Bevan that it would never suffer from fuel shortages because the British Isles were built on coal, discovered that the massive supplies were not actually on the surface. Webb's Bindery in the City Road, London, ingeniously harnessed its sewing machines to bicycles and the 'industrious apprentices' both kept warm and provided power by pedalling furiously.

As a result of the fuel shortage, the paper quota was cut in March to 70 per cent and in May to 60 per cent plus this time 20 per cent for export. It remained at that level for many months until in March 1949 it was brought to an end, almost exactly nine years since its first imposition. The palmy days were ending.

They had not proved palmy for new publishers starting up post-war. One of them wrote an interesting and pathetic letter to the *Bookseller* in April 1947 under the heading: 'My Expensive Freedom. The Truth about Publishing on 6 tons a year by a new publisher'. It began,

I gave six years of my life to military service in a fight for freedom. Freedom from fear. Freedom from want. Freedom to write. Freedom to think. *Freedom* to express ideas. So I thought. So indeed I was authoritatively informed.

He then gave an analysis of costs. Allowing 200 pages per book, he reckoned that 6 tons of paper would produce 30,000 books a year; say, six titles each of 5,000 copies, published at 8s 6d. On those figures, the costs per title would be £85 for paper, £140 for printing, £38 for the jacket (including the artist's fee), 1s per copy for the binding, making a unit cost of 2s 0½d.

After giving discounts to wholesalers and retailers, his actual price received per copy worked out at between 5s 1d and 5s 8d. The author's royalty would then have to be deducted, which he calculated at 15 per cent of the published price – a high percentage, unless the author happened to be a bestseller. That took about another 1s 3d off his net receipts. Advertising would account for 6d per copy and, after paying commission to freelance salesmen and distribution costs, he would be left with between 2s 8d and 3s 3d on every copy sold.

Thus, his average working margin comes out at 11d per copy, a total of £1,375. But now he has to take into account his fixed overheads. His office rent (two top floors in London, WC1), with heating, lighting and telephone, amounts to £200 a year. His secretary's salary is £275, printing and sending out two catalogues a year costs another £100, petty cash £150 and bank interest £90, an overall total of £815 a year. Thus, *if he sells every book printed* – and no publisher in history has ever done that – he is left with £560 for himself after a year of unremitting toil and anxiety. One single failure would wipe him out. His letter concludes,

> It is, of course, accepted that a new publisher must inevitably make his way by his exceptional pieces of luck by exploiting his bestsellers. But I have no bestsellers – there is no paper for them.

One can only hope that the anonymous new publisher was able to struggle on for another two years until the end of paper rationing – but it seems highly doubtful.

Contrast that story with the success of Michael Joseph, who had published *How Green Was My Valley* shortly before the war broke out and thus enjoyed an enhanced paper quota for the next nine years.*

* He was also helped by Purnell, the printers, who let him use their excess paper quota.

At the end of the same year, 1947, he announced with pride that his firm had published nineteen new novels of which no less than nine were *first* novels. The average sale of those in the year was 9,740 copies. Any three of them would have cleaned up the new publisher's paper quota but would at least have left him with a working profit.

Peter Cheyney advertised in July 1946 that his audited net English language sales for the previous eighteen months amounted to 1,563,441 copies, split approximately 55 per cent in the United Kingdom and 45 per cent in the USA. In that October, MGM, which had instituted an annual novel award the same year, selected Mary Renault's *Return to Night* for the first $100,000 (then £40,000) prize. In March 1947, Collins announced that sixteen of their novels, thirteen of them by British authors, were to be made into major films. Later that year, Staples Press claimed to have sold 50,000 copies of *The Black Robe* by Thomas Costain in one month. Similar announcements and advertisements appeared regularly in the trade papers throughout those bountiful years. Publishers do not spend good money advertising failures – but it was harder to fail in the immediate post-war years than at almost any time in the history of British publishing; unless, that is, one happened to be a new publisher with a tiny paper quota.

But already there were some warning whispers. As early as 13 June 1946 a leading article in the *Bookseller* had this to say:

> Most publishers would agree that they have been 'spoilt' in the last year or two. Conditions of trading have in many ways been too easy for them, despite the torture of EPT [Excess Profits Tax] and the hazards of keeping a table at The Ivy after one o'clock. But there are signs that they will soon have to work for their living again.

Three months later, Michael Joseph in a BBC broadcast said: 'Publishing during the past few years has been far too easy'. A few months later there was an oblique warning in an Allen & Unwin advertisement that said, 'Limited supplies still available'.

In June 1948, Ernest Benn Ltd took a full-page advertisement in the *Bookseller* to declaim:

> Now we must *sell* books!
> Some booksellers tell us of a decline in sales, others repeat that books are 'expensive' . . . books are *still cheap*. The public needs reminding that whereas 50 cigarettes now cost 8/9d; the railway

charges 4/3d for a journey of 20 miles; a London theatre still costs
13/6d or 16/6d – many a new book of 100,000 words to last a lifetime
can still be bought for 9/6d or half a guinea!

Brave words. But the Christmas issue of the *Bookseller* that same
year had the heading 'Poor fiction sales' in its round-up of bookshop
sales and went on to speak of the 'rapidly shrinking market for the
many [titles] by less well-known writers'. Normality was returning
to the publishing trade.

For the first two or three post-war years, publishers sold out an
edition of a new title within a few months of its publication. Unless
the book was of some abiding interest or the public demand unusually
high, they were rarely able to reprint it. With paper stocks strictly
rationed and other new titles pressing for publication, they could not
afford to use up precious paper or tie up their often limited capital with
a reprint of a slower-selling title. But with the end of paper rationing,
a new method began to develop. If a publisher calculated that the
initial demand for a new novel by a relatively unknown author would
be 2,500 to 3,000 copies, he would often deliberately print 4,000 or so
copies but would only bind up the stocks that would be sold quickly.
Then, six months later, he would bind up the residue of perhaps
1,000 copies and announce, 'The first large cheap edition – by public
demand!' If the first edition had been published at 8s 6d, the cheap
edition would be priced at 5s. By these means, perhaps another 500
or 750 copies would be sold. Six months later, the remaining stocks
would be remaindered at 6d or 9d a copy. Publishers have never
paid royalties on stocks remaindered below cost; the unit cost of an
8s 6d novel, in the order of 2s, would have been reduced through
printing more copies than were initially required. By far the largest
single item in the publisher's analysis of his production costs was
printing, which worked out at almost 50 per cent of the total. The
expense of the setting remains the same, whether one copy is printed
or 100,000. So it paid publishers to spread their setting costs, provided
that the extra copies could be sold within a reasonably short time.

It was a neat idea but it only lasted a few years, killed off by the
growing spread of paperback publishing. The reading public would
not pay 5s for a book that could be obtained at half that price in paper
covers; the paperback publishers, moreover, who had by contract to
wait a minimum of one year from the date of first publication of a
novel in hard covers, would not have welcomed competition only

months before their own edition was launched. From the early 1950s to the present day, the paperback has had an increasingly important effect on the market, especially on the fiction side.

Penguin did not enjoy its virtual monopoly for long after the war. On 3 May 1947, the formation of Pan Books was announced. Alan Bott, already responsible for creating the Book Society and Guild Books, was the founder, with the backing of finance and supplies of likely titles from Collins, Hodder & Stoughton and Macmillan. None of these big publishers had paper to spare for the newcomer and so, in order to get a sufficient quota from the Ministry of Supply, the original idea was that Pan Books would export more than 50 per cent of their printing. The first batch of titles included works by Kipling, James Hilton, Margery Sharp, Agatha Christie, J. B. Priestley, Harold Nicolson and J. P. Marquand. Production took place in France and because of a dock strike at French ports only six titles appeared on 26 June. None the less, Pan prospered and within a matter of months began to make its mark. Initially, as with most of the new paperback houses, Pan had to rely on buying in successful hardcover titles, mainly from the publishers who had a financial interest in the firm.

As a counter-measure, in January of the following year, Chatto & Windus, Faber, Hamish Hamilton, Heinemann and Michael Joseph made an exclusive arrangement with Penguin for publishing the cream of their back titles under a joint imprint. The early lists included such names as J. B. Priestley, W. Somerset Maugham, T. S. Eliot, Joyce Cary, Lytton Strachey, Aldous Huxley, Raymond Chandler and James Thurber. Already, the first sighting shots in the paperback war were being fired.

The next newcomer on the scene was Pocket Books, founded in the USA by Robert de Graff, who vied with Allen Lane as the creator of the mass-market paperback. (Pre-war, there had been on the continent of Europe the Albatross and Tauchnitz English language editions in paperback but they never achieved a wide enough circulation in the USA or the UK to be considered mass-market; indeed, their licences excluded them from being sold inside the United Kingdom.) One condition laid down by the Ministry of Supply was that Pocket Books should invest at least $125,000 in Britain under the Marshall Aid plan. The company largely used the British market as a means of selling off its American stocks in titles where British softcover rights were available. That it did so successfully can be seen from the fact that in May 1950, Pocket Books was permitted to repatriate

$218,000 from sales made in the United Kingdom. Even so, Pocket Books was not a permanent visitor to these shores and no further mention of its presence occurs in the *Bookseller*.*

In March 1951, Victor Gollancz introduced non-fiction paperback original titles – what are nowadays called 'trade paperbacks' – on to his list which showed that a clever publisher with his eye on the main chance had realised that the day of the paperback, whether fiction or non-fiction, had arrived.

Transworld created Corgi Books, which launched its first list of four titles in April 1951. One of them was *Shane* by Jack Schaefer, which has been in print continuously ever since and which has now sold over 750,000 copies. Around the same time, Collins brought out its Fontana list, Hutchinson its Arrow list, Hodder its Pocket Books (later re-christened Coronet), while Panther Books was steadily expanding. In 1957, Macmillan began its St Martin's Library series and that maverick publishing genius Gordon Landsborough became editor of the new Four Square Books, backed by Godfrey Phillips, the tobacco company.

The watershed years for the paperback industry were 1956 and 1957. In a talk given to the Society of Young Publishers on 22 March 1956, J. H. Barrett, Secretary of the Book Society, spoke of the post-war revolution in subsidiary publishing. He referred to the book clubs which were then distributing over 10 million books a year and mentioned the sale of paperbacks, 'which had been truly colossal'. He believed that the other factors in the 'revolution' had been the growth of condensed books (mainly Reader's Digest) which were then selling close on 1 million copies a year and the vast increase of magazine serials, pointing out that Reader's Digest and *John Bull* were jointly responsible for a circulation of 60 million copies a year. The reasons he gave for the dramatic change were threefold: 'the ever-increasing cost of production has virtually blotted out ordinary trade reprints'; there had arisen a vast new reading public that did not go into bookshops; and 'the new media of radio and television has [*sic*] created a fresh search for knowledge.' Mr Barrett pointed out that Pan Books alone had by then sold over 4 million copies of eight different war titles.

In June 1956, Corgi Books announced yet further reprints of their

---

* Now owned by Simon & Schuster in New York, Pocket Books in the latter half of 1988 came back to Britain in conjunction with the Simon & Schuster London operation.

three bestselling war novels: John Brophy's *Immortal Sergeant*, Guthrie Wilson's *Brave Company* and Eric Lambert's *The 20,000 Thieves*, each of which had by then averaged over 250,000 copies. On 4 August, a headline in the *Bookseller* read: 'Hodder Pocket Books are a Success'. In October, World Distributors set up a paperback list with titles by Paul Scott, Alan Moorehead and Henri Troyat among its opening choices and three weeks later Pan announced that it had sold 1 million copies of Paul Brickhill's *The Dam Busters*, the first British paperback, it claimed, to have reached that magic figure. The very same month, Ralph Vernon-Hunt of Pan Books estimated that 50 million paperbacks at 2s and over would be sold during 1956 for a retail turnover in excess of £6 million.

Digit Books (Brown Watson) were in business before the end of 1956 and Panther Books moved to larger premises, citing its 'remarkable expansion in the past eighteen months' and the fact that it had over 7 million copies in stock. By the end of the year, Hodder Pocket Books had taken a double-page spread in the *Bookseller* to announce titles by Leslie Charteris, Edgar Wallace, Zane Grey, Winston Graham, Victor Canning and Ruby M. Ayres. The year closed with a proposal to form a paperback group within the Publishers Association; Walter Harrap, the shrewd head of George G. Harrap, pronounced:

It has become abundantly clear that more than three-quarters of the picture-covered paperbacks are being sold outside the bookshops.

He was right. The paperback houses had discovered the corner shops, the newsagents-cum-tobacconists with their racks of daily papers and weekly magazines. For many decades, the man (and woman) in the street equated going into a bookshop with going into a church; that gravity, that sepulchral hush, applied in both cases. But newsagents' shops are different. There is no ceremony to buying a daily newspaper or a packet of cigarettes. In the late 1950s and early 1960s, the paperback firms were to try even wider distribution through the forecourts of petrol stations, usually with unhappy results.

1957 continued the paperback success story. In January that year, Corgi announced that its first ten titles had collectively sold over 2.5 million copies. Odhams Press set up Beacon Books to sell paperback editions at half a crown. Ace Books, with Frank Rudman as editor, put out a distinguished list. (It is ironic that the eccentric J. D.

Salinger left his hardcover publishers, Hamish Hamilton, because he disapproved of the picture jacket used by Ace for the paperback edition of *For Esmé: With Love and Squalor*. The neutral observer now can only see it as pleasant and innocuous.) In February 1957, Corgi claimed that it had sold 6 million Westerns and a month later proud Penguin announced that it was joining the majority by putting picture covers on its novels. The four leading book clubs (Companion Book Club, The Reprint Society, Foyle's, and the Readers' Union) had claimed a combined readership of just under 1 million in March 1955 but, two years later, the total had dwindled to 650,000. 'The threat from paperbacks' was given as the cause. In March, Thorpe & Porter started a paperback list, as had Macmillan. That June, Pan celebrated its tenth anniversary by publicising the fact that it expected to sell its fifty millionth copy during 1957, fiction representing about 60 per cent of that total. Paperback sales, which earned over £5 million in 1957, represented about 10 per cent of the total UK publishing turnover.

Even so, in those early days, hardcover publishers tended to look on the lusty newcomer as an adjunct to, not a supplanter of, the traditional form of publishing. Only a man with the Calvinistic self-righteousness of Billy Collins could take a one-third share of Pan Books and run his own paperback list, Fontana. But at first the latter served to mop up rights in the hardcover novels issued by Collins – as indeed Pan tended to do with the output from Heinemann and Macmillan, its other two joint and equal owners.* And there was no immediate curb, as one might have expected, on the hardcover sales of big-selling novels. For example, in May 1956, Collins announced that the first printing of Hammond Innes's *The Mary Deare* was to be 75,000 copies. Three months later, Heinemann advertised a sale of over 100,000 copies of *The Quiet American* by Graham Greene. In October, Collins claimed to have sold close on 300,000 copies of Alistair MacLean's *HMS Ulysses*, while Victor Gollancz, not to be outdone, said that his first printing of Daphne du Maurier's *The Scapegoat* would be between 100,000 and 200,000 copies – a somewhat vague pronouncement. On 31 August 1957, Cassell proudly claimed a record in the biggest-selling hardcover fiction phenomenon since the war – *The Cruel Sea* by Nicholas Monsarrat.

* Hodder & Stoughton, a previous part-owner, had conscientiously sold its share when deciding to develop strongly its own paperback imprint.

Exactly six years after its first publication, the novel had sold one million copies at the original price of 12s 6d, with no cheap editions and no paperback sales, through the normal trade outlets. It altogether sold more than 1.2 million copies – no other post-war novel has sold even two-fifths as well without benefit of book club or paperback sales.

During this period and for perhaps a further five years or so, hardcover publishers continued to look on the paperback industry as a court of second resort. They bought titles and arranged advances for the authors on the basis that the hardcover edition would clear the advance and that a paperback sale when the moment arrived would be a dollop of jam on the author's bread-and-butter – and on their own. They clung firmly to the belief that the paperback was merely an extension of the 'volume rights' that they had brought into being through their offer to publish – and they claimed 50 per cent of the paperback proceeds as a matter of right. Even as early as spring 1954, the Publishers Association, basing its figures on 'nine of the most successful fiction publishers', claimed that the average profit per copy of a published hardcover novel was 3.6 per cent of the published price *before* the writing down of stocks. It proposed that its members should as a matter of course claim a *minimum* of 25 per cent of TV and radio rights, 10 per cent of film, dramatic and translation rights and 50 per cent of digest, book club (on a royalty basis) and reprint (including paperback) rights. A few years later, Ian Parsons, the then head of Chatto & Windus, told me that his firm operated on a 10 per cent loss on its normal hardcover trading and only made a profit through its share of subsidiary rights. It was not until the mid-1960s, when the large numbers of previously available titles had been mopped up by the paperback houses, that, thanks to the Society of Authors and the efforts of individual literary agents, novelists began to get a substantially larger share of the paperback 'cake'.

In the middle of 1955, the Society of Authors carried out a survey among its members, of whom novelists were approximately half. The survey showed that 15 per cent earned between £500 and £1,000 a year, mainly through their writing; 18 per cent earned between £250 and £500; 40 per cent earned under £250. (One needs to multiply by 9.5 to obtain the present-day equivalent.) Two years later, the society carried out a more detailed survey. This second time, the 607 replies to the questionnaire broke down as follows:

4 per cent earned over £2,500
8 per cent earned between £1,500 and £2,500
10 per cent earned between £1,000 and £1,500
15 per cent earned between £500 and £1,000
18 per cent earned between £250 and £500
40 per cent earned under £250.

Only a fifth of those replying claimed to derive between 80 per cent and 100 per cent of their total income from the proceeds of their book-writing; 44 per cent of the replies came from novelists. It is a fair assumption, although there are insufficient details to endorse it, that the 20 per cent whose main income came from writing books would be among the top 22 per cent who earned upwards of £1,000 a year. It is also significant that the percentages of lower earners remain exactly the same over the two-year period. Nevertheless, taking the multiple of 9.5, over a fifth of those answering – one assumes that the least successful would be less inclined to reply to the questionnaire – showed themselves to be earning a useful living by modern standards largely from their book-writing.

Between 1956 and 1960 the average published prices of novels remained remarkably steady, rising from 11s 8½d to 12s 10d, an increase of less than 2 per cent per year. During that same period, the average published prices of paperbacks remained equally constant, ranging between 2s and 2s 6d depending on length and the numbers printed. It was usually reckoned that a reasonably successful novel should sell ten times as many copies in paperback as in its hardcover edition. If we take a representative, and reasonably successful, novel of the period, selling 10,000 copies in hard covers at 12s 6d (with a third of those sales exported) and 100,000 copies in paperback at 2s 6d (again with a third exported), the results are interesting. It is assumed that the hardcover royalty rates would be 10 per cent of the published price on the first 3,000 copies sold, 12½ per cent on the next 2,000 and 15 per cent on all sales exceeding 5,000 copies. The export sales would be at 10 per cent of the price received. The paperback royalties would be a flat 7½ per cent on home sales and 6 per cent on export sales.

On the hardcover edition, the author would get about £406 on his UK sales and about £109 on his export sales, a total of £515. The paperback edition would earn in royalties about £609 on home sales and £262 on export, a total of £871. *But* the publisher would keep 50 per cent of those proceeds, leaving the author with £435. Even so, he would almost have doubled his hardcover earnings. If we were to leap back a decade to the point when the paperback market would not have been available to the author, he might perhaps have sold another 2,500 copies in hard covers at the full price or in cheap editions but, even taking 1956–60 prices, his extra hardcover royalties would only have amounted to some £230. Thus, the rise of the paperback industry proved to be a beneficial forward step for the professional novelist's income, as well as gaining for him many additional readers.

The growth of paperbacks had adversely affected book club membership during this period. It also dealt a mortal blow to the commercial lending libraries. W. H. Smith, one of the two largest in the field, announced the closure of its libraries in February 1961. Boots, its closest rival, carried on for a few years but finally closed on 1 May 1965. (Older readers will fondly recall the tags with their green shield emblems that served as a bookmark and the fact that the library shelves were always craftily sited at the back of each shop so that the borrower on his way in and way out might be tempted to buy other items in the shop.) The official statement announcing the closure of Boots' Booklovers Library, which had been started in 1899, said:

> Factors leading to the decision have been the rival attraction of television, *the buying of paperbacks* [my italics] and competition from public libraries . . . it was plain that this kind of library did not attract the younger generation.

Several other large chains such as Countryside Libraries staggered on for a while but were ultimately doomed, squeezed between the public libraries on the one hand which allowed ratepayers to borrow novels free of charge, and on the other hand by the paperback houses which provided a permanent book at only four or five times the borrowing rate of the commercial libraries.

And yet, conversely, one of the attractions of the paperback book was its disposability. A businessman going on a long journey by train – short-haul aircraft flights were not yet widely established – would buy a paperback novel at a railway bookstall to read on the journey and he would then quite often leave it in the carriage or throw it away at his destination. (One of the early American 'think tanks', set up by Hermann Kahn, calculated that the paperback book was the ideal product consistent with its aims, being readily portable, affording several hours of pleasure or information and being either disposable or ending up as a permanent piece of furniture.) Hardcover editions have survived partly through the long-upheld British tradition that they alone are eligible for detailed reviewing in the press and in periodicals, partly because (until recent years) their binding in sewn sheets survived the wear and tear of library usage better than the so-called 'perfect' binding – and partly because we lack that fine sense of logic so well displayed by the French.

CHAPTER VIII

# The 1960s and 1970s

You know, I've met bigger villains in television and the
literary set-up than I ever met in prison.
Frank Norman,
quoted in the *Sunday Times*, 1960


The second post-war phase of publishing occupies the period from
the early 1960s to about 1981. During much of that time, it was a
case of 'the mixture as before – but more so'. There were, however,
certain significant changes, both in America and Britain. For one
thing, the 'media industry' reared its head. Television companies
and newspaper groups, the latter often with substantial interests in
television, began to consider book publishing as a desirable commodity. There was a strange belief, rarely borne out in practice, that the
various aspects of the media would each help the other and thereby
reinforce the strength of the resulting conglomerate. Examples are
the Thomson group; Granada Television when it took over Panther
Books, but the height of optimism – or folly – occurred in the USA
when CBS bought Holt, Rinehart & Winston for *forty-two times* its
profit-earnings. A normal price/earnings ratio applied to an efficiently
run publishing house might be in the order of ten times, fifteen at
the most.

*The Times* in an article on the trend towards bigness in publishing
(June 1961) made the prescient remark:

Personality in publishing seems to be on the way out. There will
probably be no more Victor Gollanczes or Jonathan Capes or
Alfred Knopfs.

In October, Thomas Tilling, which already owned two-thirds of the
Heinemann group, bought up the outstanding third and a few weeks

123

later sold the firm of Rupert Hart-Davis, which it had acquired, to Harcourt Brace Jovanovitch of New York.*

The big men were beginning to close in. On 25 April 1962, the Society of Young Publishers (SYP) held a debate at the National Book League, with the motion, 'Big Deal or Slow Death: Take-Overs and the Independent Publisher'. Paul Hodder-Williams, the managing director of Hodder & Stoughton said,

> Growth depends not on money but on ideas. If the ideas are good, money will always be available to a publisher who wants to expand.

He forbore to add that money only comes at a price; bank managers charge interest on their loans.

At the end of May 1962, the SYP came up with an interesting historical note when it published details of its survey of 'Salaries in Publishing'. An ambitious young man, according to the survey, would expect to earn £1,000 a year between the ages of twenty-four and twenty-eight, £1,500 by his early thirties, £2,000 by thirty-four and £3,000 in his late thirties. Of those who answered the survey, just over 50 per cent had university degrees (mainly Oxbridge), and three-quarters had been to public schools. Forty per cent had private incomes.

Sex equality was not a prominent feature. Of the twenty-eight women who answered the questionnaire, twenty earned less than £800 a year, seven earned between £800 and £1,000 and only one earned more than £1,000.

As a comparison, anyone entering advertising or journalism should have expected to start at £800 and be earning £2,000 at the age of thirty. Civil service (administrative grade) rates were a starting salary of £750, with increments up to £900 after three years.

On those statistics, it must be deduced that publishing was still looked on as a preserve for the educated middle classes, who could afford to forego top-of-the-market rates because of their love for or loyalty towards 'working with books'. A comparison today would probably produce the same answer.

Paperbacks went on flourishing. It was announced in May 1964 that twelve titles in paperback had each sold over 1 million copies. Ten of them were from Pan: seven James Bond titles by Ian Fleming, *The Dam Busters* by Paul Brickhill, *Saturday Night and Sunday Morning*

* Harcourt Brace sold it back to the UK – to Sidney Bernstein of Granada – in September 1963.

by Alan Sillitoe and *Peyton Place* by Grace Metalious. The other two were Penguin titles: E. V. Rieu's translation of *The Odyssey* and, of course, Lawrence's *Lady Chatterley's Lover*. Other houses too had their triumphs. Fontana sold over 2 million assorted Agatha Christie titles in their Agatha Christie National Fortnight and Four Square announced sales of 2.5 million copies of various 'Tarzan' titles. But success was bringing its own strains. At a SYP meeting in June, Tony Godwin of Penguin said that there were too few fiction 'star' titles with the result that the advances being sought (and paid) were becoming ridiculously high. The paperback advance for the new Norman Mailer was £15,000 and for Harold Robbins's *The Carpetbaggers* £32,000. Gareth Powell of Four Square Books forecast that some idiot would pay an advance of £75,000 'this year'. (One must recall that inflation did not become rampant until the late 1960s and so it is necessary to multiply by a factor of about eight to reach a present-day equivalent.)

Another outcome of paperback success was that in March 1965 Granada bought Panther Books from its owners, Harry Assael and Joe Pacey, who had started the firm with their gratuities from RAF wartime service. They received £475,000-worth of Granada 'A' shares. In 1964 Panther had sold over 10 million books and had made a pre-tax profit of £100,000.

In July 1966 Robert Maxwell, addressing the Booksellers Association Conference, forecast that there would be increased vertical integration through publishers buying bookshops. This has indeed happened to a limited degree – with the Penguin bookshops, and the Hatchards chain owned by Collins. The report continued: 'By 1975, he [Maxwell] expected the book-vending machine to be playing a very major role in book distribution.' A nice idea – but it did not happen.

Later that year, under the new Labour government, the Board of Trade announced a 'standstill' policy for the book trade. Publishers were forbidden to increase the price of titles in stock or the price of straightforward reprints. New titles were exempted, as were new editions where extra text or material was incorporated or where substantial editorial revision required considerable re-setting of the text. The policy bore especially hard against houses like Penguin which had a very strong and steady, if often slow-selling back list. The cost of paper had been rising, as had printers' wages. Three years before, Pan Books, announcing price increases from 2s 6d to 3s 6d for some back list titles, stated: 'In the last three years the paperback profit margin, never very large, has narrowed to impractical limits.' Inflation had begun to bite.

Two significant events occurred in 1967. The first, which showed the highly beneficial effect on book sales of a successful and long-running TV serial, was the BBC's adaptation of Galsworthy's *The Forsyte Saga*. Each week, orders of 1,000 copies of the hardcover editions of the various titles flowed in to Heinemann and by mid-April, 75,000 new orders had been received. Penguin, meanwhile, had sold some 250,000 assorted copies of their paperback editions. For the next two decades – and particularly after the advent of colour television later in 1967 – increased sales (mainly of paperback editions) have almost always followed any novel that becomes a successful TV serial.

The other important event that year was the growing recognition of the computer. In May, the *Bookseller* included an article headed 'Libraries in the Computer Age'. In the same issue, Paul Hamlyn, always in the van, announced that his Books for Pleasure distribution company had purchased an IBM computer for all invoicing and accounting. In September, J. M. Dent recorded that its new edition of *Everyman's Encyclopaedia* would be the first major encyclopaedia in the world to have used computer-aided typesetting.

For the next four or five years, increasing inflation and worsening economic conditions turned the screw harder yet against the publishing trade. The British Federation of Master Printers recorded that in just under nine years printing costs had risen by 77 per cent. That was in January 1969. The following July, Sogat and the NGA demanded wage increases of 14 per cent for male employees and 19 per cent for women. Michael Sissons, of the A. D. Peters literary agency, at a Publishers' Publicity Circle meeting in March 1971 reported that in the decade to 1970 the hardback royalties flowing into his firm had decreased from well over 50 per cent of the business to under 30 per cent. It is not surprising that some months earlier Jonquil Trevor, the wife of Elleston Trevor, should have written a letter to the *Bookseller* in the following sad terms:

> . . . a bestseller can no longer be counted in tens of thousands; today a sale of 5,000 copies is considered gratifying . . . (I don't of course include the occasional freak sales or the carefully manufactured sexpot novels.)
>
> Reprint houses are cutting back on their fiction titles and have

slashed royalty advances to a fraction of what they were as recently as 1966. The film industry is flat on its face for the moment and television is getting by with tatty old films and well-tried serials. There are few magazines in the market for serial rights.

By late 1972, inflation was 55 per cent up on the levels of 1966. One consequence with a direct bearing on publishers was that office premises in central London that had averaged £3.25 a square foot in 1965 were now costing between £7 and £10 per square foot. The prices standstill policy had not been withdrawn, although publishers had been allowed to increase the published price of any reprint that had not been issued in the past eighteen months.

The problem was not confined to London. New York, too, was suffering. A *Publishers Weekly* article of 7 May 1973 pointed out that Harcourt Brace Jovanovitch, which had enjoyed a price/earnings ratio of 121 in 1967 was now rated at $22\frac{1}{2}$; even McGraw Hill, whose price/earnings ratio had been $56\frac{1}{2}$ in 1967, had sunk to 10. Charles Rolo, a Wall Street expert, was quoted as saying, 'Hell hath no fury like a crowd of badly burned investors.' It seemed an age and not just a dozen years since the heading of another *Publishers Weekly* article: 'In 1960 US publishers and stockbrokers met and fell in love.'

The miners' strike at the beginning of 1974 produced an inevitable fuel crisis. It lasted for eleven weeks and during that time shops were only supplied with electricity on alternate mornings and afternoons; publishers, along with most other trades, were limited for electricity to three days a week. Many of us will recall sitting on the other days in our overcoats – we had 'a cold coming of it' that January and February – working by the light of a guttering candle. Hardship may or may not bring out the best in the British character but it certainly brought increased business to bookshops and libraries. During the first half of 1974 – and in spite (or perhaps because) of the fuel crisis, the output of new fiction actually *rose*. The number of titles published in that period was 2,102, as opposed to 2,066 in the first half of 1973. The output of all other categories fell during those first six months – perhaps demonstrating that in arduous times escapism takes precedence over the factual. All the same, publishers were much concerned with inflation and the shortage of money; Penguin put forward a scheme whereby paperback editions, instead of being freshly set, should be offset (for a fee) from the text of the original hardcover editions.

Penguin was indeed suffering. On 1 February 1975, under the heading 'The Trouble at Penguin', Peter Calvocoressi, then running the firm, wrote an article in the *Bookseller*. Part of it ran as follows:

> . . . we face a paradox. In spite of bumper sales and respectable profits, we have, like businesses of all kinds, a cash problem. We are not generating enough money to finance such large new book and reprint programmes as we have had in recent years. To put it at its crudest, if we continued at that rate we would need to borrow more than £1 for every £1 we earn, which would quickly produce an intolerable debt.

Penguin was not alone in its problems. Although the average price of new hardcover fiction rose by 13.8 per cent in the first half of 1975 – to £2.56 – printing and binding costs had increased by 30 per cent in the past year, according to the British Printing Industries Federation. One immediate result was the slashing of new lists. Milton House, which had published eighty-five novels in the previous two years, suspended all its forthcoming fiction. David & Charles halved its list from 300 new titles (basically non-fiction) to 150. Faber & Faber announced cuts and Hodder & Stoughton suspended its library reprint programme. Collins announced that it would spend more on promoting big titles but far less on the smaller ones; Cape, noted for its support of new novelists, accepted only one first novel in the autumn of 1975; Deutsch reported, 'We have cut back on fiction quite a lot'.

It was now actually cheaper for British publishers to print their books in the United States than in Britain. That November, John Boon of Mills & Boon, speaking at the Holborn Conference, pointed out that in the three years to October 1975, inflation had risen by 61 per cent; the unit costs of hardbound fiction were up by 111 per cent and good-quality paper for book printing had risen from £158 per tonne to £342 per tonne – a rise of 116 per cent. And at the same conference Gerald Bartlett, president of the Booksellers Association, stated that if the value of the 1946 pound had been 100p, by 1960 it had dropped to 59p and by 1974 to 27p – almost fourfold inflation in under thirty years.

With its smaller average printing runs, hardcover fiction publishing had to price itself dangerously high in the market as compared to the published prices of paperback fiction. Ever since the launch of Penguin Books in 1935, there had always been a factor of up to ten – and never less than five – between the two average net prices. But by the end of 1975, the average price of new hardcover fiction had risen to £2.98, a rise of 16 per cent over the price for the first six months, while the average price of paperback novels was still around 25p to 30p. The dual result was that the paperback share of the market rose from 30 per cent to 32 per cent during 1975 and in the first three months of 1976 the number of new hardcover novels fell by exactly 25 per cent as compared with the same period in the previous year.

Philip Ziegler, then a senior editor at Collins, pointed up the historical facts in an address he gave to the Booksellers Association in May 1976. Defining a hardcover bestseller as one that sold at least 30,000 copies in its first year, he compared the Collins results in the five-year period 1952–56 (before paperback sales had reached their full power) with the five-year period 1972–76. In the first period, Collins had published thirty-two bestsellers; in the second period, twenty-two. In 1975, Fontana, the Collins paperback subsidiary, had sold 18 million books, predominantly Collins titles. The individual authors had not suffered, since what they lost on the hardcover swings, they had more than gained on the paperback roundabouts – but it was evident that the 100,000-plus first printings enjoyed in the early 1950s by authors like Nevil Shute, Daphne du Maurier and Nicholas Monsarrat were, except with substantial book club support, part of history.

During this second phase, several large American publishers decided to buy their way into the British market. For many years, there had been a gentleman's agreement that for most general trade books, including fiction, the American publisher would concentrate on his home territory and the Philippines, while the British publisher would have the United Kingdom and the Commonwealth (including South Africa, even after it had become a republic). If the book was of British origin, Canada usually went to the British publisher and, if it was of American origin, to the American publisher. The rest of the world for English language rights, apart from certain territories like Egypt, Iraq and Jordan – traditionally mandated to the British – was to be looked on as an open market for both publishers to exploit.

In the summer of 1976, the US Justice Department considered that the friendly arrangement constituted a cartel; it promulgated a Justice Decree forbidding the practice. For speed and convenience, most British and American publishers had (and have) printed contract forms, which up till then printed out the list of territories the publisher expected to acquire. The simple way of getting round the Justice Decree was to leave the territorial details blank in the printed contract forms and merely type in exactly the same territories as before. That kept the cosy arrangement in being but made it appear that each contract had been the subject of special negotiations.

Thus, any publisher on either side of the Atlantic who wished to enjoy the benefits of the book market across the water either had to open an overseas branch or acquire a local publishing house. American publishers were well aware that the turnover of the British industry was just under £100 million (43 per cent of which was exported) in 1964 and ten years later had nearly trebled to £283 million. They were also well aware of the export potential to countries like Australia, New Zealand and South Africa. So the overall British territory became a plum worth plucking from the tree. Early in this phase, McGraw Hill nearly acquired the Heinemann group, which by then included Secker & Warburg. How the attempt was foiled at the eleventh hour is dramatically told in Frederic Warburg's *An Occupation for Gentlemen*. It led to the demotion and eventual retirement of A. S. Frere, until then the leading force in Heinemann. Some years later, Crowell Collier Macmillan acquired Cassell and by exercising remote and delayed control effectively ruined that splendid house, Churchill's own publishers, as a major force. (It has been pleasant in recent years to watch Cassell reviving 'under entirely new management'.) Time/Life bought a 40 per cent share in André Deutsch but after a brief period sold back its shares to the redoubtable André.

Doubleday, in conjunction with W. H. Smith, formed the Literary Guild (Book Club Associates) in Great Britain and ensured that the new book clubs would quickly become, along with its various offshoots, the most powerful in the country. Harper & Row and W. W. Norton each set up London offices but more as scouting centres and to sell in Britain American books in which they respectively held British rights than as the publishers of British books. Simon & Schuster spent years looking for a large British acquisition but in 1986 decided to set up its own branch office in London, not only to sell books in which it controlled the British rights but to establish as well an aggressive semi-independent house to buy and promote local British rights. J. A. Sutherland estimated in 1977 that about 12 per cent of British publishing was in American hands.

The trade was not all one way. Collins bought World Publishing in New York, which turned out to be a disastrous purchase, and towards the end of the second phase Pearson, the British owners of Penguin/ Allen Lane Books and Longmans, made a shrewd buy in acquiring Viking Press, New York, from the Guinzburg family.

The presence of several large organisations with allied hardcover and paperback houses on both sides of the Atlantic is bound to have a major effect on the future of popular novelists, both British and American. For the first time, one publisher is in a position to bid for the complete English language market in an author's next book. The sums offered, as will be shown in detail later, are bound to be very tempting. Publishers like to spread their risks as widely as possible on a 'swings and roundabouts' principle. It is likely that the large international groups are already chasing the relatively few global bestselling novelists with enormous offers for world English language rights deals.

During the unconscionably long death-throes of the Labour government of 1978–79, the convulsive jerkings in labour relations were neatly summed up in a cartoon showing a Cabinet minister confronted across the table by senior trades union officials. He is saying, 'We're going to wield the big stick.' In his hand, he is holding a large carrot. The official annual inflation rate at the start of 1977 was 19.7 per cent. In the *one* month of August 1978, printing costs rose by 11.1 per cent, a rise of 23.5 per cent over the full year. By May 1979, as a result of an agreement between the NGA and the British Printing Industries Federation, printers increased their prices by a further 17–20 per cent. (Already, up to the end of 1978, the average published prices of all books had risen 125 per cent – from £3.24½ to £7.34 – in five years.) Even several months into Margaret Thatcher's first Conservative government with its monetarist policies, in February 1980 NGA and Sogat put in a claim for a 28.6 per cent rise for their members. One need hardly be surprised that in the same month the Hong Kong Trade Development Council announced that its print sales to the United Kingdom the previous year had risen by 39 per cent nor that, three months later, R. R. Donnelley & Sons of Chicago, one of the biggest American printing firms, decided to open a London office at 45 Lower Belgrave Street. The trades union printing lemmings were throwing themselves over a cliff marked Greed.

The spiralling rise of inflation, already blown up by wage demands on all sides, was by now having an adverse effect on publishers, large and small. In April 1978, Collins had announced that its pre-tax profits on the year were down from £5.2 million to £3.1 million; Penguin's pre-interest profit was reduced from £3.2 million to £1.7 million. (Five months later, Peter Mayer was appointed chief executive of Penguin Books.) In July 1979, a survey by Jordan Dataquest entitled *Book Publishing* revealed that W. H. Allen, Barrie & Jenkins, Dent, Sidgwick & Jackson, Phaidon and Sphere Books were all making losses. To add to the strain, the pound, for some unfathomable reason, had become unusually strong against the dollar, having risen to a value of $2.3625. This in turn meant that British publishers were now losing 20 per cent on their American earnings. (The pound fell to $1.85 that November but rose again to $2.30 in March 1980.)

As 1979 went on, publishing conditions worsened. The Collins results for the six months to 1 July were 'extremely disappointing'. Turnover was down by over £2 million to £27.16 million and there was a loss of £828,000 before tax, as opposed to a profit of £1.23 million for the previous six months. The *Bookseller* reported that Collins was vulnerable to a take-over, with a going price of around £26 million, and Collins later admitted that about that time they had to scratch around at each month-end to make sure there was enough to pay the wages.

Penguin's results were equally disappointing. For the six months to 30 June, turnover was actually up by over 10 per cent to £11.09 million but the pre-tax loss had increased to £478,000. Collins indeed was planning for 600 redundancies out of a workforce of 2,600 at its Bishopbriggs printing works and was on the point of selling its US company (formerly World Publishing Company) to help reduce bank interest charges, which at the mid-year were up by £382,000 to £1.1 million. A month later, it announced extra job losses of thirty to thirty-five, this time among its Glasgow publishing staff.

1980 was the year of retrenchment. During the first half, the government in its efforts to squeeze inflation out of the economy held the Minimum Lending Rate (MLR) first at 18 per cent and then at 17 per cent. On 3 July, MLR came down a point to 16 per cent and in November two further points – to 14 per cent. Even so, a private investor or public institution had no incentive to invest in the publishing industry. When you can leave your money entirely without risk on deposit at a bank and receive interest nicely into double figures, 'there is no percentage', as Damon Runyan would have said, in buying shares in a publicly quoted publishing firm that might at the best pay a dividend of about 5 per cent and at the worst could lose you a large slice of your investment.

And publishers had grown fat in the soft inflationary days of the late 1970s. New Americanised terms for appointments had become fashionable. There were now chief executive officers and deputy chief executive officers instead of managing directors; salesmen had become marketing executives, publicity and subsidiary rights departments had spawned additional staff; secretaries were now personal assistants. Publishing had rapidly become not an occupation for gentlemen but for functionaries.

The sudden hard times brought about a swift and drastic reduction. Collins sold the freehold of its St James's Place offices, which had a book valuation of £500,000, to Rothschild's for £3.6 million. Penguin decided to cut its publishing programme by 22 per cent and its staff by 17 per cent, which involved the loss of a hundred jobs. The reason given was that the strong pound (at $2.30 to the pound) had hit overseas sales. In the five years to the end of 1979, Penguin's annual volume sales had dropped from 42 million to 39 million, its pre-tax profits were down from £1.8 million to a £300,000 loss and its net borrowings had virtually doubled from £3.4 million to £6.7 million.

Macdonald/Futura announced 10 per cent job cuts – including the post of 'marketing director' – out of a staff of 155. That same month of June 1980, the Thomson book companies revealed an £800,000 loss for the previous year on a turnover of £28.7 million. In August, Hodder & Stoughton was negotiating with the unions for a staff reduction of fifty out of 438 persons. ABP cut its sales force by seven, Hutchinson's previous pre-tax profit of £600,000 had been turned into a loss of £1.5 million, Marshall Cavendish was sold to Times Printing of Singapore for £7.7 million and Oxford University Press forecast a loss of £2 million on its UK operations, with an overall loss of £1.5 million. In September, Penguin's loss for the first half year rose from £478,000 to £1.62 million and later in the year Macdonald/Futura were discussing with the unions a further twenty job cuts, Hutchinson negotiated for thirty and Cassell for twenty. Hamish Hamilton and Macmillan were each making 10 per cent of their staffs redundant – out of sixty and 750 respectively.

There was a triple squeeze on all publishers during this difficult period. The strength of the pound was hitting their overseas sales and making them less competitive in the open market against their American rivals. (With the pound at $2.20, the British edition of *Smiley's People* by John le Carré was 97p more expensive than the American edition; the Cape edition of Kurt Vonnegut's *Jailbird* was 98p more expensive than the Delacorte edition. Even Frederick Forsyth's *The Devil's Alternative* and Judith Krantz's *Princess Daisy* were each 6p more expensive than their respective American editions.)

The economic tightening not only hit bookshop sales but public library issues as well, through the reduction of government funds. As a leading article in the *Bookseller*'s issue of 2 August 1980 put it:

> The shrinkage of the public library sector as a market for publishers is having an effect on the very identity of publishers' lists.

It was estimated that in the period 1978–79, 72 per cent of all public library book issues for adults comprised fiction.

The net prices of hardbound novels, which had been restrained in happier times when increases in manufacturing costs could be absorbed, had rocketed throughout the inflationary seventies. In the first half of 1971, the average price had been just under £1.25. Six years later, it had risen to £3.49 – an increase of 179 per cent. In the first half of 1978, it rose to £4.02 (up 15.2 per cent), in the first half of 1979, to £4.57 (up a further 13.7 per cent) and in the first half of 1980, to £5.37 (up yet a further 17.5 per cent). So, in under a decade, the average net price of a novel had risen by a factor of well over four.

The printing unions, NGA and Sogat, failed to see the warning lights. After their February claim for an overall 28.6 per cent increase, in March, the NGA threatened stoppages as a means of pressing their further claims for a working week reduced to $37\frac{1}{2}$ hours and a minimum wage of £80 per week. Official figures to April 1981 revealed that compositors had become – after coalface workers – the second highest paid manual workers in the country, with average gross weekly earnings amounting to £164.20. Print machine minders, whose job could be adequately performed by almost anyone with a rudimentary knowledge of printing machines, had risen in the wages scale from the twenty-first place in 1976 (£70.90 per week) to fourth (£155.20). Over 60 per cent of practising novelists then earned far less than £8,000 a year from their writings. Another five painful years were to pass before Rupert Murdoch's News International first broke and then tamed the print unions through the sudden move to Wapping and direct inputting by journalists, aided by the electricians' union.

Few in the book trade probably realised it at the time but the end of the decade also saw the end of the very hard times. Publishing house staffs were leaner and fitter than before and those who had been quick to shed their excess 'fat' were already looking to slightly improved results. Collins, for example, had turned its £828,000 loss for the first half of 1979 into a pre-tax profit of £175,000 for the first half of 1980. The country's economy was also looking better, inflation was coming down, as were interest rates. The seven years that had followed the boom-bust of 1973–74 were about to be followed by nearly seven years of boom – until the inevitable Stock Exchange 'bust' of October 1987. That is another story.

CHAPTER IX

# Conglomerates and Aggregates

> Every successful company has a 'soul', that amorphous
> combination of cameraderie, talent and shared ambition.
> You can't measure it with p/e ratios, net asset value or
> earnings per share, but it is vital to all of them and
> you can't buy it, not even for £540 million. I am afraid
> Octopus lost its soul last Friday; so goodbye, Octopus,
> may you rest in peace.
>
> Extract from a letter to the *Bookseller*,
> 17 July 1987, from Timothy Clode,
> managing director of Octopus 1977–86

The publishing industry's move from cottage to office block was almost
certainly inevitable: the inflationary processes through the 1960s and
1970s, the American efforts to break into the once traditional overseas
markets, the demands of the printing unions, the tendency of British
companies in other fields to merge or be bought out – these were only
some of the important factors that confined survival to either the large
and well-based firms or the small and quick-witted. The change has
had a profound and in some ways unsettling effect on novelists.

I would like first, to draw a distinction between the word 'conglomerate' and the word 'aggregate'. A conglomerate is a group of
companies, usually of international outlook, consisting of radically
different units making their livings in unconnected areas. For example,
Thomas Tilling had been mainly a manufacturer of buses when it
was nationalised under the first post-war Labour government. It
shrewdly invested its payoff funds in diverse companies, including
Pretty Polly stockings, and later in Heinemann. At first, it took a
two-thirds interest in the group, which included as well as William
Heinemann, Secker & Warburg, Heinemann Educational Books and
World's Work. In 1961, the purchase was completed when Tilling
bought the outstanding shares. And when, in June 1983, BTR, a

smaller but sharper conglomerate, bought Tilling's, it automatically acquired the Heinemann group, which it sold on to Paul Hamlyn at Octopus two years later. Sir Owen Green, the head of BTR, gave as his reason for the sale the fact that the Heinemann group with its £40 million annual turnover and about £6 million profit before tax was 'too small a base'.

Again, in spite of its ownership of Longman, Penguin, Viking, Hamish Hamilton, Michael Joseph, George Rainbird and Sphere Books, the Pearson group counts as a conglomerate through its separate ownership or control of a merchant bank, a financial newspaper, a long-established maker of china and a world-famous French vineyard.

An aggregate in my terms is a group of companies operating in the same or related fields. Examples would include Collins with its own very substantial list and the Fontana (adult) and Armada (children's) paperback lists, its allied printing works, its Hatchards and Claude Gill bookshops and the Grafton hardcover and paperback lists, together with the recent acquiring of a half-share in Harper & Row of New York; or Hodder & Stoughton with its adult list, its children's books (formerly Brockhampton Press), along with Coronet and Sceptre paperbacks, and Knight paperbacks for children, and its ownership of New English Library and Edward Arnold, the academic publisher. Collins does indeed have a Damoclean sword – or perhaps one should call it a 'digger's spade' – hanging over it in the shape of Rupert Murdoch's 42.5 per cent shareholding; if he were ever to exercise his right over a period to add an annual increment to his shareholdings, the Collins group would then become part of a conglomerate.*

In its 13 April 1985 issue, the *Bookseller* published a leading article on the recent spate of take-overs in the publishing trade. One sentence ran: 'In the big world of books, it is being argued, those who do not integrate vertically . . . will stand less chance of survival.'

Vertical integration – the very phrase is like a cracked bell that has rung many times in the past. One of the early integrators was Clarence Hatry, an entrepreneur and visionary who had a roller-coaster career for over forty years from before the first world war to the 1950s. Seeing how cut-throat competition between the Wars was killing off many otherwise healthy firms, he was responsible for amalgamating the jute industries in Scotland and all but succeeded in doing so later with the iron-founders of England. The Wall Street crash and the slump that followed ruined his plans for the iron-founding industry

* See footnote on page 159.

and indeed saw him receive a fourteen-year sentence at the hands of Mr Justice Avory on the charge of forging scrip to cover his shortfall. There are grounds for believing that one of his lieutenants had committed the forgery and that Hatry took the blame without being fully aware of what had happened.

An avid reader and the author of a book, *Light out of Darkness*, which advocated cutting the vast unemployment of the 1930s and building up the strength of the Dominions by planned mass emigration from Britain, Clarence Hatry emerged from gaol in 1939, borrowed £500 from his wife, used it as a 10 per cent down payment to buy Hatchards from the elderly Shepherd brothers who owned the bookshop – and was in business again. Hatchards had never believed in dunning a lord and half *Debrett*, it seemed, owed collectively thousands of pounds in unpaid debts, having treated the famous bookshop as a free library – except that the books were never returned. But CCH, as Hatry was always known to his associates, threatened to remove the books from Hatchards' front windows and instead mount a list detailing the noble debtors with the amounts owed and the length of time they had been outstanding. There was great huffing and puffing, threats of writs and the cancellation of accounts, but virtually all the debts were paid within the set period and Hatry was able to pay the balance of the purchase price (£4,500) out of the windfall. With his persuasive charm, he then managed to get the major publishing creditors to give him a moratorium. The war had begun, the blackout kept people at home – and the boom in books was on. Hatchards, which had been on the verge of bankruptcy when he stepped in, survived and flourished.

Clarence Hatry's one great fault was over-expansion. He almost never ploughed back profits to establish a sounder financial base for the companies he controlled but used those profits to buy yet more companies. He read balance sheets in the way ordinary people read thrillers and he could spot dormant assets that would be invisible to most of his contemporaries. He was one of the first of the asset-strippers, decades before Clore or Slater Walker. But he had to follow his visionary dream – and buy and buy. Before 1950, he had acquired a publishing house (T. Werner Laurie), a couple of printing works including Riddle, Smith & Duffus, the Argosy & Sundial commercial libraries, a remainder merchant (Arandar) and, of course, Hatchards itself. The plan was simple. Werner Laurie would publish the best books, one of the printing firms would print them, Hatchards and the commercial libraries would sell or lend them – and there was always

Arandar in reserve to mop up the mistakes. Vertical integration had reached its shining hour.

But the plan, which looked so foolproof, never worked in practice. The printing works, knowing that Werner Laurie had to deal with them, had no incentive to offer competitive prices. If Werner Laurie tried to force Hatchards or Argosy & Sundial to buy more copies than they could reasonably dispose of, they were left with useless stock; sales were always 'firm' in those days. The tight-knit structure soon began to unravel. Tipped off by an unworthy colleague, Hatry had bought the rights to Brehmer, a German book-stitching machine, from the Custodian of Enemy Property. Manufactu ing it from scratch in Britain cost tens of thousands of pounds, which the other companies in the Hatchards group had to denude themselves to provide – and still the machine never worked efficiently. His health ravaged by the mounting cash problems, Clarence Hatry resigned his position as the driving force of Hatchards Associated Interests in 1952 and the group gradually disintegrated. Theodore Cole, a property speculator, bought the head lease of Hatchards for £100,000 and not long thereafter sold it on to Collins.

This is not to say that vertical integration never works. The Collins aggregate has proved that it can and does, if supervised with proper Scottish caution. But there is an inherent 'tail-wagging-dog' risk. A decade later, when Wilfred Harvey's master company, the printing firm of Purnell, had Macdonald, Sampson Low and Juvenile Productions in tow, there was quite often a strong demand from the printery in Paulton, Somerset, to buy a book – any book that was long and might be saleable – to keep the big quad printing machines running. Publishing successfully is difficult enough without such extraneous pressures.

In order to function efficiently, conglomerates need to set up an accounting system that will homogenise and make sense of the profit and loss accounts of their disparate members. It can be argued that any group of companies must be susceptible to the same business principles, no matter how much they diverge from one another; there is no particular mystery, the argument would go, in the processes of publishing. In Pearson Longman's view, there is presumably little difference in balance sheet terms between the claret *vendange* in one year and Viking Penguin's autumn list. The number of books or bottles sold and the price obtained is what finally matters. But the inherent problem in publishing that has led to ever-increasing numbers of titles published every year is exacerbated once the men with the xylonite brief-cases and the pocket calculating machines take over.

As long ago as April 1949, Michael Joseph wrote an article in the *Bookseller* explaining the need to increase the output of individual titles. He predicated the publisher's fixed overhead at £5,000. If that publisher brought out ten titles in a year of which four made a profit and the other six lost £50 each, the four successful titles would need to show an average profit each of £1,325 to reach break-even point. But if that publisher brought out fifty titles in the year, of which twenty made a profit, the deficit to be covered was £6,500. Divided amongst the twenty successful titles, that meant that each of them only had to average £325 profit to break even. So the more you published, the more you spread the risk, just so long as your guesses were at least 40 per cent right. A shrewd and experienced man like Michael Joseph had made the system work but, when driven by accountants who believe – in Philip Jarvis's famous phrase – that books can be sold like soap, the publishing side of a conglomerate can be pressed into producing for volume and not because the editor concerned has fallen in love with a particular book.

By kind permission of the *Bookseller*, a detailed list of the major purchases of publishing houses or groups in the past few years appears on the opposite page and so I do not intend to set down each and every such purchase as it occurred in the body of the section. But certain generalisations can be made.

To the big businessman whose education may have stopped when he was in his teens and whose staple reading matter is balance sheets and company reports, there is often something glamorous about books and authors. Who can now say whether Lionel Fraser of Tilling's acquired Heinemann because it was a sound business proposition, which at the time it hardly was, or whether deep in his heart he wanted to be closely associated with such exciting figures as Somerset Maugham, J. B. Priestley and Graham Greene? And why did Howard Samuel, having made a fortune in the post-war jungle of property developing, acquire several small publishing houses and, only a few weeks before his accidental death from drowning while swimming near Athens, attempt in 1961 to buy ABP from the Crosthwaite-Eyre trusts, having already purchased a 20 per cent holding from Pitman? The answer cannot be based on strict business principles. Over the whole period under review, an efficient publishing house would be doing well to average a 10 per cent pre-tax profit on turnover;

# Major Purchases of Publishing Houses and Groups

*W. H. Allen.* Bought Virgin Books, 1986; Allison & Busby, early 1987. Virgin Group then bought 67% of WHA late 1987, which valued WHA at £4.5m.

*Allen & Unwin.* Merger with Bell & Hyman to become Unwin Hyman, 1986.

*Associated Book Publishers* (principally Methuen, Chapman & Hall, Eyre & Spottiswoode, Sweet & Maxwell). Bought Routledge, Kegan Paul 1985; Croom Helm, and Pitkin, 1986. Bought by International Thomson 1987, for £210m, who sold Methuen to Octopus (see below).

*Book Club Associates.* Founded by W. H. Smith and Doubleday. Bertelsmann bought Doubleday, 1986. At end-1988 BCA's equal joint owners were Bertlesmann and Octopus.

*Butterworths.* Bought Bowker, 1985, for *c.* US$ 90m; K. G. Saur, 1987. Itself owned by Reed International.

*Cassell.* Bought out from CBS Inc., 1986, by British consortium. Bought Link House Books and Blandford, 1987, for £2.7m.

*Century.* Bought Hutchinson, 1985, for £5.5m; Muller, Blond & White, 1987.

*Chatto, Bodley Head, Cape.* Bought by Random House Inc., 1987, for *c.* £17.5m.

*Collins.* Bought Granada Publishing (Grafton) 1983; Claude Gill Bookshops, 1985; 50% Harper & Row Inc., 1987, for £95m. Hostile bid by News International in train as this book goes to press. Initial bid of £293m seen as small.

*Hodder & Stoughton.* Bought New English Library, 1982; Edward Arnold, 1987.

*Longman.* Bought Pitman, 1985, for 17.7m; Addison-Wesley Inc., 1988, for US$ 283m. Itself owned by Pearson (see also Penguin).

*Macmillan.* Bought Sidgwick & Jackson, 1986. Became sole owner of Pan Books, 1987, by buying Octopus's 50% for £22m.

*Octopus.* Bought Brimax, 1983; Webster Group, 1984; Secker and Warburg, and Heinemann, 1985, for £100m; Hamlyn Publishing, 1986; Mitchell Beazley, 1987; Methuen, 1987; 50% BCA, 1988, from Bertelsmann for £52m; George Philip, 1988; Rigby International, Australia, 1988. Itself bought by Reed International, 1987, for £535m.

*Maxwell Communications Corporation* (Macdonald-Futura). Bought Macmillan Inc (USA), 1988, for US$2.6bn.

*Penguin* (Viking Penguin Inc. in USA). Bought Frederick Warne 1983; Thomson companies, vig. Michael Joseph, Hamish Hamilton, Rainbird, and Sphere, 1985, for £20.7m; New American Library, 1986, for US$65m. Itself owned by Pearson (see Longman above).

*Weidenfeld.* Bought J. M. Dent (Publishing), 1987. (Receivers sell J. M. Dent Distribution to AA, 1988.)

15 per cent would be considered an exceptional return. For example, in 1970–71, when the state of publishing was by no means in the doldrums, Jonathan Cape showed 3 per cent profit on turnover, as did Hodder & Stoughton, Macmillan were at 4 per cent, Harrap at 6 per cent, OUP at 7 per cent and only Heinemann looked bright at 13 per cent. Granada showed a profit of £27,000 on sales of £2.8 million, just under 1 per cent. Anthony Blond, Paul Hamlyn (bought in 1964 by IPC for £2.275 million), and Pitman, among quite a few other houses, showed actual losses. These are not results to excite the acquisitive City magnate.

During the 1960s and 1970s, there was a theory, which has still not been abandoned, that there was a kind of strength and prosperity to be found in grouping together different parts of 'the media'. If, for instance, the argument ran, a television network or a national newspaper were to buy one or more publishing houses, the whole would mysteriously become greater than the sum of the parts. We have seen how Roy Thomson, already a substantial shareholder in Scottish Television and the owner since 1959 of the *Sunday Times* and its provincial newspapers, acquired Michael Joseph in 1961 when he bought the *Illustrated London News*. The following year, he added Thomas Nelson and in 1965 Hamish Hamilton, the eponymous owner having just reached the age of sixty-five. Jamie Hamilton was quoted as saying somewhat forlornly at the time, 'Running an independent medium-sized publishing house is increasingly uphill work nowadays'. It could not really be said that the Thomson publishing houses benefited greatly from their close association with the *Sunday Times* – nor vice versa. Indeed, it was an outsider, the nimble André Deutsch, who developed most publishing plans with Harold Evans, editor of the *Sunday Times* for much of that period.

In like manner, Sidney (later Lord) Bernstein took Granada Television into publishing when, late in 1963, he acquired Rupert Hart-Davis from its recent American owners, Harcourt Brace. He already owned MacGibbon & Kee and in 1965 had bought Panther Books. It was some twenty years later, when Lord Bernstein was in semi-retirement, that the Granada publishing group was sold on to Collins, who shortly afterwards renamed it Grafton.

The zenith – or, more accurately, the nadir – of the media mergers was reached in New York in 1966 when CBS bought Holt, Rinehart & Winston for $275 million. In 1966, Holt had shown pre-tax profits of $6.6 million. Thus, the price/earnings ratio was in excess of forty.

Harold Latham, the dean of publishers at Macmillan Inc. for some years after the Second World War, once told me that the script of *Gone With The Wind* had been handed to their Deep South representative and remained in the boot of his car for many weeks until one wet weekend he felt guilty, read it and realised that his bosses in New York ought to see it. Even if Holt, Rinehart had ransacked the car-boots of all their salesmen and by some great stroke of luck discovered half a dozen unread *Gone With The Wind*s, the firm would still never have reached the level of profits to justify the price paid by CBS.

In May 1978, London Weekend Television decided, somewhat late in the day, to diversify into book publishing and so bought the Hutchinson group for £4 million and a further £2 million in loans. It proved a disastrous purchase; one wondered at the time how anyone with the slightest knowledge of the book trade could have been induced to offer even half that sum. In March 1985 LWT was no doubt relieved to merge Hutchinson with Anthony Cheetham's new and thriving firm, Century. The so-called merger was effected by an additional £3.9 million private placing of shares, which left LWT with a 25 per cent interest and various institutions with another 53 per cent. Just two weeks later, Penguin bought the Thomson publishing companies – Michael Joseph, Hamish Hamilton, Elm Tree Books, George Rainbird and Sphere Books (Jane's was excluded from the sale) – for over £20 million.

As far back as June 1978, the *Bookseller* published a major article advocating conglomerates in the publishing world. Its arguments in favour were threefold. To be purchased by a conglomerate would 'remove financial worry from individual houses'; the conglomerate with its greater financial 'muscle' would be able to stand up to the unions – the Callaghan Labour government then following the path of successful negotiation through surrender; and 'the reserves of management skills' would be available to the individual publisher. The *Bookseller* went on to point out that of the major independent houses Faber & Faber were showing £8,000 profit on a £2.5 million turnover, that Bodley Head had lost £114,000 in 1975 and Gollancz had lost £45,000 the same year, that Chatto had lost £100,000 over three years and that even Dent with nearly £3 million turnover had shown losses of £276,000.

By the mid-1980s, other powerful voices were raised in defence of the conglomerate and the aggregate. On 22 February 1984, Ian Chapman, chairman of Collins and one of the shrewdest publishers, gave a lecture entitled 'The Book Business: Art, Craft and Trade' at the Royal Society of Arts. His opening words were:

> Until the middle of this century, publishers were individuals who carried on their businesses with relatively meagre financial resources at their own risk. The publisher was the proprietor, the shareholders were likely to be composed of members of his family and, broadly speaking, he could publish what he liked so long as he remained solvent – which many failed to do . . . He did not have to worry about his bottom line. His list was meant to look like his library. It was a reflection of his tastes.

Mr Chapman went on to point out that eleven major companies were now responsible for some 60–65 per cent of the United Kingdom book production. Competition was increasing, US companies had made inroads into the British traditional markets and into the UK itself. British publishers had to be large enough to fight off that competition and gain their own footholds in the American market. Security lay in strength.

Commenting on the Penguin purchase of the Thomson companies, the *Bookseller* on 13 April 1985 wrote: 'For a largely paperback firm like Penguin, the way to survival and growth is clearly seen as being by way of increasing control over the rights of books'.

Peter Mayer, chief executive of Penguin, said at the same time in an interview with the *Sunday Times*:

> What a publisher wants these days is access to book rights, and these are obviously easier to get if they are in-house. You must also remember that rights are only leased, not owned.

He should have shouted that last sentence into the ear of Paul Hamlyn, who throughout his career has always shown a basic contempt for authors by endeavouring to buy, and in most cases succeeding in buying, their copyrights for a lump sum. In August that year, Mr Hamlyn took over the Heinemann group for £100 million in new shares, which left its previous owners, BTR, with a 35 per cent holding in the enlarged Octopus group. Within two years, Mr Hamlyn had sold Octopus/Heinemann on to Reed International for £535 million.

Even before the sale to Reed took place, Britain's eight largest publishers – the Pearson companies, Longman and Penguin (£240 million turnover); Octopus (£150 million); Collins (£140 million); Reed (£95 million); OUP (£80 million); Associated Book Publishers (£80 million); Macmillan (£75 million); and Hodder (£50 million) – accounted for more than half the United Kingdom's publishing turnover. Bigness was here to stay.

It is significant that none of these advocates of size or easier access to rights pauses to mention the possible effect on authors and their future status inside the publishing community. Collins would not so successfully have fought off Rupert Murdoch's predatory approach in 1981 had their authors not rallied to their defence.*

What does the professional novelist expect from his publisher? He should rightly expect a fair contract, an expeditious publication, thorough and efficient selling of his book and of whatever subsidiary rights he has assigned to the publisher, and prompt payment in full, when contractually due. But even more than all of these, he should expect – and receive – personal attention, the feeling that he is one of a family, among friends. He wants to see jacket roughs and specimen pages and be consulted over blurbs for catalogue and jacket copy. If he has a writing problem – sometimes even a personal problem – he wants to feel that he can pick up the telephone and without undue delay get through to an editor who knows him well and who is a friend. As I have said, novelists, like spiders, spin their works out of their own entrails. They lack the props afforded to the historian and the biographer – the existence of previous research, the study of original documents by other hands, even the discussions and debates with fellow workers in the same field. And so they need, as spiders also do, to find a secure framework on which to hang their webs. Their agents should and usually do provide part of that framework but novelists require further friendly allies in their editor and the people around him. When one works alone for months on end, unsure of the value of those words that are added to the growing sheets of paper each day, even the switchboard operator who recognises the voice and greets him by name before he has time to announce himself is balm to the harassed novelist.

Thus his sense of security is shaken when he receives a letter from his editor or from the managing director, announcing that the house is about to be taken over by a conglomerate – or sometimes discovers

* For the details, see page 158.

it for himself from an item in the national press or the trade papers. The apparent changes may be minimal if the reins are loosely held, as they were with the Thomson publishing houses under the calm and wise Gordon Brunton's aegis. But when the accountants get to work and decide that rents and staff would be saved if all the various houses were brought together under the same roof, the novelist may well find that his friendly switchboard operator has been declared redundant and, far worse, that his editor's immediate decisions have given way to a central editorial board to which requests are submitted in triplicate and decisions not taken by the board this week may wait in the queue for several more weeks.

The author's view was trenchantly expressed by P. D. James in her speech as chairman of the Booker panel of judges at the announcement dinner in October 1987:

> Writers are not happy to be bought and sold as if they were filing cabinets or other disposable office furniture. Our sometimes fragile self-confidence is not helped by finding that familiar faces, particularly those of trusted editors, have disappeared overnight.

Of course, a publishing house must be efficiently run and account-ants, kept in their right place, help towards ensuring that end. No one would disagree with the remarks of Ian Irvine, previously a senior partner at Touche Ross, the international accountants, and then – in June 1987 – group chief executive of Octopus, when he said:

> Editors must be profit conscious. The managers of imprints are responsible for profits – each is virtually running his own small business.

It was when he was reported a month later as telling a meeting of Heinemann editors that, after the forthcoming move to Michelin House in the Fulham Road, authors would not be allowed in any of the publisher's offices or in the 'work area' (a subtle distinction?) of the building, that eyebrows might tend to shoot upwards. Even a P & L figure-pusher ought to have grasped the ineluctable truth that authors were the prime providers of those offices and 'work areas' and should be looked on as honoured guests if they felt inclined to penetrate as far out as the Fulham Road.

One no doubt direct result of the Octopus take-over of Methuen occurred in May 1988 when Harold Pinter, who had been published by Methuen for more than twenty years, decided to move to Faber for the publication of his new play, *Mountain Language*. A few weeks later, Nick Hern, who had been his editor at Methuen and who had spent fifteen years with the firm helping to build an impressive drama list, left to set up his own list at Walker Books. Even though the take-over had not been in force for more than a year, he was quoted as saying: 'The Octopus influence began to be felt in unwelcome ways'.

Bigness often has real advantages when it comes to selling books but the acquiring and, if necessary, editing of those books usually depends on a one-to-one relationship. Authors need personal allies at court – allies with the power to get things done in a way that keeps the author satisfied. Big publishing houses do not attract major authors just because they are big. The men and women at the head of the company should not be too busy acquiring other firms or holding conferences or too ignorant to realise that without authors to pay for their Concorde flights to New York, their large company cars and their lavish expense accounts, none of these privileges would exist.

Even worse for the novelist who is not yet a 'brand name' and who perhaps never will be, conglomerates are in business, in Lloyd George's phrase, 'to squeeze the orange until the pips squeak'. Or, to borrow a sentence from Oxford University Press's annual report of 1987 in the section dealing with recent publishing trends:

> Another [effect] has been to place control of publishing more in the managers of very large concerns, to whom book publishing is but one concern and to whom profits earned are the decisive factor.

Penguin had paid some £20 million for the Thomson companies. To justify that purchase price, their collective annual pre-tax profits would need within a year or two to reach a level of upwards of £3 million – a level far exceeding their best previous results. There has to be a drive for big and quick answers, which may include the closing or radical restructuring of a whole list and will certainly include the pursuit of 'name' writers from other houses – often at inflated prices. An example of the former is Penguin's closure of the distinguished George Rainbird list, announced in October 1987, which evoked from Valerie Reuben, Rainbird's managing director, the bitter remark:

My own observation is that they are so busy acquiring businesses that they don't have time for long-term strategy to enable them to digest what they buy.

Paying too much to acquire several big names for the list inevitably means that lesser-known authors will lose out. I met Marc Jaffé of Bantam Books a few days after he had contracted to pay $3.2 million advance for the softcover rights in *Princess Daisy* by Judith Krantz. Tongue-in-cheek, I remarked that the purchase price would have paid for the same rights in more than sixty novels with an advance of $50,000 each. He replied, 'In my book, there's no such thing these days as a $50,000 novel!' Adjusting the figures for Britain, one begins to wonder whether there will soon on this side of the Atlantic be no such thing as the £5,000 novel. In February 1985, before the real onset of merger mania, Tom Rosenthal of André Deutsch said significantly:

Yesterday's promising book worth a shot has become today's marginal.
Yesterday's marginal has become today's regretful rejection.

Will the delicate talent that needs fostering patiently over several novels be able to find a niche with a publishing house that is part of a conglomerate? And will the smaller independent houses have long enough purses to develop that talent over the often lengthy period until it starts to show a profit for them, always realising that at such a stage the predators may swoop and lure that author away with the promise of advances and promotional budgets that an independent house may not be able to match?

Three other factors may affect a conglomerate's ability to deal properly with the authors it acquires through the purchase of one smaller house or a group of publishing houses. Most authors have a sense of style and continuity. To be ushered into that eighteenth-century house in Albemarle Street, the abode of numerous generations of Murrays, and to be shown the lock of Byron's hair on the mantelpiece of the chairman's room is to feel heir to a long and honoured tradition. In Bedford Square, the managing director of Michael Joseph used to occupy the room that had been Lady Ottoline Morrell's salon. Now he has a more or less open-plan office on one floor of a large but nondescript modern building in Kensington. In pounds and pence terms, publishing can be conducted just as efficiently in a partitioned neo-brutalistic building as in an elegant Georgian house – probably more so – but is it fanciful to think that the spirit and the style of 'making books' has been largely lost?

Next there is the 'shake up and shake down' factor. Most publishers these days have computerised their accounting systems. Problems may well occur if, for instance, the acquired publisher's ITT computer is not compatible with the head company's IBM system. Authors' accounts can be seriously delayed while the original publisher's royalty data are arduously transferred to an alien system. A close watcher of publishing results remarked recently that Viking Penguin's profit levels remained static – indeed fell – for a year or two after the Thomson houses were acquired. Buying a publishing house is rather like having a heart transplant: it takes time for the immunising drugs to work and the new organ to become a working part of the old body. On top of this, as already mentioned in the case of Penguin and its owner, Pearson, with a wide variety of companies under control, the publishing house has to adjust itself to a sophisticated accounting system, adapted to make sense of several disparate businesses. After Heinemann was acquired by BTR a senior Heinemann executive told me that it was impossible to take on a junior secretary *sub rosa*; the extra, though modest, salary would show up in the group accounts within a fortnight. That is good business for a hard-driving conglomerate that keeps a tight rein on its overheads. But the reverse side of the coin is that a major publisher, largely responsible for a £40 million turnover and pre-tax profits over £6 million, has to waste time sending an indent – no doubt, in triplicate – to his head office whenever a new and junior staff member is required.

The third factor is the 'musical chairs syndrome' – the tendency for editors to feel unhappy under the new restraints or to be declared redundant through the streamlining process applied by their new masters. An example is the knock-on effect achieved by a series of apparently unrelated events during 1987. In January, Bob Gottlieb, editor in chief at Knopf, which is part of the Random House group in New York, left to become editor of the *New Yorker* magazine. Sonny Mehta, editor of Pan Books in London, was invited to replace him. In the spring, Random House bought the Cape/Chatto/Bodley Head group and not long afterwards asked Simon Master, the managing director of Pan, to run the group. A little later, Helen Fraser, a stalwart of Collins/Fontana, fell out with the new management in Grafton Street and resigned: she was soon to be invited to join

Heinemann as publisher. By this time, Heinemann had in a period of two years moved out of the ownership of Tilling in to BTR and thence to Octopus and thence to Reed International. Upset by all these chops and changes, Brian Perman, the managing director, Peter Grose, the deputy managing director, Fanny Blake, the publishing director, and Kate Gardner, the production director, all announced their resignations. Around the same time, Pan, having been owned by Collins/Heinemann/Macmillan in equal shares and then by Heinemann (now Octopus) and Macmillan on a 50/50 basis, became solely owned by Macmillan, whose deal with Octopus had included – at Paul Hamlyn's insistence – the clause that if either company were to change ownership, the other had the right to buy it out. Octopus had, of course, sold itself to Reed International. Pan replaced its missing two top executives with two 'refugees' from Hodder & Stoughton, Alan Gordon Walker, head of the Australian company, and Ian Chapman jr, editor of Coronet. And at the end of the year, David Machin, who had been running Bodley Head for several years, resigned over a policy disagreement.

A further factor is what one might call 'the Football League syndrome'. The directors of professional football teams need quick results – promotion to a higher division or the winning of the League Cup or the FA Cup. They appoint managers at high salaries and with an open cheque-book for the purchase of outstanding players to achieve those results for them. The manager who wins a trophy this year is his directors' darling; but if his team next season gets knocked out in an early round of the FA Cup or loses half a dozen League matches in succession, yesterday's darling soon becomes today's scapegoat. Some managers in difficult straits will pay well over the odds to acquire a player with a name, who may or may not fit in with the existing team and its style of play. This week, this month, this season, take precedence over a patient build-up of the players into a team.

One can see this kind of frenzied approach being applied to the more subtle process of publishing. Up to the last decade, many houses had a kind of personality, often derived from the tastes of the founder or one of his descendants. There was a definable 'Cape novel' or a 'Collins adventure story' or a 'Secker book'. With a few exceptions – and those still among the independent ranks, such as John Murray, André Deutsch, Robert Hale, Hodder & Stoughton, and Weidenfeld – that no longer applies. The successful novelist, like the professional footballer, is considered to be up for grabs, liable to move from house to house for ever increasing money. The footballer has the strong excuse that his career is unlikely to span more than a decade and so he must play the market while he is still in demand. And no one who has ever asked for a pay rise should fault novelists for achieving their market value – and sometimes more. But what the long-term effect is likely to be on a novelist whose career may cover forty or more years is a question yet to be answered.

It must be said that many, perhaps the majority, of established novelists have remained faithful to one publisher for many years. William Golding has been published by Faber throughout, as Iris Murdoch has been by Chatto & Windus. Hammond Innes, Jon Cleary and Victoria Holt are only a few of the many novelists who have stayed happily with Collins as did Alistair MacLean until his death in 1987. Anita Brookner is just one of those who have been published only by Cape throughout their careers. John le Carré, Jeffrey Archer, Noel Barber (until he died in 1988), Gavin Lyall, and James Clavell have been steadfast on the Hodder lists for many years between them. But these are all authors who have reached a peak – or a plateau – in their careers and most of them are of an age when familiarity breeds not contempt but a sense of security. It is the newer writers who seem to be more at risk, more restless, more ready to look longingly at the rosier apples in the next-door orchard. Whether the increased pressures on their consciences and on their writing integrity to justify the tempting advances they are offered – and the risk of instability through being a 'gun for hire' to the highest bidder – will in the end be justified and will prove not to have a deleterious long-term effect on their actual work has yet to be seen.

But British publishing has not reached its Stonehenge – a circle of monolithic slabs. We have seen since 1986 the launching of two new and so far successful general imprints – Bloomsbury and Headline. A little earlier, Century proved that with energy, determination and a slice of well-earned luck to hit the computer book market at the right moment, publishers who knew what they were doing could do it well. Existing independent houses, from Macmillan and Hodder & Stoughton through André Deutsch, Souvenir Press, John Murray, Severn House, Constable, Gerald Duckworth, Faber & Faber, Victor Gollancz, Weidenfeld and Robert Hale, are all keeping their heads above water even if, like the proverbial duck, a few of them may be paddling away furiously beneath the surface.

In October 1986, Ian Chapman said: 'The big will get bigger for the next three or four years. And then, I think, they will have grown beyond the optimum size, and they will divest.' New York editors have been more wont to move from house to house during their careers than their British counterparts have done – until the last few years. For a long time now, authors with sufficient power in New York have been able to insist that options and future contracts will only be valid as long as Editor X remains with the contracting publisher. There have been a few such cases recently with London publishers as well. But again, it is only the powerful who can insist on this form of editorial continuity. The mid-list and the new novelist will still have to dance to the music of a carousel whose riders may jump off or be flung off before the music stops.

CHAPTER X

# Fiction Publishing in the 1980s

Some books are an author's soul, others a publisher's
product.

Aidan Ellis,
in a letter to the *Bookseller*, 25 May 1985

The worst possible way for an author to begin with a
publisher is with the potential of an unearned advance.

Deborah Rogers, August 1985

If one had to sum up the publishing trends of this present decade to
date in one sentence, it would be: the cottage industry is dead, long
live big business. The grouping of individual units into large bodies has
produced internal problems but it has also introduced a much needed
professionalism, often from outside, into the trade. For example, late
in 1985, Hodder & Stoughton appointed the advertising agency of
Saatchi & Saatchi, with a budget of £250,000, to run special promotion
campaigns the following year for seven of the house's leading novelists.
Again, in February 1986, Penguin employed Conran Advertising to
create 'a new series style' in the advertising and display material for
King Penguins. Such moves would have been unthinkable in the more
cosy days of earlier decades.

Apart from the growth of conglomerates, four factors have especially
influenced the present decade. They are: vertical integration; the
continued growth of paperback publishing; and the development of
bookshop chains, sometimes through the participation of publishers,
which is a further aspect of vertical integration. There was also the
threat, both external and internal, of the imposition of VAT on
books, coupled with pressure from home and abroad to break the
Net Book Agreement.

Up to the mid-1960s, a hardcover publisher keen to sell paperback rights in one of his books had the choice of at least half a

dozen independent firms: Ace Books, Corgi, Four Square (later New English Library), Mayflower (the British offshoot of Dell in New York), Panther and, above all, Penguin. Pan had three masters in Collins, Heinemann and Macmillan but it operated with considerable independence, buying many titles from outside. And even though Sphere Books, Coronet, and Fontana were owned respectively by Thomson, Hodder & Stoughton, and Collins, they could not make the necessary turnover from buying solely 'inside the house' and had to compete for paperback rights from outside firms. Thus, there was wide and healthy competition to acquire rights from any hardcover publisher, however small, who had a desirable title to sell.

That situation still obtains where the small publisher has an outstanding bestseller to place but overall the room for manoeuvre has become more and more limited. There is now no major paperback firm that is not allied with (or owned by) a hardcover house.

Vertical integration has aided the novelist in one sense in that, if there is a joint 'hard/soft' offer from one large group for the rights in his next novel, he gets the full royalty on both editions and does not have to share the paperback earnings with the hardcover publisher. But, equally, it has the disadvantage of a pre-sale – if the hardcover sales prove to be exceptionally good, he cannot improve the paperback advance – and thus limits his freedom of choice. And, conversely, if the hardcover edition does badly, the publisher may cut his losses and withdraw the expected publicity and advertising budget for the launch of the paperback edition.

In July 1979, Robin Denniston of OUP gave a paper entitled 'The Academic Publisher' to the Library Association. In it he said:

> Hardback publishing has become in the last ten or so years, quite specifically and quite willingly, a market research operation exploited by paperbackers, who can select from a thoroughly tested range of products those items most suited to their needs. Of course this is an over-simplification. Often paperbackers stick their necks and their cheque-books out early in the game in the hope of a greater proportion of the eventual profit.

For example, in December 1978, Pan Books paid an advance of £150,000 for paperback rights in *Overload* by Arthur Hailey. That was then the highest-ever advance paid for softcover rights in Britain for a novel. Almost exactly five years later – when inflation had risen by

70 per cent i.e. £150,000 would by then be equivalent to £225,000 – Corgi paid £800,000 for the British paperback rights in *The Fourth Protocol* by Frederick Forsyth. (A sale of between 2.5 million and 3.5 million copies throughout the UK and Commonwealth would have been required to earn back that advance – and Corgi has not yet announced that it has done so.) It appears that there were exceptional factors involved in pushing Corgi to such a high figure – Arrow Books, the in-house paperback firm of Hutchinson, which controlled the rights, was apparently prepared to bid up to £600,000 – but, even so, the efficient management of Transworld/Corgi would presumably have avoided the temptation of making a bid that bore no relation whatever to the financial calculations.

In 1974, British hardcover fiction turned over a total of £24,558,000, of which export sales accounted for about 31 per cent. That same year, paperback fiction turned over £21,156,000, of which the export percentage was 35 per cent. Ten years later, hardcover turnover had increased to £66,793,000 in the year but paperback turnover had passed it with a total of £71,424,000. (It had done the same in 1983 by a larger margin – £68,346,000 to £57,800,000.) Thus, in a decade, the overall earnings had increased threefold – largely due to the effect of inflation on published prices – but the proportions had switched from 55/45 in favour of hardcover sales to (in 1983) 45/55 in favour of the paperback side.

In January 1981, it was announced that the Pentos bookshop chain was heavily in debt to publishers, several of whom had even stopped supplying the group. By then the borrowings and loan stock of the Pentos conglomerate – of which the book chain was a substantial part – were over £13.5 million – against shareholders' funds of £18.5 million. Interest of £1.62 million payable for the first half of 1980 was almost as much as for the whole of 1979. It was an inauspicious start to the new decade but by retrenchment, the cutting of overheads and several shrewd purchases, Pentos was within a year or two up and running again. With the purchase and refurbishment of Dillons in Gower Street, London, in mid-decade and the opening of new branches in Oxford and elsewhere, Pentos fairly quickly reversed its fortunes. Waterstone's has been another entrepreneurial chain, which in a few years has opened some dozens of new bookshops in city centres. Each of its main bookshops is run as a separate entity, so that lack of success in one place cannot adversely affect the rest of the chain. Waterstone's displays something of the hustle and bravado of

American bookselling. It seems prepared to take short leases, recruit bright young staff and, if turnover does not reach the required level within a short time, cut its losses and close that particular branch. One recent example is that of the Regent Street, London, branch, which was closed when the rent and rates proved too high for the volume of business. Again, when a large store that had once been the local Woolworth and latterly a supermarket fell vacant in Hampstead High Street, Waterstone's moved in fast with an external design in darkest black – much to the annoyance of local and less go-ahead bookshops, two of which have since closed. Significantly, the paperback department was immediately accessible with a very wide-ranging stock.

It was a far cry from the days of forty years before, neatly caught in verses attributed to Gerald Bullett:

> They praised the book in Leeds and Pimlico,
> In Leicester Square and Paternoster Row,
> Filling the town with tidings of its wit
> Till even booksellers got wind of it,
> And this unwelcome thought their slumbers shook,
> That now at last they'd have to sell a book.

Indeed, by the end of 1987 and through 1988, there was some risk that certain city centres were becoming 'over-bookshopped'. In January 1988, Waterstone's announced that it was to open a shop in Nottingham. Bookshops already present there included W. H. Smith (two branches), Sherratt & Hughes, a newly refitted Dillons, and Penguin. The overall annual bookshop turnover in Nottingham was estimated at £3.5 million to £4 million, with Dillons having the biggest share. Would there be room for another aggressive newcomer?

At the same time, Pentos decided to open a Dillons store in Manchester, which already supported its own Athena bookshops, as well as Blackwell, Waterstone, Hatchards, Sherratt & Hughes. Room for one more? And there was the case of Oxford – with Blackwell, Dillons, the Oxford Bookseller and W. H. Smith, all within a short walking distance of one another.

Between 1984 and the end of 1987, the six major chains *excluding* W. H. Smith (Blackwell, Hammicks, Hatchards, Pentos, Sherratt & Hughes and Waterstone) added a total of ninety-eight bookshops to their lists. Their total trading space had increased from 372,000 square feet to 659,000 square feet. In the same period, W. H. Smith had increased its own square footage from 581,000 to 651,000. And yet, by mid-March 1988, the six majors between them announced a further expansion of twenty-four new sites, totalling 134,000 square feet – an increase of 20 per cent.

Many of the locations acquired over that four-year period were in main streets or shopping centres at high rentals. Most bookselling chains work on a rental level of 8 per cent to 10 per cent of turnover. Thus there had to be a drive for increased turnover, either by selling more books or by pressing publishers to increase their discounts. Waterstone's announced that its sales target per employee on the shop floor was to be raised from £68,000 to £100,000 a year.

And yet . . . Nigel Sisson, Penguin's hardback sales director, was quoted in the *Bookseller* for 25 March 1988 as saying that there was 'no evidence that volume sales have increased despite the expansion of the chains'. In fact, the volume of sales for mass-market paperbacks had decreased by 25 per cent in the four-year period 1982 to 1986, although unit sales of all titles (including hardback) to 30 September 1987 were up by 2.5 per cent. Even so, that modest increase in no way matched the more than 40 per cent increase of trading space acquired by the six majors and W. H. Smith in roughly the same period.

Variety of choice is splendid for the customer but, as Roy Thomson's verdict in the context of serious Sunday newspapers put it, 'There is always room for two but rarely room for three.' Unless the numbers of potential book buyers have mysteriously increased in recent times – and there is no clear evidence that this is so – some of the rival bookselling chains may have a hard time over the coming years.

In trade terms 1981 largely belonged to Rupert Murdoch, whose all-conquering progress was halted – at least on one front – by 'author power'. In January, News International bought Times Newspapers (*The Times* and the *Sunday Times*) from Thomson, to add to its existing stable of the *Sun* and the *News of the World*. The master's vulgarising touch was soon evident in both newly acquired papers. And in May that year, Murdoch bought 30 per cent of Collins from the family holdings. There had been something of a palace revolution shortly beforehand; Jan Collins, the eldest son of Sir William, had been persuaded to become non-executive, rather than executive, chairman, much to the distress of his mother who had long been closely involved with the company's fortunes. The next month, Murdoch made a formal bid for the remaining Collins shares – £2 per ordinary share and £1.50 for the non-voting shares. At that stage, he held 31.3 per cent. The offer would go unconditional once his holdings passed 50 per cent.

The Collins board put up a stout defence against the invader, forecasting a pre-tax profit of £4 million in 1981 and the payment of a dividend 150 per cent up on 1980. Borrowings were steeply down, it claimed. In addition – and this in retrospect was the master-stroke – a letter was sent to the leading one hundred Collins authors, seeking their support.

Robert Maxwell, who has always appeared to have more fingers than there are worthwhile financial pies to probe, had earlier bought 9.4 per cent of Collins ordinary shares. In July, Murdoch, having acquired the Maxwell holding, thus increasing his own to over 42 per cent, raised his offer on the outstanding ordinary shares to £2.25. Maxwell had just bought the printing firm of Eric Bemrose from Murdoch's News International for £3 million – with payment over ten years – and had settled a long-running dispute over the printing of the *Sunday Times* colour magazine. The City Takeover Panel investigated these actions in case they constituted a 'concert party' between the two marauders but quickly decided that they fell within the usual cut and thrust of City dealings. Collins had already complained of the Murdoch bid to the Office of Fair Trading but when the latter decided not to refer the matter to the Monopolies and Mergers Commission Collins seemed to be an inevitable victim of the ever-hungry Murdoch.

It was their authors who saved the day. Letters signed by such major bestsellers as David Attenborough, Sir Arthur Bryant, Winston Graham, Jack Higgins, Victoria Holt, Hammond Innes and Alistair MacLean appeared in the press, citing the signatories' complete support for the existing management and threatening to remove their books if the unwanted bid won the day.

Murdoch soon realised that it was no bluff and that a house without its biggest authors would be like a three-legged racehorse when competing in the publishing Derby. He settled for his existing holding of 42 per cent-plus with the right to appoint two members to the Collins board. Under the take-over rules, he would not be allowed to add to his holdings for two years and then was limited to acquiring no more than $2\frac{1}{2}$ per cent of the ordinary shares in the market in any one year. As it happens, he has maintained the status quo for the past seven years and appears to have developed a cordial relationship with the Collins board. But knowing that your largest shareholder can take you over in three to four years may serve to concentrate the collective Collins executive mind.*

Although statistics for the first quarter of 1981 showed paperback sales 20 per cent up in turnover compared to the first quarter of 1980 – from £14.62 million to £17.55 million, well ahead of the inflation rate – and unit sales up 2 per cent to 28.5 million, returns of unsold copies were rising at a worrying rate. For example, Pan Books' returns were up from 11.9 per cent in the first quarter of 1980 to 22.9 per cent and Granada from 16.1 per cent to 20 per cent. Star (owned by W. H. Allen) was running at 25 per cent, Futura at 17.8 per cent and Hamlyn at 16.4 per cent. Only Penguin with 10 per cent and Fontana with 12.2 per cent were at a manageable level. It was significant that those houses most dependent on wholesale distribution were the worst sufferers. (Penguin only did 20 per cent of its turnover through wholesalers, whereas Pan did 43 per cent and Hamlyn a massive 60 per cent.)

Pat White, the chief buyer of Bookwise wholesalers, pointed to the reason – over-production – in a talk quoted at length in the 15 August issue of the *Bookseller*. She said that of the 300 titles she was offered each month, only one hundred could be rated, with probably twenty-five to twenty-eight of them getting an A rating (suitable for all outlets) and a maximum of eight getting 'Pick of the Paperbacks' support. She added that there might be ten or more titles in any one month that would merit this status but, 'physically, the outlets could not cope, with books getting fatter and displays getting bigger. There are just too many strong titles.' Hugh Campbell, chief executive at Hamlyn, gave the other side of the picture when he said, '. . . the big wholesalers are going for the big, established writers and those books with major promotional efforts behind them, and the lesser books are being ignored completely'. Thus, although the overall paperback market looked healthy – with sales in the first half of 1981 16.4 per cent up on the same period in 1980 and with adult books earning £31,265,000 from a sale of 46,539,586 units – novels by authors without a strongly established name or which were too subtle to attract a wide stock response were likely to get a poor showing – or none at all. In the paperback mass market, the outlook for the 'literary' novelist was depressing.

* In November 1988 Rupert Murdoch made a further bid to take over Collins.

Luckily, for several there was a new (or newish) niche – the trade paperback in 'B' format, which was more akin in shape and size to the old Large Crown octavo hardcover novel than to the small mass-market paperback. As far back as the early 1960s, Panther had developed its Paladin list under the inspired editorship of Tony Richardson, who died tragically young, and Pan had its Picador, also under an editor of great flair, Caroline Lassalle, who became a successful novelist. Later, Sphere introduced its Abacus list, Coronet its Sceptre list and Transworld its Black Swan list. In addition, there were Faber Paperbacks, largely catering for its own authors, and Virago paperback editions. All these lists had – and have – a special interest in 'quality' novelists, who might well sell up to 10,000 copies in a more expensive and restrained softcover format but who would be unlikely to achieve a minimum sale of 20,000 to 30,000 copies, which mass-market publication requires in order to make a small profit.

Indeed, there are signs that good novelists can fare very well in a trade paperback edition. In recent times, Black Swan paid an advance of £60,000 for the latest novel by Isobel Allende; with P. D. James's *A Taste for Death*, Faber cleverly interposed a trade softcover edition between the hardcover and the mass-market edition. It announced that the hardcover edition would be published on 9 June 1986 at £9.95 and a 'C' format paperback (the same size as the hardcover) on 20 October at £5.95. The Sphere mass-market edition was to be published in the autumn of 1987, Faber having undertaken to withdraw the 'C' format edition that August. Faber printed 65,000 copies for the hardcover and 'C' format editions, with the idea of binding them up into whichever edition was required. In the upshot, *A Taste for Death* had a very considerable success, selling almost 44,000 copies hardcover and 125,500 in the 'C' format edition. This clever innovation will no doubt be repeated by Faber and its rivals when the right opportunity presents itself.

That novel-reading was still a minority interest, like real tennis and sword-dancing, was proved early in 1982 at the conclusion of the Book Marketing Council's 'Best of British' campaign. It had chosen twenty famous living novelists and their current works to promote at considerable advertising expenditure and a nationwide publicity drive. But a poll revealed that half of those quizzed who recognised the name of Anthony Burgess thought he was the traitor, Guy Burgess. The name of John le Carré was often confused with that of Robert Carrier, the chef and cookery writer. Little wonder, perhaps, that although British publishing turnover exceeded £1 billion for the first time during 1981, there had been a 4 per cent decrease in paperback unit sales in the year, at least partly because of a 17.6 per cent rise in the average price.

In an article in the *Author*, Richard Findlater wrote: 'The number of full-time authors has fallen by a half in the last decade to less than one-sixth of those who responded [to his questionnaire].' He also revealed that 118 novelists, who replied, averaged a writing income of £1,600 a year, less than a fifth of the wages paid to printing union machine minders. In fact, by the end of 1982, British printing prices were seen to be some 10 per cent to 25 per cent higher than the continental rates.

As if these problems for the publishing trade were not enough, a new problem arose in 1984 – in the words of Grant Paton, president of the Booksellers Association, 'the threat of VAT on books'. There were rumours in Whitehall that September that the Chancellor Nigel Lawson might be considering the imposition of VAT on books and newspapers in his next Budget. For the rest of the year there was great controversy and many protesting letters in the press, arguing against 'a tax on knowledge'. The *Bookseller* headed a leading article in its 8 December issue, 'VAT – Protests build on all fronts'. That week, there was a two-hour debate on the subject in the House of Lords. Finally, in parliament in March 1985, Mr Lawson declared that there would be no VAT on books. But the subject refused to disappear. Many of the continental members of the EEC charged VAT (or the equivalent) on books and there was continuing pressure on Britain to fall into line. By the end of 1987 and, in spite of his promise over two and a half years earlier, Nigel Lawson was believed to prefer indirect to direct taxation and might thus eventually favour spreading the VAT tax to cover books, newspapers and magazines. Apart from the 'tax on information' plea, publishers had few solid grounds for fighting against the tax. During the five years to the end of 1987, the Thatcher government had kept inflation down to an average of 5 per cent (or less) per year. In that same period, the average price of hardbound novels had risen in 1983 by 11.2 per cent, in 1984 by 10.6 per cent, in 1985 by 1.5 per cent, in 1986 by 8.7 per cent and in 1987 by 10 per cent – an overall rise of almost exactly 50 per cent, *double* the inflationary rate. To the pleas of the trade, a Chancellor might well point out that any industry that could increase its profit margins thus and get away with the higher prices could easily stand a modest extra tax. The argument that most publishers were making up for lost time, having failed to raise their published prices to a proper degree two decades earlier, would be likely to fall on deaf ears.

As if VAT were not enough of a menace, resale price maintenance through the Net Book Agreement came under scrutiny in October 1987. In that month, British and Irish delegates, with representatives of the Publishers Association and the Booksellers Association to the forefront, appeared in Brussels to argue against objections to the NBA raised by the EEC – on the grounds that it runs counter to Article 85 of the Treaty of Rome 'because of inter-state applications'. Mr Jeremy Lever, QC, presented the British defence to the EEC's case which, as reported in the trade press, was thus:

> The operation of retail price maintenance is an element of the NBA. The working of r.p.m. within the UK is not a concern of the European Commission, but when price-maintained books – exported, imported or re-imported – cross the frontiers of EEC countries it is the Commission's business.

At the time of writing, no decision has come out of Brussels. If the British delegates do lose their case, the result could be at the least a substantial nuisance and at the worst a major catastrophe for the future of the Net Book Agreement.

Throughout the decade, the annual output of titles has risen year after year – apart from 1981, which showed a modest decrease on the 1980 results. The totals of all titles published annually has run as follows:

1981: 43,083
1982: 48,307
1983: 51,071
1984: 51,555
1985: 52,994
1986: 57,845
1987: 59,837

A *Bookseller* headline on 28 September 1985 asked, 'Are publishers digging a grave by expanding their lists?' The previous week, Michael Sissons of the A. D. Peters agency wrote a cogent article which in part said:

162

It appals me to be still hearing from publishers that next year they must publish twenty more titles, any old titles I guess, simply in order to meet budgetary targets . . . When North Sea oil runs out, this country will have one natural asset left, the English language . . . We must above all nurture and not abuse those who write and who, through their developing skills, guard and develop the language.

Some notable publishing fortunes have been made on books which owe little to the writing, let alone the quality of the writing, and where in many cases no royalties are paid. Surely, looking ahead, this is a time for publishers to value particularly the words that they print and those who create them.

As if on cue, three weeks later, also in the *Bookseller*, Peter Mayer, the chief executive of Penguin, wrote:

We shall have to be very much better at business and recognise because of all this (and the time it takes) that in a *de*creasing number of cases will the editor-publisher any longer be the head of the house.

The shape of the future is in any case increasingly international.

One can only ask – if the editor is no longer the man in charge, or at least with real influence over the shape of the list, who will be left to 'nurture and not abuse those who write'? Commuting between New York and London in that 'international future' seems hardly the ideal way to attract, develop and keep real writing talent.

Late in the year, Penguin announced that it was going to group all its publishing companies in Wrights Lane, Kensington, and that redundancies were likely. Two or three weeks later, Collins reported that it was about to unify/integrate its hardcover and paperback publishing: in December it also bought the Claude Gill chain of bookshops. 'Verticalism' was on the move. It was not altogether a smooth progress. In March 1986, 40 per cent of the Michael Joseph staff, 60 per cent of Sphere staff and just under half of the Hamish Hamilton staff – three of the Thomson companies acquired by Penguin – opted to take voluntary redundancy instead of relocating in Kensington when the move took place in May. Moving to new offices is a chaotic and time-consuming process at the best but when so many unhappy staff vote with their feet, the problem of having to replace most of them either just before or just after a major move is hazardous indeed. So, although it was announced in March 1987 that the Penguin Group was *six times larger* than it had been when Peter Mayer became chief executive officer nine years before and although the group turnover for the year 1986 was up from £113.3 million to £133.3 million, the trading profit was *down* from £10.8 million to £9.3 million – a drop of from just under 10 per cent of turnover to 7 per cent. The reported reason was the expense of time, energy and money through absorbing the Thomson houses. A much improved 1987 suggested that the absorption was nearly completed.

Around this time, Susan Howatch left Hamish Hamilton for Collins and Danielle Steel left Michael Joseph/Sphere for Transworld. In each case, a massive advance was paid, perhaps more than the option-holding publishers were prepared to put up. Both authors have demanding agents, well able to look after their interests. One is more concerned for the new and developing authors, who may have lost an editor's services and friendship through the redundancies or, worse, have found themselves jettisoned because of the reductions or because their work did not fit neatly into 'the new policy'.

Three welcome developments that ran contrary to the trend towards bigger, if not better, occurred during 1986. In February, Tim Hely-Hutchinson, Sue Fletcher and Sian Thomas, all of them senior directors of Macdonald, announced that they were going to leave and set up a new publishing house, Headline. They had proved their merit by pulling Macdonald round from a trading loss of £1.5 million at the end of 1982 to a pre-tax profit of around £550,000 in 1985. Headline Book Publishing was indeed launched on 7 July that year with a working capital of £1.5 million, with institutional backing from Rothschild Ventures and with private investors as well. Tim Hely-Hutchinson's father, the Earl of Donoughmore, was a well-known figure in the City whose contacts no doubt proved most helpful to the youngish entrepreneurs. One hundred titles a year, both hardcover and paperback, were planned.

On 19 July, Simon & Schuster, the huge New York house whose annual turnover of $900 million was some three to four times bigger than that of the largest UK house and which since 1975 had been a subsidiary of Gulf & Western, one of the biggest international conglomerates, announced that it was to set up a branch in London, with Clyde Hunter, late of Heinemann, in charge. Richard Snyder, chief executive officer in New York, said, 'We're positioning ourselves to be a truly global publisher, which has long been our goal'. From the early evidence, the London office is not to be a repository for American titles in which the parent holds British Commonwealth rights. Simon & Schuster, London, indeed, has been making positive efforts to find and encourage local writing talent.

Finally, Nigel Newton, David Reynolds, Alan Wherry, and Liz Calder – all of them experienced and successful publishers in different fields – announced the launching of another new house, Bloomsbury Publishing, in September 1986. As with Headline, it too looked forward to publishing at least one hundred titles a year when in full swing. Bloomsbury introduced one bold innovation, to set up an Authors' Trust with 5 per cent of the issued capital of the parent company, which I discuss in greater detail in the final chapter of this book.

In October 1986, Collins sold its one-third share of Pan Books to Macmillan and to Octopus-Heinemann for £10 million. Up to the end of 1985, the latest accounts submitted for Pan showed a pre-tax profit of £2.4 million on a turnover of £25.9 million and net assets of £2.7 million. The Collins sale valued the company at £30 million which, judging by the 1985 results, appeared to be on the modest side.

In January 1987, the *Guardian* published its regular list of the 'Top 100' paperbacks for the year just ended. The figures showed that there had been an 18.7 decrease in the total sales achieved by the 'Top 100', as compared with the 1985 results, and there was also a significant drop in the number of titles exceeding a sale of 100,000 copies. Pan, as so often, was the paperback house with the best results, having four titles in the top ten, the three best export sellers, seventeen titles in all in the 'Top 100', on which £17 million had been earned in turnover, and 24 per cent of the total sales. In September, less than a year since Collins had sold out, Macmillan bought Octopus's half-share of Pan for £22 million – on a price/earnings ratio of sixteen. Thus, on paper, Pan's value had increased by almost 50 per cent – from £30 million to £44 million in eleven months.

1986 and 1987 saw a hotting up in the 'Battle of the Atlantic'. Simon & Schuster had set up its London branch in July of the former year. In May 1987, Random House of New York bought the Cape/Chatto/Bodley Head group for over £17 million – as with second marriages, a triumph of hope over experience. In June, International Thomson, with its headquarters in Canada, bought Associated Book Publishers* for approximately £210 million. In July, Robert Maxwell abandoned his $2 billion take-over bid for Harcourt Brace Jovanovitch in the States. Rupert Murdoch, having acquired Harper & Row in April for around $300 million through his subsidiary company, News America, sold a half-share on to Collins for £95 million. Bertelsmann, the huge German printing and publishing group, which already owned Bantam Books in New York, bought Doubleday in September 1986 for $475 million and in August 1987 added to Doubleday's 50 per cent share of Book Club Associates by buying the other half from W. H. Smith for £60 million, after considerable discussion with the Department of Trade and Industry. The recent strengthening of the pound and other European currencies against the dollar may see an increase in the transatlantic purchases, at least from the eastern side.

What can individual authors make of all this international buying and selling? There was a wartime black-market story in which a consignment of tinned fish kept changing hands at ever-increasing prices. Finally, the last buyer decided to open up a tin and inspect the contents. A putrid stench assailed his nostrils – the fish was rotten. He opened another and yet another tin with the same results. Then in anger he telephoned the man who had sold him the consignment and bitterly attacked him. 'My boy,' came the reply, 'that fish is for buying and selling – not eating.'

That story was echoed by a publisher's remark about the 1986 Frankfurt Book Fair: 'This fair is more about publishers buying publishers than publishers buying books.' The counterpoint was put by Michael Pountney, a shrewd observer of the book trade, in an article he wrote for the *Bookseller* on 22 February 1986, on the smaller, independent publishers:

> They live for the publishing of books, not for the business of business.
> An agent said that after twenty to thirty visits to Collins he still had no idea what Ian Chapman (the chairman) looked like, but after one visit to Deutsch, André was unforgettable: the personal touch.

* Methuen, Chapman & Hall, Spon, and Sweet & Maxwell.

166

Somehow, the very large publishing groups with their international branches must learn to acquire – or re-acquire – that personal touch. And the smaller houses, which can more easily provide it, must go on fighting to retain and increase their share of the market. In the end, authors are individuals – and it is individuality that most appeals to individuals.

CHAPTER XI

# The Editorial Function Today

What is an editor but a cross between a fall guy and a
father figure?

Arthur Koestler

In September 1976, Sir Robert Lusty addressed the Oxford Book
Association. *Inter alia*, he said:

> The role of the writer in publishing is the only role that really
> matters and this cannot be said too often and too loudly . . . Authors
> don't much care for dealing with departments. They require, rightly
> in my view, access to an identifiable human being at the top who
> is capable of saying yes or of saying no and able to do what is
> necessary when he has said it.
>
> Today in publishing editors breed like rabbits gone wild. In
> publishing they were unknown until after the war. From recent
> advertisements in the *Bookseller* and in addition to editorial directors,
> house editors, copy-editors, commissioning editors, I have found a
> need for copywriter editors, processing editors and project editors.
> I think they have come to stay.
>
> Editorial direction and selection has been taken over by editors
> and the publishing of their acquisitions is done by committee. The
> all-round man has become a square.

More than a decade has gone by since Sir Robert made that
speech. *Laus temporis acti* is a virus to which the old and the retired
are especially prone; and yet subsequent experience gives some extra
credence to his remarks. To explore how things stand today, this
chapter is based on interviews with eight representative editors.*

* The interviews all took place in the months of June and July 1987, except for the one with
Liz Calder which was at the end of September.

168

Each of them received in advance six questions which were framed to stimulate discussion. They were:

1   To what extent do you discuss with professional novelists on your list (a) what they are going to write next and (b) the work when it is in progress?
2   Would you steer a professional novelist away from a particular theme or plot if you felt it would be wrong from a literary or commercial point of view?
3   Do you ever put up ideas of your own for a new novel to any of your professional novelists?
4   What are your thoughts on auctions and are there too many of them?
5   Do you think it is as easy as it was five or ten years ago to publish a promising first novel?
6   Has the 'literary' novel a future?

The eight editors had entered publishing by various routes, several bearing out the adage, 'It isn't what you know but whom you know.' After Winchester and National Service, and having stayed on in the army for a few years and winning the Military Cross for gallantry in the Aden 'troubles', Mark Barty-King spent two years in a menial job with Abelard-Schuman in New York, a year in California in the rare books trade, then eight years with Heinemann, eleven years at Granada and the last four helping to develop Bantam Press, London, from scratch.

Liz Calder, whose parents had emigrated to New Zealand, took a BA in English at Canterbury University, returned to England, married, spent several years travelling in North and South America with her then husband, who worked for Rolls-Royce, and their two small children, came back to the UK and spent a year with the MGM Story Department. When that closed down, tipped off by Deborah Rogers and Giles Gordon, she became publicity manager at Gollancz for four years and then did another four or five years there as an editor. Towards the end of 1978, Tom Maschler invited her to join Cape as a senior editor. She stayed eight years, then left to help form Bloomsbury Publishing.

Rosemary Cheetham was educated at 'one of those grim little public schools where they taught you how to curtsy and weren't terribly interested in their teaching'. She then read English at Girton

College, Cambridge, took a secretarial course and became secretary to Anthony Cheetham at Sphere Books. When he left in 1974 to start Futura, several of the staff went with him, including Rosemary. She had taught herself by trial and error to become a copywriter of blurbs and then an editor. After two years, she was given the chance to develop a women's fiction list. By the end of the decade, Cheetham had moved on to begin his own company, Century, and Rosemary, who was now his wife, was very much a partner in the enterprise. She has continued to build up a (mainly women's fiction) list at Century.

After Downside, Cambridge, a spell of teaching and some magazine sub-editing, Richard Cohen became a junior editor at Collins through a contact. He stayed there five years, then moved to Hodder & Stoughton as senior editor for fiction. Seven years later, he moved on again, this time to be publishing director at Hutchinson where he has remained since the merger with Century.

On leaving Charterhouse, James Hale worked briefly as an assistant at W. H. Smith and then, influenced by the first ever non-family director of Hodder & Stoughton, took a job there on the bottom rung – as a packer and looker-out. A year later, he was promoted to do a graduate two-year course at Hodder, getting to know how each department functioned. At the end of the course, he became an editor on the paperback side and after a year or two moved to the hardcover side under Robin Denniston. He stayed for twelve years until 1976, when he temporarily left full-time publishing to act as reader and editorial adviser to the Literary Guild. In 1982, he went back into publishing by joining Macmillan and becoming in due course editorial director.

Harold Harris was a scholar at St Paul's School, where he studied classics. He went into journalism and by the early 1950s had joined the staff of the *Evening Standard*, becoming literary editor in 1957. Five years later, having developed the book pages and doing much to make the *Standard* by far the best of the (then) three London evening papers for arts coverage, he was offered the job of editorial director at Hutchinson. He joined in February 1962 and retired some eighteen years later.

Chris Holifield was educated at a 'middle-class boarding school' and at Cambridge where she read modern history. After a six-month secretarial course, she spent a year in that capacity at Granada. Her private ambition was to become an editor; when she realised that the Granada management was against women editors, she left to become secretary to Philip Evans at Coronet. Not long afterwards, he promoted her to the rank of junior editor. That was 1973 and for over two years Chris Holifield remained happily learning her trade. But when Philip Evans was involved in a terrible motoring accident that left him semi-paralysed and in a coma for sixteen weeks – he has since made a remarkable part-recovery and acts as a reader and consultant for several publishing houses – Chris Holifield moved not long afterwards to Pan Books as fiction editor. In 1976, she was invited by ABP, who had just launched the Magnum imprint, to come and run the list. When she realised that ABP was unlikely to invest the amount of time and money required to make Magnum wholly successful, she left to become editorial director at Sphere Books, where she improved the market share and revived the Abacus list. But again it seemed that her new bosses, the International Thomson Organisation, had no long-term plans for their publishing houses and when David Machin invited her to join the Bodley Head as publishing director of adult books, she accepted.*

The eighth editor, Robert McCrum, followed the classical path into publishing – prep school, Sherborne, a history scholarship to Corpus Christi College, Cambridge, a Transatlantic Award to Pennsylvania University, then in 1976 a job at Chatto & Windus, where he was ostensibly publicity assistant but did 'practically everything', including the in-house reading. He moved to Faber & Faber in 1979 as editorial director and has remained there ever since.

The eight editors were split in their response to question one – the extent to which they discussed the next book with novelists on their respective lists. As Mark Barty-King put it, 'I've always looked on the editorial role as being basically a responsive role, giving an author what that particular author needs . . . I also feel that authors should have a pretty clear idea of what they're doing.'

This was echoed by Liz Calder: 'It's always been my experience that novelists write the novel they're burning to write. If they tell me it's about, say, South American tin mines, I'm not the person to say, "Don't do that, it's a terrible idea." If they're burning to write it and you know they're good, it's going to be a good novel, no matter what it's about.'

Robert McCrum too shared this view: 'I've noticed the two kinds of writers behave in two different ways; the more commercial think

* A year after our interview, in June 1988, she resigned from the Bodley Head.

commercially and the literary writers tend to think in a literary way
. . . Most literary novelists . . . even the quite young ones . . . you
let them talk and then say, "That sounds like what you want to do,"
rather than say, "I think you should write a book about the civil
war in America." You find out what's in their minds. Over dinner
or lunch, you talk and talk and you hear what they're saying . . .
They want confirmation of a path they've already adopted.'

On the other hand, Rosemary Cheetham, who in turn at Sphere,
Futura and Century had to develop (or re-develop) her particular
list from scratch, replied when asked if she discussed themes and
plots with her authors, 'Endlessly. In some ways, I find that quite
exhausting – the amount they rely on me to tell them what to do
. . . There isn't a single author on the list who doesn't believe that,
given the right advice, they could become Barbara Taylor Bradford
or Len Deighton. Or, perhaps more likely, Jack Higgins, who after all
was an apprentice for a long time and then suddenly broke through.'
She added that she had been convinced that Sarah Harrison had the
ability to write a big novel and so she suggested the First World War
as a theme. At first, Miss Harrison refused, perhaps through lack of
confidence in her ability to tackle such a theme and so large a canvas.
Then, a few weeks later, she telephoned Rosemary Cheetham and
said she would try. 'She turned in an absolutely cracking synopsis.
It had that spark of originality. She'd taken a mundane idea and
she'd created it into a story where you could see there was going to
be real emotion and real characters and a really serious theme.' The
resulting novel was, of course, *The Flowers of the Field*, which brought
the author an immediate reputation and considerable earnings.

James Hale expressed his views thus: 'How much one involves oneself with preliminary discussions with a professional novelist depends
on two things – how much they want and how much you think they
need.' He gave two differing examples. With Alexander Fullerton,
he has long and detailed discussions on the plot and the characters
before the novel is started. He then usually hears nothing from the
author until the finished typescript is delivered. In all probability,
few changes to the text will be needed. The other example was of
a novelist with whom he works closely both before the start of the
novel and during its development, 'virtually on every line'. As he
summed it up, 'All a professional novelist wants is to get the book
in his view right and to make money from his book . . . A professional
author cannot afford to put a book on one side for two years, then

look at it again, then do what is necessary . . . All that an editor can do is to see the book as best he can through the author's eyes and do what the author would himself or herself do after that lapse of two years.'

Most of the editors interviewed were chary of either steering an author away from a particular theme or plot and of putting up ideas of their own. But Mark Barty-King made a good commercial point when he said, 'There are certain instances where one steers an author away from a specific subject if one knows that another author is writing about it. I wouldn't encourage an author at the moment to write yet another book about Iran or Beirut. There will be many more terrorist novels, I'm sure, but I wouldn't want an author of mine to be up against dozens of terrorist novels.'

Chris Holifield also felt that editors should take the lead, if required. 'It is the editor's job to be available and to fit in to the degree to which the author wants an advance involvement . . . Quite often, someone who is writing "literary books" wants to know why he's not reaching a wider audience. That's one way an editor can discuss what he's doing and perhaps encourage him to tackle a larger subject rather than to continue writing a series of miniature-scale books, which I think an awful lot of serious English writers still tend to produce.

'. . . Younger writers are often very uncertain which way to go. The more you write, the more confident you get and the more clear you are about what you want to do and how to find your audience.'

An interesting issue that arose from the interviews, not covered in the list of questions, was the amount of actual editing of the finished typescript that the interviewees expected to carry out. Harold Harris, with his wide newspaper experience before his eighteen years as editorial director of Hutchinson, had several pertinent comments to make.

'I came to the conclusion that the authors who like to talk about [the work in progress] and who like to have an editor looking over their shoulder are journalists. Almost without exception . . . They've been brought up knowing that an editor or a sub-editor is going to be looking at their work and that they'll have certain instructions on how to write it.

'Almost always, American editors expect to do more to books than English editors do. I used to feel, when I was editing full-time, that English editors on the whole do too little editing and American editors do far too much. I tried to steer a course between the two.

My editing was usually on points of detail, things that I hadn't properly understood, rather than a major criticism of the book.

'In what I would call the commercial novel, I would certainly criticise the structure of the book. For instance, one of Freddie Forsyth's novels [*The Devil's Alternative*] has a lot of different themes – there were five different plots going through the novel. In the first chapter, he brought all five strands in and I persuaded him that this was making it difficult for the reader. One of the strands, for example, was completely unnecessary until halfway through the novel. I suggested he should make the first chapter about one specific strand and then introduce the others after that – but get the reader interested in the one particular strand. This is the commercial outlook about a novel that one has to take into consideration.

'. . . Koestler used to say to me, "Well, do you understand it, Harold?" I would say, "Yes, I understood it." Then he would say, "Well, if you understood it, it's all right!" Once I said, "Arthur, you just use me as a fall guy." There was a long silence and then he said, "What is an editor but a cross between a fall guy and a father figure?"'

Richard Cohen also had firm points to make on this score: 'Early on, I once said to an author, "I think my job is to stretch you to the point where you almost lose your temper with what I'm asking of you." I wouldn't put it so baldly now, but the point about *stretching* an author is an important one. It's a matter of realising what an author can take, whether he's a good reviser or not.'

Speaking of several highly successful commercial novelists, he said, 'It's odd how many are actually a-literate; they often can't spell or punctuate, they're not serious or regular readers of fiction, they have little interest in words. It's almost as if that lack of intellectual interest goes with the peculiar gift of story-telling they have. And it's often the biggest sellers who most need to be made literate.

'. . . Jeffrey Archer will listen to a number of people giving him advice and will do major plot changes, extra scenes and character shifts – but he remains his own man. He is not academically trained and in several ways is very humble about his writing, but at every stage of editing it's he who decides what goes in, however much he takes from other people.

'It's very dangerous for an editor to think it's he or she who "makes" an author. Not necessarily hubristic, just wrong-headed. Peter Benchley has never had a more productive editor than he had in Tom Congdon over *Jaws*, when Tom was at Doubleday. But Tom has never had the same success in his later editorial jobs. The same is true of Robert Ludlum and his one-time editor, Dick Marek. The lesson in both cases is that a commercial author often gives up close editorial help at his peril; but it is exactly the big-selling commercial author who, independent of editorial assistance, has a quality which is his and his alone, a quality that can't be grafted on.'

And what of the book that, after it is delivered, does not work – at least, to the editor's satisfaction? James Hale had one solution: 'It is always done much better face to face but, twice in my life, I have asked novelists to put the book they have written in a drawer – certainly for a period of time – as publishing it would do their careers real harm. Both of them did. In neither case was an agent involved. It was quite a frightening moment both times, as they were extremely promising authors . . . In one case, it was the third novel of a writer in the surreal area and this time he passed so far through the glass wall that there was no visibility at all. It took a hard day's drinking [to convince him] but it did in the end work.'

Chris Holifield's approach is somewhat different: 'I've frequently asked them to try to rewrite it and if they still don't manage to, then it seems to me one should try to get them to shelve it. It is very important, if they are going to be persuaded, that their agent agrees with me. Quite often, if the agent does agree with me, we can be quite formidable. I'm talking, of course, about the younger author . . . The good agents [will] have read the novel and will have an editorial view of it as well as an agent's view.'

The consensus of opinion was that auctions were on the whole a necessary evil which, having once been invented – see Appendix A by Scott Meredith – could not now be reasonably disinvented. As Mark Barty-King put it, 'There are too many auctions, too many inexperienced agents going out to auction unnecessarily and often coming away with disappointing results. One responds better, because it's more flattering, to an agent who says, "Look, I've got something I want you to have first crack at because it's going to fit Bantam Press/Corgi – or because you did so well with such and such a book." We will often come up with a very big advance to keep a book out of an auction and to pre-empt. Often, I think that's the happiest outcome. The agent gets the money he wants but he also gets the house he wants.'

Liz Calder tended to echo his remarks, although she did make a good point about sauce for the goose *and* the gander. 'I just accept that auctions are a fact of life. I'd much rather someone came to me and said, "This is the best thing I've read in years and it's all yours. Go away and make me an offer." *But, after all, publishers do it.* We hold auctions to sell paperback rights and to sell foreign and American rights.

'. . . Auctions are time-consuming and take up energy and resources that may be totally wasted. I feel that Bloomsbury has to show itself to be competitive, as we're new and we have to try harder . . . The "auctioneer" doesn't always get the publisher he wants and doesn't always get the best deal for the author, although it may be the most money.'

Richard Cohen felt that the instant communications that have existed between London and New York for some years now often lead to an increase in auctioning. 'A New York publisher buys a big book and within twenty-four hours ten London publishers will have heard of it. So the London agent gets ten phone calls and often has no option but to auction it: he has his long-term relationships with all those publishers to consider.

'An auction is by definition an affair where the winner pays more than the others think it's worth. If everybody else is wrong, the winning publisher has gambled well. But if the publisher spends too much time and money trying to regain his outlay, then he's either harming other books on the list or maybe harming that author – in the sense that he's pushing for that book to get a certain readership and a certain sale, and if he gets lots of returns the market may well perceive the book to have failed . . . So an auction may be setting up an artificial situation for that book then to exist in, and a promising career may be spoilt. I don't think agents generally look enough into the *total* effect of an auction.'

Chris Holifield raised two practical problems when she said, 'One of the great problems of auctions is that you don't have enough time. Sometimes a very large script will arrive with a two-and-a-half-week limit on it. That is very self-defeating. If you are expected to pay a lot of money for it, you should be able to get several readings . . . and probably talk to your paperback house, which means they've got to have time to read it, too. And then you need time to discuss it with them and come up with an offer.

'Apart from everything else, auctions create two classes of books. The books that come in in the normal way from an agent with an ordinary letter are continually overtaken for attention by the books that come in with a date on them – which you have to keep on top of. That's very unfair and quite infuriating as well, because one of those [the normal submissions] might be something you'd be far more interested in.'

James Hale felt there were pros and cons in the whole subject. Dealing with the latter first, he mentioned how he had had photocopies made of three novels which had just been auctioned and sold to other publishers, one of them fetching an advance of £130,000 and the other two having been 'sold for such high sums that the publishers who bought them must expect to sell many thousands'. He arranged for some of Macmillan's professional readers and some in-house editors and others to read the photocopies. 'We all sat round scratching our heads afterwards. We still didn't understand why they had been bought for such large sums . . . There is a certain madness going round and it has more to do with competition between publishers and has nothing to do with professional writing. Very often, the writing just isn't professional. It's probably very damaging to the whole business.'

And yet his summing-up returned a 'not guilty' verdict. 'Auctions are not necessarily a bad thing. They do make you concentrate very hard on exactly how you're going to publish the book and exactly how much you have to offer. It's certainly also true that they can tie up your time . . . We keep a diary on upcoming closing dates and there are never less than three, sometimes as many as six, dates always in it . . . Consider the functions that are tied up in a key auction which you really want to win. You have your managing director involved, your editorial director, probably in most cases the editor who was originally approached. You then have to bring in your sales director and your marketing director to put together a marketing plan. If it's an efficient plan, the design department will get involved in producing a jacket and leaflets, which will be a considerable expense because you may need to get some of them printed. There's a lot of money spent and a lot of expensive managerial time when you could be out there selling books.*

'There is a plus side to auctions. Part of an editor's job is to get everyone inside the company excited about particular books. It's a very exciting moment when you've got the entire company wound

* Compare Deborah Rogers's remarks on page 69.

up to acquire a book – they really want it. And then you get it. That does wonders for the morale of the company.'

The last word on auctions must go to Robert McCrum, who only participates on a strictly selective basis. One recent coup was *Lake Wobegon Days*, which was offered by A. P. Watt with high hopes. McCrum liked the book greatly and put up an advance of £12,500, half expecting that he would be outbid. But of the six or so publishers in the auction, some did not make an offer at all and the others proposed small advances: his bid was accepted. Then the American bandwagon began to roll. The book shot to the top of the *New York Times* and *Publishers Weekly* bestseller lists and the buzz spread across the Atlantic. Faber has had a big success with *Lake Wobegon Days*, selling 60,000 copies in hard covers and 120,000 in paperback.

All the same, Robert McCrum has reservations about auctions in general: 'The difficulty with auctions in a company like Faber & Faber is that we simply don't have that kind of money for individual books, given the money available for the whole list. We haven't got £150,000 to spend [on one book] and it would skew the whole list so badly to have to buy a book that way that on the whole we have to try to avoid those situations or buy when it's a low-key auction – though most auctions by definition can't be low-key.'

He considers it would be unfair to the novelists already on his list if he were to pay a very large amount for a literary novel, nor would they like it once the news was out. He instanced Peter Carey, 'who, after all, is trusting us to be sensible and run an old-style publishing house which looks for quality. If we suddenly start behaving like somebody else, then we've betrayed that trust.'

The editors were generally in accord in their answers to the fifth question – is it as easy as it was five or ten years ago to publish a promising first novel? As Mark Barty-King put it, 'It's as easy to publish a first novel today as it's ever been. I don't think there's a first novel in existence that is really good that isn't under contract. We would not resist a first novel, however small, which was well written by somebody with talent . . . Everyone is crying out for talent.'

Rosemary Cheetham went further: 'In a funny kind of way, it's easier [to launch a promising first novel] because of all this hype. I don't think there's any problem in getting out there and hyping a first novel. When all the razzmatazz has faded and you've got a track record to rest on, the author wants you to do something as exciting the second time round. *That*'s the difficulty.'

Richard Cohen developed two interesting points: 'Publishing isn't like the car business. Get the production line moving! Most people are in it not to make a fortune but for the fun. Part of that fun is finding new fiction, in particular new literary fiction, and that means not working for huge conglomerates and having to publish what an editor overseas has already discovered for you . . . Good first novels will continue to be published for ever . . . Hardcover fiction will be a long time a-dying but I feel that more and more it may become a test run for the paperback.

'To what extent in the last thirty years have people who might have written novels of quality gone into film and television writing, producing, directing? A generation of talent has been lost to the novel in the way a generation was lost in the First World War – one feels the gap.'

And James Hale expressed his confidence thus: 'We are publishing four first novels in the early months of next year. I have high hopes for all of them and think they are all reasonably outstanding in their own way. The actual sales [of first novels] are not large; they're probably as small as they've ever been. But publishers are much more efficient and paperback houses are far more prepared to publish the literary novel. These two factors make it possible to go on publishing them . . . The emergence over the last few years of the [paperback] trade fiction format – without that I'm not sure we could have continued to the same extent with literary fiction.'

Chris Holifield was more cautious in her comments: 'It's both easier and harder to publish a promising first novel. If it's perceived as being really promising, then there's a lot of competition for it as more houses try to get on to this particular bandwagon and are looking for promising new British talent. The less obvious ones – those that are very much first novels and which may need a lot of work done to them – could be far harder to place . . . I do try to publish first novels in the spring because the autumn is such a difficult time.'

But Robert McCrum struck a positive note in his summing-up: 'There never was a better time to be published . . . There's a greater receptiveness – perhaps it's more accurate to say as great a receptiveness – than ever before. Although there've been many mergers, there are as many smaller publishers starting up. There's a great hunger among editors for new writers. At the risk of sounding very elitist, books that should get published do get published and the books that don't get published probably shouldn't be. I don't believe in talent languishing unpublished in garrets.'

The final question – has the 'literary' novel a future? – received unanimous assent. As Liz Calder put it, 'I think the literary novel has a future – and always will be the thing that represents the heart of literature. As long as the book itself has a future, I'm sure that good novels will have.'

This was echoed by Rosemary Cheetham, who said, simply, 'More than ever, the literary novel has a future.'

And by Chris Holifield, who referred back to the recent assistance from trade paperbacks: 'There's more interesting serious fiction writing being done now than there has been for some years. It's partly to do with the expansion of the trade paperbacks, which has found a market that previously was being dissipated.'

Perhaps the only discordant note of warning came from Robert McCrum: 'It's easy to take a book on but after that . . . probably at least half of the new books each year barely make it. Most books fail in some sense. There are very, very few books which are really successful . . . The list is always carried by a handful of books . . . 10 per cent do really well and everyone's delighted; 60 per cent, say, fall short of the author's expectations and the remaining 30 per cent are a catastrophe! . . . It's a Sisyphean task publishing first novels. What you're really hoping for are reviews and that special buzz, so that when the paperback comes out, which we [at Faber] automatically do a year later, people will go out and buy 7,000 to 10,000 copies. But of course we're talking about very modest sales.

'Quality does seem to sell, as long as one's expectations aren't too high. The threat to the literary novel lies outside. The merchant banks and the overseas buyers [of publishing houses] – if they try to get the Jonathan Capes jumping through a fiery hoop – 15 per cent profit a year [on turnover] – it won't happen. That's where the threat to the literary novel comes, when houses like that lose their sensibility and their ethos through the new owners.'

Several other points arose through the various interviews that fell outside the list of questions. As a counterpart to Robert McCrum's remark about 'hoping for reviews', James Hale had an acid comment: 'The standard of reviewing is as low as I've ever known it and the standard of literary editorship is in many ways appalling . . . It's dangerous for us as publishers. We used to say, "Well, at least it'll get reviewed", and that will help. You can no longer say, "I know this novel will get reviewed." You simply can't. And that is frightening.'

He spoke at some length of the actual cost to a publisher of assessing incoming manuscripts, including those that were unsolicited. Macmillan pay their readers £15 for a detailed report on one script and that would include a synopsis of the story. For a submission that was clearly unpublishable, where the professional reader need only read twenty or thirty pages, a fee of £5 would be paid for a brief condemning report. These do not sound like handsome fees, if one considers that even a quick reader would need perhaps the better part of a day to read carefully a long script and write a detailed report on it. But a sizeable publisher might well receive 2,000 or 3,000 scripts in any one year, most of them unsolicited. On the assumption that 500 out of, say, 3,000 required at least one detailed report, perhaps several, and the rest warranted a brief one, that would constitute a cost of at least £20,000 a year. The result might be one hundred publishable and eventually published books; each of them would thus carry an invisible overhead of £200 in editorial fees.

Robert McCrum quoted Philip Larkin as once saying that 'Most novels have a beginning, a muddle and an end.' When I asked him if he found that being a successful novelist caused problems for his editorial relationships with his own authors, he firmly rejected the possibility. 'If you write yourself, you can get inside a writer's head more quickly and understand how difficult it is . . . Writing a book is one of the most difficult things anyone ever tried to do. It's incredibly lonely, it's very demanding – it has great satisfactions but enormous frustrations. If you can do that, you will have rapport and a sympathy with the people who write for you.'

Without in any way accusing Mr McCrum of falling into this particular trap, there is a counterpoint to his claim that the writer/editor will best understand and sympathise with his author. It is the risk that such an editor, whether an established writer or manqué, may, probably subconsciously, try to make over the submitted text as he himself would have written it. James Hale, earlier in this chapter, when saying that an author cannot afford to put a book aside for two years and then come back to it with a fresh eye, remarked, 'All that an editor can do is to see the book as best he can *through the author's eyes* [my italics] and do what the author would himself or herself do after that lapse of two years.'

If the writer/editor were to apply his creative talent and end up seeing the book too much through his own eyes, he would divert the author from his original intention. Numerous novelists have complained over the years, when checking the proofs of their books, that the narrative and the dialogue have been substantially altered by their editors, away from the text they delivered in the first place.

We have also seen – in the case of Alberto Moravia and Frederic Warburg – that the publisher who has written a book may spend valuable time discussing his own work and neglect the author's new submission, which was the reason for their meeting. Another such instance emerged from my interview with A. S. Byatt, which also emphasised the risk of getting on too friendly terms with one's editor. In the early days of her association with Chatto & Windus, Cecil Day Lewis edited her novels. As she put it, 'You can get to know an editor too well. My novel ceased to be the centre of our conversation, which was about everything including his poetry. So when I actually wanted help, the formal relationship had gone . . . It's what the [author/editor] relationship is for. It's a business relationship, it has a purpose. And it means, as if you were consulting a psychotherapist, you have the right to go on talking about what you're doing without the feeling that you're being bad-mannered.

'I don't ever actually take advice [before writing] but I do like to lay out what I'm thinking to see if it even sounds coherent, every now and then . . . I've never shown anybody anything I'm writing until it's finished and then I get to hate it, so that, when Chatto says this is far too long and take the best bits out, I just sit there gloomily and let them! And about two years later, I hate them because I feel they were wrong; but I feel very defenceless at the moment when it's gone in, as I always have this terrible reaction against what I've just finished and can't stand the sight of it.'

Robert McCrum, I had discovered, was particularly worried about what he called 'an astonishing level of unreality in the British publishing community as between the relationship of what is expected and what actually happens . . . the gap between what people expect to sell and what actually sells, the gap between the advances that are being paid out for some books and the actual sales – it's as though publishers believe their own propaganda. "If we can generate enough enthusiasm for the book when we pay £100,000, somehow that will be translated into sales" – which of course never happens. That level of unreality is catastrophic, very dangerous.'

In her turn, Chris Holifield voiced much the same sentiment: 'I don't think the amounts of money being paid for Graham Swift or Fay Weldon have very much to do with the realities of what the books are going to earn . . . I suspect that in the long run there's going to be a backlash against the prices being paid for those books and others. I can't believe that the frenetic interest in publishing in the City will continue. Publishers are particularly after brand names, a classy kind of brand name . . . The reason is because they think they really can market those names to a much bigger audience. I'm not sure that's true. In the end, there must be some kind of limit to the number of people who want to read, say, Graham Swift, however good he is.

'There's too much money washing around in publishing in relation to the kind of business it is. Eventually, the people who are investing in it, whether they are conglomerates, the City or whatever, are going to realise what a relatively low return it will bring.'

She spoke with some force on the editor's role and accountability: 'What the editor does is . . . rather intangible. If you're dealing with a lot of tangibles, looking at the financial picture or the structural picture or the personnel picture, all the editor has are vaguely defined skills. The only way you learn is on the job. In the end, it must come back for an acquiring editor – most importantly – to judgment . . . When we get down to doing profitability studies on the computer, it will be very useful in many ways. It'll also be very easy to code something in for the editor – and then you'll be able to see which editor's books make money for the company.

'It all comes back to more financial controls. In the most enlightened publishing managements, editors are seen to be important – and where it all starts. Yet there are a great many publishing houses where editors are seen to be very unimportant, merely part of the whole picture, and not to be given too much voice in publishing policies or in deciding the overall direction of the company.'

The editorial valediction must go to Harold Harris, the oldest of the eight and the man who has had the dual distinction of editing one of the greatest of twentieth-century novelists and one of the most successful – in Arthur Koestler and Frederick Forsyth. He said, 'An author doesn't just want his editor's admiration because it goes without saying that, unless the work was admired, the book wouldn't be published. What the author wants is his editor's love.'

The eight editors interviewed were chosen to represent a wide variety, ranging from those who worked for a privately owned house, one of them of very recent creation, to an editor in an international conglomerate. It is interesting, therefore, and to some degree surprising that their views are in broad agreement, one with another. All of them feel that auctions are inevitable nowadays but are none the less too frequent, too time-wasting and too much blunt instruments when it comes to putting the right author with the right firm at the right price. All of them, too, feel that there is a distinct future for the literary novel, especially with the quite recent growth of 'quality' paperback lists. Nearly all think that the writer of 'literary' fiction knows what he is about and is best left to get on with it without editorial intervention. It is the 'commercial' story-writer, quite often an ex-journalist, as Harold Harris points out, who tends to welcome advance discussion of themes and plots and, later, close editorial attention to the structure of his stories. Again, as Rosemary Cheetham has shown, popular women-novelists, usually with some journalistic background, are susceptible to proposals on subjects and themes.

What emerges clearly from the interviews is the devotion to a demanding job and the long hours an editor expects to put in without any public recognition and, if a particular book comes unstuck, with a large measure of private blame from the management of his company. Many executives in other businesses would happily fly to Australia and back to secure a contract running into hundreds of thousands of pounds, perhaps millions, but how many, like Robert McCrum, would undergo the expense and the tedium of a flight round the world to spend time with an author when, although the quality of his new novel might be helped, the commercial improvement in terms of extra sales might be a few thousand pounds at the most? Or whose wives, like Hilary Hale with James, could observe that he had worked full-time every weekend for the past two years?

If one eliminates Harold Harris, who came to publishing fairly late in his working career and remained with Hutchinson for eighteen years until retirement, the other seven editors have had twenty-one jobs in publishing between them – a neat average of three jobs per editor. This is in contrast to the 'old school' of editors in the years just before and for fifteen years after the Second World War – men like David Farrer of Secker & Warburg, Roger Machell of Hamish Hamilton, Charles Monteith of Faber, and F. T. Smith of Collins, who spent the whole of their publishing careers with the one firm. There is no particular merit either in staying still or in moving around. Most of the seven editors are now in their forties or early fifties and if one assumes that they first became editors in their mid-twenties, they have averaged roughly seven years in each job – hardly a sign of a grasshopper mind.

All the same, the modern frenetic activity in the buying and selling of publishing houses has inevitably brought on a bewildering spate of job-changes. Ed Victor, the literary agent, put the authors' and agents' view forcefully, as quoted in the *Sunday Times* on 4 October 1987:

Two years ago I signed a contract for Douglas Adams with two companies called Heinemann and Pan. Then Heinemann was owned by BTR, now it's owned by Reed. Pan was owned by three publishers: Macmillan, Collins and Heinemann. Now it's owned by Macmillan. Heinemann was run by someone called Brian Perman. Now it's Helen Fraser. His editor was David Godwin, then Fanny Blake, now there's no one. Pan was run by someone called Simon Master, now it's Alan Gordon Walker. Douglas's editor at Pan was Sonny Mehta. Now there's no one in that job. Every single element in his publishing life has changed.

That is a significant statement. Once an author is happily settled with a hardcover and a paperback publisher, he seeks continuity. Life is tough enough in the solitude of 'the lonely art' and, once the author delivers his new book, he wants to be dealing with familiar faces, not strangers. He gets used to one editor and his ways; over a period of years, he has developed a respect for the editor's strengths and a knowledge of his weaknesses. A new editor may be as good, perhaps better. But it is 'an expense of spirit' for the novelist to make the required adjustment and heed the advice of a newcomer, who has not proved himself or herself to that novelist's satisfaction.

In the previous chapter, I recounted the wartime story of the black market and the consignment of tinned fish. One sometimes gets the same feeling when international entrepreneurs get involved with the purchase and sale of publishing houses: ('My boy, those publishers are for buying and selling – not publishing'). The Newhouse brothers buy the Random House group and later the Cape/Bodley Head Chatto & Windus group. They acquire Sonny Mehta from Pan to be editorial vice-president of Knopf in New York and, within weeks, Simon Master, also from Pan, to run the Cape group. Shrewd moves, no doubt, and equally doubtless tempting offers to the two men concerned. But what happens to the wretched authors, without whom there would be no Random House, no Knopf and no Pan? Does Douglas Adams follow his editor to Knopf in the States – and leave Heinemann to join Simon Master at the Cape group?

There is, as I say, no law that says an editor must stay put. It is perfectly honourable, sometimes desirable, that the ambitious man or woman editor should move to a house where the opportunities and the matching salary and perks are greater. But authors hate to feel that they are pawns in a game in which they are not in fact players and where the rules have little to do with them. It may well be that over the coming years the privately owned houses, the André Deutsches, the Faber & Fabers, the Victor Gollanczes, the John Murrays and the Hodder & Stoughtons, will gain by an influx of worthwhile authors who look to a calm and relatively settled future.

CHAPTER XII

# The Crunch

Beautiful! beautiful! And money in every word of it!
Hall Caine, after reading aloud
from his own novel, *The Bondsman*

One recent and in many ways disturbing development has been the
trade's and the reading public's preoccupation with the large sums
earned by bestselling novelists. Between the wars and even up to
the 1960s newspapers did not speculate and trade magazines did
not pronounce on how much Rudyard Kipling or Warwick Deeping
or Nevil Shute or Graham Greene made from the publication of
any one of their novels. A publisher might advertise the fact that
a particular novel had sold 100,000 copies and Victor Gollancz was
never backward in proclaiming that the umpteenth impression was
rushing off the presses. But no one saw fit to translate those high
sales into an approximation of the earnings they represented. The
world waited decently until the successful author died and the value
of his estate was published.

We live in an age when success is counted in terms of money.
Young men today can and do earn more in a year than their
grandfathers earned in their working career. And just as transfer
fees in the footballing world suddenly rose to hundreds of thousands
of pounds, even millions, for a man whose career would be limited
to under ten years, so major novelists now have their market value,
sometimes inflated beyond their actual earning capacity.

When there are fewer and bigger publishing houses and groups
competing for the major successful authors, the price they are willing
to pay is driven higher. Something has to give way – even a very
large publisher's access to funds is not unlimited – and that tends
to be the 'mid-list' book. Publishing is always a matter of dealing
in 'futures'. An author with a proven if fairly modest track record

can never be as exciting a prospect as the newly acquired bestseller, real or potential, and the beginner-novelist who may break through. We live in a world of brand names and slogans. Guinness may be good for you – indeed it may be 'Pure Genius', whatever that means, and perhaps Persil does actually wash whiter. But just as the man in the public bar will ask for a Guinness or a Heineken or a Hofmeister and the bewildered housewife in the supermarket, faced with a dazzling array of detergents, will pick the one she knows, so people entering bookshops will ask for 'the new le Carré' or 'the new Forsyth' or 'the new Wilbur Smith'. To some degree, this has always been so, but for at least twenty-five years after the war, publishers seemed to have the time and the money to seek out and nurse interesting writers of talent who might never develop beyond a middle range of sales.

Just as several large publishers on both sides of the Atlantic appear to be paying well over the odds at times to attract the bigger authors, so individuals and companies with access to enormous funds often pay extraordinary amounts to acquire those very publishers. In 1987, Rupert Murdoch bought Harper & Row for around $300 million, which worked out at fifty-five times its annual earnings. In publishing circles, it has always been reckoned that to pay ten times earnings (plus the value of the assets) would be a comfortable purchase. After all, not many publishing houses earn more than 10 per cent of their turnover as annual pre-tax profit. So presumably Mr Murdoch saw some 'hidden gold' in the Harper & Row balance sheet that had hitherto been invisible to other expert eyes or he felt that a new management and drastically cut overheads would dramatically increase the profit ratio – or it was a crazy purchase. The early signs are that it was a smart purchase: Rupert Murdoch owns over 40 per cent of Collins and his sale of half of Harper to Collins will provide the latter with a well-established bridgehead into the New York publishing front.

Only a few weeks after that deal, Random House of New York had reversed the action by buying the Cape/Chatto/Bodley Head group for a reliably reported sum of £17.5 million. The news gave me a nostalgic twinge. In 1957, when Jonathan Cape, the majority shareholder, was in his late seventies and his son David, who had been briefly with the firm, had decided four years earlier that publishing was not for him, I was approached by a City consortium. They asked me to call on Jonathan, whom I knew quite well, and offer him £175,000 for his shareholding. They had done their sums carefully and it was a fair, even somewhat generous, offer. In the event, Jonathan Cape waved it aside – and then enchanted me for an hour or more with stories from his career; of how in his teens he had been office-boy at the London office of Houghton Mifflin and had been sent out to The Pines at Putney with some proofs for Swinburne. As he walked from the station, he was drenched by a sudden thunderstorm and rang the doorbell, dripping wet. Theodore Watts-Dunton opened the door, bustled him inside and made him take off his jacket and trousers and wrap himself in a blanket while his clothes dried in front of the fire. Nothing untoward happened – even then, Jonathan was probably too tall and bony for the taste of the two small round men – but it was many years before he realised what risk he had run. And there was his favourite story of how for over thirty years his only contract with Ernest Hemingway had been scribbled on the back of a Paris menu. And, among many others, the story of how T. E. Lawrence came to lose the unique manuscript of *The Seven Pillars of Wisdom* on the railway station at Bletchley.

In those days, Jonathan Cape was a moderately prosperous and efficiently run firm. Allowing for inflation over thirty years, £175,000 in 1957 would be worth about £1.52 million today. One must also take into account the value of the Howard family's minority shareholding and the fact that the Random House purchase also included the Chatto & Windus and Bodley Head shares. (In that same year, 1957, Stanley Unwin who had previously acquired the complete Bodley Head shareholding sold it on to Max Reinhardt for £75,000.)

If one stays long enough in the publishing trade, the same things seem to come around again. Early in 1986, I was approached by a director of Kidder Peabody, the merchant bankers. He had a very wealthy client who was thinking of investing up to £10 million to acquire a British publishing house. We looked at various 'situations' and perused balance sheets. In a memorandum I drew up for him, I stated that among other possible purchases the Cape group would make an interesting 'buy' at around £2.5 million – £3 million at the outside!

Even then, it was common knowledge in the trade that the group had problems. By the early summer of 1987, it was trading at a loss and was beginning to pile up debts. The management may have failed to recall some wise remarks made by Leonard Woolf, himself the co-founder of one of the houses in the group, Hogarth Press. In his volume of memoirs, *Beginning Again* (1964), he said:

In business the road to bankruptcy is paved with what the account-ant calls 'overheads' and too many publishers allow their 'over-heads' to dictate to them the size of their business and the kind of books they publish.

The purchase has given Random House a useful foothold into the United Kingdom and Commonwealth markets and access to some solid back lists with continuing paperback potential. But £17.5 million does appear to be a very large entrance fee to a not very exclusive club.

The deal has also placed on every staff member of the Cape/Chatto/Bodley Head group 'the pressure to perform'. The two Newhouse brothers, who own on the American book-publishing side Alfred A. Knopf and the Fodor travel guides as well as Random House, and who also own the third largest newspaper chain in the United States and the Condé Nast magazine empire which in Britain alone includes *Vogue*, the *Tatler*, *House and Garden* and *Brides*, must be businessmen first and philanthropists second. They expect their money to work for them. In its last profitable year (1984), the Cape group showed a net profit of £216,300 on a turnover of £16.25 million. Somehow, that profit has to be increased *eight times* to at least £1.75 million to show a reasonable return on the investment. There could be both conscious and subconscious pressure to bid wildly for commercial books of little artistic merit, seeking quick returns instead of investing in long-term authors, thus undermining the traditions carefully built up in over 200 years of collective publishing. Within a month of the purchase, a new 'overlord' was appointed – Simon Master, who had learned his trade at Pan Books under the tutelage of Ralph Vernon-Hunt and who had latterly run the large mass-market paperback house with real success. The appointment was a sign of major changes to come.

The next part of this chapter is taken up with two fictitious but all the same cautionary tales. They deal with the two extremes of fiction publishing and try to give an accurately costed profit-and-loss account of the perils and pleasures of novel-writing and publishing.

John Meek, who is twenty-nine years of age, has written his first novel under the title of *It Springs Eternal*. It is the story of a young man who left Oxford with a Third and took various temporary jobs until on answering an advertisement in *The Times* he finds himself as tutor to a backward boy who cannot pass Common Entrance. The boy is thick and thuggish but he does have an attractive elder sister with whom our hero promptly falls in love. She treats him with contempt and prefers the company of older, more sophisticated men. One evening, when a dinner date has fallen through, merely to amuse herself with a novice, she takes our hero to bed. He looks on the event with wonder as showing that she now returns his deep love. His dream is shattered when she tells him contemptuously that she only bedded him to amuse herself – and the amusement was slight. He leaves the logarithms and the irregular verbs and eventually finds himself a job in a West End bookshop. It will come as no surprise to members of the trade that Mr Meek himself took a Third at Oxford, had a brief and unhappy love affair and now works at Hatchards.

John Meek happens to be the nephew of Shirley Beauford, the famous novelist, who doesn't actually bother to read his painfully typed script but recommends him to her own agent, Michael Tenper. He reads the script. It is derivative and gauche but he thinks it shows a few touches of talent; anyway, he is not in business to upset his best client, Ms Beauford. So he agrees to represent it. Five publishers turn it down, three almost by return of post. This is no time, they all say, to try to launch a modest first novel. So Tenper tries his last shot. He leans heavily on the medium-sized house of Gollmasch, whose brightest star just happens to be – Shirley Beauford. He doesn't actually go so far as to threaten that she will leave if they don't publish her nephew but he does stress how pleased she will be if they do. And so they do.

They pay John Meek through his agent an advance of £1,250 on account of a starting royalty of 10 per cent of the published price. The book appears before a largely unheeding public. ('It's really a case of privishing,' the managing director of Gollmasch said to his cynical sales director.) There are two or three reviews that tend to cancel each other out: 'Stylishly written but unoriginal' – the *Observer*; 'Fresh insights embedded in a plodding style' – the *Sunday Times*. *It Springs Eternal* sells 900 copies in the home market (300 of which are bought for public libraries) and 250 copies overseas. Home sales bring in royalties of £981 and overseas sales £137.50, a total of £1,118.50. Gollmasch fail to sell book club or paperback rights and Michael Tenper has no success in selling foreign, film or TV rights. So there is an unearned balance on the advance of over £130, which Gollmasch have to write off. They had printed 2,000 copies as being the minimum economic first printing and gave away 150 copies for reviews and promotion. So the 700 surplus copies have to be remaindered at 10p a copy, bringing in £70. As the remainder price is below cost, John Meek gets no further royalties.

Now let us do a 'time spent/income earned' accounting in turn for the three parties involved. First, John Meek, the author. As a beginner, working at nights and weekends with plenty of crossings-out and false starts, he managed to average about one hundred words an hour during the writing of his novel. It is 80,000 words in length and thus it took him some 800 hours to finish. His total earnings are £1,250 less his agent's commission and VAT – £1,108.70. Even if we discount all the other time he spent after the novel was accepted in visits to his agent and to the publishers, correcting proofs, attending the sales conference and so on, his earnings work out at a rate of £1.38 per hour. And he is one of the lucky ones. For every hundred novels written and submitted to publishers, probably one at the most ever gets published.

And what of his agent? Michael Tenper is the senior one of three directors at Tenper & Co. They occupy two floors – about 1,500 square feet – of a Georgian building in Bloomsbury. The rent and rates come out at over £25,000 a year. They have three secretaries, a receptionist, a senior book-keeper and a royalty clerk. The total overheads have been rising steadily each year and are now approaching £200,000. To cover that amount and show a reasonable profit, Tenper himself has to bring in over £100,000 in commission a year by his own efforts. He works at least a forty-hour week and usually takes two or three scripts home for reading at weekends. Forty hours a week for forty-eight weeks a year equals 1,920 hours. Thus, every hour of his working day, Tenper needs to earn £52 to keep on target.

How does that work out with *It Springs Eternal*? He spent four hours reading the script, another four hours in meetings with the author, six hours in dictating letters and making telephone calls to the five publishers who rejected it, another hour or so over an expensive lunch encouraging Gollmasch to accept, two hours drawing up the contract and a further three hours in chasing up the publisher to sign the contract and pay the instalments of advance, as and when they fell due. And so he has spent at least twenty hours in achieving and servicing the sale; an expense of time that should have brought in £1,040 in commission earnings. On top of that, his secretary spent perhaps eight hours typing letters to the author, offer letters to the various publishers, parcelling up and sending off the typescript on six different occasions, making telephone calls on behalf of the script, typing the contract details into the standard contract form and fetching her boss innumerable cups of coffee. She receives £8,000 a year, which works out at £4.76 an hour for a thirty-five-hour week. So, even without allowing a percentage of overheads, one has to add a further £38 to the debit balance.

The agency received in all its commission of £125 on the operation, which resulted in a notional loss of £953 – not a recipe for business success.

Messrs Gollmasch fared even worse. It is a medium-sized publishing house which publishes on average 120 trade books a year and achieves a turnover of around £6 million. Being reasonably efficient, it manages to keep its overhead expenses down to 40 per cent of turnover, i.e. £2.4 million per annum. In other words, each of the books it publishes has to carry an overhead of £20,000. On *It Springs Eternal*, it turned over £5,850 on home sales and £1,375 on export sales, a total of £7,225. It also earned £70 on the 700 copies remaindered at 10p each. The manufacturing costs of £4,400 have to be set against the income of £7,295, as does the unearned balance of the advance, £141.50. Thus, the contribution to overheads ended up at £2,753.50, representing a notional loss of £17,246.50.

And for this result, a senior editor, the production director, the marketing director, the publicity director and their respective staffs, together with the salesmen on the road and the various overseas offices or representatives in South Africa, Australia, New Zealand, Canada and the continent of Europe probably spent a total of 500 hours collectively. Unless John Meek's next novel contained some special sales-inducing ingredient, one could hardly blame Gollmasch for regretfully declining to publish it. Nursing new talent can be injurious to your financial health.

Now let us turn to the happier side of publishing economics. Shirley Beauford has delivered her new novel under the title of *The Buck Stops at My Bank*. It is a searing tale of high life in the jet set in which the beautiful and elegant Stella Orbitt, heiress to a gigantic perfume company, finds herself subject to an unwelcome take-over bid from the even bigger scent combine run by the arrogant and satanically handsome Baron Maxim de Printemps. The shenanigans range from the film star colony at Malibu Beach through Manhattan's Trump Tower where our heroine has a duplex apartment, Claridge's and the

Costa Smeralda where Stella is kidnapped by the Baron's emissaries and subjected by him to a fate which sounds much better than death. Finally, to the surprise of no reader, the two of them find true love for each other and the merger takes place in every sense of the word.

It is easy to sneer at the Shirley Beaufords of the literary world. They run no risk of ever winning the Nobel Prize for Literature but for all their clumsy handling of words and their writing at inordinate length, they do have a certain narrative strength and an ability to keep the reader turning the pages. Fiction exists on many different levels and at least the very popular novelists do attract readers who may eventually graduate to more demanding and rewarding reading.

Not for Shirley Beauford the expense of muscular energy tapping away at a typewriter or word processor. She has a special voice-actuated recording system in her penthouse suite. When working on a new novel, she either lies on a divan – no hurly-burly for her – or walks up and down the forty-foot room talking the story aloud. Each afternoon, a relay of secretaries transcribe her words in triple-spaced drafts, which she corrects next morning before starting her two or three hours of dictation. She reckons to average about 400 words an hour by this method and, as her novels are very long – around 300,000 words each – it takes her about 750 hours to write one.

Gollmasch pay her an advance of £350,000 for United Kingdom and Commonwealth (excluding Canada) rights in her novels. In addition, she gets $1.5 million for USA and Canadian rights, around £400,000 (in local currency) for translation rights and, in the case of *The Buck*, $500,000 for motion picture rights – in very round figures, a total of £2 million. (It is technically incorrect to say that she receives the payments. Thanks to a clever accountant, the Beauford copyrights are 'owned' by a Swiss company, which pays all her considerable expenses plus a comfortable annual salary on which, of course, she pays her due British taxes. But the bulk of her vast earnings is subject only to the very modest level of Swiss taxes.) At any rate, her notional hourly rate of earnings after agents' commission has been deducted comes out at £2,400.

The senior staff at Gollmasch seize on the new Beauford with whoops of delight. The print order of the hardcover edition is set at 75,000 copies of which 50,000 are sold in the home market and 25,000 for export. The published price is £10.95 – the same as John Meek's novel; although his aunt's novel is nearly four times as long as his, the setting costs are spread by the enormously bigger first printing. Ms Beauford gets a flat 15 per cent of the published price as her royalty on home sales and 12½ per cent of the price received on export sales. The whole edition sells out and so her royalty earnings amount to £99,190.

Gollmasch sell book club rights for £40,000 on which the author gets 60 per cent (£24,000) and paperback rights for £250,000 advance on which her take is 80 per cent (£200,000). These sums are set against the overall advance paid by the publisher, which means that she was paid an advance of £350,000 and her earnings amount to £323,190, a deficit of £26,810. But the publisher has received £16,000 as his share of the book club sale and £50,000 as his share of the paperback advance, £66,000 in all. So, even when he sets a £20,000 share of his overheads against *The Buck Stops at My Bank*, he is, as they say in publishing, ahead of the game.

And now we come to the concealed profit margin. Allowing for discounts to wholesalers and retailers, Gollmasch was paid an average of £6.50 a copy sold in the home market – £325,000, and £5.50 on the copies sold for export – £137,500. From that total of £462,500 the production cost (£2.50 per copy) has to be deducted – £187,500. So the publisher ends up with a manufacturing profit of £275,000 on the operation. No wonder that the managing director always sends Ms Beauford a case of Dom Perignon on her birthday and at Christmas.

Although all the figures quoted to date in this section are reasonably representative, no allowance has been made for 'fine tuning' or special expenses incurred. For example, Gollmasch might have approached the famous advertising agency of Satchel & Handbag and spent at least £100,000 in advertising *The Buck* on television and hoardings. They probably did spend several thousand pounds on a publicity tour for the author with bookshop signing sessions thrown in. Even so, the net profit they made out of her would underwrite their losses on half a dozen John Meeks. It is, in fact, the rich and successful author who without realising it pays his or her publisher to seek out and cherish new talent. My final chapter goes into this point in greater detail.

Let us now examine what might have happened if Shirley Beauford had been published by the conglomerate, Octopencoll, which has a couple of paperback houses in its stable. We can assume that the advance of £350,000 would have been the same, as would the level of book club earnings. But Octopencoll would have issued the paperback edition through one of its in-house softcover firms. They could well have sold 500,000 copies at a published price of £3.95 a copy – 375,000 copies being sold in the home market and 125,000 for export. The author's royalty rates, as she is a bestselling novelist, would have been 12½ per cent of the published price on home sales and 10 per cent of the published price on export sales. Thus, her royalty earnings overall on the paperback edition(s) would have amounted to £234,137; when these are added to her hardcover royalty earnings, the total is £333,327. And so her advance of £350,000 would have been unearned by the amount of £16,673.

*But* the publisher would have achieved a turnover of £900,000 on the paperback home sales (375,000 copies at £2.40 a copy) and £250,000 in export sales (125,000 copies at £2 a copy). The manufacturing costs for the whole edition at 90p a copy came to £450,000. Thus, there was an overall gross profit of £700,000 minus the unearned advance. Octopencoll publishes 400 titles a year and its overheads come to £12 million; therefore each title has to carry an overhead share of £30,000. Even so, *The Buck Stops at My Bank* has brought the publisher in more than £300,000 in profits. Lucky the publisher who has a sprightly filly like Shirley Beauford in his stable.

How has Michael Tenper, her devoted agent, fared? Whether she is published by Gollmasch or Octopencoll, he still makes his 10 per cent commission (£35,000) on the advance. She has a separate film agent and so Tenper does not share in those proceeds but his firm gets half commission (5 per cent) on her American earnings through an associated New York agency – which amounts to $75,000, and 5 per cent of the foreign rights, which brings in another £20,000. So in return for several cherishing telephone calls every week, regular and expensive luncheons and dinners, flowers from Moyses Stevens and judicious gifts from Aspreys, Michael Tenper Ltd makes over £100,000 in commission on every novel she writes – which she does at the rate of about one every two and a half years. His only problem – and it is one that other agents would be delighted to assume – is that she represents about 40 per cent of his personal commission turnover each year, nearly 20 per cent of his whole firm's turnover, and if she were suddenly to leave him on a whim, the firm's profits would be badly dented. London agents do not have forward

contracts with their clients, who are thus free to leave at any time.*
The fact that big authors tend to be more faithful to their agents
than they are to their publishers says much for the nature and
quality of the relationship and is something that publishers might
care to ponder.

Up to around 1960, there was a saying in the trade, 'It takes five
books to make an author.' A publisher could afford to invest in a
promising writer and back him over the three or four unprofitable
books through which he was gradually making his name. This might
take seven to ten years but the investment was comparatively modest
– a total of around £750 for advances on the four or five novels
and an overall £2,000 in production costs. The earnings in sales
would at least cover both outlays and leave a small contribution
to overhead expenses. Today, as we have seen from the example
of John Meek, a publisher would need to be extremely rich or
successful to afford nursing a tyro over that formative period. So
the fiction publisher is left with two alternatives – either to bid in
the market-place for the established bestsellers or to try to create his
own, usually with the help of an enterprising agent. A bestseller *can*
be created, as was convincingly shown in 1987 with *Destiny* by Sally
Beauman or a few years previously with Shirley Conran's *Lace* and
Sarah Harrison's *The Flowers of the Field*. The necessary ingredients
are professional skill on the part of the author – to be successful,
a commercial novel needs to be written with as much skill as a
literary novel – detailed market research to spot existing trends and
possibly introduce a new one, a large slice of luck and that modern
discovery, 'hype'.

The word has been considered a contraction of 'hyperbole'. Indeed,
a few years ago, Samuel Vaughan, then of Doubleday, said in a lecture:

> Hyperbole has become so common that we now refer to it by a
> cosy contraction. We call it 'Hype'. We decide to apply it, as if
> it were a wax compound for shining up a car.

However, the redoubtable William Safire, H. L. Mencken's direct
descendant in the spiritual sense, will have nothing of that derivation.
In his book, *What's The Good Word?*, published in 1982, he says:

---

* Agents can get round this factor by arranging for the publisher to agree to a three-book
forward contract for the bestselling writer.

. . . the notion that 'hyperbole' gave birth to 'hype' is folk etymology. 'Hype' comes from 'hypodermic needle', such as the one used by narcotics addicts; to be 'high' was to be 'hyped up'. Billy Rose, in a 1950 newspaper column, carried that euphoria a step away from drug lingo in writing about a movie: 'No fireworks, no fake suspense, no hyped-up glamour.' It was a short leap from the compound adjective 'hyped-up' to the noun 'hype' and its most current compound noun, 'media hype'.

Curiously, both 'hyperbole' and 'hype' now mean 'exaggeration' – the first intended, the second as a result of sensational attention . . . But 'hype' [also] means 'artificial, phony', as if in a dream induced by drugs.

Hype is the exaggerated promotion of a product, first by word of mouth and then by publicity and advertising. In the late 1970s, Ed Victor took a first novel entitled *The Four Hundred* and by acumen, sheer energy and force of personality parlayed it into a multi-million-dollar property. The book was not a success when published in London and New York – unkind friends in the trade whispered that it had been called *The One Hundred* before Mr Victor got to work – but the author ended up as a rich man and his agent must have been consoled for the book's lack of success through his share of the proceeds including the large outright film sale, although no film has as yet been made.

There are several different ways of exercising hype but perhaps the most typical is as follows. The agent sits down with a needy but skilful client, preferably a photogenic woman of not too advanced years. Between them, they hammer out a scenario or detailed treatment of around thirty pages. They have already analysed the ingredients that have led to success in recent years. These might be lurid tales of Hollywood 'from the inside' (Jackie Collins and Jacqueline Briskin) or the story of the young woman who either inherits or painfully acquires an industrial empire (Sidney Sheldon's *Bloodline* or Barbara Taylor Bradford's *A Woman of Substance*) or the young American girl who inherits a crumbling mansion or castle in Connemara and the spooky events that occur when she moves in. Stir in some soft porn, preferably with a sexual twist or two derived from Kraft-Ebbing, and add a sufficiency of exotic backgrounds and the trappings of wealth such as executive Rolls-Royces and Ferraris (Lamborghinis have been 'out' for some years now) and the mixture is ready for the oven. Many of the successful *genre* novels of recent years have been based, often quite loosely, on the Cinderella theme, although in most of the modern versions Prince Charming might think of other destinations for the glass slipper.

The author then goes off and writes two or three chapters, not necessarily in sequence. They will be revised again and again until the agent is satisfied. Preferably, the author will have no track record in the United States but if she has had a few books published there without success, it will be important to invent a pen-name for her. At this point, the agent flies over to New York to begin the hard sell, usually in co-operation with his associated agency there. He has already picked off his likely targets on the transatlantic telephone, warning them that he has a 'hot property' which he is coming over to auction; he has chosen them specially, he says, to be among the lucky bidders.

Why didn't he establish the 'once and future' book in England first before looking overseas? Because, whether we like it or not, America is the modern Eldorado of publishing. Although British publishing has followed the American pattern of larger groupings and aggressive bidding, the potential American readership is between four and five times as great, which is reflected in the levels of advances paid. Shirley Beauford received £350,000 from her British publisher and $1.5 million from her American one – almost three times as much. In addition, it has to be accepted that Europe looks westwards for its fashions, its eating habits, its films and television and its political influences – whereas America looks at itself. In fiction terms, success in the USA is almost always reflected by success in Britain and on the continent of Europe. The reverse rarely operates to any great degree.

The agent auctions the unfinished book in New York. He has the advantage of being 'a visiting fireman', present for a limited period. Five publishing houses have been invited to bid after reading the available material. One doesn't like it and drops out right away. Among the other four, the best bid on the first round is $175,000. The second round creeps up to $305,000, the top bid being a sneaky attempt to slip past what was imagined to be the outstanding offer of $300,000. At that stage, two of the four publishers still in decide to drop out. They think the book could do well on their respective lists but they do not see it as a contender for the top of the bestseller list.

Luckily for the agent and the author, whom he has been telephoning each day with a progress report, the two big houses left in are old and deadly rivals. An element of wanting to deny the prize to the other man rather than desiring it entirely for itself creeps into the bidding. They slug it out by $20,000 increments until at last one of them calls the agent to say that $750,000 is his absolute and final bid. The agent prevails on the other to top it by 5 per cent – and so United States rights, including Canada which has had to be 'thrown into the pot', have gone for $785,000.

Now the real hype begins. Mentions appear in the US and British trade magazines; gossip-column items are planted in British national newspapers, accompanied by shots of the author photographed under soft lights with a vaseline-smeared lens; she is invited to join the Society of Authors and make an appearance on the *Wogan Show*. A dozen London publishers, including the top six, queue up for the chance to bid for British volume rights. Women's magazines demand to be shown a typescript as soon as the novel is finished, in case it could be fashioned into a serial, and several film companies offer options. The hype has worked and now all the agent has to do is sit back and pick the best bids from those that come tumbling in. All the author has to do is sit down and write a book that will live up to the advance publicity, the buzz, the pre-hype.

One cannot imagine that Hardy or Conrad or Galsworthy or D. H. Lawrence or Evelyn Waugh or Graham Greene would have allowed any one of their novels to be packaged or promoted thus, even after it had been written and delivered to the respective publisher. Perhaps Arnold Bennett or H. G. Wells, who prided themselves on being men of business as well as writers, might have succumbed. Nor, to be fair, can one imagine present-day novelists of quality, Iris Murdoch or William Golding or Patrick White, pursuing a similar Klondike. It is the pressure to perform that drives large publishing groups, and the pressure to compete among the surviving medium-sized houses, to play the 'futures' market, to suffer the agent's hype and in their turn to subject their potential readership to all the hype that they can muster.

CHAPTER XIII

# Films and Television

Take a few months off and write it as a book.
H. N. Swanson, the Hollywood agent,
gives advice to screenplay writers.
Quoted in *Publishers Weekly*, 1956

Away from the sound of gunfire, Hollywood continued to make films
and money throughout the Second World War. Already by 1935,
it had become the second most powerful industry – after oil – in
California, employing over 9,000 people in its thirty-nine studios; it
had assets of close on $100 million; and especially during the war
years, the population of Great Britain included 'going to the pictures',
largely to see American films, among its most popular pastimes. Each
week throughout 1943 and 1944, 25 million cinema tickets were sold
in Britain, which meant that every man, woman and child in the
country averaged some twenty-five visits a year to the local cinema.
As Eric Rhode pointed out in *A History of the Cinema from its Origins
to 1970* (from which the above statistics are taken), writing about the
immediate post-war period,

> Fortunately for the film industry, the US State Department,
> acknowledging the propaganda value of Hollywood movies, put
> pressure on the bankrupt nations of Europe to exhibit these movies
> as part of a package deal which included trade and cash concessions
> [Marshall Aid].

Samuel Goldwyn, who concealed great shrewdness under his much
publicised indulgence in malapropisms, had already declared that the
author was the indispensable requirement for a good picture – not the
star, the producer or the director. He said,

> A great picture has to start with a great story. Just as water can't
> rise higher than its source, so a picture can't rise higher than its story.

201

Many of the other heads of studios shared his opinion. They believed fervently that a story that had proved successful in another medium, in book form, would be as or more successful when adapted for the screen. From there it was a short step to entice, as they did during the 1930s and 1940s, recognised novelists to write screenplays under the studio roofs. Raymond Chandler, F. Scott Fitzgerald, Aldous Huxley, Christopher Isherwood and William Faulkner are just a few of the authors who were tempted and who succumbed.

Many of the most successful novelists in the early post-war years could confidently expect to sell the full film rights – not just a twelve-month option – on virtually every novel they wrote. Leading examples are Nevil Shute with *Pastoral*, *The Pied Piper*, *No Highway*, *A Town Like Alice* and *On the Beach*; or Graham Greene with *The Third Man* and *Fallen Idol* (both based on short stories), *The Power and the Glory*, *The End of the Affair*, *The Heart of the Matter*, *The Comedians* and *Our Man in Havana*. As early as July 1945, Collins announced that the film rights in five of its new novels had been bought – Nigel Balchin's *Mine Own Executioner*, Norman Collins's *London Belongs to Me*, Marguerite Steen's *Rose Timson*, *Saplings* by Noel Streatfeild and *The Noble Savage* by Doreen Wallace. The following year, film rights in *The White Tower* by James Ramsay Ullman were bought by RKO for $100,000, then held to be a record sum.

But Hollywood was not getting things all its own way. The British film industry was enjoying a renaissance under entrepreneurs like Alexander Korda and the high-minded J. Arthur Rank. In September 1946 a *Bookseller* article pointed out that 'American film companies are said to be concerned at the way in which film rights in so many bestselling English novels are being snapped up by English companies before Hollywood even gets a chance to bid for them.' It instanced the latest two novels by Daphne du Maurier, Howard Spring's *Fame is the Spur*, Thomas Armstrong's *The Crowthers of Bankdam* and the novels by Norman Collins and Nigel Balchin just mentioned.

Archibald Ogden, the story editor for Twentieth Century-Fox (Europe), residing in London, responded to the *Bookseller* article by saying that the extraordinary situation had arisen whereby film rights in likely bestsellers now had to be bought pre-publication, thus eliminating the opportunity of testing them first in their own market. This meant that American film companies would need to offer a large fixed sum for the rights plus an 'escalator' of perhaps $25,000 if the novel in question later became a Main Selection of the Book of the

Month Club or the Literary Guild. Less than a year later, the point was made that

> current film contracts in America tend to be based on a rising royalty in proportion to the sales of the original book, which suggests that the film company puts a value on the book sales and resultant publicity and on the creation of a waiting public for the film.

In April 1949 MGM, having two years earlier publicised its $100,000 annual award for a novel to be turned into a film, announced that it had twenty-seven new films, either in production or recently released, that were based on bestselling books. The British authors concerned included Margery Sharp (*The Nutmeg Tree*), John Galsworthy (*The Forsyte Saga*), Bruce Marshall (*The Red Danube*), Margaret Irwin (*Young Bess*) and Rudyard Kipling (*Kim*).

The Labour government in Britain during the first five post-war years fought back in two ways against the Hollywood barrage. It set up a 40 per cent quota for foreign (i.e. mainly American) films. It also instituted the Eady Scheme, whereby films produced and shot inside the United Kingdom were entitled to receive a share of box-office receipts, levied by Customs and Excise, in direct proportion to their earnings inside Britain. The idea was not only to aid British film companies but to attract the American studios to make films locally.

The Eady Fund achieved some useful results, which were shortly to be increased by Senator Joseph McCarthy's demagoguery and witch-hunting for 'reds under the Hollywood beds'. Liberal-minded American film-makers such as Carl Foreman and Joseph Losey moved to Britain and worked here more or less permanently until driven out again by Denis Healey's Budget in the mid to late 1970s. But within seven years from the end of the Second World War the Hollywood studio system was beginning to crumble. As in the classic Westerns, the studios might draw the wagons into a circle against the smoke signals of the surrounding Sioux or Apache bands – but there was no Seventh Cavalry to ride to the rescue.

Already in 1947, the US State Department had begun to break the studios' monopoly and in 1950 a Justice Department decree forced them to separate the means of production from the means of distribution. Hitherto, the studios had both made the films and owned the cinema chains that showed them. They had been able to make block-bookings and fix the prices of admission. Henceforth, the studios were prevented by law from owning cinemas as well. This step gave the public greater freedom of choice at competitive prices. But the paddling pool was about to be engulfed by a different kind of tidal wave.

By 1949, 40 per cent of the American population was able to watch television. The TV companies' revenue in 1951 was double that of 1950 and *seven times* as much as in 1949. Correspondingly, cinema receipts in the USA fell by exactly one quarter between 1946 and 1952. In spite of the temporary boosts afforded by the new inventions of Cinerama, 3D and Cinemascope, the decline continued. As Eric Rhode put it, 'The days of Hollywood as an industry were numbered. The market no longer needed a steady day-to-day output'. The studios marched on through the 1950s, like mastodons sinking deeper and deeper into the mud, until in 1960 Twentieth Century-Fox sold off 256 acres of land to Alcoa for $43 million. Towards the end of that decade, five of the seven major studios announced overall losses of $110 million. Paramount and Warner Brothers closed down many facilities and cut their staffs. MGM sold off various studios, reduced its labour force by 40 per cent and auctioned off its wardrobes, set departments and stock footage library. Two years later, in 1971, Warner Brothers and Columbia decided to concentrate on the Warner lot alone. Paramount became a division of Gulf & Western, United Artists sold out to Transamerica (itself a subsidiary of the Bank of America) and not long afterwards Warner Brothers merged with Seven Arts and became in turn part of a very large conglomerate, Kinney National, which also owned car parks and car rental firms. The Hollywood of Sam Goldwyn, Louis B. Mayer, Harry Cohn, Jack Warner and Irving Thalberg was, like the statue of Ozymandias, a broken part of history.

With it went the star system, which had been the fulcrum of Hollywood's power. Since the days of the silent films, the studios had put leading actors and actresses under contract, paying them a handsome salary whether they were working or not but giving them virtually no choice over which film they would make next. In *The Moon's a Balloon*, David Niven tells an amusing story of how, when under contract to Samuel Goldwyn, he refused to take part in a social comedy as his next 'vehicle'. He still had to complete another film for Goldwyn who arranged that, as he came on the set each morning, Niven would see Dana Andrews, in full evening dress, white tie and tails, lounging in the background – a silent reminder that if Niven felt the new part unworthy of him, there were other good actors ready and willing to undertake it. The studio heads were despots, who tended to look on actors as prize cattle which they had bought and could just as easily sell.

The first film to undermine the star system was reputed to be *Winchester '73*, a Western that told how the new repeating rifle had 'changed the West'. James Stewart, then a highly 'bankable' star, was persuaded by an independent producer to play the lead for a guaranteed sum and a percentage of the box-office receipts. The film was a success and Mr Stewart earned far more for himself than he would have received under the old system. Other stars followed his lead until within a few years the big names who drew the public into the cinemas were able to pick and choose the stories and screenplays they wanted to make as films and to receive enormous guaranteed sums, even for a 'cameo' appearance. The point was reached where the Salkind brothers paid Marlon Brando the sum of $3 million for a fleeting appearance in one of their *Superman* films, which was being shot in Budapest. On arrival, the star was shocked to discover that he had only a few lines to speak and would be on the screen for no longer than two or three minutes. He wanted to give more value for his ridiculous fee and insisted that the writer of the screenplay, the novelist George MacDonald Fraser, be summoned to Budapest at once to expand the walk-on part. For a substantial extra writing fee and all expenses paid, Mr Fraser was happy to fly out to Hungary for the week, meet Marlon Brando to discuss his requirements and then sit down to write in some new dialogue and action.

The great advantage enjoyed by independent producers was that they had no large fixed overheads to support. The major Hollywood companies had vast studios to look after, back lots where a Western cow town or the forum in Ancient Rome could be simulated, actors, writers and technicians on the payroll, accountants, secretaries, receptionists and security guards to pay each week. All the independent producer needed was a room and several telephones. He would set up an off-the-shelf company to make one particular film, secure a twelve-month option on the novel or play he wanted to make as a film – with the right to renew the option for a second period of twelve months, if needed – find the 'seed' money to hire a professional writer to produce a draft screenplay, then look hard for a leading star (or stars) and a director to make at least a tentative commitment. Once he had assembled his 'package', he might seek his overall financing from City institutions or merchant banks or from one of the large film distributors, who would end up with 50 per cent of the distribution income. Eventually, on the principle of 'if you can't beat 'em, join 'em,' the Hollywood companies would take the more aggressive independent producers under their wing.

Television may have eroded the appeal of the cinema as mass entertainment but it did not destroy Hollywood. Indeed, as Paul Mayersberg wrote in *Hollywood: The Haunted House*,

> Television was going to be the end of Hollywood in the late fifties. It wasn't. Hollywood saw the danger and assimilated television and what looked like being the destroyer turned out to be the saviour of Hollywood. There are about 20,000 jobs in Hollywood. Half of them are television jobs, the other half movies.

That was written in 1966.

How did these various developments affect the professional British novelist's chances of selling film rights in his work? The answer is, on the whole, adversely. Up to the early 1960s, each of the large Hollywood companies maintained a sizeable office in London with an industrious story department. Kathleen Bourne, who was MGM's story editor in London, claimed to cover every single novel published in the UK each year. The Paramount, Warner Brothers' and Twentieth Century-Fox story departments were not far behind. Brief synopses of every likely novel were airmailed to 'the Coast' by these assiduous sifters, who realised they were in competition not only with their American rivals but with the local talent in London Films, the Boulting Brothers, Powell and Pressburger, Ealing Studios, the J. Arthur Rank companies at Pinewood and Denham, and Associated British at Elstree. If the film rights in any novel remained unsold, it was not for lack of exposure. Indeed, it was sometimes due to over-exposure. Film agents quickly learned to avoid putting their most attractive projects through the story department mill and preferred to offer them direct to a Hollywood producer, whose vanity might make him sheer away from a story that was second-, third- or even tenth-hand by the time it reached his desk.

Apart from offering novelists the possible bonus of an extra sale of rights, films – and, to a lesser degree, television – may have had a direct effect on the way some of those novelists construct their stories. 'Pre-credit sequences', to employ the technical film term, are a case in point. Until the end of the 1940s, nearly every film began with 'mood' music to which the title, the author, the stars and cast, the dress designer, the make-up artist and the producer and director were displayed against an ornate background. Once the credits had rolled, the film itself began. Leslie Halliwell, the *cinéaste*, claims that the first film which deliberately changed the sequence was *Rommel, Desert Fox* in 1951, but few who have seen Fred Zinnemann's *High Noon* (1952) will forget his apt use of pre-credit sequences. Against Dmitri Tiomkin's thudding music and the plaintive singing voice of Tex Ritter, the film opens with the shot of a solitary horseman motionless on a hill. In the distance, two tiny figures, who turn out to be horsemen as well, come galloping closer until they join the lone rider. Looking grim and without exchanging a word, the three hitch up their gun belts and ride down from the hill, through the little town, to the railroad track. The hands of the station clock point to eleven. The men dismount and wait for the train, due in at 'high noon'. And *then* the credits start rolling. Since that opening, which set the mood and heightened the suspense of the whole film, the pre-credit sequence has become a stereotype through over-usage, copied in turn in the mood-setting preliminary shots of numerous TV series. One thinks of *Starsky and Hutch* with the car-chase through a narrow alley, sheets of paper being scattered under the wheels of the vehicles, or *LA Law* with the main characters introduced at their morning conference.

The spirit of an age must never be ignored. It is possible that, just as the movie makers – or the more progressive and intelligent of them – decided to launch straight into the action and initially ignore the demands of the cast and technicians, so the same energetic spirit influenced novelists to omit the leisurely approach of the Georgian period and start with a bang. But it is equally arguable that novelists through their visits to the cinema quickly saw the advantage of opening with a dramatic scene, that might chronologically be taken from the middle of the story, and then flashing back to the literal starting point. In the same way, cross-cutting, fades and dissolves, the staple techniques of the movies, have been effectively employed by fiction writers. And hours of watching television series and individual dramas, many of which employ the same techniques, may well have subconsciously affected those same novelists.

One of the most experienced film and theatrical agents in London is Douglas Rae. His career stretches back nearly a quarter of a century from the time he joined GAC/Redway, having previously been himself a successful writer of television plays and film scripts. After two years at GAC/Redway where he built up the literary department from scratch, he was wooed away by Sandy Lieberson, then the London head of CMA, and became head of the literary department that was to be created. That was in 1966 and he stayed for close on eight years. Freddie Fields and David Begelman, both of whom were later to run studios, were the American heads of CMA, and they gave him complete freedom to develop his department as he saw fit.

As he put it: 'Being at CMA was rather like going to the right school. When you graduate, your buddies all go into the right jobs and you have a network. The agents in America that I was continually dealing with moved around. Mike Medavoy became head of Orion and Alan Ladd Junior went on to be head of Fox. McIlwaine was at one time head of Columbia – they had all been agents I knew well.'

When he heard that CMA was going to merge with IFA to make one gigantic corporation, he moved to Robert Stigwood's organisation. When Stigwood announced that he was going to pull out of the United Kingdom, Douglas Rae decided to set up his own firm. That was in 1974 and in the intervening years Douglas Rae Management has prospered.

I asked him to comment on the situation that prevailed when he was a writer and in his early days as an agent. He said: 'American interest was very, very strong in the 1950s and the 1960s. Especially in the 1960s. There was "swinging London"; Antonioni's film *Blow Up* did a great deal to give London its image. And there was *Time* magazine with its cover story of King's Road and Carnaby Street. It was all . . . hyped, I think, but it did give foreigners the idea that this was the place to be. The Beatles were also largely responsible. There was so much happening in music; there was a great flurry in London and foreign investment in films.

'The James Bond films were born, Chaplin came over to make a film, Sophia Loren made films with Marlon Brando and Peter Sellers who was at his peak . . . Universal was financing the new Chaplin picture out of England, Columbia made a series of pictures that were financed by Columbia Europe. Some were made with English directors and some with American directors. Columbia made *The Looking Glass War* by John le Carré. British books were turning into international films. The Alistair MacLean novels were all done at that time, too, several with Elliott Kastner. There were the Joseph Losey pictures [*The Servant* and *Accident*, based on British novels], which were the art pictures, and John Schlesinger had just emerged. Lindsay Anderson had made his film *If*, which had a great impact, Jack Clayton was making films – *The Pumpkin Eater* and *The Innocents* [based on novels]; there was a really exciting group of British talent functioning.

'British Lion, the Boulting Brothers, EMI and Hammer Films were still in the business of making pictures. What with them and the American companies, it was a healthy state of affairs. Then the Americans began to pull back, there were problems over dollars and exchange rates. One or two of the films didn't work out and so they began to retrench.

'It was just about that time that Leon Uris, although he had made big sales to movies with *Exodus*, suddenly sold *QB VII* to television. That was the first major mini-series that I can think of – selling a big book right off to television. From time to time, movies go through a stage of everyone not knowing what to do. They say, "We shouldn't make cowboy pictures any more," but they don't know what to do instead. Then they stopped making John le Carré movies. They were still top bestsellers but you couldn't interest film companies in Cold War and spy stories – and yet a few years previously *The Spy Who Came in from the Cold* [1965], had been one of the biggest successes. Fashion began to change. It was partly fashion and partly because television was beginning to grow up. In America, the belief had been that everything had to be contained in one evening [for a TV drama]. They got a shock when *Upstairs, Downstairs* was brought over and they found that people all over America were rushing home to see [each episode] and that it was possible to do an infinite series.

'Television was changing America and films were becoming more and more expensive and the [money] people wanted assurances. So they started doing the sequel films. They made a film with Barbra Streisand named *Funny Girl*. I remember a meeting at CMA with David Begelman saying, "What's going to be the fashion? It's going to be sequels to stories that have already made it. So we're going to make *Funny Lady* (1975)". And so they created a sequel to the Fanny Bryce story. And it went on. *Love Story* [1970] was a great success, so they created *Oliver's Story*. *Planet of the Apes* appeared in 1967. When that became a success, they did a "prequel". Out of that spawned something that is going on today, which is *Omen I, II* and *III* and *Rambo I, II* and *III* and the Rocky films. This is the rut they've now arrived in because for big money-making films they almost want an assurance that it's going to be successful. So they go back to the format of the picture before – *Romancing the Stone* and *Romancing the Stone II*, using the same characters – or they will do another James Bond. All

209

these make them feel secure today. In a funny way, these films have taken the place of bestsellers. I don't think they look for bestsellers so much any more . . . They say, "So many million people have seen *Rambo*, we're safe to make *Rambo II*. They'll know who he is."

'At the same time, television was buying bestsellers and doing them over four hours or perhaps six or even seven hours and you found that the story could be told in full – it wasn't the filleted version any longer. People . . . liked the whole thing spread out before them. In many instances the author can make more money. Television carries residuals, whereas with a film you usually make an outright sale. Authors like Judith Krantz and Barbara Taylor Bradford have found their way into producing and wheeling themselves in as producers of their own book. There's another piece of the pie there for them which they'd never have got under the old film structure.'

Douglas Rae went on to explain how the author of a bestselling novel can make $500,000 or even more out of a TV sale with those residual rights firmly in place, whereas for a film sale, a more likely 'top line' would be $200,000.

'I remember one top executive saying to me in California, "I buy a big bestseller book and I get the writer who's just been awarded an Oscar and hopefully a director who's won an award and I put all these together. If it's not a success, nobody can blame me!" One forgets that all these very powerful executives who are styled president of this and that are *employed*. They are all looking to keep their jobs and so they protect themselves.

'Today there's a great escapism going on. In the 1930s, which was the last great escapist period, there were musicals but they're far too expensive to make now. We do it by fantasy and horror films mainly. We are also getting into biography pictures, which they also made a lot of in the 1930s, Paul Muni and Gary Cooper were always playing someone well known. There was *Pasteur* and *Madame Curie* and *Sergeant York*. You don't make a life story of someone who wasn't a success. Everyone identifies with success and feels a bit better [after seeing the film]. The biogs and fantasy pics are not usually based on books. The books come afterwards, which fits in with the decline of literature.

'If you look at the bestseller list today, they're there as books but they don't go anywhere else. There are books on the bestseller list that couldn't be filmed like the "How To" books. So many books have been created 'in house' by publishers that there's very little in the way of literature these days . . . A very interesting thing has happened. Piers Paul Read was emerging as a remarkable novelist and then was suddenly pulled away to write the bestseller [non-fiction] book, *Alive*. Then, to follow that financially, he had to do the Great Train Robbery book.

'There are very few film writers in this country, although there are some very good writers for television. In America, boys leave college and don't write novels any longer, they write screenplays and by the age of twenty-six they're touting three or four screenplays – that is, if they want to write at all. There are no novels. In this country, young people will still sit down and try to write a novel or perhaps a stage play but they never dream of writing a film script – and still wouldn't write a film script unless someone said, "I'm going to pay you!" Films are something you have to be paid for – it's a big money thing. And so there's no speculation on films. The whole renaissance of small films is really an offshoot from television films in this country. What is exciting is that in America they've found a different way to distribute them and so the films are getting seen over there.

'In this country, we're nothing like the cinemagoers we used to be. In New York, people go to the cinema all the time. It's the same all over America. They *talk* about films. This only happens in London with a particularly interesting film. This is a small country . . . and the screen is a big canvas. Television perhaps suits us better because it observes detail.'

Douglas Rae did not consider that the few 'bankable' stars – the Brandos, the Hoffmans, the Newmans and the Redfords – had to any great degree used their considerable influence in the buying of film rights in novels, although he mentioned that Burt Lancaster, when he had a production company, Hecht-Hill-Lancaster, had bought rights in several novels. However Meryl Streep had been instrumental in getting both *Sophie's Choice* and *The French Lieutenant's Woman* made into movies. Novelists must consider it a great pity that there are not more actors and actresses with the discrimination and influence of Ms Streep.

Douglas Rae's summing-up is worth recording. 'I've always been fascinated by the reaction of people in America. Their history is of a country without people in it, so over there when they see someone, they greet him. Here, we are holding on to our territory; we want to know someone before we greet him. I think this is reflected in the way we write. Some of the best writers in this country have written in miniature.'

The growth of television in Britain in the fifteen years or so following the Coronation in 1953 certainly presented new openings for the aspiring writer – but more in the shape of original scripts for television than TV adaptations of their existing novels.

When novels were successfully adapted for the TV screen, the author and his publishers discovered a useful bonus in sharply increased sales. At the end of 1954, the television version of George Orwell's *1984*, which had had one sensational showing, was repeated. In the next five days, Secker & Warburg, the hardcover publishers, received 1,000 new orders, while Penguin Books had orders for an extra 18,000 copies of the paperback edition.

By the early months of 1956, with the BBC transmitters now covering virtually the whole of the United Kingdom, and Independent Television, having started the previous September, proving a lusty infant, book publishers were still unsure whether they should try to fight the new medium, ignore it in case it might go away or actively exploit it. In the upshot, they wisely took the third course. In January that year, Cassell, Chatto & Windus, Heinemann, Allan Wingate and W. H. Smith combined to form Television Book Ltd, which would provide a regular programme on books for ITV. It was entitled *The Living Page*; Graham Greene's *The Quiet American* was the first novel to be featured. Not to be outdone, the BBC commissioned J. B. Priestley to 'front' a regular programme under the title of *Books and Authors*. ITV quite quickly discovered that non-fiction books are often superior to fiction for TV features, unless the novelist happens to be world-famous, and so their future programmes concentrated on books like *Seven Years in Tibet* or *The Scourge of the Swastika*. In April 1956, the BBC began to televise a regular series, *The Murder Club*, devised by Heinemann and chaired by its then author, Eric Ambler, 'to promote interest in detective and thriller fiction among the reading public'. On both sides of the television fence, the companies were showing themselves to be just as eager as the national press to give free publicity to books.

That June, Dan Lacy, chairman of the American Book Publishers Council, proved himself a shrewd prophet when giving the Bowker Memorial Lecture. He forecast the time when a householder would be able to keep an outside engagement but leave his television set on – and there would be a device that would record a particular programme for his future enjoyment; the video cassette recorder (VCR) was still at least twenty years ahead in its practical application. The tired business-man, he said, would have 'a play projected on his home screen, or a tape-recorded voice reading him a novel or a poem'. And so it came to pass.

Hollywood was still fighting back. That same month, Harry Cohn, President of Columbia Pictures, announced that his company intended to subsidise 'novels of outstanding promise'. Authors or their agents were invited to submit an outline and some sample chapters to Columbia. If the material was viewed favourably, Columbia would agree to underwrite the author's living expenses in completing the book, on the understanding that the company had an exclusive option on the film rights. If those rights were eventually taken up, the company would go further by joining in co-operative advertising with the publisher. The scheme was an interesting one that might have proved helpful to young novelists on their way up but it does not seem to have borne fruit.

In July 1956, Eyre & Spottiswoode claimed the first ever British 'TV spin-off' novel. Frank Tilsley and his son Vincent had written a popular TV serial, *The Makepeace Story*, each episode of which was seen by an average of 10 million viewers. They had now written a novel, *Seth Makepeace*, based on the serial, and the book was shortly to be published. Nowadays, one would expect a paperback, not a hardcover, publisher to cash in on the success of a TV series, to achieve the widest circulation in a short time and to keep the published price accessible to the man and woman in the street. Nevertheless, the novelty value seems to have worked quite well for Eyre & Spottiswoode.

A month later, T. Werner Laurie was the first British book publisher ever to advertise on television. It was a modest enough beginning – £55 for a five-second advertisement on the Midland transmitter – and the novel featured was *A Single Soul* by Alexander Steward. A few weeks later, Ernest Benn bought two ten-second spots on ATV (Birmingham) for *The Gilbert Harding Question Book*.* Off and on over the next thirty years, publishers have flirted with TV advertising, usually featuring established bestselling authors such as Morris West, then published by Collins, or Hodder & Stoughton's large campaign in 1986 through Saatchi & Saatchi for novels by John le Carré and Jeffrey Archer. It is highly doubtful whether the high costs of TV advertising can be

---

* Gilbert Harding was at the time an important television (*What's My Line?*) and radio (*20 Questions*) personality.

covered through the income derived from extra book sales directly attributable to that advertising – but at least the author feels cherished!

It must be remembered that up to 1 July 1967 when the BBC colour system was officially launched, television transmissions in the United Kingdom were made in black and white on the same 405-line picture that had been used in 1937. Nevertheless, the BBC Annual Report of 1959 estimated that there were 26 million viewers, the majority of whom were women. The average viewer watched the screen for nine hours a week during the summer months and thirteen hours in the winter months – but one-third of all viewers watched for more than eighteen hours each week. The 1959 general election broadcasts had attracted 8 million viewers, 20 per cent of the adult population. Strangely enough, ITV had drawn 52 per cent of those viewers to the BBC's 48 per cent.

One casualty of the increasing popularity of television was the topical illustrated magazine. *Picture Post*, which had led the field for what would later be called 'investigative journalism' where excellent photographs supplemented the text, closed on 1 June 1957. Its proprietor, Sir Edward Hulton, said that the main reason for its closure was that 'television does the job better'. Other illustrated weekly magazines like *Everybody's*, *Illustrated* and *John Bull* staggered on for a few years but were eventually beaten by the sheer speed of television reporting. Shots of an earthquake or a riot appear on the TV screen the same evening; weekly magazines could not vie with that degree of immediacy.

It may seem strange that, as the general illustrated magazines were being forced out of business, the shrewd Canadian entrepreneur, Roy Thomson, having bought the *Sunday Times* in 1959, should institute a colour supplement for that newspaper in February 1962 to be followed by the *Observer*. The *Telegraph* quickly jumped on to the colour supplement bandwagon but at first stole a march by publishing it with the Friday issue of the *Daily Telegraph*. It was not for several years that its colour supplement 'moved in' with the *Sunday Telegraph*, which had been started in February 1961.* Roy (later Lord) Thomson, who was in middle-age before he settled in Britain, sensed that the years of 'conspicuous consumption', the 'never had it so good' era, were about to blossom. The increasingly prosperous middle classes would soon be buying fashionable clothes, furniture and motor cars

* In autumn 1988 it was moved again to Saturday publication.

and holidaying abroad in the trendy leisure places. Goods would not be expensive, handmade and lovingly maintained for years: they would be relatively cheap, mass-produced and discarded when a new fashion decreed. Colour advertisements, he instinctively knew, were more seductive than monochrome and a service ITV could not supply for several years – and advertisers would pay large sums per page for a guaranteed circulation of a million or more of the right class of potential buyers. And thus the Sunday colour supplement flourished and became imitated to the point where almost every self-respecting Sunday newspaper had to publish one. The lead time was usually around six weeks and so only rare – and expensive – efforts were made by the supplement editors to deal with topical subjects. Indeed, the more cynical readers would quickly consider that the general text and photographs were largely 'stuffing' to keep the full-page colour advertisements apart.

In February 1987, the *Sunday Times* published its Silver Jubilee colour magazine. It consisted of 132 pages including the covers: $65\frac{1}{2}$ pages were colour advertisements, 18 pages were black and white advertisements and the remaining $48\frac{1}{2}$ pages were text, approximately 36 per cent of the whole. The very first colour supplement in 1962 had included a short story by Ian Fleming. The Silver Jubilee issue was made up of nostalgic and self-congratulatory articles with no original fiction. This is perhaps an unfair comparison but it helps to bear out the point that the Sunday colour supplements were no effective substitutes for the previous illustrated general magazines which had provided outlets for writers of fiction.

Nevertheless, from time to time, the more conscientious supplement editors did buy short stories from authors or commission well-known novelists to revisit their favourite city or write a travel article. Only to that modest degree did the advent of the colour supplement (or magazine) prove beneficial for the professional novelist.

British television has been relatively good to the novelist in its arts programmes and in publicising such events as the Booker Award but, even in the more experimental 1960s and early 1970s, it played safe – and infrequently – in its choice of novels to adapt as a 'one-off' sixty- or ninety-minute programme or as a multi-part serial.* Throughout the

* In this context, a 'serial' is one complete story split up into several episodes; a 'series' is a succession of ongoing episodes dealing with the same group of characters with a climax or finale occurring at the end of each episode. John Mortimer's *Paradise Postponed* would be classified as a serial, whereas his *Rumpole* programmes would constitute a series.

period, on average over 4,000 new novels a year have been published, of which at least a few hundred have probably merited close consideration as likely television material. In the upshot, well under ten of them in any one year would end up on the TV screen. Those that did were either big bestsellers or novels by household names. One reason for this has been that Hollywood, although far less opulent than in its great days, has still been in the market for the 'big' novels and British television cannot compete with its levels of payment. Both the BBC and ITV have found it cheaper and safer to commission a television writer to write an original drama or a series, which he might afterwards adapt into novel form. It costs roughly ten to twenty times as much to produce one hour of television as it does to print and bind a popular novel. Clearly it is cheaper to find a writer to deliver an original shooting script than to invite him to transform a novel into a shooting script *after* the company has first paid a copyright fee to the author of that novel. And, unless the author happens to be an experienced writer for television, to invite him to tackle the adaptation involves the company in an initial risk.

Commercial companies, in particular those with a weekend franchise, have always had to attract and hold a large viewing audience. Thus, except at those periods when the licences are shortly due for renewal and 'prestige' becomes the order of the day, they have found that programmes like *Sunday Night at the London Palladium* or a simple give-away-money quiz show are a more certain magnet than a drama based on a novel. Some long-running fiction series have proved successful, such as *Robin Hood* or *The Saint*, which began in 1962, ran for some years and made Roger Moore a star. But the fourteen *Saint* titles published in Hodder & Stoughton Paperbacks were exhausted within months and thereafter new stories, based on the main characters, had to be introduced.

Up to the end of 1966, the motion picture production companies had formed an association known by its acronym as FIDO (Film Industry Defence Organisation). Every member of FIDO had to agree that it would not sell the television transmission rights in its films until at least seven years after their respective first public screenings. But with costs rising and box-office receipts falling, one company after another broke the agreement and by the middle of 1967, BBC and ITV were eagerly bidding against each other for Hollywood's 'treasures'. At first, the prices paid were very small. In 1967, Leslie Halliwell, bidding on behalf of ITV, bought British transmission rights from Paramount in *The Greatest Show on Earth* and about one hundred other films for $3,000 each, and in 1968 he bought rights in the first six James Bond films for a total of £828,000. Hollywood soon realised, however, that, as long as there were two rival bidders, prices could be pushed upwards. By the early 1970s, the BBC had paid £3 million for *The Sound of Music* and in the middle of the decade ITV went as high as $4 million for *Star Wars*. Any film that costs several million dollars to buy has to be shown on the television screen once or twice a year for several years in order to cover its costs – and thus is using up screen time that might otherwise be made available for an original script based on a novel.

There is a further aspect to the costing side. In spring 1988, Thames Television announced that it cost £245,000 to make a one-hour episode of *Rumpole* but only £30,000 to buy in a one-hour episode of *LA Law*. Since the viewer ratings would be roughly equal, one can understand the pressures there must be from financial controllers on the creative departments of television companies to play safe – and save money.

British TV companies also have the chance of buying 'the film made for television', usually produced in a Californian studio with an economy budget, no major stars and often shot in one location. This development has perhaps afforded the best opportunities for the purchase of film/TV rights in popular or unusual novels.

Another recent move has been the making of the two-hour 'pilot' film for television which, if well received, can quickly be expanded into a multi-part series. Several novels by Arthur Hailey have enjoyed this treatment, in particular *Gold* and *Hotel*. The latter became a very long-running series in which Mr Hailey's setting of a luxurious, rather old-fashioned, hotel was preserved but which depended on new plot lines and new characters provided by professional scriptwriters.

To help determine the extent to which the professional novelist benefits from television as a source for adapting his work to a large audience of viewers, I made a close study of programmes from all four channels during the month of February 1987. February was selected as a typical month during the winter schedules, midway between the peaks of Christmas and Easter and a time when the average viewing audience would not be distracted by holidays or the long summer evenings. The study focused on weekdays from 6 p.m. to midnight and on Saturdays and Sundays from 2 p.m. to midnight – the hours when the working population, as well as their families, had ready access to the TV screen. Fifty hours' viewing a week per channel constituted a total of 200 hours a week, or 800 hours over the four-week period.

As the saying goes, there are lies, damned lies – and statistics. Focusing on a different month might have thrown up quite different results, although one has doubts that it would be so.

*Percentage Analysis of Major Types of Programmes during February 1987*

| | News | Arts & Current Affairs | Entertainment | Old Films | 'Soap' | Sport |
|---|---|---|---|---|---|---|
| BBC 1 | 16.35 | 14.00 | 10.25 | 12.10 | 7.80 | 14.80 |
| BBC 2 | 10.75 | 20.00 | 7.70 | 20.45 | 1.20 | 21.33 |
| LWT/Thames | 10.15 | 13.90 | 4.90 | 17.50 | 8.25 | 11.00 |
| Channel 4 | 10.80 | 25.70 | 10.15 | 32.80 | 5.40 | 4.33 |

Before undertaking the analysis, I would confidently have forecast that quiz shows and situation comedies ('sitcoms') would feature high among the programmes occupying large segments of the viewing time. In fact, they jointly account for less than 6 per cent of BBC 1's fifty hours, less than 5 per cent each for BBC 2 and Channel 4; even for the major commercial channel, LWT/Thames, the home of give-away quiz shows and sitcoms embellished with raucous 'canned' audience applause, they represent together around 15 per cent – or not much more than one hour per day through the week.

And where does the novel, adapted for television, stand in the ranking list? The sad answer is – almost nowhere. During the four weeks under scrutiny, BBC 1 transmitted an adaptation of an Agatha Christie 'Miss Marple' story in two weekly instalments, each of fifty-five minutes. BBC 2 showed four weekly instalments, each of fifty minutes, of *The Citadel* by A. J. Cronin; the version was a repeat, having previously been shown a few years earlier on BBC 1. LWT/Thames brought out two thirty-minute episodes of *A Little Princess* by Frances Hodgson Burnett. Channel 4 transmitted no novel adaptations at all.* The three novels concerned had all been first published before the Second World War and their respective authors had been dead for a considerable time. The living professional novelist might well consider himself ostracised by the television companies when it came to seeing his own work transformed for the TV screen. Old films, bought in by

* Channel 4 did transmit the film *Cal* with a screenplay by Bernard MacLaverty, based on his novel of the same title, but that was a film which had already been successfully exhibited in cinemas.

the four companies, took up well over twenty per cent of the available viewing time and had virtually ousted him from the potential market. The learned judge who declared that justice is open to all – like the Ritz Hotel – might nowadays have added, 'or like the sale of television rights by an aspiring novelist'.

In fairness to the TV companies, it must be added that the situation had improved somewhat when the 1987–88 Autumn/Winter schedules were announced. There were seven prominent TV tie-ins of various novels and one collection of stories. They were:

*Fortunes of War* (The Balkan Trilogy) by Olivia Manning
*Vanity Fair* by William Makepeace Thackeray
*Small World* by David Lodge
*Mr Stimpson and Mr Gorse* by Patrick Hamilton
  (entitled *The Charmer* for the TV serial)
*The London Embassy* by Paul Theroux
*A Perfect Spy* by John le Carré
*Lake of Darkness* by Ruth Rendell.

The Autumn/Winter schedules for 1988–89 were even more beneficial for novelists. Apart from the established film or TV 'performers' – such as Len Deighton with *Game, Set and Match*, P. D. James with *A Taste for Death*, D. H. Lawrence with *The Rainbow*, and Ruth Rendell with two offerings, *Shake Hands Forever* and *No Crying He Makes* – there were welcome newcomers. Derek Robinson's fine sardonic novel about a RAF squadron before and during the Battle of Britain, *Piece of Cake*, had a major 6-part series on London Weekend, Maureen Duffy's *Gor Saga* (re-titled *First Born*) featured on BBC1 as did Mary Wesley's 'first'* novel, *Jumping the Queue*, and four Margery Allingham stories featuring Albert Campion. Other BBC series or plays included *Gentlemen's Club* by Richard Gordon, *The Franchise Affair* by Josephine Tey, *Deadline* by Tom Stacey and *Shalom Salaam* by Alexandra Hine. ITV's offering was *Act of Betrayal* by Michael Chaplin. Even though the hours devoted to these dramatisations of novels represented a minute percentage of the schedules, they were a considerable advance on the previous concentration on old movies and American imports.

Nevertheless, only a few of the more distinguished or successful

* Macmillan has been blameworthy in heavily publicising the novel as Mary Wesley's first. It would have taken minimal research to establish that she had published at least two novels with Macdonald more than a decade earlier.

novelists have found a real niche in television adaptations of their work; even fewer have had the double benefit of both selling the television rights and being invited to adapt their own work. There is often a certain topicality in the subjects and themes of the novels that do get chosen. J. A. Sutherland in his book *Bestsellers* made the pertinent point:

> The bestseller, for example, has an intimate connection with the news. Frequently, it presents itself as 'tomorrow's headlines' . . . In Britain in 1979–80 the whole Blunt affair melted miasmically into the bestseller ethos of the televisation [*sic*] of le Carré's immediately prior *Tinker, Tailor, Soldier, Spy*, so that one could hardly tell when headlines about moles finished and fiction started.

A little later in the same book, Mr Sutherland makes a more debatable claim:

> But just as the cinema's increasing reliance on special effects in the 1970s brought a lateral pressure to bear on fiction, so too television's appetite for 'bestsellers' to process can be expected to inspire novelists to produce many more segmented narratives in the 1980s.

As the analysis of TV schedules has shown, the novelist who deliberately wrote a story with readily identifiable 'natural breaks' to make the task of adaptation into a TV series that much easier would have a very small target at which to aim. John le Carré, three of whose last five novels have become extremely popular television serials, has never had any thoughts of a TV outcome in mind when contemplating a new novel. Indeed, a detailed study of the novels and the corresponding TV scripts, often written by Arthur Hopcraft, would show – particularly in the case of *Tinker, Tailor* – how much the latter differed from the former in structure and chronology. Nor should one forget that, to an internationally bestselling novelist today whose overall income from any one book will run into several million pounds, a sale of television rights, no matter how successfully concluded, represents 10 per cent or less of that overall income. He does not have, therefore, any great inducement to follow Mr Sutherland's precept of 'more segmented narratives', particularly if, by so doing, he might risk damaging the sales of the novels themselves.

There is in fact a little-discussed but inherent risk for the novelist whose work is adapted for television. Mr le Carré has stated that he can no longer contemplate writing a novel that features George Smiley because in his mind's eye the character is indissolubly linked in appearance and gestures with Sir Alec Guinness's brilliant TV impersonation. He apparently made one abortive attempt but found himself wondering how Guinness (and not Smiley) would react to a particular situation. One imagines that John Mortimer similarly must visualise Leo McKern whenever he writes a Rumpole script. A novelist needs the freedom to draw his characters from the well of his own inspiration.

Television has presented one main opening to the aspiring novelist. It is to abandon the novel and seek a career in writing TV scripts or, as authors such as James Mitchell, John Mortimer, Fay Weldon and Frederic Raphael have managed, to combine both careers with perhaps the emphasis on the television side. Had television not coincided with their best creative years, it seems likely that writers like Alun Owen, Denis Potter and David Hare would have stretched the technical resources of the novel. Television's gain has been fiction's loss.

In a previous work, *Fiction and the Fiction Industry*, Mr Sutherland made this comment:

The various deviations of literary genius caused by commercial incentives and inhibitions are usually too fine to trace, except in those large drifts which one can see, for example, towards drama in the seventeenth century, lyric poetry in the early nineteenth or fiction in the late nineteenth century. In the 1960s one main drift has been that which draws creative writers out of fiction and into television.

One cause for surprise is that the drift has not been greater. Mr Sutherland went on to quote Melvyn Bragg and his three reasons for being a 'teleperson':

1: 'you can't live off fiction'; 2: television work offers a 'world – a society to which the author can belong'; 3: television offers an outlet for the writer's evangelical desire to instruct a large audience on the value of fiction.

It sounds like special pleading. Several critics or reviewers such as Hermione Lee, Joan Bakewell and Bernard Levin have fronted book programmes on television with authority and enthusiasm; Miriam Gross, previously of the *Observer*, runs the excellent weekly *Book Choice* on Channel 4; Melvyn Bragg's own *South Bank Show* is justly renowned. But this activity is an addition to, not a substitute for, their continuing to write – reviews and articles in the case of Lee, Bakewell and Levin and successful novels (and 'the book' of a musical stage play) in the case of Bragg.

The greatest potential danger to the novel lies perhaps with the would-be or disappointed novelist who turns his creative energy into scriptwriting or directing television programmes. They almost never go back again.

CHAPTER XIV

# Trade Winds

Authorship is a hopelessly middle-class thing, a lottery
subject to uncontrollable market forces and it is better
not to do it.

Mervyn Horder, reviewing
*The Common Writer: Life in Nineteenth-Century Grub Street*
by Nigel Cross, 1986

Most novelists do what they can do. The writer of tough adventure
novels is unlikely to switch successfully to tender romantic fiction: nor
can one imagine Iris Murdoch or Muriel Spark suddenly emulating
Shirley Conran or Sally Beauman. The few adaptable writers of fiction
are usually those who have been journalists, trained to write to a length
and to a closely defined readership, and who have a private overdrive
to succeed. (Very occasionally, a 'spoof' novel will make its mark: one
such a decade ago was *Naked Came the Stranger*, compiled by a circle of
American journalists, who each wrote a chapter with his or her tongue
firmly in the cheek. But these are rarities and the success is usually
fleeting.) The others write what is in them to be written. If they have
an extraordinary talent that is readily recognised by serious reviewers
or the luck to write a novel that hits, or even helps to formulate, the
public taste, they will break through into commercial favour. If they
have the skill to repeat the recipe, they will continue to enjoy that
level of sales, as long as the recipe remains popular with readers.

In this context, one thinks of John le Carré, who wrote two
stylish but modest suspense novels before hitting the jackpot with
*The Spy Who Came in from the Cold*, which acted as a corrective
to the sexual fantasies of Ian Fleming. Le Carré's Leamas in his
shabby raincoat, worrying about the rent and his expenses, seemed
a far more convincing agent than the invulnerable Bond with his
brand-name belongings, the Dunhill lighter, the Aston Martin car,

and the schoolboy smut of the heroines' names – like Pussy Galore. Le Carré wrote two more good espionage novels after *The Spy* – *The Looking Glass War* and *Small Town In Germany*. Then he wrote a 'straight' novel, *The Naive and Sentimental Lover*, which was flawed to some extent but which developed his talent in a serious area that might have led to remarkable heights.

But it was attacked by the British critics and the sales, both in Britain and the United States, were well below the previous levels he had attained. He went straight back to the field of his earlier success and wrote the Karla Trilogy, featuring George Smiley. Since then, two more novels in a similar vein have followed – *The Little Drummer Girl* and *A Perfect Spy*. Thus, it could be argued that John le Carré has been trapped by his own extreme success. It is not just a question of money. In the last twenty-five years, he must have earned a very considerable amount, more than enough to provide ample comfort for himself and his family for the indefinite future. It is as much a question of status, of being accepted as a top-selling author. To break the mould that a large and receptive reading public has forced upon him and chance an ignominious critical reception and inferior sales is often more than a successful author dares risk, particularly when he has reached an age when safety beckons.

Since the end of the Second World War, there have been close on a dozen factors that have had either a direct or a tangential effect on what the novelist writes and how he writes it. They include the influence of publicity and advertising; the impact of book clubs, all the greater since they became 'simultaneous' in 1967; the Net Book Agreement (NBA) and the bookselling trade; public libraries and the Public Lending Right (PLR); the existence of the Arts Council the prizes and awards that are available to novelists, especially the Booker Prize; the professional bodies, the Society of Authors and the Writers' Guild; and the effect of high taxation for much of the period. Some of them occur before the event and some afterwards. For example, there have been few, if any, novelists with the courage and self-conceit to sit down and deliberately attempt to write a novel that will win the Booker Prize. But it is equally clear that the careers of those novelists fortunate enough to win the prize have been favourably affected thereafter.

## Publicity and Advertising

> Half the advertising is wasted – but *which* half?
>
> Lord Leverhulme

For the first few years after the war, while the boom in book sales lasted, most publishers would have looked on publicity as not only unnecessary but even somewhat caddish. If the American cousins wished to bang the big drum, good luck to them. That was not the way we did things here. Advertising was the right and proper way to bring a good book to the attention of likely readers. And so the book pages of the *Sunday Times* and the *Observer*, the *Daily Telegraph*, the *Manchester Guardian* and the *New Statesman and Nation* were enfiladed with those two-inch and four-inch single and double columns, each with a special border and the publisher's colophon to distinguish it from its rivals. Victor Gollancz, never a shrinking violet, used to take a column in the *Observer* on the leader page to flaunt his wares.

It all became too much for Dorothy L. Sayers. In October 1945, she wrote:

> One trick that I believe to be extremely dangerous is the 'ponging' of one particular book so as to manufacture a monstrous and unnatural boom for it; and this is especially harmful in the case of a first book. The unfortunate author is never able to get away from or live down his bloated reputation.

That was a strange remark for someone who in her days as an advertising agent was credited with inventing that long-running slogan, 'Guinness is good for you'.

Even as late as February 1958, Alfred A. Knopf, writing in *Atlantic Monthly*, remarked:

> When Samuel Butler asked Darwin, 'What sells a book?' he got the classic answer, 'Being talked about is what sells a book.' And the answer still holds.

But neither Mr Knopf nor any of his successors on either side of the Atlantic has ever completely solved the big question that lies behind Darwin's answer. 'Yes – but what gets a book talked about?'

By the early 1950s, the Americans were well aware that books had to be *sold* in competition with other rivals for the public's spare time – such as television which, with its proliferation of local stations as well as networking companies, was by 1952 available to virtually the whole population coast to coast. At this time, the word 'marketing' entered the New York and Boston publishing vocabulary. 'The market' was the goal and marketing managers were the centre-forwards. As Jon Cleary has put it, 'In 1952, Scribner's sold *The Sundowners* to Pocket Books and I had lunch with the marketing manager. I saw that the whole thing was so different from selling hardbacks – it was selling sausages! It was the first time I'd heard the term "marketing".'

Even in 1958, Frank Morley, the American who worked at different times for Harcourt Brace in the States and for Faber and Eyre & Spottiswoode in London, was able to compare the two approaches from first-hand knowledge:

> In New York we tried to sell the baby before it was born and in London we merely brought it to birth and exposed it and hoped for a sale.
>
> There are now indications that if you merely expose the baby on the hillside, nobody is going to pay much attention to its cry.

As far as novels were concerned, that 'exposure' took place along the following lines. Every publisher had a review list consisting of the names of perhaps a hundred national newspapers and magazines, leading provincial papers, and details of specialised periodicals. A senior secretary would be deputed to mark up the list and one of her juniors would type out the appropriate labels. Three weeks or so before the book was published, the review copies would be sent out, each with a slip inside stating the actual date of publication. Already, if the novel was likely to enjoy reasonable sales, an advertisement would have been placed in one or more of the trade papers then existing – certainly in the *Bookseller* and possibly also the *Publishers Circular* and *Smith's Trade News*. On or shortly after the book appeared, there could be two or three small advertisements in the book pages already mentioned. Then everyone in the publishing house sat back and waited.

'And yet it moved.' In that very decade, Michael Joseph published a slim little book entitled *The Snow Goose* by Paul Gallico. There was hardly any advertising and no reviews at all in the national press. But the novella was 'talked about' in Alfred Knopf's phrase – what we would now call 'word of mouth' recommendation – and the eventual sales ran into hundreds of thousands of copies. As Ronald Pollitzer of Collins said in a *Bookseller* article in May 1960, 'Books get more publicity than any other commercial product, more even than films, I believe'. He should have known because he was one of the first and certainly one of the most outstanding publicity managers in post-war British publishing. Older members of the trade still recall with awe his handling of Chester Wilmott's *Struggle for Europe* and, a little later, Field Marshal Montgomery's and Field Marshal Alexander's memoirs. And the way he bludgeoned the book trade over *The Wooden Horse* and *Reach for the Sky*, forcing them to the top of the bestseller list at different times, is still memorable. These were, of course, dramatic true war stories, appearing when the war was still fresh in the minds of adult readers and when a younger generation that had grown up during the war was excited to find out what it had missed. By now, autographing sessions in bookshops had become fashionable but only those novelists who were household names or who had been catapulted into fame through successful films of their books – for example, Richard Gordon and the *Doctor* series or John Masters after *Bhowani Junction* – could hope to emulate the war heroes.

As with so much else in the book trade, the early 1960s were the watershed. Many larger and medium-sized houses set up for the first time a separate publicity department. No longer were they prepared just to send out review copies, advertise modestly and hope for the best. As the previous paragraph shows, the main impact was on the non-fiction side – the autobiography of a famous person or an important book on a topical subject or a true-life adventure story is always easier to publicise than a 'made-up' story – but the successful novelists were not ignored. In December 1962, *The Times* in a special article pointed out that in the period from 1 October 1961 to mid-November 1962 it had reviewed 256 novels. The article went on to point out that its reading public was 'more cosmopolitan-minded and less capable of being shocked and more prepared to face world problems in fiction than ever before'. It mentioned also 'the large number of novels treating of human complications arising from differences of colour or of national and anti-semitic prejudices'.

For the first time in 1967, the *Bookseller* began to report publicity tours carried out in the United Kingdom by American novelists – John O'Hara for New English Library, Robert Crichton for Hodder & Stoughton, and Irving Wallace for Cassell. They might well have been considered 'visiting firemen' and the thought that they had travelled 3,000 miles especially to grace our shores would stimulate interest from local newspapers and radio stations. But by then both national television and BBC radio were, apart from the press, affording outlets for novelists. The BBC had started its *Monitor* arts programme under Huw Wheldon's editorship in 1960; later in the decade came Radio 4's *Bookshelf* and in 1975 a BBC programme devoted to newly published paperbacks, mostly fiction – *Read All About It* under Melvyn Bragg. Two years later, the *Bookseller* followed the lead of the *Sunday Times* by starting a weekly set of bestseller lists, which must have served to accentuate the already successful but added to the general publicity for books.

In the past decade, with publishing houses often grouped together and with more money available both for the purchase of big-selling novels and for their promotion, the publicity tail has quite frequently wagged a weakly mongrel. As Per Gedin, the Swedish publisher, put it in an address to the Booksellers Association Conference in the summer of 1978:

> In the old society, authors, publishers and booksellers knew exactly where to find their public. It was well defined, easy to get at and had a strong motivation to read books. In modern mass society everyone is a prospective reader but – to exaggerate somewhat – few are natural readers.
>
> There is no social motivation to read, but it is possible to create a tremendous interest in *one* book.

He went on to point out the effect that television had on book sales, instancing *I, Claudius* and *Claudius the God*, which had together been selling 15,000 copies a year in the Penguin edition before the TV series appeared; one year later, the joint sales were 186,000 and, in 1977, 260,000. A similar case was *The Forsyte Saga*, which had been 'selling poorly in Penguin' before the first TV run.

Only a week after Mr Gedin's speech, Futura announced that it would be spending £50,000 on promoting *The Thorn Birds*. It was a case of reinforcing success. The novel had already been sold for record sums throughout the world. Indeed, before a single edition had appeared anywhere, the novel had earned $2,722,900 in advances. The US paperback rights had gone for $1,900,000, the British and South African rights for $266,000, German language rights for $265,000 and the Australian rights for $125,000. So Futura had a stake to protect.

In 1986, Collins announced that its promotional budget for a thriller entitled *The Mahjong Spies* by John Trenhaile was also to be £50,000. The house had contracted for two books from that author 'for a six-figure sum'. In other words, *The Mahjong Spies* was carrying an advance payment of at least £50,000 on top of the budget, a minimum total of £100,000. The book did figure briefly in the lower reaches of the hardcover bestseller fiction lists and, a year later, for a short period in the same area of the paperback list. But, unless Collins has written the large sum down or off as a long-term investment – in which case, why only a two-book contract with the author? – one cannot help feeling that it was largely money down the drain. To employ Dorothy L. Sayers's strange verb, 'ponging' a moderately successful novel by lashing out comparatively enormous sums of money – probably £2 or more per copy of the anticipated hardcover sale – does neither the publisher nor in the long run probably the author any real good.

The old military maxim is – reinforce success. Hodder & Stoughton were on much safer ground when, four months later, it announced that Saatchi & Saatchi had been commissioned with a budget of £250,000 to set up a publicity and advertising campaign for the forthcoming novels of seven of its leading authors – Jeffrey Archer, Noel Barber,* John le Carré, James Clavell, James Herbert, Stephen King and Morris West. Each of them was (and is) an accepted bestseller; all of them would figure well up in the top twenty-five highest selling writers of fiction in the United Kingdom. The scheme appears to have worked well, although whether the £250,000 cost of the budget has been more than earned back through additional sales and turnover that would not have been achieved without the glossy campaign is a secret locked in accounting files on the south side of Bedford Square.

A good part of the Saatchi budget, particularly for Archer and le Carré, was spent on television advertising on the eve of the respective publication dates. A decade earlier, when Morris West was on its list of authors, Collins had undertaken an extensive TV advertising campaign on a co-operative basis with Mr West for his novel *Salamander*. The cost was reputed to be £30,000 – allowing for inflation, the equivalent of over £60,000 today. There was, it seems, an increase of sales above his fairly high normal level but the improvement was not permanent and, within a year or two,

* Noel Barber died in July 1988.

the author, dissatisfied with the sales level of subsequent books, left Collins for Hodder & Stoughton. (He has since moved on after three further novels to Century Hutchinson.)

Apart from pleasing the writer and his family, television advertising – and, indeed, most other forms of advertisement – has never been a guaranteed method of enhancing a book's sales. It will certainly bring the fact of the novel's imminent publication to the attention of the author's existing readership and may even attract new readers. But the amount spent can never be great enough to ensure a wide impact. The manufacturer of soap or detergents or dog food or fish fingers knows that he has a large potential market for his product. He can afford to undertake detailed market research, both of the product itself and of its name and packaging. He can then carry out test marketing in specific areas and, as a direct result of that research, refine the appearance of the product. He may spend £1 million on the research and promotion. The publisher of novels cannot afford that scale of expense. If we take just three of the bestselling novelists on the Saatchi & Saatchi list – Jeffrey Archer, John le Carré and Stephen King – their readership will overlap by probably less than 50 per cent in each case. Stephen King's 'horror' novels will not necessarily attract Jeffrey Archer's readership, nor is it likely that either of them will have the same reader 'profile' as John le Carré. So it is not merely a question of one type of breakfast cereal competing with other rivals for the first meal of the day. In effect, every novel competes with every other novel.

In the early post-war years, the rule of thumb policy pursued by publishers was to spend in advertising 6d for every copy printed. Published prices were then 7s 6d or 8s 6d for a hardcover novel. When discounts to the book trade were allowed for, this meant that approximately 10 per cent (or somewhat less) of expected turnover went in advertising. Nowadays, the published price would be £10.95 or £11.95 and the discounted turnover figure per book between £6 and £7. For a novel liable to sell 10,000 copies, which should guarantee it at least a brief appearance on the bestseller lists, it is improbable that the publisher would spend up to £7,000 in advertising and promotion. His big 'throw' is reserved for the major novelist who will sell well over 30,000 copies in hard covers and probably over 300,000 in paperback.

So what can a novelist do to help sell his own books? Here we can turn to Jeffrey Archer and Jon Cleary, as two tough professionals with a strong urge to succeed. In his interview with me, Jeffrey Archer said, 'What is the point of writing a book if nobody reads it? . . . I want everybody in the world to read me. I don't mind people saying, "I don't enjoy him and I don't want to read another one".... Hodder can show you the figures – 82 per cent of people who've read one Jeffrey Archer have read *every* Jeffrey Archer. My aim in life is to get you to read one ... So I get all the salesmen putting me in the window, I get all the others working hard, I make people work. I fail sometimes. If they think I'm too aggressive or they find my attitude wrong, they don't want to join the game ... I know the name of every single one of the salesmen at Hodder Paperbacks, *every single one*. In many cases, I know their wives and families. And why? Because I like people. You'd tire of it if you did it as an act every time. I particularly like salesmen because they actually go to the shops, get out of their cars and deal with selling books. They bring home readers for me and so I adore them.

'I would say to young ambitious authors who wish to be read, the great secret when you're unknown is to do anything and everything. For example, I did a show in Newcastle – I think it's called *Midnight to One* – where I was on for three and a half minutes at five to one. The producer felt very guilty and was most courteous afterwards ... That producer went on to become the producer for *This Is Your Life* and when he read *Kane and Abel*, he talked Eamonn Andrews into doing me when I was not very well known. I *became* very well known, launched into the stratosphere overnight, because 18 million people watch that show. And many of them were reading *Kane and Abel* next day. What I'm getting at is that if someone asks you to do LBC at midnight, you do it, because the LBC producer or director may well be the head of the biggest BBC show in two years' time and say, "I had that author on – he's great, he works hard and he delivers." That's all *they* care about.

'When I was a new author, if I could get ten people to read a book, I'd go and get those ten. I knew that if I could build and build, the floodgate would eventually open. If it [success] hadn't happened, I'd have given up very quickly. I'd have said, "Listen, I don't write very well, they're not very interested in me, I think I'll make violins." . . . I could see that few authors were professional about publicity. Agents were professional, publishing houses were professional, authors imagined that when they handed the book in, that was it. I believe you are exactly halfway when you have handed the book in. Any author who does not realise that is either a snob or a fool – he can take his choice.'

As a realistic professional whose career has run for nearly forty-five years, Jon Cleary's advice is worth careful attention. 'My feeling on promotion and publicity is that you can over-expose yourself,' he said to me. 'In Australia, they try to publish me to catch the Christmas and summer market . . . by bringing out the hardback and at the same time the paperback of the previous novel plus three backlist titles, to make a package. I only consent to do publicity every second book. I feel you can be over-exposed if you come up every year. I'm selective about what I do. I go on certain radio programmes and I usually only go on two television programmes.

'But probably the most effective thing, which a lot of authors overlook, is to go into a shop, pay your respects to the manager and then ask to talk to the girl on the floor, who's the one who *sells* the books. She's surrounded by thousands of names and she can't distinguish one from the other – except for the top names. If a real, living author steps up and says, "I'm Joe Blow", the face connects in her mind with the name. People have told me, when some little old lady comes into the shop, starts browsing around and says, "I'm going on holiday, what can you recommend?" the girl remembers that last week she met Joe Blow or Jon Cleary. I've found that the most effective way of getting publicity. I've been doing it for thirty years and more and have found it's paid off.

'I don't know that newspaper advertising has that much impact. It's more public relations than publicity. Even if one of my fans notices an advertisement, I haven't gained a new reader, which is the whole purpose of advertising.

'You do much better through radio interviews and TV . . . The first thing I always ask before I'm interviewed, whether it's a three-minute clip on radio or a five- to seven-minute appearance on television, is, "How long have I got?" They're always a little surprised . . . because most people don't ask them that question. They think it's a vanity thing and say, "Why do you ask that?" It's got nothing to do with vanity: if you know you're only going to get three minutes, you don't burble on but keep your answers short. I have a clock in my mind that tells me I've got a minute to go. If the interviewer hasn't mentioned my book, *I* mention it. That's because I've been at the game a long time.'

Jacqueline Susann, author of one of the biggest-selling of all post-war novels, *The Valley of the Dolls*, was a tireless advocate of her own work. She had married a trained publicist named Irving Mansfield and the couple were indefatigable in arranging her appearances on almost any radio or television chat show in the length and breadth of the United States, where a mention of her latest book might stimulate extra sales. According to her unofficial posthumous biographer, Barbara Seaman, whose book *Lovely Me: The Life of Jacqueline Susann* was published in America towards the end of 1987 and in Britain a few months later, Ms Susann was about to embark on a publicity tour when she heard of the tragic assassination of President Kennedy. Her heartfelt comment was, 'Why the fuck does this have to happen to me? This is gonna ruin my tour!' Professional zeal in self-promotion can occasionally be carried a step too far.

*Book Clubs*

As with so much else in the 'service industry' world, book clubs originated in the United States. The first of them all, the Book of the Month Club, was founded in April 1926 and the Literary Guild, created and owned by Doubleday, in the autumn of the same year. The initial printings of main selections were around 25,000 copies but twenty years later in the early post-war period these had risen to between 400,000 and 600,000 copies. By 1976 the Book of the Month Club (BOMC) had 1.25 million members, sent out 12 million books a year to those members and spent something like $12 million a year (or a dollar a book) on promotion, advertising and circulation.

In the United Kingdom, the Book Society began in 1929 and Victor Gollancz's Left Book Club in 1936. By the time war broke out, the Readers' Union and Foyle's Book Club were also active. The Left Book Club often published original works (e.g. *Guilty Men*) but the others were bound by the strict rule whereby a year had to elapse from first publication before a book club could issue its edition. That edict remained in being until 1967; the reasons for change will be explained later. The Left Book Club, which did not long survive the war, never had a membership exceeding 60,000 but the Reprint Society, founded in 1939, announced on its tenth birthday that it had 'an entirely authentic' membership of 150,000.

By the mid-1950s, book clubs were booming. Odhams started the Popular Book Club in April 1954, three months later Reader's Digest introduced its Condensed Books. In August that year, it was announced that 750,000 books a month were being distributed through book clubs in Great Britain. In March 1956, J. H. Barrett, in his talk to the Society of Young Publishers, claimed that book clubs were distributing over 10 million books a year and that a 'vast new reading public' existed that did not go into bookshops.

What goes up sooner or later tends to come down. By March 1957 the overall membership of the four main book clubs (Odhams Companion Book Club, the Reprint Society, Foyle's Book Club and the Readers' Union) which had been between 950,000 and 1 million in March 1955 was now down to some 650,000. The 'threat from paperbacks' was the main reason for the decline.

In 1964 the situation had become quite desperate. By that time, virtually every major paperback house had become well established; book clubs were thus competing head on with the paperback houses, as both parties had to wait a full year from first hardcover publication before distributing their respective editions. As far back as 1937, Foyle's Book Club had announced that it would bring out its edition of *Brynhild* by H. G. Wells two weeks after Methuen's trade publication but several large booksellers cancelled their trade orders with Methuen and the plan was hastily abandoned. Shortly afterwards, the Publishers Association recommended that a six-month interval should be the norm but that was later amended by a Publishers Association/Booksellers Association *ad hoc* committee to twelve months.

In 1966 the American Literary Guild, headed by the friendly but formidable Milton Runyan, formed Book Club Associates (BCA) in Britain in a 50/50 partnership with W. H. Smith. To give themselves a flying start, they bought up the Reprint Society and then World Books, the latter from Odhams. And then heavy pressure was applied to the PA and the BA to remove the twelve-month stop. After much arguing, all concerned agreed that simultaneous publication with the trade editions could start from 1967 with the following provisos:

(a)   that book club editions should be under the club's own imprint and should be 'different in appearance' (the latter proviso was soon dropped);

(b)   that in their advertising the book clubs should make only 'limited comparisons' with the published prices of the trade editions;

(c)   that the trade publisher must announce immediately the fact that he had sold a sub-licence of a title to a book club. The sale and the announcement must be not less than four months before trade publication;

(d)   that the price of the book club edition must be not less than

25 per cent below the published price of the trade edition (it was eventually stabilised at 35 per cent).

The agreement effectively set the pattern of book club publishing over the next dozen and more years, which were to see BCA becoming ever more prominent and the other clubs either dwindling or attempting to specialise. In 1977, Bertelsmann, the huge German publishing combine, set up the Leisure Circle in Britain which, two years later, had built up a membership of 130,000 of which 80 per cent were thought to be female. And in 1979 Collins, Heinemann and Bonniers, the large Swedish publishing house, formed the Nationwide Book Club. In spite of the expertise of the owners and over £3 million in start-up costs, the club only managed to attract a membership of 170,000 and was still showing a loss two years later. It was sold in 1982 to Readers' Union for 'well over £1 million'.

In 1987, Doubleday was sold to Bertelsmann which had already bought Bantam in New York. Through the former purchase, Bertelsmann had automatically acquired Doubleday's 50 per cent holding in BCA. That helped to concentrate W. H. Smith's corporate mind and, on the grounds that 'BCA is essentially a mail order business and we believe we should concentrate on our principal retail operations', Smith sold its half-share to the Germans for £69 million. (W. H. Smith's initial investment had been £3.5 million, so in just over twenty years, during which inflation had increased by a factor of just under seven, it had made almost twenty times profit on the stake.)

The French group, Les Presses de la Cité, which already had a 50/50 partnership with Bertelsmann in a leading French book club, France-Loisirs, at once bought on the W. H. Smith share of BCA for £59 million and 50 per cent of the Leisure Circle in Britain, wholly owned by Bertelsmann. It was, according to *The Times*,

a strategic move which will open up new opportunities for selling English language books in the rest of Europe, Africa and Asia.

At the time of the sale, BCA had 1.7 million members in Britain with 200,000 more overseas. To April 1987, it showed a year's profit of over £7 million on a turnover of around £75 million. Its nearest competitor, the Leisure Circle, had a membership of around 400,000 and Readers' Union, owned by David & Charles, about 200,000.

Previously, in 1983, there had been a growing feeling in the trade that the 'big battalions' were making life too hard for the specialist clubs. In September that year, Sir Gordon Borrie, the director-general of the Office of Fair Trading, issued a concordat for book clubs, which required the following points to be observed:

1 the exclusive licence they received from the original publisher was to be limited to three years. Thereafter, if required, the licence would be non-exclusive;
2 in order to qualify for an exclusive licence, the book club would have to order a minimum number of copies – either 1,500 or half the original publisher's print run;
3 every exclusive book club edition must have its own imprint, crest or legend. The title page must indicate clearly that it was a book club edition;
4 there must be reasonable access to the rights for specialist clubs, which would be entitled to exercise a non-exclusive licence two months after the first book club had published its edition.

In October 1987 Bertelsmann aimed a Teutonic V-1 at the British printing industry by announcing that in future all BCA and Leisure Circle book club editions would be printed by its own (German) printers. That implied that the trade editions of all book club main choices would also have to be printed in West Germany, since it would be a pointless and expensive duplication of effort to have two identical editions printed in two different centres. The BPIF at once lodged a complaint with the Monopolies and Mergers Commission.

Late in January 1988, Lord Young, the Secretary of State for Trade and Industry, announced the verdict. 'Merger would be against the public interest'; BCA would not be allowed to take over Leisure Circle. He pointed to the problem over printing contracts:

Bertelsmann will be able to manage the allocation of printing contracts from a central position, and we know that it plans to use that position – within the limit described – to control as many of the long print runs as possible.

The Germans had flexed one set of muscles too many. It is possible – even probable – that the merger would have been approved if there had been no overt threat to take away the printing of book club editions from the original hardcover publisher.

So the deal with W. H. Smith had to be unscrambled. Until

August 1988, a year after the original attempt to sell BCA, the status quo prevailed. Then, presumably after delicate soundings had been taken, W. H. Smith made a new deal with Bertelsmann by selling its half-share of BCA for £60 million. Previously, the Office of Fair Trading had stipulated that any new partner must be neither 'sleeping' nor concentrated in the book club business. In September, Bertelsmann to the surprise of many sold the half-share on to Octopus for £52 million. Paul Hamlyn himself, a long-time friend of Reinhard Mohn, the founder of the Bertelsmann group, was directly concerned with the negotiations and must have bargained shrewdly to whittle the purchase price down by £8 million – almost one-seventh of the price paid to W. H. Smith a month earlier. It was a great bargain when one considers that in the thirteen-month period to 31 May 1988 BCA's audited net profit was £8.8 million.

With Paul Hamlyn agreeing to become chairman of BCA for its first year of operating under the new flag, Octopus had made a significant forward move into becoming a more all-round publishing operation. All the group now needed to complete the circle was a powerful paperback house; Reed, the parent company, was already eyeing hungrily the Pearson group with the Penguin bird in its large nest. But that is another – and likely to be a long-running – story.

Over the past decade, book clubs have tended to go down the market in search of wider membership. The *Bookseller* pointed out that since 1975 clubs have swung towards popular non-fiction, 'Royal' books, cookery books and the like. On the fiction front, authors of the calibre of Graham Greene and John le Carré were giving way as main selections to Wilbur Smith and Jackie Collins. There was in fact a backlash in 1982 – though not on aesthetic grounds – when Robert Lacey and Jeffrey Archer refused to allow their publishers, Hutchinson and Hodder & Stoughton, to license their latest books, *Princess* and *Kane and Abel* respectively, to BCA because they felt that book clubs were undercutting their substantial sales through normal retail outlets.

Critics have not been slow to dismiss book clubs as providing pre-selected pap for people who lack the initiative to form their own tastes and venture into a bookshop to buy their choices. J. A. Sutherland, for example, hits out with

a strong drive towards automatism; £7 million spent on adver-tising each year conditions readers into making the proper, unison responses. This, if anything, is the culturally sinister feature of the book club habit – that it is a habit, not a free intellectual act.

And Per Gedin in *Literature in the Market Place* says in a splendidly Nordic disparaging tone, 'The form of distribution best suited to the mass society is . . . the book club. But anything that encourages people to pick up a book and read it is in itself worth encouraging. Even if book clubs need like-minded subscribers and so encourage like-mindedness, the mere act of reading can and may lead upwards. The non-reader is the author's worst enemy.'

To survive in times of heavy postal costs and advertising charges – they spend £6 million to £7 million annually in advertising – book clubs have to pursue the lowest common factor, the guaranteed popular choice. So only the bestselling or the *genre* novelist has any real chance of featuring as a main or joint selection. Once again, the rich get richer and the poor get poorer – but that is a sad if inescapable fact of writing life.

## *The Net Book Agreement*

In March 1890 Mr (later Sir) Frederick Macmillan wrote a letter to the *Bookseller* under the title of 'A Remedy for Underselling'. He pointed out that publishers depended on healthily profitable bookshops for their livelihood and that unless all bookshops adhered to the practice of selling each title at the published price set by the respective publishers, the smaller, less well capitalised bookshops would quickly be squeezed out of business – to the eventual detriment of the whole trade. Nearly a hundred years ago, the firm of Macmillan, which had been founded almost fifty years earlier, was, as it still is, one of the four or five most powerful publishing houses. The trade, both the publishing and the bookselling side, rallied to the call and in 1900 the Net Book Agreement came into force. Certain kinds of publication, mainly educational, were to be classified as 'non-net' but virtually all books for sale through the general trade fell within the Net Book Agreement. From time to time, large stores that stock books as a sideline have attempted to breach the Agreement by selling popular titles as 'loss leaders' but the Publishers Association would swiftly threaten a blacklisting by their members and the stores would soon come to heel. Even when a National Book Sale came into being in February 1955 (to be repeated annually) when for one week publishers' and booksellers' overstocks were sold at substantially reduced prices, at the end of the week those copies still unsold would revert to their original published prices.

The United States has never had a similar agreement. Indeed, for many years past, it has had specific laws declaring any form of cartel to be illegal. American publishers do print the published price of each book on the dust-cover and many bookstores do in fact sell those books at that recommended price. But simultaneously the large chains in major cities indulge in heavy discounting and price-cutting. While the Scribner's Bookstore was still in being at 597 Fifth Avenue, New York, it might be offering a bestselling title for the recommended price of $17.95 but across the street the same book would be on sale at Barnes & Noble for $12.50 or even $10. This system could help to explain the gloomy prognostications of Ronald Mansbridge, the New York manager of Cambridge University Press, when he said in a speech made in July 1956:

> Like the buffalo and the whooping crane, the [American] bookseller has already been allowed to go a long way on the road to extinction. There is now only one of him for every 100,000 Americans.

Earlier that same year, the British trade was severely shaken when a Restrictive Trade Practices Bill was introduced in the House of Commons. It promised (or threatened) that all restrictive practices were to be examined by a special court to be set up and that collective measures for enforcing restrictive practices were to become unlawful. The *Bookseller* set the tone by a headline that read: 'End of Net Book Agreement'. In March 1956 it was announced that books, along with pharmaceutical products,* were to be included in the list for the Monopolies Commission.

The legal mills ground slowly. In August 1961 the Restrictive Practices Court reserved judgment in the case of the Newspaper Proprietors Association and retail newsagents. Six months later, the Publishers Association decided by a two-thirds majority to defend the Net Book Agreement at a likely legal cost of £40,000–£45,000, which today would be about £350,000. The defence was scheduled to start on 25 June 1962. Arthur Bagnall, QC, was to lead the defence with D. A.

---

* In September 1959 the Restrictive Practices Court ordered manufacturers and wholesale chemists to discontinue price-fixing.

Grant, QC, and Jeremy Lever as his juniors. The witnesses to be called included John Attenborough of Hodder & Stoughton, R. W. David of Cambridge University Press, Peter du Sautoy of Faber & Faber, Ian Parsons of Chatto & Windus and Frank Sanders, formerly Secretary of the Publishers Association but then in charge of the distribution organisation, Book Centre.

All the defence witnesses played their part well in the face of searching, at times hostile, questioning. Perhaps the two most dramatic statements came from Mr Balleny, the accountant who specialised in publishing accounts and audits, and later from Frank Sanders. Balleny gave it as his expert opinion that any publisher with a turnover of under £100,000 would almost certainly be making a loss. Sanders, with his previous close knowledge of the Publishers Association, reckoned that at least half the members of the Association had a turnover of less than £100,000!

On 31 October the Restrictive Practices Court gave its judgment. The Net Book Agreement, it declared, *was* in the public interest. The trade rejoiced, as well it might. A 'famous victory' had been won and in the quarter of a century that has followed, no government has publicly attacked the Net Book Agreement. Early in 1976, during the post-OPEC slump, Mrs Shirley Williams, then Secretary of State for Prices and Consumer Protection, did ask publishers to take part in a voluntary scheme for freezing the prices of their back list titles but that was only a temporary measure which did not whittle away the effect of the NBA.

However, in the spring and summer of 1988, several of the more aggressive owners of bookshop chains such as Terry Maher and Tim Waterstone strongly advocated the abandonment of the Net Book Agreement. In their view, it subsidised inefficiency and prevented the go-ahead shops from attracting new customers through attractively priced bargains. Controversy quickly developed; among the prominent defenders of the status quo were, understandably, the Publishers Association and, as an individual, Lord Stockton, whose family firm Macmillan had recently left the Publishers Association. At the time of writing, the argument rumbles on.

More of a long-term threat, perhaps, is what may happen in 1992 when Britain becomes fully integrated in the European Community. The Treaty of Rome frowns on any form of resale price maintenance (RPM). Many European countries, including France, have long since dropped RPM for the sale of books and many other goods.* Will our then government care sufficiently to fight its corner against substantial pressure? And, even if so, will one objector prevail against the majority vote? It does not seem likely.

Has the professional British novelist benefited from the existence of the NBA? The answer has to be a qualified yes. Many leading booksellers and not a few writers have complained through the years that it is the publisher's prerogative alone to set the published price of his books. Although most publishing contracts do include an approximate net price, the preamble usually states that the number of copies printed, their production, distribution and the eventual published price 'shall be at the sole discretion of the publisher who shall bear all expenses in connection therewith'. The important author or his agent will very often be consulted but if the publisher declares his firm conviction that the book will sell far better at £10.95 than if priced at £12.95, the author is unlikely to demand the higher net price.

There is a strong argument to be made that since 1945 a whole range of titles, including novels, was consistently under-priced. Between 1950 and 1976, the average price for all books rose from £0.605 (converting the pre-decimal currency) to £5.85, an increase of almost ten times. Adjusted for inflation, the rise was from £0.605 to £1.33, a little more than double. Yet the cost of paper and binding in real terms more than trebled in the same period. Thanks to the NGA and SOGAT, whose exorbitant demands in the 1960s and 1970s effectively decimated the British printing industry, printing costs between 1 January 1962 and July 1979 rose by 502.9 per cent; in the four years from July 1975 to July 1979 by 79.6 per cent; in the two years to July 1979 by 33.3 per cent and in the year from July 1978 to July 1979 by 20.1 per cent.

According to F. A. H. Timms, formerly the chief accountant at Cambridge University Press, writing in the *Bookseller* in September 1971, the 1960 edition of Sir Stanley Unwin's *The Truth about Publishing* had stated that an efficient publisher's overheads should be about 30.5 per cent of his turnover. Mr Timms pointed out that by 1967, the average for several representative firms had risen to 35.47 per cent and three years later to 42.47 per cent.

In the face of all these upward pressures, it is surprising that average net prices for fiction in the ten-year period covered by Mr Timms only rose by 80 per cent – from 13s 10d (£0.69) in 1961 to £1 4s 11d (£1.25)

---

* The French have recently re-imposed a form of RPM for books.

in 1970. Although inflation was rife, the decade had been a particularly prosperous one: book prices could have risen by at least another 50 per cent and have continued to rise *pari passu* with inflation thereafter. Comparisons between the cost of a book and the cost of a seat in the stalls or at a Festival Hall concert are on the whole pointless but it is perhaps worth mentioning that a good novel provides more than the same length of entertainment – and continues to exist as a possession after the first spell of entertainment has been completed.

With their production costs rising inexorably and their overheads increasing annually to squeeze their profit margins, publishers took the alternative to raising net prices properly: overall, they cut the royalty rates paid to their authors. In *A Sort of Life*, his first volume of memoirs, Graham Greene tells how Charles Evans of Heinemann offered him a starting royalty of $12\frac{1}{2}$ per cent of the published price on his *first* novel – and that was almost sixty years ago. Tennyson had received a $33\frac{1}{3}$ per cent royalty on his later volumes of poetry and well into the 1950s successful novelists received 20 per cent or even 25 per cent on their home sales. Today, the bestselling novelist might obtain a flat 15 per cent or even $17\frac{1}{2}$ per cent on home sales, but the less successful would have to be content with 10 per cent, rising to $12\frac{1}{2}$ per cent after a sale of several thousand copies and rising again at a much higher level to a maximum of 15 per cent. As Anthony Burgess succinctly put it in a 1979 article:

No author can ruin a publisher by withdrawing his labour.

Even Christopher Sinclair-Stevenson of Hamish Hamilton, that noted friend and encourager of authors, having signed the Writers' Guild minimum terms agreement, wrote in the *Bookseller* in November 1980 that he could not afford to print 1,500 copies of a novel at a tolerable published price if the starting royalty were to be 10 per cent, the Guild's minimum, and that $7\frac{1}{2}$ per cent would have to be his figure, thus breaching the agreement. 'The axe will fall most viciously on novels' was his sombre conclusion.*

The Monopolies Commission's report, which came out against the

---

* He has, in fact, on two occasions – once with a novel and once with a non-fiction book – concluded contracts where the royalty rates were lower than those set out in the Minimum Terms Agreement but in each case the only alternative would have been to refuse publication on financial grounds.

proposed merger of the BCA and Leisure Circle book clubs, also cast a beady-eyed glance at the Net Book Agreement. Without the NBA, there could not be a fixed and binding published price for a book, set by the original publisher; on that fixed price depended book clubs' discounted price, set at 35 per cent lower. No positive action was recommended but when a government whose ideal is a free market economy focuses on an ancient barrier, its removal may not be all that far distant.

The great problem – and the great appeal – about books, in particular, novels – is that they are not interchangeable units. It is probably a fair statement that, in spite of television advertising, one brand of detergent will wash clothes just about as clean as any other brand. Thus price reductions or gift schemes may help to shift the stocks of 'Brand X' more quickly off the supermarket shelves. And the very siting of quick-selling goods in supermarkets has become a psychological art in attracting the transient attention of the hurried shopper. But, apart from the small minority of popular authors who have become 'brand names' – such as 'the new Jeffrey Archer', 'the new Wilbur Smith', or 'the new Danielle Steel' – impulse buying of books does take place at airport racks and railway station bookstalls but not to any great degree in town and city bookshops.

Most potential readers enter a bookshop with the intention of buying one or more particular books, because their interest has been whetted by newspaper reviews or advertisements or word-of-mouth recommendation from a friend whose judgment they respect. If that book is not available, they may buy something else in the same price range – but *price* is not the basic incentive. I believe that if the NBA were scrapped, very few would-be readers would walk round every bookshop in their home town comparing prices and buying the cheapest copy of the book they are seeking. Indeed, price-cutting would only work effectively when the potential buyer wants the equivalent of 'junk food' for a journey.

Even an aggressive bookselling chain needs a solid profit margin if it is to afford to carry a representative stock of titles and not just depend on the rapid turnover of a few discounted blockbusters. Without the NBA, smaller bookshops in country towns or in the suburbs of cities could soon be forced out of business. As J. A. Sutherland put it in *Fiction and the Fiction Industry*, 'the Net Book Agreement acts as a *de facto* subsidy for small retailers'. The shop that has limited space and even more limited funds must needs keep a close watch on its stocks and cannot represent each of the more than 4,000 novels published each year in Britain.

But even if those shops can only stock the more popular and quicker selling titles, they are providing the potential buyer with a wider choice of purchase. Had the judgment in 1962 gone against the NBA, bookselling outlets today might well have been reduced to a few large chains like W. H. Smith, John Menzies, Waterstone, Dillons and Hatchards, with the occasional privately owned shop in small towns. (Even as things are, the spread of the large chains must be responsible for the steady diminution of the private bookshop.)

The author who puts his heart and his spirit for many months, even years, into the writing of a novel does not want its success or failure to depend on the whim of half a dozen big buyers nationwide.

## Public Libraries

Public libraries came into being in 1850, following the Public Libraries Act; they were to be a free source of information for the aspiring artisan and the humble seeker after knowledge. The Education Act of 1832 had helped to speed the growth of literacy and the day of Samuel Smiles and 'self-help' was on its way. For many years, even into the present century, the books that could be freely borrowed from public libraries were mainly non-fiction – technical, instruction and reference books.

Gradually, during the 1920s and 1930s the balance swung towards the providing of fiction. By 15 February 1947, a Mr F. W. Lovell could write to the *Bookseller* in these terms:

> Of course, a lot of the novels priced at 7/6d (or now, usually, 8/6d or 9/6d) are not worth that amount to the book-buying public; what is more, they are not bought by the public. They are published with an eye on the main chance, the library which is the true support of the novel and its writer.

The following year, it was announced that the public libraries' expenditure on books worked out at 7d per head of the population, double the purchase rate of 1939. This is perhaps not surprising when one recalls that 1947 and 1948 were years of great privation, with most staple items of food and clothing still rationed and continuing shortages of coal and other items of fuel. Reading a good book was one of the best ways of forgetting the daily miseries.

A decade later, the niceties of life had clearly improved for £16 million was now being spent annually from public funds on public libraries, yet less than a quarter of the population was making use of libraries. Statistics showed that in 1924 there had been 2.7 million borrowers whereas in 1958 there were 13 million. Again, 76 million books had been issued in 1924 against 392 million in 1958. A simple calculation reveals that on average the 1924 borrowers each drew just over twenty-eight books a year and the 1958 borrowers slightly over thirty books – not a significant difference. It was estimated in the latter year that 68.6 million copies were available in the library system.

By late 1960 the total expenditure had risen to £18.75 million, which worked out at 7s 4d per head of the population. But the breakdown of that overall figure is interesting: 40 per cent went on salaries, 28 per cent 'on other items', 6 per cent on binding, 1 per cent on newspapers and magazines, which left just 25 per cent to be spent on new or replacement books. A month or two later, the public libraries were warned by a Publishers Association committee against buying paperback books and binding them up in a durable 'library binding', thus saving the cost of having to buy the more expensive hardcover edition.

It was around this time, too, that the Public Lending Right Bill was first presented to the House of Commons on its weary route march that would last over fifteen years, partly because public librarians, with a few honourable exceptions, were firmly against supporting the authors in their quest.

In June 1961 the chairman of Associated Book Publishers in his annual report repeated a regular complaint of publishers – that the libraries with their free issues were reducing bookshop sales: 'The more probable reason for the sluggishness of the home market in ordinary (i.e. hardbound) books is the combined effect of the free libraries and the paperbacks'. Three years later, it was estimated that eleven books were borrowed from public libraries for each one that was sold through a bookshop.

In the spring of 1969, Mr Bryan Luckham, staff tutor in sociology at Manchester University, published *The Writer in the Market Place*. It demonstrated that whereas (free) public libraries were increasing their borrowings – there were 600 million issues in 1967 – the commercial lending libraries were declining at a rate of 10 per cent per year. W. H. Smith and Boots had already closed their library chains and the remaining ones were in serious financial trouble. Collectively, the commercial libraries had made 150 million issues just after the war. By 1950 the figure had declined to 75 million, which was further reduced to 20 million by 1969 – under 4 per cent of the total achieved by the public libraries that year.

Mr Luckham provided some other interesting statistics, such as the following table, taken from *The Writer in the Market Place*:

*Consumers' Expenditure on Leisure Items*

|  | 1957 | 1967 | *Plus or Minus* |
|---|---|---|---|
| Books | £46m | £86m | +87% |
| Cinema | £95m | £62m | −34% |
| Newspapers | £120m | £216m | +80% |

The table does not take account of inflation, which rose almost 27 per cent in the decade, and the consequent rise in prices, but it does serve to show that in spite – or partly because of – the increasing public library issues, the overall sale of books was holding up.

Three years later, in July 1972, according to Margaret Thatcher, then Secretary of State for Education, public library issues were static at 600 million a year, even though £60 million was being spent on library funds. She gave a breakdown of 50 per cent spent on wages and salaries, 25 per cent on incidentals and 25 per cent on the purchase of books – the same percentage as in 1960. A long tail to wag a smallish dog, one might conclude.

Then came the slump. Oil prices more than trebled, property values declined steeply, secondary banks crashed. Interest rates were forced upwards until towards the end of the decade the Minimum Lending Rate stood at 17 per cent. Government spending was slashed and with a Labour government back in power under the 'white heat technologist', Harold Wilson, now more ashen than in previous premierships, it was perhaps surprising that even public library expenditure was more than halved – to just under £20 million in 1974–75, £25,435,000 in 1975–76 and £27,854,000 in 1976–77.

In a paper read to the Library Association in July 1979, Robin Denniston, of Oxford University Press, said, 'Paperbacks are for the young – hardbacks are for libraries, the middle-aged and the well-heeled'. It was a shrewd remark. J. A. Sutherland had already pointed out that in 1976 the average age of library borrowers was between forty-five and sixty-five.

A leading article in the *Bookseller* in the issue of 2 August 1980 stated:

> The shrinkage of the public library sector as a market for publishers is having an effect on the very identity of publishers' lists,

and went on to point out that 72 per cent of all adult book issues were novels. Just six years earlier, John Bush of Victor Gollancz Ltd had written the following in a letter to the *Bookseller*:

> While it is well-known that the sales of bestselling authors have declined with the modern habit of borrowing rather than buying, this is certainly not true for the general run of fiction authors.

By 1980 it had, alas, become true. Fiction sales had polarised, both in bookshop and library outlets. The very successful novelist had not suffered greatly in either area, the moderately successful had lost perhaps 25 per cent of his sales in both areas, while the averagely unsuccessful had suffered disastrously in the two outlets. Even with the end of the slump at the beginning of the 1980s, the situation had not greatly changed.

In February 1985, a National Book League survey, covering the previous year, demonstrated that library funds in real terms had been reduced by 19 per cent when compared with 1979. The libraries were 'beleaguered'. For example, Somerset County Council had been ordered to cut £100,000 from its budget for 1985–86 and as a result had decided to buy no fiction in the next financial year. (By August, the cut was restored and the buying of fiction was resumed.) In the period 1983–84, public libraries generally in England and Wales bought 13.5 million books for £64.25 million, an expenditure of £1.15 per head of population. Superficially, this compares favourably with an expenditure of 42p per head in 1974–75 but we have to take into account the fact that the average price per volume in the earlier period was £1.80 as compared to £4.77 for 1983–84. Thus, expenditure had risen by a factor of 2.7 whereas the price of books had increased by a factor of 2.6, which broadly cancel each other out.

An analysis of public library expenditure in the successive years 1984–85 and 1985–86 shows the total rising from £359 million to over £465 million but in each case a huge tail was wagging a not very frisky puppy. Just over half the costs went on employees' salaries and benefits, premises cost around 11 per cent, establishment and capital charges about 15 per cent and so on – leaving in 1984–85, 17 per cent to be spent on books and pamphlets and in the next year 15.7 per cent. It is passing strange that a government avowedly looking for value for its money has not in over eight years turned a bleak eye on an organisation that spends only one-sixth of its income on the one 'commodity' it exists to distribute.

Even a shift of 2 per cent from public library overheads to purchases would provide more than £9 million pounds extra, much of which would inevitably be spent on novels. There was a glimmer of hope in December 1987 when Richard Luce, Minister for the Arts, in a written reply to a House of Commons question, stated that £250,000 a year for three years would be set aside from government funds to seek 'a more effective partnership between public and private sectors'. He promised a feasibility report would be published in the following spring.

It appeared in February 1988. Apart from stressing that the basic free service was sacrosanct, it came up with various suggestions for closer collaboration between the two sectors. These included:

(a) 'a premium book-subscription service providing newly published novels and biographies on demand';
(b) subscription services for specialist information and specialised materials for businesses, the professions and the academic world;
(c) general information publishing services, i.e. booklets on topics of local interest, information for house-buyers etc;
(d) fee-based research, e.g. family genealogies;
(e) scope for using public libraries as outlets for the sale of cultural products, i.e. 'books, records and videos'.
(f) contracting out to private firms such items as cataloguing, labelling, jacketing and binding;
(g) competitive tendering from private firms for providing

library services to local old people's homes, video tape lending services and the running of branch library services.

All in all, it was a positive and significantly far-reaching study. One should not be too surprised to learn that the response of the Publishers Association and that of the Booksellers Association was tepid to cool.

An efficient free library service is bound to reduce the sale of hardcover books through normal bookshop channels. There do not seem to be any statistics, since facts and hypotheses would be inextricably involved, on whether novelists in general gain or lose through the 'swings and roundabouts'. If novelists were liable to sell more copies if there were no free service available to readers, the blow has been cushioned in recent years by PLR earnings.*

Thus no one could argue effectively, as J. A. Sutherland tries to do, that the presence of the public library system has had a marked influence on the subjects, methods and lengths of modern novels. He is correct in claiming that the pressure of the public library has made for traditionalism as opposed to avant-gardism – which is little more than to say that middle-aged, mainly middle-class readers are liable to read traditional novels. It cannot assume that potential Russell Hobans or Angela Carters are going to imitate Jeffrey Archer or Barbara Cartland in their quest for larger sales to libraries.

In *Fiction and the Fiction Industry*, discussing the turnround rate of library borrowings, he writes: 'The two week, four/six book rule encourages a shortness and broad readability.' But librarians do not want to buy short novels because their borrowers prefer *short* novels. The reason is far more hard-nosed. Judging by the fiction bestseller lists over the past decade and more, fiction readers actually prefer longer novels – the 'good long read'. Librarians prefer short novels because the turnround is that much quicker and so they need buy fewer copies of a popular but short novel.

Twenty years ago, the public libraries did encourage the publishing of new, even experimental, fiction by subscribing well before publication. Mr Sutherland quotes two examples given by Michael Dempsey, then the editor of Hutchinson New Authors. Novel A, published in 1967, sold 2,243 copies out of a printing of 3,000, of which 2,050 copies went to public libraries. Novel B, also published

* See pages 255–7.

in 1967, sold 1,500 copies, of which 1,300 went to public libraries. Today, the public library orders for those novels might be in the 500–600 copies range. But no publisher can afford to put out a hardcover novel with a maximum potential sale of 800 copies. Reflecting on those New Authors results with the hindsight of twenty years, one might add the rider that Hutchinson's bright idea might not have come to grief quite so soon if less reliance had been placed on the public libraries.

## The Public Lending Right

So many hundreds of thousands of words have been uttered and written on PLR – for and against – that one hesitates to add to the number. But, as it is the one commercial factor that has affected most professional British novelists in the last few years, a brief chronological sketch and some observations are indeed necessary.

PLR was implemented in Denmark in 1946, in Norway in 1947, in Sweden in 1954 and in Holland in 1971. Two to three years later, both Australia and New Zealand had also adopted it. In Britain over thirty years was to elapse from the first efforts through a series of indifferent or hostile parliaments before the first PLR payout. Even then, the parliamentary draftsman responsible for drawing up the bill went on record in the autumn of 1982 in these terms. It had fallen to his lot, he wrote,

> . . . to draft a bill for the implementation of an entirely new – and in my opinion wholly bogus – legal conception called 'public lending right'.

Authors may wish to note his name – Godfrey Carter.

On a heavenly plane, the still, small voice will work wonders but in public affairs the shrill, loud voice is an essential if results are to be achieved. Proper tribute is paid later in the chapter to the sterling work of Brigid Brophy and her associate Maureen Duffy; it was not until 1972 when Ms Brophy and her newly formed Writers' Action Group (WAG), with an initial seventy-five members drawn from the Writers' Guild, got to work that things began to move vigorously forward. Even so, nearly another seven years were to pass until in March 1979 the PLR Bill became law – and a further five years still before registered authors received their first annual payments. (Ms Brophy was in no way actuated by self-interest – unlike some of her numerous opponents. Her first PLR payment was £240, £21 below the average payout.)

The story begins in 1951 when her father, John Brophy, himself a distinguished novelist, along with A. P. (later Sir Alan) Herbert, proposed what became known as the 'Brophy Penny'. The simple idea was that every time a book was borrowed from a public library, the borrower should pay one penny to the library staff, who had to keep file cards in any event. The money could be held until the end of the year, earning interest for the borough, incidentally, and then it could be paid through a central fund to the individual authors by checking the number of borrowings on each card. The public libraries were loud in their objections, claiming they had neither the time nor the staff to cope with the extra chore.

Six years later, in a House of Lords debate on state assistance to the arts, the Earl of Huntingdon, whose wife happened to be the writer Margaret Lane, made a further eloquent plea for the 'Brophy Penny'. He referred to Richard Findlater's 1955 survey on authors' earnings and pointed out that the main reason for their plight was the public library system. The estimated life of a book in the libraries varied from 120 to 200 borrowings, although naturally not every book reached that range. Even so, it was highly unfair to the author that one of his books might be borrowed 200 times and he receive nothing apart from the original royalty paid by his publisher on the single copy.

The counter-blast came at once. Mr Lionel McColvin, the Westminster City Librarian, in a letter in the 15 July issue of the *New Statesman*, said the idea was preposterous:

> I think that public authorities should be free to do what they like with their own property and if they choose to lend books free of charge, as they are legally entitled to do, there can be no objection. They are merely carrying out their responsibilities under the Libraries Act.

Mr McColvin did not appear to recall that 'public authorities' are funded partly by the local ratepayer and partly by central government. His definition of 'their own property' is a breathtaking one.

Many librarians were under the mistaken impression that they would be responsible for marking off each issue against the author concerned. Others took the ineffable view, though in a different context, of the director-general of the British Lending Library Division, who proudly said in August 1974: 'We do try to acquire all currently published English language books above a certain level (i.e. we don't buy . . . fiction)'. That type of librarian reckoned that as approximately one-third of all home sales of books were made through their libraries, the author should consider himself lucky enough and not imitate Oliver Twist. It probably never struck the thinker of such thoughts that, without authors, he would have no comfortable and secure job to go to each day.

In 1960, Woodrow Wyatt, then a Labour MP, introduced a Libraries (Public Lending Right) Bill in the House of Commons. It was talked out that December. July appears to have been a significant month in the 'one step forward, two steps back' progress of PLR because – and he should have been the last man to speak thus in view of *The Two Cultures* – Lord Snow, the government spokesman in the House of Lords, said on 3 July 1965:

The concept of a library royalty is one which must be abandoned.

But the following year Lord Goodman, the chairman of the Arts Council, announced the setting-up of a working party to study PLR. Two years later, in February 1968, the council published a pamphlet, *The Arts Council and the Public Lending Right*, which proposed an annual grant out of public funds and a parliamentary Bill to establish a compensation fund for authors. Nothing much seems to have happened, unless one includes an Arts Council 'dry-run' on PLR at Hove in Sussex. Even so, the *Daily Telegraph*, in a leading article at the end of April 1970, uttered a prophecy that the then editor might prefer to forget: 'The long-drawn-out battle, launched by Sir Alan Herbert and his cohorts some ten years ago, looks all but won'.

That September, a concerted effort on behalf of PLR was launched through letters to the *Bookseller* from Michael Holroyd and Victor Bonham-Carter of the Society of Authors. The Society joined forces with the PA and, the following February, came out with a joint brief on PLR. It proposed that on each in-copyright book sold to a public library an additional 15 per cent of the published price

252

should be set aside. For example, if 1,000 copies of a £2 book were sold to the libraries, £300 would be raised in this way. The extra funds would be split 75/25 between the author and the publisher, so that in the case quoted, the author would get £225 over and above his normal royalties and the publisher would get £75.

In May 1972 the same two bodies produced a refined version in a joint statement. It advocated 'blanket licensing' – i.e., one annual licence fee per library. 'The resulting revenue would be distributed as a percentage of the published price of each copyright work sold to libraries.' The overall fee should be a sum equivalent to 20 per cent of the total amount spent annually by libraries. That percentage would work out at about £4 million; £500,000 would be required for administrative costs, the remaining £3.5 million was to be shared in the proportions of 75/25 by authors and publishers. The individual author would end up by getting roughly the same amount as his royalty payment on a single copy sale – i.e. he would receive the equivalent of a double royalty on his UK public library sales, 'which are around 8 per cent of the total world sales [at published prices] of British books'.

There is a strong whiff of 'without whom etcetera' about the publishers' claim for a share. But, if one does not accept Mr Carter's argument that the entire legal conception of PLR is 'wholly bogus', the authors' claim must be based to a large extent on the contention that at least some of the often one hundred or more readers who paid nothing to borrow a particular title from their local public library might well have bought a copy from a local bookshop. That contention needs little extending to include the publisher, who could claim to have lost additional sales (on which he would have paid the author a royalty) through the free availability of the book in the public library.

But the vigilant Ms Brophy was having none of it. Two months later, in a letter to the *Guardian*, she strongly criticised the PLR Working Party report and suggested that the Society of Authors should 'renew the quest for a PLR scheme from scratch'. Later in 1972, she wrote again, this time in the *Bookseller*, to announce the formation of WAG.

The notion was slowly – very slowly – gaining ground. By March 1976, thanks to or in spite of the flustered efforts of the then Minister for the Arts, Hugh Jenkins, a PLR bill was given a first reading in the House of Lords. The bill allowed for an allocation of £1 million for distribution; it was given an unopposed second reading by the Lords in April but in July the Commons adjourned its second reading. That October, the bill passed its second reading in the Commons and was published in November 1978.

It became law in 1979 as the Public Lending Right Act, which required that the rules for its administration were to be laid down in a scheme. That gave rise to the Public Lending Right Scheme of 1982. Amending orders were made in March and November 1983 and in December 1984. For example, the initial proposal allowed for a cut-off point for the most popular authors at £5,000 and a minimum payout per head of £5. The latter was later reduced to £1. The first year was to run from 1 July 1982 to 30 June 1983, with the first payout taking place in February 1984. (The works of dead authors could not be registered; it is a pity that one exception could not have been made for George Orwell in his 'own' year.)

This brief chronological sketch does far less than justice to Brigid Brophy, nobly backed up by Maureen Duffy. Throughout the whole period from 1972 she was both vehement and persistent in promoting PLR to all who would listen – and to many who would not – through letters, speeches, public meetings and private lobbying. Senior civil servants and ministers, in particular Hugh Jenkins, must have cringed whenever she demanded yet another appointment. When the bill became law, there were many justified tributes to her in the press. On publishing the details of the Act in its issue of 17 July 1982, the *Bookseller* added this eloquent statement:

It is to Miss Brophy that a great many writers will wish to pay a special tribute; and it is to be hoped that her great service over many discouraging years will also be widely acknowledged.

Compliments must also be paid to John Sumsion, the Registrar, who without any previous experience of the book trade set up the administration swiftly and highly effectively with very modest staff and funds. Throughout its so far short life, the scheme has run smoothly and with total lack of fuss. Potential applicants would do well to read his résumé of the system in *The Writers' & Artists' Yearbook*.

The results of the first year are worth some close study. Already in June 1983 over 6,000 authors had registered, accounting for some

254

52,000 titles – an average of 8.7 titles per author. Although details of the payments were confidential, many authors disclosed what they had received, from which it was demonstrated that, other things being equal, the prolific author was – fairly obviously – liable to figure high on the ranking lists. For example, Ursula Bloom, who was then aged ninety-one and who had not published a new book for five years, received £4,992, whereas M. M. Kaye, the successful author of comparatively few novels, earned about half that sum. Claire Rayner was on the £5,000 limit, as was Jeffrey Archer, who handed over his earnings to help the Spastics Society publish a book of contributions from their handicapped members. J. L. Carr, a novelist of some distinction – shortlisted twice for the Booker Prize – but who wrote sparingly, earned £103. Statistics showed that 62 per cent of the shareout went to fiction, 23 per cent to non-fiction and 15 per cent to children's books.

The idea that publishers should get a share had been dropped well before the Act was passed but when the first payments were announced, the PA gamely fought its corner. After all, it was argued, if an author wished his publisher to reprint in hardcovers a book long out of print, why shouldn't the publisher reply, 'Fine. You keep the PLR money – and I won't pay you a royalty'?

The second PLR shareout in February 1985 showed that the number of authors registered had risen from 7,562 to 9,395 but that, as a consequence, the average payment had decreased from £261 to £216. This time, forty-seven authors had reached the cut-off point of £5,000 – but 1,715 had notched up no earnings at all. The statistical analysis revealed that Catherine Cookson and Barbara Cartland were *ten times* as popular as Beryl Bainbridge, Margaret Drabble, William Golding and Fay Weldon. The general euphoria was only marred by some remarks from Mr E. H. Browne, the Hertfordshire County Librarian, who wrote:

> If authors had joined with librarians and the book trade to wage a campaign for the protection of library book funds as vigorously and successfully as that conducted for PLR, they would be a good deal better off than they now are.

(It could be added in parentheses that, the following year, the public libraries of England and Wales spent a total of £359 million of which employees (52 per cent), premises (11 per cent), establishment and capital charges (15 per cent) and miscellaneous (5 per cent) amounted to 83 per cent of the total, leaving a meagre 17 per cent to be spent on the one thing that gave credence to everything else on the list – books.)

Further analysis of the PLR results showed that of the authors who received over £1,000, 81 per cent were fiction writers, 6 per cent non-fiction and 12 per cent children's writers. The most popular categories of fiction in descending order were: romance (25 per cent), mystery and crime (24 per cent), general fiction (20 per cent), war stories (4 per cent), historical novels (3 per cent) and Westerns (2 per cent).

The most borrowed authors, again in descending order, were Catherine Cookson (with an average of 23 borrowings per novel), Wilbur Smith (10), Victoria Holt (7), Dick Francis (6) and Evelyn Anthony (6).

The fourth PLR payment, made early in 1987, revealed a further increase in the numbers registered – now up to 12,990 among whom eighty-six West German authors were included. (As West Germany already accepted 'qualified' British authors for its local brand of PLR, it was felt proper that the compliment should be returned to qualifying West German writers.) The fifth PLR payout, announced in January 1988, showed yet another increase in registrations – this time up to 14,635. The lump sum to be allocated was still £2.75 million – the government had announced a 27 per cent increase to £3.5 million for the 1989 payout – and so the average slices of the cake to be cut were that much smaller. Here is a breakdown for the four years 1985 to 1988 inclusive, with the numbers falling into each segment of earnings.

|  | Feb 85 | Feb 86 | Feb 87 | Feb 88 |
|---|---|---|---|---|
| £4,990–5,000: | 47 | 63 | 59 | 57 |
| £2,500–4,889: | 83 | 141 | 129 | 123 |
| £1,000–2,499: | 247 | 345 | 353 | 345 |
| £500–999: | 343 | 470 | 487 | 508 |
| £100–499: | 1,681 | 2,425 | 2,536 | 2,603 |
| £1–99: | 5,221 | 6,182 | 7,473 | 8,624 |
| NIL | 1,773 | 1,631 | 1,995 | 2,375 |

It is hardly surprising that over 90 per cent of the registrands should earn less than £500 a year from PLR. (The exact percentages for the years under review are: 1985 – 92.35 per cent; 1986 – 91.68 per cent; 1987 – 92.37 per cent; 1988 – 92.94 per cent.) No wonder that Graham Swift was moved to comment in 1987: 'I'd much rather make bookshop sales than collect PLR'. Again, a year later, another author was quoted as saying:

> Based on the estimates of sales and royalties paid I am losing about £3,000 a year in royalties to earn £500 (less tax) on PLR . . .

But was he? There is no certainty that, without a countrywide free library service, that author or any other would have sold the same or more quantities of copies through bookshops and the trade channels. £3,000 in royalties would represent an additional sale of between 2,000 and 3,000 extra copies in the trade – a substantial number when one recalls that even a fairly successful novel may sell fewer than 5,000 copies in the home market nowadays. And surely that author's royalty earnings would be equally subject to tax as his PLR earnings?

More to the point, I feel, was the recent comment from another unnamed author:

> The secret of PLR is to write lots of short books. Write *War and Peace* and you're in dead trouble; it takes the average Englishman six months to read.

As might be expected, among the hundred most borrowed books in the results announced in 1988 were those by Jeffrey Archer, Catherine Cookson, Dick Francis, Wilbur Smith and Danielle Steel. Less expected was the fact that Anita Brookner's *Hotel du Lac*, still fresh from its success as the Booker Prize winner of 1984, also featured in the top one hundred.

On the latest figures, over 12,000 authors are better off – thanks mainly to the Brophy family – than they would otherwise have been, without doing any extra work. And that must be considered a bonus. But there was another – unexpected – bonus.

Before the advent of PLR, a novel, once bought or borrowed, was a private compact between two strangers – the writer and the reader. Now there was an extraordinary psychological advantage for the writer, apart from the welcome income. In 1987, Philip Roth was quoted as saying:

I have virtually no sense of my impact upon the general audience, nor do I really know who these people are . . . They're as remote as the onlookers are to a chess-player concentrating on the board and his opponent's game – I feel no more deprived or lonely than he does because people aren't lined up around the block to discuss his every move.

Not every novelist is as stoical as Mr Roth. On receiving their first PLR results, several authors wrote to the *Bookseller*, enthused with the thought that strangers were *reading* their books, that they did have an invisible audience that liked their work. Typical is an extract from a letter from Margaret Potter, the author of thirty-five novels under several pen-names: 'But now, suddenly, the reading world is flooded with light. There are people out there – borrowing the books I have written and going back for more'.

Four years later, in February 1988, her feelings were echoed by Simon Brett, ex-chairman of the Crime Writers Association.

. . . the most significant effect of PLR, from the author's point of view: the effect it has had on confidence . . . [Removing] the awful fear that has always been lurking at the back of their minds: *there is really no one out there. You are sending your books out into a total void.*

Apart from the encouragement provided by these unknown borrowers, a prolific novelist who has half a dozen or more fairly recent books readily available through public libraries could set up a kind of self-critical study by closely analysing individual results. If all else was equal, why did Novel C attract far fewer borrowings than either Novel A or B? How does the graph of sales compare over several years? If he has more than one publisher, are the offerings from Publisher X more in demand than those of Publisher Y – and, if so, is there a good reason apart from Y's apparent inability to make public library sales?

A playwright or screenplay writer or TV scriptwriter has the advantage – sometimes the disadvantage – of an immediate response from his audience. Perhaps now at last the novelist has achieved a similar status through PLR?

## The Arts Council

In the mid-1960s a certain outspoken England footballer wrote his memoirs with the help of a professional 'ghost'. One chapter was entitled: 'What the Average Football Club Director Knows about Football'. There followed a blank page. If the history of the Arts Council were to be written now, over four decades since its formation in 1946, the chapter entitled 'What the Arts Council has done for Novelists' would contain a few paragraphs at the most.

Many people might take the view that the novelist is not a fit subject for state patronage. State subsidies for an opera company, a national theatre, symphony orchestras and art galleries – in the days when no individual patron, however rich, can afford to look after them for an indefinite period – can be justified, for they usually have the upkeep of bricks and mortar to contend with, high travelling costs and the hiring of outstanding performers or, in the case of art galleries, the purchase of very expensive paintings. If a large part of their function is, as it should be, making 'culture' readily available to the general public, they can never be in the modern term cost-effective. Thus there is a strong and realistic argument that part of the taxes collected from the public by the state should be returned for the public's edification and enjoyment in the form of subsidies for those arts.

Novel-writing in its higher reaches may be an art form but it has always had a commercial bias as well. As long as he has the corner of a desk, some sheets of paper and a pen or typewriter, the novelist is in business. All he is spending is his own time. If he finds he cannot support himself from writing novels, he can take a job and write in his spare time. So, while it is proper for the state through the Arts Council to subsidise poetry magazines or literary periodicals or small avant-garde publishing houses, all of which do have external costs – and thus indirectly assist the new or unusual writer – direct grants to novelists could end up as a form of 'feather-bedding' that will not produce novels of higher quality.

There is also a case for supporting non-fiction writers, in particular, biographers and literary critics who may need to spend several years in research before writing their books. In any event, as the statistics later in the chapter show, no promising writer of fiction or non-fiction has run the risk of being overwhelmed – 'killed with kindness' – by the Arts Council.

In our interview in April 1988, I asked A. S. Byatt: 'Do you feel – in general, not personal terms – that the Arts Council since 1967 has helped to improve the lot of the "literary" novelist? Are you in broad agreement with state sponsorship for individual novelists?'

She replied, 'I don't feel the state has an absolute duty to support the arts. On a personal level, I am very grateful. The bursary they [the Arts Council] gave me made it possible for me, psychologically, to make the decision to stop university teaching. The recognition is in some ways as important as the money.

'I am never quite sure about giving large sums of money to very young people who are starting out – before they've managed to make themselves produce something. If you are going to give state sponsorship, it should either be to particular projects like magazines . . . because a literary magazine publishing short stories can almost never make ends meet in this country and most good writers want to write short stories . . . or to well-established writers who in fact just need to clear the space to write their book . . . It's terribly important for anyone to be paid for work they have done rather than for showing promise or for being somebody. That's why PLR is so important because the state provides library systems which use people's books; to get money that is related to the number of times which your book has been borrowed feels terribly good.'

Jennie Lee, as Minister for the Arts in 1966, produced a White Paper entitled *A Policy for the Arts*. That same year, the ubiquitous Lord Goodman, then chairman of the Arts Council, announced that, whereas in 1965 only £15,000 had been spent on literature as a whole, in 1966–67 the sum of £66,000 would be spent – £16,000 for poets and the rest for 'general literary purposes'. A Literature Panel was to be formed and grants to authors would be made on a pound for pound basis with their publishers' 'subsidy' (whatever that might be). PLR, he declared, was a good thing; that useful political standby – though he did not phrase it thus – a working party, would be set up to study PLR.

Sure enough, in December 1967 the Literature Panel came out with a list of bursaries, each of £1,200, for authors who included Lettice Cooper, Jean Rhys, Gilbert Phelps, Kathleen Nott, Christine Stead and Julia Strachey.

In 1968, the Council spent £5.75 million on the arts – £61,500 (1.07 per cent) for 'literature'. Things had improved somewhat by 1970, when the total grant was £8.2 million of which £116,333 went to literature – an increase of all of 0.35 per cent. There were fifty grants made to authors of sums ranging from £400 to £1,000, a total expenditure of £40,000.

In July 1975, Peter Owen in a letter to the *Guardian* proposed that the Arts Council should subsidise small publishers. He cited his production costs in 1971 and 1975 of two different titles, each of 160 pages and a first printing of 2,000 copies. In the earlier year, his production costs had been £580 and he had been able to publish the book at £2. Four years later, even though he had been able to share some production costs with an American publisher, they had amounted to £1,420, two and a half times as much, and his published price had to be increased to £3.25. No immediate subsidy appears to have been forthcoming from the Arts Council but the Council of Europe later stumped up along the lines of his suggestion.

During the middle three years of the 1970 decade, when inflation was increasing at an annual rate of around 20 per cent compounded, government grants to the Arts Council kept pace as the following table shows:

| Year | Total Grant | Allocation to Literature | Grants to Authors |
|------|-------------|--------------------------|-------------------|
| 1973–74 | £17,542,000 | £146,278 | £41,500 |
| 1974–75 | £25,069,000 | £199,500 | £47,800 |
| 1975–76 | £29,089,000 | £255,286 | £35,600 |

In each year, the allocation to literature worked out at around 0.8 per cent of the total grant and the amounts handed on to individual authors varied from just over 28 per cent in 1973–74 to just under 14 per cent in 1975–76. In other words or figures, about one-thousandth part of the 1975–76 grant ended up in the hands of the lucky few authors whose applications had been accepted.

In February 1974 the Arts Council took a bold step. It initiated the New Fiction Society, which was to be a 'simultaneous' book club, administered by the National Book League. Promising new novels would be chosen; unlike commercial book clubs, the published price would not be discounted by 35 per cent but a Book Token of equivalent value would be made available for encashment at the local bookshop. Editions of between 500 and 2,000 copies were anticipated. In the year 1974–75 the Arts Council subsidised the scheme to the extent of £34,500 and in the following year by £26,000.

On the lines that 'a camel is a horse designed by a committee', the scheme was soon to become a failure. By January 1977, the New Fiction Society announced that in the previous two and a quarter years 13,000 volumes had been sold at a cost to the Arts Council of £60,500 – over £4.50 per volume. (The average price of a hardbound novel in the period July–December 1976 was £3.42.) It is not perhaps surprising that Mr Sebastian Faulks, who was then in charge of the NFS, should write in a *Bookseller* article in December 1978:

> The past few weeks have been the best in the New Fiction Society's history. In one peak spell of five days we sold 300 books.

'No comment' is the only possible comment.

The inevitable was not long delayed. In July 1981 the Literature Panel announced that the New Fiction Society had been receiving a grant of £35,000 a year and had achieved a membership of under 3,500, which worked out at over £10 per head per year. (At that rate, it would have been cheaper for the NFS to have handed out six or seven *free* copies of good novels in their paperback editions to the membership.) The panel announced that the Society would be closed down at the end of 1982.

In principle, the idea behind the New Fiction Society was both interesting and potentially useful to up-and-coming novelists. But like so much that is organised by bureaucratic committees, it was not handled to the best advantage. It would not have cost the Literature Panel much – in fact, probably far less than they did pay in salaries – to have acquired the services of an experienced retired publisher – someone like Sir Robert Lusty who had been largely instrumental in starting Hutchinson New Authors, or a retired book club 'expert' like J. H. ('Tony') Barrett – who could have brought years of expertise to running the society, or an Ian Parsons or a David Farrer, men of the knowledge and calibre to exploit the idea to its full extent.

In 1980, the Arts Council, always adept at spotting wild geese before they took to the wing and throwing wads of public money at them, decided to emulate Booker McConnell and Whitbread by making three awards, each of £7,500, to the best books in various categories published that year. The three judges were to receive £2,000 apiece for their pains, which brought the annual outlay to not far short of £30,000. In the first year, Hugh Thomas was awarded the non-fiction prize for his *Unfinished History of the World*, published by Hamish Hamilton – but he honourably refused to accept it on the grounds that his book was critical of state intervention in the arts. Booker and Whitbread, the latter of whom had for several years given three similar annual awards to a total value of £10,000, publicly voiced their displeasure over the competition from a state body; the Arts Council decided to drop its national book awards at the end of its 1981–82 schedules.

That was in March 1981. Some two months later, Charles Osborne, the director of the Literature Panel, made a controversial announcement. He expressed the view that the council should spend more on distribution and less on individual authors. 'Arts Council money,' he said, 'has been awarded to mediocre writers because of the shortage of writers of stature.' Instead of many small grants, he proposed that there should be five bursaries, each of £7,500, for authors of outstanding literary quality who had 'a proven record' of achievement. The overall budget for literature should be reduced from £930,000 to £852,000 but more resources should be given to small presses.

The Writers' Guild and the Society of Authors both demanded an early meeting with Mr Osborne; the Writers' Guild went further in calling for his immediate resignation. (It is hard to see how the meeting could have taken place if the 'target' had accepted the Guild's advice.) But once again the events reveal that the Literature Panel either lacked coherent aims for the expenditure of the public moneys entrusted to it or had failed to reveal those aims to the people directly concerned. Was the comparatively modest annual budget to be spent in discovering and encouraging new (or newish) talent? Or was it to be an award in recognition of talent that had already proved itself? Or a mixture of both? Would it have been better spent if the whole budget had been shared among deserving publishers whose role had always been the discovery and support of gifted authors? No doubt all these – and other – questions were discussed each year by the part-time members of the panel but, as one of them sadly, even sourly, put it around that time, the members might propose in their infrequent meetings but it was the director and his staff who did the disposing in their absence.

On 19 September 1981, the novelist and critic Margaret Forster wrote an article in the *Bookseller* on why she had just resigned from the Literature Panel. One of the main points she made was that the panel met four times a year for a three-hour session. Most members acted for two years but some for as long as four years. Thus the membership of the panel was continually changing and continuity of purpose was virtually impossible:

> So much talk, so few actual decisions, so many things shoved off on to sub-committees, so little sense of general direction.

Her summary, almost a threnody, was:

> The Arts Council is *about* money, state money, and what should be done about the distribution of it. Money is what causes the trouble, the resentment, the suspicion. The Literature Panel has, at ground level, lost control of its purse. The great sums spent, for example, on the New Fiction Society are in my opinion not nearly as important as the 'trivial' little grants once decided so earnestly and anxiously by a sub-committee.

The very next week, the Arts Council budget for 1982 was publicly announced. The total was £71.7 million of which the grant to literature was to be £680,421 – under 1 per cent. (Interestingly, the Council's employees were to receive £1.85 million in salaries and pension schemes.)

The grant to literature, slightly more than one-third of the wages and pensions bill, was to be allocated as follows:

(a)  grants to publishers – £48,000 (of which the Calder Educational Trust would get £20,000 and thirteen other publishers would share the rest);
(b)  eleven 'creative fellowships' – £70,000;
(c)  awards and supplements to writers' and translators' prizes – £84,000;
(d)  to various establishments – £210,000 (including £50,000 to the NBL and £70,000 to the Poetry Society);
(e)  to literary magazines et cetera – £164,000 (including £37,000 to *London Magazine* and £20,000 to *Bananas*, with a further £50,000 to five 'little presses').

In subsequent years, the shift of emphasis from individual authors to publishers and literary periodicals appears to have been maintained. Previously, it could well have been argued that, whatever the panel's plans or lack of plans, an annual budget of around £50,000 was neither here nor there when it came to implementing them. To give thirty or so authors £1,000–£1,200 apiece would be a pleasant bonus for those who did not need it and perhaps three months' grace for those who did. But even if Dashiell Hammett wrote the last third of *The Glass Key* in one thirty-hour stretch, there are few post-war novelists who can write a tolerable novel in three months. So, *pace* the Writers' Guild and the Society of Authors, Mr Osborne's remarks in 1981 did face reality.

The following year, the Council cast about for new ways of spending its budget. Although Marghanita Laski, then the chairman of the Literature Panel, expressed real doubts, the Council arranged for Peter Mann of Sheffield University to investigate a plan whereby public libraries might be given additional funds for ordering extra copies of 'literary' novels. His report must have been sufficiently damning; the idea was not followed up. Alas: some innocent fun might have resulted when it came to choosing the titles that qualified and deciding what would eventually happen to those copies – possibly the majority – that remained inviolate on the public library shelves.

In May 1982, the Literature Panel came up with a more practical idea. It was to back Secker & Warburg against loss in their reissues of minor classics of the twentieth century. (The first two titles were *The Revenge for Love* by Wyndham Lewis – first published by Cassell in 1937 – and *Siren Land* by Norman Douglas – first published by Dent in 1911.) However, in the event of success for the series, the Arts Council would claim half of any profits that accrued. The step accorded with Charles Osborne's already declared policy of diverting the panel's budget towards publishers and, for once, showed a businesslike approach in requesting a share of profits.

By April 1984, the philosophy, as expressed in the Arts Council's *The Glory of the Garden*, took yet more account of market forces. Apart from proposing to cut the National Book League's grant by 25 per cent and wiping out entirely the annual grant to the English Centre of International PEN, the Literature Department's 1984–85 grant of £898,500 was to be cut precisely in half for 1985–86. This was on the grounds that a subsidy for literature, except poetry, has a very marginal impact on the production and availability of good books because they are sustained:

by a large and profitable commercial publishing industry . . . a basic ingredient in the school curriculum . . . [and] available to the public through the public library system.

The following week, in an article published by the *Bookseller*, Mr Osborne wrote:

My own view, formed as the result of reading the report we commissioned some years ago on the efficacy of grants, is that, although we undoubtedly made it a little easier for a few writers to live while they were writing, we had no discernible effect on the work written. No books, good, bad or indifferent, were written with the aid of Arts Council grants which would not have been written without them.

He expressed the same belief in stronger terms in his book of memoirs, *Giving It Away*, published by Secker & Warburg in October 1986:

Spending hundreds of thousands of pounds on encouraging medi-ocrities to think of themselves as 'full-time' writers was both pointless and cruel. Also, it did absolutely nothing for the con-dition of literature in Great Britain.

Whether Mr Osborne had 'bitten the other generals' before he left his post at the Council is unknown. But it may be significant that the Arts Council's allocation for literature in the 1987–88 budget was £467,000, which worked out at 0.3 per cent of the government's total grant-in-aid to the Council. Or roughly the sum a conglomerate would pay in advances for two or three books from a rising novelist. Perhaps the lunatics have all escaped from the Council asylum and found places for themselves in general commercial publishing?

*Prizes and Awards*

*The Writers' and Artists' Yearbook* lists a total of 116 prizes and awards, of which seventy-five are nominated for children's writers or poets or overseas writers or for non-fiction. Of the remaining forty-one open to novelists, the most important are as follows:

266

The Booker Prize, the Whitbread Literary Awards, the W. H. Smith Annual Literary Award, the James Tait Black Memorial Prize, the Boardman-Tasker Award, the Geoffrey Faber Memorial Prize, the *Guardian* Fiction Prize, the Hawthornden Prize, the Somerset Maugham Award, the Nobel Prize, the John Llewellyn Rhys Memorial Prize, the Sinclair Prize for Fiction, the *Sunday Express* Prize, the Betty Trask Awards and the *Yorkshire Post* Book of the Year.

On the grounds that no sensible novelist sits down in advance and deliberately aims his next book to win one or other of these prizes, it can be said that they constitute a form of *post hoc* recognition. But any novelist fortunate enough to win one of the more publicised awards or prizes – especially the Nobel or the Booker – will find his future career comfortably enhanced.

The James Tait Black Memorial Prize is the oldest of the existing prizes for full-length fiction, having been started in 1918 in memory of a partner in the publishing house of A. & C. Black. It was followed the next year by the Hawthornden Prize, founded by Miss Alice Warrender and now administered by the Society of Authors. The remaining prizes have been post-war creations, the earliest of them, but no longer existing, being the Atlantic Awards. In 1946 the Rockefeller Foundation put up the sum of $50,000 as grants for promising novelists. Six hundred applications were received and forty-seven awards were made up to June 1949 when the grants ran out. Few of the original award winners established themselves as novelists, although J. F. Burke, who won an Atlantic Award for his novel *Swift Summer*, became a successful professional science-fiction and thriller writer.

It was not until 1968 that a large commercial corporation, hitherto unconnected with the arts, stepped in with a substantial prize for fiction. This was Booker McConnell, until then known largely as a major producer of cane sugar, molasses and rum in the West Indies. Some five years earlier, the company had first turned its attention to the world of writing by setting up an ingenious tax avoidance scheme for authors.* But the Revenue had quickly plugged the tax loophole and it was an act of genuine patronage, although not unmindful of the useful publicity that might accrue, that led Booker to bless the new scheme. The real

* See 'The Inland Revenue and its Effect', pages 283–4.

credit for instituting the prize and loyally sustaining it during the difficult early years must go to certain Booker main board directors – David Powell, chairman, Roy Rock, vice-chairman, and especially Charles Tyrrell, who was also in charge of the tax scheme – ably aided by a Booker executive, John Murphy, and Lord Hardinge of Penshurst, then the editor of the 'Crime Club' department at Collins.

The original idea was to call it the Charles Dickens Prize but after Lord Hardinge in particular had pointed out that (a) the award had nothing to do with Dickens and (b) that it would be a quixotic gesture to put up a large sum of money and forego the publicity of associating one's name with the deed, the board of directors forsook their modest approach. Hardinge had been responsible for much of the early research and had closely studied the details of the Prix Goncourt.

Announced early in October 1968, the Booker Prize for Fiction, a cheque for £5,000, was to be awarded to what the panel of judges considered the best novel published in 1969. The first panel was to be W. L. Webb, literary editor of the *Guardian*, Dame Rebecca West, Professor Frank Kermode, David Farrer, editorial director of Secker & Warburg, and Stephen Spender – a fit selection of the 'great and the good'. Moreover, Booker's guaranteed the prize for a period of five years.

The first winner in 1969 – in those early days selected and announced in the spring – was P. H. Newby for his novel, *Something To Answer For*, published by Faber. The following year, again announced in April, Bernice Rubens won with *The Elected Member* (Eyre & Spottiswoode). On that occasion, Jennie Lee, Minister for the Arts, presented the trophy and the £5,000 cheque. For the third year, another distinguished panel of judges – Saul Bellow, John Fowles, Lady Antonia Fraser, John Gross and Malcolm Muggeridge (later replaced by Philip Toynbee) – chose V. S. Naipaul as the winner with *In a Free State*.

If prizes and awards were items that a writer could consciously strive for, one could almost accuse Mr Naipaul of being a 'pot-hunter'. His tally is remarkable: the John Llewellyn Rhys Memorial Prize (1957), the Somerset Maugham Award (1961), the Hawthornden Prize (1963), the Phoenix Trust Grant (1964), the W. H. Smith Annual Literary Award of £1,000 (1964), culminating in the Booker Prize (1971). When one considers that his (late) brother

Shiva, also in 1971, won both the John Llewellyn Rhys Memorial Prize and the Jock Campbell/*New Statesman* Prize and the Whitbread Literary Award in 1973, one's admiration for the family's prize-winning abilities overflows.

Basically, literary critics tend to select literary novels. The generous Booker Prize had certainly benefited the individual winners in the early years but had not brought Booker itself the kind or range of publicity it could have reasonably hoped for. The winning novels had increased their sales, but on the whole to a fairly modest degree. They were mainly not the stuff of bestsellers. Moreover, the prize initially attracted fewer candidates because of its announcement date in April each year; many publishers held off their big novels for publication in the run-up to Christmas, the months of September and October. Despite a change in 1971 to an autumn prize-giving, by November 1974 Booker McConnell was expressing its doubts in public over whether to continue to offer the prize after the guaranteed period. Three years later, Michael Caine, the chairman, when Paul Scott's *Staying On* (Heinemann) was the winner, said somewhat wistfully that Booker 'would like to see a winner that would command a more universal acceptance than that of the literary world alone'. (Paul Scott was too ill to accept the prize in person and died a few months later – on 1 March 1978 – at the age of fifty-seven.)

That autumn, with the award money doubled at £10,000, Iris Murdoch, already a highly popular novelist, was the winner and the prize gained greater publicity thereby.

For the next year, further changes were made to the format. The usual short list of up to six titles* continued to be announced a few weeks before the award ceremony, thus whetting potential readers' interest, but the winner was no longer to be chosen when the rest of the short list was announced. Inevitably, the name of the winner and the title of the winning novel would leak out – and the publicity impact lost. Henceforward, the winner was to be chosen from the short list on the day of the prize-giving and the details kept secret until the announcement itself. Previously, the directors of Booker McConnell had invited the shortlisted novelists, their families, their publishers (but *not* their agents) and the principal literary editors to dinner in the ballroom at Claridge's but now the dinner was arranged for the

---

* The short list was not always uniform. In 1975, there had been a two-horse race (Ruth Prawer Jabhvala's *Heat and Dust* and Thomas Keneally's *Gossip from the Forest*). But objections were raised, as they were in 1980 and 1981 when there were seven titles on the short list.

Stationers' Hall in the presence of BBC Television cameras. That in turn led to radio broadcasts and press interviews for the winner.

The effect on book sales, with the increase in publicity for Booker's, was remarkable. In 1980, Faber's first printing of *Rites of Passage* by William Golding had been 20,000 copies. Within three months of its winning the Booker Prize, the sales had virtually doubled to 38,000 copies. The following year, Jonathan Cape printed 3,000 copies of Salman Rushdie's *Midnight's Children* and had sold 2,000 when the award was made. By January 1982, sales had increased to 19,000. Perhaps the most outstanding recent example is Kingsley Amis's *The Old Devils*, the 1986 winner, where Hutchinson's first printing was 15,000 copies but the eventual hardcover sales exceeded 70,000. Two years previously, the value of the award had been raised yet again – this time to £15,000.

By now the Booker format had been firmly established. It is administered by the National Book League, now Book Trust, and is open to novels written in English by citizens of the British Commonwealth, the Republic of Ireland, Pakistan, Bangladesh and South Africa, and published for the first time in the UK by a British publisher. Novels to be published only between 1 January and 30 November in the respective year can be candidates and each publisher is limited to submitting a maximum of four* 'full-length' novels from his list, although the judges have the discretion of calling forward further novels which they may consider worthy of consideration. Only proofs or finished copies, not typescripts, are eligible.

Professor John Carey, the chairman of the 1982 Booker panel of judges, said in his speech announcing the winner,

> Publicity breaks down the barrier between ordinary readers and contemporary writers that half a century of modernism has built up.

A gloomier view was expressed three years later by Bill Buford, the editor of *Granta*, with

> The Booker is an uneasy marriage of literature and hype. When hype serves literature, that is fine; it is much less satisfactory when literature is serving hype.

* As a result of a meeting held in November 1987 between Michael Caine, chairman of Booker, Martyn Goff of Book Trust and six leading fiction publishers, the regulations were slightly altered. Publishers would henceforth be limited to three submissions plus any eligible novel from a past winner. The judges could call forward a minimum of five and a maximum of fifteen additional titles from publishers' supplementary lists.

No one is entitled to decry Booker McConnell's feelings of triumph in providing the most publicised and most discussed literary prize after many years of patient subsidy and, initially, little to show for it. And it would be unthinkable that Booker would directly or indirectly attempt to influence the choice of the judges, once selected. But five individuals are very unlikely to make one unanimous choice: any award, chosen by a panel, is bound to be a compromise. This may well explain why in 1983 the choice fell on a 'difficult' novel – *The Life and Times of Michael K* by J. M. Coetzee – which evoked the following comment from W. H. Smith, which had sold fewer copies of Mr Coetzee's novel than of the previous three winners: 'If there is a succession of unpopular winners, the impact of the prize will diminish'. In 1984 the judges chose a 'mainline' novel in *Hotel du Lac* by Anita Brookner. Again, the 1985 choice was a 'difficult' novel – *The Bone People* by Keri Hulme, to be succeeded the next year by a 'mainline' book in Amis's *The Old Devils*. Both the Brookner and the Amis novels were very substantial sellers in hardcover and paperback – highly popular choices in the trade.

A plausible complaint over the selection process for judges was voiced by Howard Jacobson in an *Observer* article shortly before the 1987 Booker announcement was made. He wrote:

An aspirant to the prize in 1971 would have had the satisfaction, win or lose, of knowing that he'd been read by John Gross, Saul Bellow, John Fowles, Lady Antonia Fraser and Philip Toynbee. In 1973 by Karl Miller, Edna O'Brien and Mary McCarthy. In 1975 by Angus Wilson, Peter Ackroyd, Susan Hill and Roy Fuller. One way or another and allowing for the vicissitudes of reputation, a candidate in these years must have felt that he was largely in the hands of those who had at least tried to close on the imp of imagination themselves. But thereafter the grounds on which judges were selected seemed to shift; the idea of including a common reader or two – though not so common as to be unknown – took someone's fancy, with the consequence that in 1976 Lady Wilson showed up on the panel, and in 1979 Benny Green.

And so it has gone. The election of a personality with a more or less passing interest in the arts is now expected . . . A prize will only ever be as good as those who judge it.

The 'great and the good' in literary/critical terms are bound to be few in number: the task of reducing a hundred and more full-length novels to a short list of six and then to a single winner is an arduous and time-consuming matter. Judges who would qualify under the Jacobson 'rules' would be liable to have books of their own to write. Nor would it be a good thing to have the same familiar faces cropping up year after year.

Nevertheless, when one also takes into account some of the people who have been nominated as Booker or Whitbread judges – Verity Lambert, Ken Livingstone, Joanna Lumley, Richard Branson and Frank Delaney – it is clear that few of them would provide a likely target for Hermann Goering's Luger.

The other lucrative prizes have attracted nothing like the publicity and sales-appeal of the Booker nor, to be fair to their sponsors, have they attempted to rival it. The Whitbread Literary Awards, first announced in 1971, go each year to one title in each of the following categories: a novel, a first novel, a children's novel, a biographical or autobiographical work and a volume of poetry. The winner in each category receives a nomination award of £1,000 and one of them is selected as the Whitbread Book of the Year, receiving a further prize of £20,000. Whitbread's give a pre-announcement lunch at their Chiswell Street brewery and the results are widely reported in the press but, until recently, no great effort seems to have been made to attract TV and radio coverage. For the 1985 results, Channel 4 arranged to transmit three programmes; BBC Radio 4 and *Kaleidoscope* also gave useful radio publicity. The 1987 overall winner, Christy Nolan's brave and artistic autobiography, received – caused – great media attention, culminating in a typically inept performance by Terry Wogan.

The Betty Trask Awards are confined to novelists under the age of thirty-five who have written a first novel, published or unpublished, of a romantic or traditional nature. One would have thought that the judges would be overwhelmed with a flood of – in Earl Camden's words – 'perishable trash' but over the few years these awards have been in existence and in spite of the prize money of not less than £17,500, there has been a paucity of entrants.

The W. H. Smith Annual Literary Award of £4,000 goes to 'the most outstanding contribution to literature', fiction or non-fiction, written by a Commonwealth (including UK) author and published in Britain within twelve months of the date of the award. W. H. Smith does not appear to seek wide publicity either for itself or for the award winner. It is in a delicate position as by far the largest seller of books in Great Britain and until recently a half-owner of the largest book club organisation; it may therefore not wish to attract additional publicity for what is largely an altruistic contribution to authorship.

Towards the end of August 1987, the most lucrative book prize of all was announced – the NCR Award, amounting to £25,000. The judges were to be Jeremy Isaacs (chairman), Baroness Blackstone, Professor Norman Stone and Victoria Wood. And just before the end of the year, the *Sunday Express* announced *its* prize for fiction – to the value of £20,000 – to be awarded in January 1988. As a circulation-builder, the newspaper decided to print in its columns a voucher for £1, which its readers could claim off the published price of the winning novel. That turned out to be *The Colour of Blood* by Brian Moore, which had recently been a much fancied short-list candidate for the Booker Prize.

At the beginning of June 1988, the first NCR Book Award for non-fiction went to *Nairn in Darkness* by David Thomson, who sadly had died some three months earlier. There was considerable publicity from the Radio 4 *Today* programme, BBC 2's *Cover to Cover*, Radio London and LBC. The author's widow made a moving televised speech at the prize-giving ceremony. Hutchinson, the publishers, had sold rather more than 4,000 copies prior to the award. On the day after the announcement, they received over 1,000 new orders and at once put a 3,500-copy reprint in hand. Small stuff, perhaps, if compared to the onrush of orders after a Booker Prize ceremony but at the least a useful start. Five other authors who had been shortlisted – Claire Tomalin, Max Hastings, Kathleen Tynan, Michael Ignatieff and Nirad C. Chaudhuri – each received a NCR consolation prize of £1,000, a feature the Booker Prize committee could usefully follow. It had begun to look as though the greatest distinction a new book could achieve would be not to win a literary award in its year of publication.

The annual Nobel Prize for Literature, worth well over £100,000, attracts international publicity – more often than not – for its strange selections. However, since the war, winners writing in English have included T. S. Eliot, William Faulkner, Bertrand Russell, Sir Winston Churchill, Ernest Hemingway (a controversial choice at the time), John Steinbeck, Patrick White, Saul Bellow and Sir William Golding. It is a continuing mystery to many that Graham Greene has never become a Nobel Laureate.

Prizes are for the lucky and talented few whose subsequent careers may well be enhanced. They have virtually no influence on any serious novelist as he sits down to start a new book, except the vague and pious hope that if he does his best and his publishers are amenable, he may be shortlisted for the Booker – and then who knows?

## The Society of Authors and the Writers' Guild

In *Fiction and the Fiction Industry*, J. A. Sutherland made this perceptive statement:

> Writers are actually in the position of artisans rather than a labour force. They sell a finished product which they make in their own time and on their own premises. This makes it peculiarly hard for them to apply direct pressures or to combine; steelworkers can do this, novelists frequently can't since the conditions of their work disperse them into single, detached units.

Earlier in the same section he had spoken of:

> . . . the formation of the commando WAG (Writers' Action Group). This group was the first move towards a trade union for writers, in contrast to the professional association represented by the Society of Authors. For a long time authors had felt themselves in need of unionisation.

But authors are not only individuals by trade, they are almost always individuals by the very nature of what they do. It is a cliché – but none the less true – that writing is the lonely art. There have been several accomplished cases of dual, even triple, writing teams, in post-war years: Lapierre and Collins, the Hardwickes, Jay and Lynn, Norden and Muir (in radio and television), but the great majority of writers work alone. They are thus peculiarly susceptible to the stresses of isolation and they are usually – indeed they often have to be – self-centred. The more successful amongst them almost invariably use an effective agent who can get publishers to agree to terms considerably above the average. Comparatively few of the really successful writers are active in furthering the cause of their less favoured brethren, although they may show 'solidarity' by joining the Writers' Guild or the Society of Authors. I have previously quoted Anthony Burgess's wise remark, 'No author can ruin a publisher by withdrawing his labour'. Thus the guild and the society have often found themselves fighting the good fight on behalf of the weak, who most need concessions from publishers but who have the least 'clout' with which to reinforce their claims. At any rate, the situation has changed radically from the days of 1911 when D. H. Lawrence, in a letter to Edward Garnett about approaching Duckworth, wrote:

> Do not, I beg you, ask for an advance in royalties. Do not present me as a beggar. Do not tell him I am poor . . . I do not want an advance – let me be presented to Duckworth as a respectable person.

The functions of the Society of Authors, which celebrated its centenary in 1984, and of the Writers' Guild, which was formed in 1959 as the Screenwriters' Guild but in 1974 widened its membership to include book authors and stage dramatists, are well described in the *Writers' and Artists' Yearbook*. The society is an independent trade union and the guild a trade union affiliated to the TUC, although non-political by nature. The former charges an annual subscription of £50 and the latter 1 per cent of the income an author makes in those areas where the guild operates – with a minimum of £30 and a maximum of around £500. Speaking personally, the society appears to me more of an 'establishment' body and the guild more abrasive in its approach but each with its permanent staff and access to professional legal and other advice will help individual authors and fight battles of principle. For example, the society backed Andrew Boyle when the Inland Revenue tried to tax the Whitbread Award he had won in 1974 and it also backed (together with the Writers' Guild) several of its members who took action against the BBC for copyright infringement; the guild fought a long and eventually successful battle to implement PLR and joined forces with the society to set up a Minimum Terms Agreement for authors.

Neither body has been helped overmuch in its quest to improve the lot of authors by the Publishers Association, which until recent years took a generally arrogant view towards the one essential link in the chain from manuscript to reader. From 1954 until 1965, the PA had fought a stout rearguard action to ensure that when paperback rights were sold to an outside publisher, the original hardcover publisher would always retain 50 per cent of the proceeds. This was on the rather specious argument that publishers *needed* half the paperback earnings to keep themselves afloat and should also be acknowledged as the originators of the rights concerned.* Even in the latter year,

* See above, page 119.

275

the PA only conceded that the split should become 60/40 in favour of the author *when* the total sales had reached 100,000 copies. Ten years later, when most large houses and groups had either acquired their own paperback house or had financial links with one, the situation had changed completely but for a long period the Canutes of the PA had tried to stem the incoming tide – and often got their feet wet.

Standard publishing contracts contain a clause that the author or his agent may demand the reversion of the rights licensed to the original publisher if the work is out of print and the publisher fails to reprint it within a limited period, usually six or nine months from the time of the request. The clause goes on to state that the work shall not be considered out of print if there shall be in existence a valid sub-licence with another publisher, nearly always a paperback house, to publish the work within a set time. In the latter part of 1963, individual agents and the Society of Authors suggested to the PA that it would be helpful to their clients/members if publishers' royalty statements were to include a notice when the work was out of print in all editions. (In those days, hardcover publishers did not necessarily send agents a copy of any sub-licence that had been granted to a paperback house.) The following Olympian statement emanated from the PA:

> The council of the Publishers Association feels strongly that clauses of this sort should be rejected because it is no part of the publisher's function to provide authors' agents with information which they should themselves be able to infer from royalty statements. The publisher's responsibility under a normal royalty agreement is to produce and publish a book and to account to the author or his agent for sales.

The statement went on to say that publishers were not liable 'to discover and declare whether any such sub-leased editions are in print'. It is the same houses, if not the same stiff-necked members of the PA Council, who nowadays fawn on major authors and are quite prepared to spend £5,000 and more in making a video to win those authors away from their present situations.

The Society of Authors has for many years published a quarterly journal entitled – not unnaturally – the *Author*. Each issue contains a number of informed articles on relevant topics and letters (often of complaint) from its members. For example, in the autumn issue of 1951 there was a discussion over whether, in a period of what were then considered to be rising prices, lowering the author's royalty by $2\frac{1}{2}$ per cent might have a significant effect on the published price. The answer was a brisk No. The effect on a hardcover book published at 10s 6d ($52\frac{1}{2}$p) would be all of 3d ($1\frac{1}{4}$p) – and twice that amount on a book published at 1 guinea (£1.05). Two years later, another issue pointed out that on a sale of 5,000 copies, of which 3,790 were sold in the home market and 1,160 were exported (the remaining fifty copies being presumably for review), the author earned a grand total in royalties of £330. (At that time the average secretary earned perhaps £400 to £500 per year.)

Periodically, the society canvassed its members with questionnaires dealing with their earning capacities and published the results in surveys put together by Richard Findlater. Those surveys of 1955 and 1963 revealed that 40 per cent of the members who replied were earning less than £250 a year from their writings. In 1962 the society proclaimed that the traditional 50/50 split on paperback rights between publisher and author was 'a dead duck', which probably had some effect on the walls of Jericho (or Bedford Square).

The Publishers Association and the society did, however, form a brief alliance in May 1972 when they issued a joint statement recommending 'blanket licensing' for PLR.* Brigid Brophy soon published a tart letter in the *Guardian*, pointing out the weaknesses in the proposition and suggesting that the Society of Authors should 'renew the quest for a PLR scheme from scratch'.

The society has played a useful part over the years in publishing letters of complaint from its writer-members in the *Author*. Many of these complaints featured late payments from publishers – occasionally, no payments at all – or cases of remaindering without first notifying the author or the rejection after delivery of a book that had been commissioned under contract: all examples of high-handed treatment that the normally solicitous publisher would have been at pains to avoid. The unwelcome publicity in a widely read journal no doubt had a salutary effect on the guilty parties.

After 1974, when book-writers featured among its members, the Writers' Guild went about things differently. Over a period, it put together a Minimum Terms Agreement (MTA), which spelled out 'the bottom line' of what any author could reasonably expect his publisher to provide when contracting for a particular book. Many of

* See above, page 253.

the clauses provided no more than any honest publisher should and would put forward spontaneously but two provisions in particular ran into opposition, both with the PA and with individual publishers. They were that the starting royalty must never be less than 10 per cent of the published price and that the licence conferred on the publisher should be terminable after a set period, preferably ten years.

The problem about any 'blanket' clause in a publishing contract is that there will always be exceptions. For example I have quoted Christopher Sinclair-Stevenson of Hamish Hamilton, the first publisher to sign the MTA in 1978, as saying that, when confronted with a novel whose first printing could only be 1,500 copies, he would either have to forego publishing it or break the MTA by offering the author a starting $7\frac{1}{2}$ per cent royalty.

The publishers' official position, when confronted with the demand for a limited licence period, is that all proper contracts contain a clause in which the rights conferred on the publisher shall revert to the author if the publisher allows the work to go out of print *in all editions* (my italics) and fails to reprint within so many months of a demand from the author or his agent. Of course, under these conditions, the work cannot be considered out of print if there is a valid paperback contract in existence. Thus, the original hardcover publisher may have let his edition of a successful novel go out of print and yet sit back and continue to draw 30 per cent or 40 per cent or even 50 per cent of the paperback royalties *ad infinitum*. And if some new development should turn up, such as the 'Pickles' omnibus series, published jointly by Heinemann and Octopus, the original publisher will happily take 50 per cent of those proceeds as well. This happened to *The Spy Who Came in from the Cold* by John le Carré, first published by Victor Gollancz in 1963. Apart from a limited edition published to mark the Gollancz fiftieth anniversary, the book has been out of print in hard covers for many years but has sold continuously and well in the Pan paperback edition for most of that time.

It can be argued – and the hardcover publisher would be the first to do so – that his perception in 'discovering' a then unknown writer should be rewarded. But how long, O Lord, how long? To earn a comfortable annual income for complete inactivity over twenty years seems an excessive reward for that early discovery of talent, which was highly recompensed at the time. It is small wonder that the Writers' Guild has aimed at a maximum ten-year licence in its Minimum Terms Agreement.

In July 1980 the guild publicly blacklisted W. H. Allen for its refusal to sign the MTA. The issue of the *Bookseller* (26 July) reporting that fact also carried an article by Keith Colquhoun, the novelist, which included the following passage:

> I have a feeling that, for very sensible reasons, publishers do not much care for authors, who are the uncertain factors in an otherwise smoothly-run business, and very often are not even good company, living in their unhealthy world of solitude and introspection.

In May 1981, although not as a result of Mr Colquhoun's sarcastic remarks, W. H. Allen came to heel and signed the MTA. Hamish Hamilton had already done so – but a haul of two out of several hundred was an insignificant catch.

In June 1982, Richard Findlater commented in the *Author* on his latest authors' survey, which, he said, 'reveals that the number of full-time authors has fallen by a half in the last decade to less than a sixth of those who responded'. He pointed out that 118 novelists averaged earnings of £1,600 a year each. It was only a few months earlier that union compositors at printing works were revealed to be now the second highest paid manual workers (after coalface workers), with average gross weekly earnings of £164.20.

Earlier in the year, the Society of Authors in conjunction with the Association of Authors' Agents (AAA) had pressed the Publishers Association to institute a Code of Practice when dealing with authors. The PA procrastinated and so elicited a tart comment from the society:

> When publishers stand to gain anything, few organisations are as united as the Publishers Association. But if concessions might have to be made, the coherence of the PA melts conveniently away.

But the society and the AAA pressed hard and towards the end of the year the PA had managed to convince most of its members that an official Code of Practice should be set up. Even so, after a year of discussion and eight months of drafting, the code was, in the words of the society, 'well below what we had hoped for'. For example, the society had pressed strongly for universal half-yearly royalty statements – on the not unreasonable grounds that accounting once a year, when inflation and loss of interest were calculated, meant that the author could lose about 15 per cent of his earnings through the delay. The point was not accepted by the PA and the society stated that it would continue to press for the MTA.

The final clause in the code (no. 20) contains the following pious credo:

> Above all, the publisher must recognise the importance of co-operation with the author in an enterprise in which both are essential. This relationship can be fulfilled only in an atmosphere of confidence, in which the authors get the fullest possible credit for their work and achievements.

Many writers might have grounds for believing that the clause merely accentuated the obvious but it was in fact a large step forward from that comment of Walter Harrap's: 'Ours would be a wonderful trade if it weren't for authors'.

In the past five years, the Society of Authors has started a new trust, the Authors' Foundation, having raised some £60,000 with a further £40,000 pledged through covenants. The foundation's aim is to help those authors who have already had a book contracted and who have been paid an advance on it but who would benefit from extra funding. Thus, its main effect would be focused on biographers and historians, although a novelist whose book incurred considerable expenses through research or travel might conceivably benefit.

In February 1986, both the society and the guild advised their members to strike out option clauses in contracts, unless the publisher were prepared to negotiate and pay an additional sum for including the option. Six months later, both bodies threatened to boycott Century Hutchinson for its refusal to sign the MTA. (In 1987 Century Hutchinson did eventually sign amid sighs of relief and smiling faces all round.) Bloomsbury, soon after its inception, went willingly to the signing table, as did Headline, although the latter refused to accept a definitive licence period, which it felt was best left to negotiation on individual contracts.

The week after Headline's signing, Gordon Graham, then president of the Publishers Association, wrote a letter to the *Bookseller* saying that the PA could not negotiate an *en bloc* deal over MTA, as it was 'against collective negotiation on an issue over which they [member companies] compete with one another.' Nevertheless, the society and the guild had picked off eight quite significant houses, although there has been no great succeeding domino effect.

Successful authors, almost all of whom have keen agents to negotiate their terms, really have no need of a union or similar body to fight their battles for them. The less successful writers who do need that support cannot bring individual pressure to bear – and their supporting body dare not contemplate collective action. (One cannot envisage the Society of Authors or the Writers' Guild blowing a whistle and shouting 'All out!' to their respective members.) So moral rather than financial pressure has to be the order of the day: within those narrow limits, it has to be said that both bodies have done rather well for their members in the past one and a half decades.

## The Inland Revenue and its Effect

For an author, dealing with the Inland Revenue is rather like playing tennis with an unscrupulous opponent who keeps moving the net closer to his own baseline, giving himself far more space for hitting winners on your side of the court and correspondingly less space for you to hit winners back.

It has to be said that the pressures of tax weighed far more heavily on writers – and indeed other self-employed people – in the thirty-five years following the Second World War than they have in more recent times. The maximum rate of tax on earned income is now 40 per cent; at one stage in the post-war years it was over 92 per cent. For example, in July 1952 H. E. Bates reported that he had had to sell thirty French Impressionist paintings from his collection to help pay his income tax. He wrote,

> If a writer makes £25,000 a year, he has difficulty in getting the income tax people to allow him even £2,000 of it.

The *Bookseller* followed up this plaintive cry by working out that a married author earning £25,000 a year, which in today's inflated currency would be worth over £250,000, would – excluding any duly incurred expenses he could charge against his income – receive £3,999 net. In other words, depending on those expenses, he would be handing up to 84 per cent of his earnings to the Revenue.

That same month, Sir Compton Mackenzie lost his appeal in the higher court against a ruling by Mr Justice Danckwerts. Sir Compton had sold the copyrights in twenty titles, all written between the years

1911 and 1930 while he had lived permanently outside the United Kingdom, to Macdonald for £10,000. He claimed that, as he had not been subject to UK tax at the time each of the books had been written, the sale of his copyrights should be exempted from tax. Mr Justice Danckwerts had ruled that it was the date of the sale, not the date of the writing, that mattered; only expenses, if properly incurred during the year of the actual sale, could be deducted from the payment received. This drew from the author the bitter remark:

> . . . it is a matter of principle for the future of authors who, in this age of mechanisation, are regarded as crops – spring wheat or potatoes – able to produce at the same time each year.

No wonder Eric Linklater added his cry of pain to the correspondence:

> Taxes are steadily ruining me. I am always writing novels. I have to in order to meet income tax demands. These come in quicker than I can make money to meet them.

In the month of August 1952, John Pudney wrote to the *Bookseller* with an ingenious plan to avoid tax when a lump sum payment was involved, such as a sale of film rights. The author, he wrote, should sell the copyright to his wife – or she to her husband – for £5. Tax would have to be paid on the transaction but it could hardly exceed £4. Then the new owner of the copyright sells it on to the film company for £50,000 – on which no tax would be payable, as it would be a capital transaction, twenty years and more before capital gains tax went on to the statute book.

One hardly imagines that the Inland Revenue would fall for that wheeze. But apparently it did fall for a not dissimilar transaction whereby Sir Winston Churchill made a dual sale after the war to *Time/Life*. He sold Henry Luce a chest containing his wartime decorations from grateful Allied governments for the sum of $600,000 and at the same time he sold the copyright in his (as yet unwritten) volumes of memoirs for some nominal figure. Very modest tax was payable on the latter but nothing on the former, since again it was a capital transaction. It was rumoured at the time that senior Labour figures wanted the matter raised in the House of Commons but Clement Attlee, then Prime Minister, quashed the idea, pointing out that, as the man who largely won the war, Churchill deserved anything he could get out of it.

In June 1957 the executors of the late Peter Cheyney's estate obtained a High Court judgment from Mr Justice Harman that royalties arising after the author's death were not subject to tax. In August that year, the Crown appealed against the judgment and in October the Court of Appeal reserved its judgment. Two weeks later, it dismissed the Crown's appeal but granted leave to appeal to the House of Lords, where again the case was dismissed. That appeared to be a fair and final verdict – but dead authors could not rest in peace for long. In the 1959 (Conservative) Budget the tax laws were altered to ensure that income arising for an author after his death was to be assessed for estate duties.

Again, in the early 1960s Booker McConnell invented an ingenious and at the time perfectly legal formula whereby a successful author formed a private company, if he did not already have one, to which his existing and future copyrights would be formally assigned. Booker McConnell then bought 51 per cent of that company, thus taking control of it. The lump sum they paid for the majority share was, in those pre-capital gains tax days, free of tax and the author had the right, if he wished, to buy back the majority shareholding for a considerably smaller sum after the lapse of several years.

The story has it that Ian Fleming, who needed to raise some capital, had approached the family merchant bank but had been turned down. He happened to mention the fact during a round of golf with Jock Campbell, the chairman of Booker, who at once offered to help. In March 1964, Ian Fleming sold the majority of shares in his private company, Glidrose Productions, to Booker but unfortunately died a few months later and so drew little benefit from the tax avoidance scheme. His estate in England was valued at £289,170 (equivalent to £1.56 million today) on which duty of £210,366 – about 73 per cent of the total – was paid.

Nevertheless, Booker continued to control Glidrose and in addition acquired several other leading authors on the same basis, including Agatha Christie, Gavin Lyall, John Braine, Harold Pinter, Francis Clifford and John and Penelope Mortimer. Several of them later took the opportunity to 'buy themselves out' and the 1984 list had been reduced to Robert Bolt, and the estates of Agatha Christie, Ian Fleming, Georgette Heyer and Dennis Wheatley. The turnover that year came to £1.2 million of which Agatha Christie's earnings amounted to close on

80 per cent, with Ian Fleming second. The Christie rights controlled by Booker included her film rights, whereas Fleming's film rights were excluded.

However, for more than the past twenty years, Booker has acted in the capacity of literary agent. The original scheme was blocked by the vigilant Revenue just a few years after its inception. As one of those closely involved with the details of the scheme has recently said:

> Mostly (but by no means exclusively) Booker's were offering present capital in exchange for future income, highly beneficial for everyone except the Revenue. So it was bound to be stopped – it seemed to me only a question of time before the chairmen of ICI and Shell started doing the same thing for each other, after which everyone else would have been at it.

As things then were, other companies, often without the stability and reputation of Booker McConnell, rocked the bandwagon with more speculative schemes of a fairly similar nature and were sufficiently blatant to attract the Inland Revenue's attention.

The early part of the post-war period can be summed up in Douglas Jay's arrogant dictum: 'The gentleman in Whitehall really does know better.' The then Labour government clearly had to subsidise the new welfare state by applying heavy taxes and there was a measure of justice in making those with reasonable earnings pay for those in want. But behind the donnish smugness of Douglas Jay there was also another Labour MP's vindictive cry of triumph – 'we are the masters now'. The brave new world of rationing, clothing and furniture coupons and shortages found little room and no sympathy for nonconformist individuals like writers.

Thus, in April 1951 the Tucker Committee recommended that authors should be entitled to spread their earnings from any one book over a five-year period, avoiding the incidence of a heavy tax rate in the year of publication when the earnings would be at their highest level. The Attlee government ignored the recommendation. It was left to R. A. Butler, the Chancellor in the incoming Conservative government, in his Budget speech of April 1953, to allow authors a two-year spread *after* publication. The following year, the Budget allowed the premiums for retirement pensions for the self-employed to be exempt from income tax and surtax, although relief was limited to premiums of not more than £500 or 10 per cent of earned income in any one year.

It was a useful step for the more successful author. But at the same time the Finance Bill made it obligatory for publishers at the end of each tax year to declare all payments made to individual authors in excess of £15. In June of the same year, the government increased the tax-free premiums for the self-employed from £500 to £750 with percentage increases for authors born before 1915.

In 1957 the Special Commissioners for Tax granted a further concession whereby an author living permanently outside the United Kingdom would be entitled to sell the copyright of a book for a lump sum which would be tax-free. It was a dubious benefit, which only assisted the author who could afford to live abroad indefinitely and who then had to gamble on obtaining the level of lump payment that would compensate him for losing the chance of selling further advantageous rights in his work, such as film or television or paperback rights.

The publishing world was rocked in 1963 when Wilfred Harvey, the chairman of Purnell, which owned Macdonald, Sampson Low and Juvenile Publications, had £59,193 of his annual expenses *disallowed* by the Inland Revenue out of a total claim of some £85,000. In present-day terms, the disallowed amount would be equivalent to £480,000. Part of the claim had been for a sizeable yacht kept permanently in the south of France where apparently major business deals took place from time to time. 'Lucky for some' must have been the muttered verdict of authors published by one of the Purnell companies.

To enter into a legal dispute with the Inland Revenue was – and indeed still is – a costly and chancy business, particularly at a time when surtax on top of the already high standard rates meant that the successful author was paying 90 per cent on the upper levels of his income. In 1960 Hammond Innes made an outright gift to his father (before publication) of the entire copyright in his forthcoming novel *The Doomed Oasis*. The Revenue reckoned that the market value was £15,425 and assessed Mr Innes for income tax on that amount. He fought the case and six years later, in December 1966, Mr Justice Goff in the High Court ruled that it was a proper gift and that no tax was due. Nevertheless, the victory was tempered by the fact that Hammond Innes must have spent several thousand pounds in legal fees and costs. The Commissioners of Revenue took the matter to the Court of Appeal, which dismissed their case – but the author was involved in further high expenses: once again, 'The law is open to all – like the Ritz Hotel'.

The situation in the mid-1960s was well described by Professor

Mervyn King, an authority on tax reform, in an article published
by the *Sunday Times* on 14 February 1988. In part, it said:

> In those days the top marginal rate of taxation was 91.25 per cent and
> in 1965–66 a 10 per cent surcharge took tax on some investment
> income to over 100 per cent. Yet despite these penal rates, the system
> yielded peanuts in revenues. People with low incomes were let off,
> while people with high incomes could get off paying such high rates.
>
> The income distribution, derived from tax returns, became sus-
> piciously equitable. Judges and senior civil servants were the only
> people earning large incomes. Everyone else found other ways, legal
> or not, of being rewarded.
>
> Far from making the pips squeak, penal rates made the perks leap.
>
> Meanwhile legitimate tax reliefs and allowances cut taxable in-
> comes to half the total of incomes declared to the Inland Revenue.
> Despite a standard rate of 41.25 per cent in the late 1960s, the
> income tax system actually only collected 14.6p in the pound.
>
> Income tax rates were twice as high as they needed to be, because
> politicians gave back in reliefs 50p in every pound which the tax
> nominally collected.
>
> The result then was a vicious circle. The higher tax rates rose,
> the more the tax base shrank and the less revenue those higher rates
> collected. So tax rates then had to go even higher.
>
> . . . High tax rates penalised people for doing useful things such
> as working, earning, saving and investing. Economic activity was
> seriously distorted. Time and effort spent trying to evade or avoid
> taxes, while immensely profitable for the individual (and his
> advisers), did nothing at all for society.

In July 1969 the Irish Finance Bill came up with an ingenious proposal. Artists and writers, irrespective of nationality but who were 'solely
resident' in the Irish Republic, would be totally exempted from paying
local income tax on their earnings from works that were recognised
as having cultural or artistic merit. British income tax regulations
stated that an individual would only be classified as living abroad if
he maintained no residence in the United Kingdom, spent the first full
year permanently out of the country and thereafter only returned for
a limited period each year, which gradually increased over a lengthy
period to a total of 180 days in any one tax year. All the same, once the
first year had passed, and with Dublin less than an hour's flight from

London, an English author could easily obtain the benefit of a tax-free existence in Eire with a lower cost of living and quick, if limited, access to his cultural centre.

Several well-known authors took advantage of the Irish concession, including Frederick Forsyth, Len Deighton and Alexander Fullerton. John Huston, the film director, also became an Irish resident in flamboyant style. Many other authors in the post-war years of high taxation have gone into exile in other places – Graham Greene in Antibes, Anthony Burgess in Monaco, Muriel Spark in Rome, George MacDonald Fraser in the Isle of Man, where Richard Adams subsequently went, Jack Higgins in Jersey, Nancy Mitford in Paris and Alistair MacLean in Switzerland, along with various American tax exiles like Irwin Shaw and Peter Viertel.

In *Fiction and the Fiction Industry*, J. A. Sutherland suggests that authors who are driven into tax exile and who realise that the American market is of paramount importance for their earnings, become more international in the settings of their novels; he instances Anthony Burgess and Muriel Spark. Those who have studied from inside the trade how and what novelists write will hardly accept so simplistic a theory. Air travel has made the world smaller; the author who is a 'quick study' and who wants to set part of his next novel in Malibu Beach, part at the Grand Canyon and Las Vegas, part in New York and part in Bali and Kathmandu, can buy a round-the-world air ticket for under £2,000 (claimable against earnings) and spend a few days in each place taking notes, living out the rest of his life in Ponders End.

Mr Sutherland is closer to the mark when he says, 'It may seem a crude observation, but where a novelist lives, or where he no longer lives, will have an effect on a product which is essentially inspirational in origins'. Later on, he quotes Brian Moore as saying, 'I have become a literary nomad.' In September 1975, Piers Paul Read in a letter to *The Times* on the subject of tax exiles mentioned the subtle but certain bond which should exist between a writer and his own people. Paris in the 1920s must have been very Heaven for the younger American expatriates, who had their own nationals for friends – including Hemingway, Scott Fitzgerald and Zelda, Henry Miller, Sylvia Beach, Nathalie Barney and Gertrude Stein – who were part of an artistic and cultural explosion of painters and sculptors and French poets and who were in the forefront of developing their own literature. But for a modern novelist to cut himself off from his roots and live permanently in a foreign country, there can be a depersonalising effect on what he writes and how he writes it.

The 1973 Budget declared that with effect from 1 April that year authors' royalty earnings arising in the United Kingdom would be subject to value-added tax. Rights licensed overseas would be zero-rated; agents would be required to charge VAT on their commission charges to individual authors. Throughout the period under review the VAT rating has remained at 15 per cent but the annual income (or quarterly earnings) at which level an author was obliged to register for VAT has gradually risen to its present level of £21,000 annually or £7,500 in any one quarter. This again has been a law that has benefited the (comparatively) rich and hit the poor. If a publisher's payment were, say, £1,000, in the case of a VAT-registered author the agent would submit an invoice for the sum due plus £150 for VAT. The author would receive the VAT quotient in full, which at the end of the quarter he would have to pass on to the Customs & Excise, plus £885 – the £1,000 minus the agent's 10 per cent commission of £100 *and* the 15 per cent VAT charge of £15 on that commission. But the author would be entitled to deduct that £15 charge from his eventual payment to Customs & Excise. The author whose earnings were too low to attract a VAT registration would also receive £885 from his agent on the same transaction – but would have no means of charging back the £15 item.

Early in 1978, the Inland Revenue decided to have a go against the winners of literary prizes by arguing that such awards fell into the category of writing income and should be taxed at the then standard rate of 40 per cent. Andrew Boyle, himself a Whitbread prizewinner, backed by the National Book League and the Society of Authors, fought a test case on the grounds that a prize or award is something granted arbitrarily after the book in question has been written and published. It is a kind of windfall that cannot be planned or taken account of in advance. A year later, he won his case in the High Court and even the Inland Revenue did not have the nerve to pursue the flimsy pretext for punishing prizewinners as far as the Court of Appeal.

All genuine authors, whether they depend solely on their writing income or whether they use it to supplement a salary or other earnings subject to PAYE, have the real benefit of being classified under Schedule D. They can charge all direct expenses exclusively incurred in carrying out their trade against their literary earnings. These charges may include not only stationery, typewriter or word processor repairs, postage, telephone calls, and travel and research expenses, but a proportion of their rent, heating, lighting and repair bills if they use one or more rooms in their home solely for their writing activities. (But they should bear in mind that if they come to sell their house or flat, the Revenue could claim that the percentage of space used for their writing would be subject to capital gains tax.)

Until the recent big reductions in the rates of personal income tax, a writer who regularly earned more than £25,000–£30,000 a year from his copyrights could have found it tax-efficient to form a private company, transferring all existing and future copyrights to that company, in consideration of which the company would pay him an annual salary. That is no longer the case, assuming that all or virtually all of his net earnings fall within the 25 per cent tax rate. Or, at the risk of being cut off from inspirational sources, he could sell up his UK home and live permanently abroad, either subject to lower local taxes (provided there was a tax-exemption arrangement between his new country of residence and the United Kingdom) or, as in the case of the Irish Republic, no tax at all.

Finally, the super-rich author may transfer his copyrights to a company in, say, Switzerland but continue to live in England and pay tax on the comfortable salary received from that Swiss company. The added advantage of such a move is that when he dies, his copyrights will escape UK estate duties, thus saving perhaps several million pounds for his heirs.* On the other hand, the patriot may feel that he owes the country of his birth and upbringing a debt of honour and, having taken advantage of all the legitimate means of avoiding undue taxes, will cheerfully pay up on the residue of his income during his lifetime and (in his unavoidable absence) on his estate after his death.

---

* At March 1988, the scheme was being investigated by the Special Commissioners for Inland Revenue, who may shortly have it declared invalid.

# Chapter XV

# 'Once upon a future time'

The real battle for English lies in our Elementary Schools
and in the training of our Elementary teachers.
                              Sir Arthur Quiller-Couch, 1920

In the forty-odd years since 1945, we have seen the growth of paperback
editions to a point where they have overtaken the hardcover side in
unit sales and annual turnover. We have seen annual production of
both kinds rise inexorably amid complaints of over-production and
the elbowing out of the worthy by the flashy instant-book. We have
seen independent houses bought by and merged with conglomerates –
and yet we have also seen new independent houses arising and many
of the older ones flourishing in their own way. Novels are still being
reviewed every week by the more serious newspapers. Novelists are
still news. Can one imagine a button manufacturer being afforded the
amount of publicity given to Tom Wolfe in 1988 on the publication
of his first novel in the United States and Britain? It seems safe to
prophesy that the novel in one form or another will survive well into
the twenty-first century. 'Tell me a story' is a perennial plea.

There could well be changes in the manner in which the novel is
'packaged' and presented to its readership. Several interesting, though
mainly unsuccessful, experiments have already taken place since the
war. In the early 1950s, for example, Gordon Landsborough launched
a series under the title of *Weekend Novel*. He bought reprint rights in
existing printed novels and published them each week in tabloid
newspaper format without any form of binding or stapling and with
line drawings as illustrations. They were priced at 1s or 1s 6d per issue,
well below the then prevailing price of a paperbound book. Had the idea
caught on, he intended to include columns of advertising to bring the
'book' more into line with a popular newspaper but his venture was
under-capitalised and had to close after some twenty or so issues had

appeared. In those days, the paperback houses had little combined power with which to fight the intruder: with more capital behind him, Landsborough would have had access to front-rank novelists and the necessary advertising and publicity required to get his new idea off the ground. As it was, he accepted defeat and shortly afterwards joined Panther Books as its editor.

Thirty years later, a similar idea was tried. Rodney Stone formed a small company, Viaduct Publications, which was soon taken over by Hugh Begg of Seymour Press, with the plan of publishing *Complete Bestsellers*. As the title suggested, a complete novel (with two or three exceptions to include very popular non-fiction titles) was published each week in magazine format with a picture cover at 95p – in Hugh Begg's phrase, 'just under the magic £1 barrier'. All the titles to be included in the series had been published in book form at least seven years previously and so had already had a good run in both hardcover and paperback editions. Some of the titles had indeed been out of print in all editions for a long time. All of them were by successful authors, as evidenced by the first five titles published: *The Moon's a Balloon* by David Niven, *Fair Stood the Wind for France* by H. E. Bates, *The Eiger Sanction* by Trevanion, *Class* by Jilly Cooper, and *The Looking Glass War* by John le Carré.

Other authors included were Morris West, George MacDonald Fraser and Ed McBain but the plan, if the series prospered, was also to include new unpublished novels. The average first printings were 50,000 copies, of which firm sales accounted for about half, although the sales graphs showed that a 60 per cent level of sales might be expected before long.

Even though, as Hugh Begg said in a talk to the Society of Young Publishers,

> There is nothing new about fiction being available in magazine form. Wilkie Collins, Charles Dickens and a host of other Victorian authors were first published in this way,

it was not long before controversy – and then opposition – arose. *Complete Bestsellers* was launched in the late summer of 1982. In November Simon Master, then managing director of Pan Books and chairman of the Publishers Association Paperback Group, sent a letter to many literary agents and subsidiary rights directors in various publishing firms, saying that legal action could be taken against the new development, which he did not mention by name, for infringement of copyright. (An author usually licenses a publisher for the volume rights in his novel. Unlike Gordon Landsborough's *Weekend Novel* where the various sheets were loose, *Complete Bestsellers* was stapled at the centrefold, as are all magazines. Mr Master's contention was presumably that this constituted a 'volume'.)

Hugh Begg was having none of it. In his reply, he claimed that the only rights granted by the author were 'one-shot periodical rights', a form of publication that had been popular, mainly in Australia, for some years after the war when books (sometimes condensed) had been printed as a 'pull-out' supplement to a Sunday newspaper. He further contended that the new form of publication was bringing extra income and publicity to authors from books that were otherwise dormant.

By now, several newsagent chains had refused to stock new issues, largely, one assumes, from fear of upsetting their bigger suppliers, the paperback houses, but also for 'legal reasons'. This, of course, was exactly what Mr Master and the PA Paperback Group wanted. Standing orders for *Complete Bestsellers* fell from 35,000-plus per issue to under 20,000 within a month. Viaduct Publications threatened to prepare a case to present to the EEC under Articles 85 and 86 of the Treaty of Rome. The battle rumbled on until the end of February 1983, when the PA Paperback Group and Hugh Begg decided to call it a draw. There were several results – the saddest being that *Complete Bestsellers* ceased publication; in addition, Corgi decided to include one-shot periodical rights among those licensed to it by authors in their contracts and Simon Master admitted that three major literary agencies at least, Curtis Brown, John Farquharson and Laurence Pollinger, strongly dissented from the PA Paperback Group's official view.

Looking back, it does seem a dog-in-the-mangerish attitude. The titles concerned had all virtually exhausted their hardcover and paperback life. One can understand a publisher's wish to defend his hard-fought ground – but not at the expense of his own authors. For example, Hugh Begg offered the original publisher of any title to be included in *Complete Bestsellers* a page free of charge in which he might list other available titles by the same author. In the case of *Flashman* by George MacDonald Fraser, Pan refused the offer, thereby denying Mr Fraser as well as themselves the chance of further sales of his other *Flashman* titles. (The author left Pan Books for Fontana not long afterwards, but not for this specific reason.)

Had the dispute ended in the High Court, it is unclear how the judge would have ruled on the basic question, 'When is a volume not a volume?' Nevertheless, authors and those who care about their prospects must always feel sad when a new opening for their work is slammed shut and bolted.

Hugh Begg, who as a director of the Thomson group started Yellow Pages in the United Kingdom, is a man of more than one idea. Undeterred by the failure of *Complete Bestsellers*, he came up in the latter part of 1983 with a more daring project. It was to take the *unpublished* novel of a bestselling writer and publish it in four separate booklets with four consecutive issues of a national Sunday paper. The newspaper would not charge extra but would use it, like a colour magazine, as a circulation-builder and to carry additional advertising.

The all-important ingredient would be the author's name. It had to be a household name, one that would give a mass market the promise of 'a good read'. Mr Begg, with whom I had co-operated on *Complete Bestsellers*, invited me at an early stage to take part in the scheme, as I already represented several internationally successful writers and had access to many others.

As an author usually licenses 'volume rights' to his book publisher and reserves for himself the serial rights, which in the case of a novel are not normally in great demand, Mr Begg and I invented the term 'complete serial rights'. (In the ordinary way, a serial version of a book does not run to more than 25 per cent – at the most, one-third – of the complete text.) The whole validity of this new or newish concept lay in the legal definition of 'volume rights'. We contended that a volume must *ipso facto* be a bound-up version of the complete book and that, even if the full text would eventually be published, to do so in four separate instalments would not infringe the volume rights licensed to the book publisher. We took counsel's opinion from a leading copyright barrister, Mr Hugh Laddie, who generally confirmed our view. An approach was made to Associated Newspapers; their managing director, John Winnington-Ingram, was delighted with the idea and approved the likely authors, including Frederick Forsyth and Jeffrey Archer, who had given tentative approval and allowed their names to be put forward. The *Mail on Sunday*, which was rebuilding after a difficult start, was to be the vehicle.

When the word got out, a gale blew up in the book trade, particularly among booksellers. It was felt strongly that the trade sales of any novel launched in this way, no matter how successful the author might be, would be damaged, especially with the paperback editions. After considerable negotiations, Forsyth's publishers, Hutchinson, then run by Charles Clark, himself a one-time barrister, who disagreed strongly with our definition of volume rights, and Transworld, who had already agreed to pay £800,000 for the paperback rights in Forsyth's forthcoming novel, persuaded him not to risk what might be a seriously adverse effect on his book sales. So he withdrew.

It was now the early spring of 1984. The only other leading novelist on the short list with a novel due for publication shortly was Jeffrey Archer with *First Among Equals*. His publisher, Hodder & Stoughton, who also issued his paperback rights through Coronet Books, was itself considerably exercised. Even though he volunteered to give it a share of his substantial payment from the *Mail on Sunday*, it was worried over what the short- and the long-term repercussions might be on the book trade. But, backed up by his agent, Deborah Owen, he was adamant.

As he said to me in our interview, 'Everything comes on the back of something you did before . . . I by nature like to be an experimenter, the man who tries something that's never been done before. It doesn't worry me to see something fail. If you throw the ball into the ring ten times and it comes back five times, you're damn lucky!'

*First Among Equals* ran for four instalments, starting on 17 June 1984. The newspaper spent about £500,000 on hoardings and television advertisements focusing more on the author and the title than on the *Mail on Sunday* itself. Circulation rose throughout the four weeks and the paper was substantially helped to find a niche for itself in the potential book-reading market. And the 'complete serial' had no adverse effect on book sales – in fact, the reverse. Jeffrey Archer's previous novel, *The Prodigal Daughter*, three weeks after its first publication, had sold some 90,000 copies – 40,000 in the home market and 50,000 for export. At the same period after its book publication, which overlapped the *Mail on Sunday Serial*, *First Among Equals* had sold 60,000 copies at home and 56,000 for export – a total of 116,000. It was also reported that the book was selling quickly in the shops.

The paperback edition, which appeared in the summer of 1985, was an immediate success. It became no. 1 on the *Bookseller* list of paperback bestsellers and by 26 October that year had spent seventeen consecutive weeks on the list, mainly in the top half. It, too, eventually outsold its predecessor, *The Prodigal Daughter*, by a margin of 20 per cent. Thus, no one in the trade could reasonably claim that the *Mail on Sunday*'s serial version had in any way inhibited the novel's book sales.

The newspaper repeated the experiment once more in the early spring of 1985 – this time with *The Tenth Man*, a novella by Graham Greene which had been discovered as a film treatment among the MGM archives and brought into book form through the pertinacity of Anthony Blond. As the story was less than 40,000 words long, the *Mail on Sunday* could only publish in two consecutive instalments but again the effect on book sales was beneficial.

One abortive experiment that might have had – and might yet have – a profound effect on successful novelists as a form of 'complete serialisation' took place in the summer of 1983. As a sales inducement, a number of American supermarket chains offer a customer who spends at least, say, $30 at a time a free china saucer. Next week, that same customer on buying at least $30-worth of goods from the store will be given a cup, the next week a plate and so on. By shopping regularly at the same supermarket, the customer can eventually acquire 'free of charge' a complete tea-service.

The experiment was a variation on this practice. It was to take the forthcoming novel of a top-selling American author – a Sidney Sheldon or a Stephen King or a Judith Krantz – and to offer one large supermarket chain the exclusive chance of buying it in four or six separately bound instalments and making each consecutive instalment a give-away week by week instead of the china tea-service. There was a certain snob-appeal involved, a form of one-upmanship, in that the housewife could upstage her friends by discussing the new Sidney Sheldon novel, which was not yet available in the book stores. It was also what the supermarket trade might call a 'grabber'; the shopper who enjoyed instalment one could hardly fail to return to the store next week and buy enough goods to be given a copy of instalment two. For a while, Bantam Books were seriously interested in pursuing the idea and a big distributing firm in southern California apparently held discussions with Safeways Stores but in the end it was decided that there were too many problems. For example, the store would need to hold surplus stocks of each instalment, as a new shopper arriving in week three would want to start at the beginning and not halfway through the story. Nevertheless, with central distribution and sophisticated computer-ordering, such problems could easily be overcome, particularly in Britain where distances between cities are so much smaller. A fifty-store supermarket chain with an average of

10,000 customers per store per week provides an enormous potential for spreading the reading habit through a captive market. I prophesy that one day soon someone, a Hamlyn perhaps or a Sainsbury, will have the courage to have a go.

The reverse process, a return to the Victorian practice of serialising a novel in weekly instalments long before it appeared in book form, occurred in October 1985 when it was announced that Fay Weldon was to write a weekly 'saga' entitled *The Hearts and Lives of Men* for publication in *Woman* magazine, to begin the following February. The first instalment was to be of 4,000 words, then 3,000 words for each of the next two weeks and thereafter 1,000 words a week. It was to be an open-ended arrangement, running for an indefinite number of weeks; at that stage, no decision had been taken on whether the long-running story would ever appear as a book. In the event Heinemann did bring out an edited version as a novel and with reasonable success.

*Woman* magazine does not seem to have repeated the experiment, from which one might assume that it was not particularly successful in attracting and retaining sufficient new readers over a longish period. It was, however, a bold and worthwhile experiment which the agents of other established women novelists might pursue. As already mentioned, most novelists work in isolation, their only editorial advice usually comes from professional readers such as their agents or their editors – and that when the full typescript is finished and delivered. To get a kind of playback from readers in the form of comments while the story and the characters are still in development could be a salutary experience.

Over the last decade, audio-cassettes have played an interesting part in bringing novels – or, rather, a severely condensed version of novels – to a wider audience. Listen for Pleasure/EMI were one of the first companies in the field, starting with *The Moon's a Balloon*, read by David Niven himself, and several of the John le Carré novels, also read by the author who happens to be a reader (and mimic) of professional standard. Many other popular novelists have had their work adapted in this way, often read by well-known actors. An audio-cassette version has the advantage that a housewife or house husband doing the ironing or dusting can be listening to the words as they work; or a motorist on a long run can slot a cassette into the recorder and listen to the story as he or she drives. The disadvantage is that the average reading speed is about 120 words a minute; the running time of one side of a cassette is forty-five minutes. Thus, a three-pack cassette box can only comprehend around 30,000 words, whereas the novel from which it is adapted may be three, four, five or more times as long. Even though Listen for Pleasure/EMI employ skilled 'digesters', as do the other companies in the market, the result can seldom be more than a taster for the full novel. All the same, if audio-cassettes attract listeners to become readers of 'the real thing', they will have achieved a worthwhile result.

A perennial surprise – at least, to me – is that people who have seen and enjoyed a film or a television series are attracted to read the book on which either has been based. Visual impressions have so much more impact that someone who has read and enjoyed a novel might well be induced to see the film or TV version, in order to compare his internal visualisation with the outward and visible version – but the reverse would not apply. Yet it clearly does. 'The book of the film' quite often succeeds. *If* VAT is eventually applied to books, I think there is a likelihood that some popular novels may be packaged with a video-cassette, either of the film if one exists, or of a specially made brief version. The viewer/reader will have the choice of reading the book first, then seeing the video, or vice versa.

In other words, between now and the next century, I see the divisions separating one form of copyright from another crumbling, both where authors and publishers are concerned. As long ago as April 1984, Matthew Evans of Faber & Faber was quoted in the *Bookseller* as forecasting that publishers will 'move into low-level production, *exploiting in other forms* [my italics] the rights they own and have developed'. (The world knows how Faber, through its control over T. S. Eliot's poetry, has earned millions of pounds from its interest in the musical-play *Cats*.) With the prime costs of making a video being continually reduced through the involvement of advertising agencies and music promoters, the larger publishers could well afford to buy a successful novelist's film and TV rights on a profit-sharing basis and exploit them through the skilful use of videos.

In the calendar year 1986, 6,002 novels were published, of which 2,806 were reprints or new editions and 288 were translations of foreign novels. In other words, that year 2,908 new novels were published in Britain, several hundred of which were of American origin. Probably 150 – at the most 350 – were first novels by British authors. Yet I have estimated (page 29) that at any given time the typescripts of up to 6,000 unpublished British novels may be circulating on a doomed path between one London publishing house and another.

At least half of that multitude – and I write from sad and prolonged experience – are wholly unpublishable. A bricklayer learns his trade before he begins to lay the bricks that will become the wall of a house. An accountant, a doctor or a lawyer has to study and pass professional exams before he can earn his living. But many people who have not really mastered the rudiments of English grammar, let alone the subtleties of dialogue or even the formation of a paragraph, believe that because English is their native language, they are qualified to compete with the master story-tellers of their generation.

Even so, when one has discounted the unpublishable and the derivative and the banal, though competently written, there could well be several hundred unpublished novels in any one year that in happier circumstances could have been published – and with at least modest success. Yet what can happen to all those 'regretful rejections', to use Tom Rosenthal's words, apart from leaving them to moulder in a bottom drawer? One answer is a form of *samizdat* publication. As Q. D. Leavis said in an essay, published in 1980, 'We may well see a return to the primitive circulation of manuscripts among a select company'. There are several photocopying bureaux in London and other main centres – one of the most important being Legastat off Chancery Lane in London – which have sophisticated Xerox and collating machines, 'perfect' binding and jacketing facilities. Such a firm can produce a few hundred or more copies of a book (from a cleanly typed script) at prices well below normal printing charges. Publishers always say – and with reason – that it does not pay them to print fewer than 1,500 copies and their preferred first printing would be twice that number. By the time orthodox printing machines have been made ready and the setting process carried out, the costs are indeed considerable. (In the future, authors using word processors compatible with computer-typesetting will cut costs through eliminating the setting process.) The author whose novel has been narrowly rejected by perhaps half a dozen publishers but who is determined to give his work a wider circulation would do well to investigate the photocopying bureaux; as indeed would publishers, who often let a book go out of print because there are only a few 'dues' on the order book. The novelist who becomes his own publisher still has to cope with the problems of storage, subscribing, selling, packing and distributing copies of his book – but at least he can always give it away to his family and friends or supply copies to the local bookshop on a sale or return basis. After all, as George Bernard Shaw said in 1895:

> All that is necessary in the production of a book is an author and a bookseller, without any intermediate parasite.

The advent of reasonably cheap photocopying and binding has, nearly a century later, brought his words that much closer to reality.

There has been a great change in the status of authors since the war. Successful writers have always been in demand and held in respect by their publishers but, particularly in the past twenty-five years authors of any potential are liable to be treated more favourably by publishers than ever before. This is partly thanks to the efforts of professional bodies like the Society of Authors and the Writers' Guild, partly due to the pressure of agents and perhaps largely due to the rise of conglomerates with greater funds that lead to greater demand and an inadequate supply of the very talented and successful writers – talent and success are not necessarily synonymous. One can hardly imagine a publisher today repeating, even as a joke, Michael Joseph's 1950s remark, 'Authors are easy to get on with if you are fond of children'. In the future, we are bound to see greater efforts made by publishers to make their authors feel part of 'the family'. It is good business as well as good sense.

Bloomsbury has already made a start through its Authors' Trust, whereby five per cent of the issued share capital has been set aside; the trust's shares are likely to be sold when the institutional investors realise their shareholdings and the resulting cash will be shared out between qualified authors on a title by title basis. This appears to be a once-and-for-all payout but it is an important step which shows that one publishing house at least recognises that its success depends on authors who deserve to share financially, if modestly, in the company's fortunes.

It may be possible for publicly quoted publishing houses to move a step further. For a very established author, an advance of £250,000 on his next book – or £350,000 or even £500,000 – is often just a status symbol; he doesn't actually *need* the money and, if he pays United Kingdom taxes, will still lose a large chunk of it to the Revenue. An author takes a large advance for one (or more) of four main reasons: because his agent thinks it will keep the publisher 'on his toes'; because he has heard on the grapevine that his rivals A and B get somewhat less and he wants to feel one up on them; because it gives him a feeling of power and gratification that his publisher thinks his new book is worth that immense sum; and because he may happen to need the money.

It would make considerable sense for the publisher, instead of his paying out, say, £300,000 in instalments, to offer that author an advance of £150,000 plus a shareholding in the company of the same amount. The shares would rank for dividends and, if the publishing house prospers, could eventually be sold on the market for a capital gain. If the book earns out its actual advance and the initial value of the shareholding, royalties and other payments in excess would be paid out in the normal way.

The scheme would require to be approved by the Inland Revenue and the author might have to pay earned income tax on his shareholding even though he had not had access to the funds. There is also the argument that, if ten or more very successful authors took part in the scheme and each over a period produced six or more books, the company might find itself with a substantial minority shareholding in the hands of a few powerful authors. That would present no great problem to a group like Reed International or Pearson or Collins – and it is very unlikely that top authors would ever band together for some power ploy over the company. The great advantage, both actual and psychological, is that the method would tie the author far more closely to the publishing house than any contractual option could achieve and it would save the house a considerable sum through paying out smaller advances.

One other ingenious plan, which is already under way and which may produce revolutionary results in the future shape and scope of the larger publishing companies, is the creation of Tim Hill of Hill & Company, Publishers, in Boston.* Having observed how the growth of television in the United States and the consequent drop in cinema attendances broke up the old Hollywood studio monopoly and gave rise to the independent producer, whose overheads were low and who assembled a new 'creative' team for each picture he made, Tim Hill decided to apply the same techniques to the top end of book publishing – initially in the USA. In his own analysis,

From an author's viewpoint, the constancy of working relationships is threatened by editors changing houses, managements changing

---

* I must register an interest by declaring that I act as a part-time consultant in the United Kingdom to Hill & Company.

policies, or companies changing ownership. The objectives of publishing house and author may no longer coincide. In many respects each book competes for attention and resources with every other book on a publisher's list. While the major author is unlikely to be subordinated to other authors, inevitably he is in the position of subsidising losses. More importantly, he may involuntarily underwrite the institution's excessive overhead or growth objectives.

. . . Major authors represent a far higher percentage of total sales than in the past. Publishers pay large royalty advances because they need the disproportionate contributions to overhead and/or profit represented by bestselling books.

The Hill answer is to have on call a freelance team of experienced editors, designers, typographers, advertising and publicity experts and marketing executives. An individual programme is worked out with each author and every step is subject to the author's approval. If, for example, the author has a long-standing association with an editor he respects and that editor is able to undertake freelance work, he will be brought on to the team. The author is shown all the costings related to his book including a *fixed* percentage of sales to cover Hill & Company's overheads. So the quality of paper, the typeface, the design, the binding, the dust-jacket and the published price are all agreed by the author before the book appears. The distribution, warehousing and invoicing can either be carried out by arrangement with the author's previous regular publisher or by a major house suggested by Hill & Company.

The plan strikes at the soft underbelly of the current publishing structure. The present practice is to set a published price which, allowing for production costs and the author's advance/royalties at one end and sales discounts at the other, will ideally leave a gross profit margin of about 50–55 per cent on every copy sold. Out of this must come a share of the publisher's overheads – rent, rates (soon to be a poll tax), heat, light, salaries etc, leaving something like 10 to 15 per cent pretax profit on the turnover achieved. But, as I demonstrated in the earlier chapter, 'The Crunch', – and as Mr Hill shows in his analysis – the big-selling author is making a surplus that goes not to him, but to defray the publisher's overheads and to support unsuccessful authors on the same list. Hill & Company, along with most major authors, would agree that profits from bestselling books should help support less commercial publishing – to a *reasonable* extent. As so often with publishing contracts, the word 'reasonable' is susceptible to opposing interpretations, depending on whether one is wearing the publisher's or the successful author's hat.

In order to maintain his profit margin, the publisher has to ensure that the big author does not receive too high a royalty, although the usual excuse is the impact of inflation. Up to the mid-1950s, a royalty of 25 per cent of the published price was paid to the few top sellers, while 20 per cent was fairly common. Today, 15 per cent would be considered the bestseller's rate, while $17\frac{1}{2}$ per cent would be exceptional.

Thus, if one takes a major novel, published in New York at $18.95 and selling 300,000 copies, under the normal publishing procedure with a flat 15 per cent royalty, the author would earn $852,750. Under the Hill plan, he would get all the earnings after the fixed editorial fee, the production costs, a modest percentage profit and overhead figure for the publisher and promotion costs had first been deducted. His 'take' would then amount to $1,550,391 – the equivalent of a 27 per cent royalty. The marketing of subsidiary rights, book club and paperback, in the main would not be affected and the author would receive his normal share of proceeds.

One important 'plank' in the Hill programme is that after ten years from first publication, all rights automatically revert to the author. This allows a paperback house, publishing one year after the initial hardcover edition, a nine-year licence, which is usually adequate. It avoids that perennial problem and complaint for writers that a publisher who undertakes a licence for the duration of copyright, provided he keeps the book minimally in print in one form or another, can retain the rights and make little effort to exploit them except through a Micawberish aspiration that something may come along – a film, a television series, sudden notoriety for the author – to reawaken the public interest. For some years now, the Writers' Guild has been pressing hard on this point in their Minimum Terms Agreement; it is significant that a new publisher, far from resisting, is in fact strongly advocating that same point in his publishing plan.

Significantly, it is named the Hill & Company Author Partnership Program. The key word is 'partnership'. Even the most considerate and author-favouring houses do often, perhaps subconsciously, treat their authors as not quite grown up enough to be told the inner secrets. Royalty statements show the numbers of copies sold at home and abroad but only a very few reveal the initial printings and almost none show discounts to the trade. Often, such details would rebound to the publisher's credit; if, for example, the royalty statement revealed that the publisher had printed 10,000 copies but had only sold 4,000, he would at least get marks from the author for having had initial, if misplaced, confidence in the book's sales appeal.

What of other aspects of the trade between now and the end of the century? When – it is not really a case of *if* – the Hill (or some similar) plan comes into being, the effect on major publishing houses, both in New York and London, will be immense. Publishers, liable to lose their 'milch cows' except for distribution, will need to take rearguard actions or advance their own attractive substitute plans for those fairly rare bestselling authors. They will argue that they cannot afford to seek out and sustain new writing talent unless they have access to the additional gross profit accruing from their top authors. But behind the plaintive cries, they will have to adapt. Faced with the choice of half a loaf or no bread at all, most big publishers will take the half-loaf and feed their lesser authors on crusts.

Agencies will prosper – and change, both in scope and size. Already, many authors have discovered that, with all the chopping and changing that has taken place and will most likely continue to take place in the ownership and staff of publishing houses, the one fixed point in a fluctuating world is their literary agent. More and more, agents will assume editorial as well as sales responsibilities. It seems likely that some of the bigger agencies will take on freelance editors who will at the least copy-edit the clients' typescripts and, if required, provide full editorial services, leaving the publisher to provide the production, promotion, sales and distribution of a ready-made product.

Agents will also, I believe, provide a wider range of services for their clients. They will set up informal or formal associations with lawyers, accountants, travel agents and even merchant banks, and thus give a comprehensive form of advice for the authors on their lists. This in turn will mean that the smaller agencies, in order to compete, will tend to merge or be bought out by the bigger firms. At present, very few, if any, literary agencies have a strong merchandising department to compete with, say, Mark McCormack's International Management Group – and yet many of them have clients who would benefit financially from that non-literary form of marketing. That will need to change – and so will the practice of sub-leasing film, television and stage rights to one or other specialist firms. Several of the larger agencies do have strong internal film/TV/stage departments but, even so, A. D. Peters towards the end of 1987 announced its merger with Fraser & Dunlop, whose forte is on the film and stage side. Others, I reckon, will follow.

In the past, it was held that companies, such as literary agencies, which have no forward contracts with their clients, would not be suitable to become public companies. Since then, we have seen how advertising agencies, who are in the same boat – or even a less watertight boat, as they are susceptible to the poaching which has so far been largely absent from the literary agencies – have gone public on giddy price/earnings ratios. There are already a few large literary agencies whose commission income approaches or exceeds £1 million a year, another half dozen earning around £500,000 in commission and perhaps a dozen more comfortably in excess of £250,000. If two or three of them were to merge, as advertising agencies have done, and reduce their overheads by occupying the same building and combining their accounting systems, they would soon be eligible for a placing of shares on the Unlisted Securities Market. The original shareholders could sell off up to 45 per cent of the equity, thus retaining overall control and still making a useful capital gain.

I mention 'the poaching which has so far been absent from the literary agencies'. There are, however, signs that, as demand increases for the relatively few 'brand-name' authors, agents may forget their well-bred reluctance to seduce an important client from another firm. The Association of Authors' Agents' code specifically bans the practice – or knowingly approaching an author who is already represented, even if the firm concerned does not belong to the Association. But, in the words of François Villon:

> Nécessité fait gens méprendre
> Et faim saillir le loup des bois.

There could be a wolf or two lurking in the Bloomsbury woods.

British authors as a whole may not be deeply religious but they should pause to light a candle and utter a prayer for a handful of great Englishmen who in a little over fifty years ensured a prosperous future for them. If Wolfe had not defeated Montcalm in Canada, if Clive and Hastings had not opened up India, if Cook had not discovered Australia, if Nelson had not won the Battle of Trafalgar, if Wellington had not succeeded in the Peninsular War and at Waterloo, French might now be the universal language and English have gone the way of Latin. (Any language that fails to create a single word for 'shallow' must in spite of its precision and elegance be deeply suspect!) Thanks to our own empire-building and the dominance of the USA in world affairs over the latter two-thirds of this century, English is the *lingua franca* – and British writers have automatically enjoyed wide export sales of books and copyrights that are denied to their French, German, Italian and Spanish counterparts.

But . . . there is still an internal battle to be won. Writers depend upon readers; good writers depend even more on good readers, men and women who understand and appreciate the nuances of the language, the rhythms and even the visual aspect of fine prose. There may be a few determined souls who would go on writing in solitary confinement, cut off from the outside world, but most authors need to know that they have a devoted readership out there.

That is why I have headed this final chapter with a quotation from Sir Arthur Quiller-Couch, written nearly seventy years ago. It is even more significant today. In our interview, A. S. Byatt mentioned the damaging effect that some hard-left teachers who despise the richness of English literature can have on their pupils, how Shakespeare could be eliminated in a couple of generations. Equally damaging is the effect that bad English teachers, themselves ill-educated and uninterested, can have on the young, apart from not encouraging them to appreciate an unparalleled legacy. The teaching of grammar in many schools seems to have gone by the board. Someone who cannot parse a sentence – who hardly knows the meaning of the verb – is often set to teach a class through the line of least resistance. The grave result, as several senior members of the English faculty at University College, London, have told me repeatedly, is that first-year students, each of them with a highish grading in A-level English, often do not know the difference between the subject and the object in a simple sentence and have to be given a crash course in grammar – something they should have learned a decade earlier – before they can be trusted to write a straightforward essay. (It is interesting to note how often reporters on *The Times* and other supposedly serious newspapers commit such solecisms as 'He laid down on the ground' or 'with we journalists' or 'X, whom it is believed is absent abroad'.)

When 'Q' wrote his Preface to *The Art of Reading and Writing*, from which the quotation comes, reading was the major, almost the only, leisure pursuit for most people. The British Broadcasting Corporation had not yet begun to send words and music into the ether, to be picked up on those early cat's whisker 'wireless' sets. Television was still more than fifteen years away; gramophones had to be wound by hand each time a record was turned over; the larger towns had a small cinema showing flickering silent films with a pianist improvising background music.

Twenty years ago, in a letter to the *Bookseller*, I suggested that the Booksellers Association should raise a statue to the memory of Enid Blyton, who had recently died. My tongue was only just touching the inside of my cheek. Her books had then sold over 250 million copies world-wide and today are still selling at the rate of around 10 million copies a year. Whatever one may think of their literary merits, they have seized the attention of innumerable children and have held them from the ages of five to twelve. She was a great story-teller and many a book-reading adult once graduated from the Blyton 'school'. Perhaps it is not too late to erect that statue.

But we still need better teachers – better paid, because pay and talent ought to become more closely linked – if the dominance of the English language that Wolfe, Clive, Hastings, Cook, Nelson and Wellington inadvertently ensured is not to be swept away by the more raucous counter-attractions of satellite TV, videos and pop records.

Writing in the *Bookseller* of 8 April 1988, Andrew Nurnberg, a literary agent much concerned with selling translation rights on both sides of the now rusty Iron Curtain, said, 'By the end of the century, China is expected to be the world's largest English reading public'. Are agents and publishers contemplating the setting up of offices in Beijing, Shanghai and Canton? In twenty years' time, will we find that the English language sales of a moderately popular British novel are over a quarter of a million and the big bestseller well over 5 million, thanks to the fecund East?

One thing is certain. Publishing conglomerates may break up into their component parts, agencies may grow larger and provide comprehensive services for their clients – we may even see some form of amalgamation between the at present separate functions of publisher and agent – but, whatever happens, the novel will survive. It may be listened to on a Walkman head-set or viewed page by page on the television screen or carried by hand, either as loose-leaf 'filofiction', as performed by Octopus in the summer of 1988, or as a 'book' book – the perfect portable piece of entertainment and artistic stimulus, which one can study at one's own speed, refer back to continually and finally display on a shelf to 'furnish a room'.

Some years ago, a woman novelist was holidaying in the south of France, when she ran short of money. She cabled her publishers: WILL YOU COMMISSION MY NEW NOVEL QUESTION MARK SIXTY THOUSAND WORDS STOP LOVE AND KISSES STOP. The publisher cabled back: IT DEPENDS WHICH WORDS IN WHICH ORDER. That is, in effect, the whole story of writing and publishing.

'In the beginning was the Word.' And in the end the word will still be there.

# Appendixes

A.  Some Thoughts on Auctions by *Scott Meredith*
B.  Subsidiary Rights – the American Way by *Paul S. Nathan*
C.  Aquisition Statistics on Selected Quoted and Unquoted Companies
D.  Select Bibliography
Index

*Appendix A*

# SOME THOUGHTS ON AUCTIONS

## by SCOTT MEREDITH

*Scott Meredith is a distinguished New York literary agent who started his firm (of the same name) in 1941. He is held to be the first to submit a book, whether written or in synopsis form, to more than one publisher at the same time.*

I've been asked about this many times over the years and have kicked myself each time, for the fact is that I simply don't remember the specifics of the first auction, which must have been early in 1949. At the time I had no sense of history and it wasn't until years later that it dawned on me that we'd been involved in something of historical importance; by then, the particular author and manuscript involved, and the outcome of the auction and the terms of the deal, had long since merged in my mind with the thousands of auctions conducted since then.

I do remember, though, thinking of the idea and being terrified, fearing that it might not just fail but could put us right out of business. In those days, of course, it was the absolute rule that you could submit to only one publisher at a time, and if you typed up two copies (in those pre-Xerox days) and submitted to two houses simultaneously, and were found out, both would return your material coldly and immediately. (Of course, coming right out and asking two houses to bid against one another would have been like committing a second murder while on Death Row for the first.)

It wasn't so much courage that caused me to continue but a sense that the existing situation couldn't go on, no matter what. The old system was designed to protect the publisher at the expense of the author and for no other reason. The author might leave his job to complete a manuscript, work for years using up his savings, make his first submission, and then sit back and wait for months only to wind up with a rejection. By the time he'd been through this process five or six times, a year or more could have

311

gone by, and if the next publisher came in with a small offer, with terribly unfair terms, the poor author was so desperate to get his book sold that he'd often give away the store rather than risk losing the deal. This has by no means disappeared today, by the way, since some books are still offered one submission at a time, and so I don't need to remember the horrors of the old era; we still live with this, as do all agents. But for the right books we can now rescue our clients from being forced to bargain from weakness, even desperation.

And so we went ahead, though I knew some of the publishers would refuse even to consider our submission when told that others would be reading it simultaneously. I felt confident that some would agree, as indeed some did. I had a ready-made answer for those who refused: 'Well, that's your privilege, but this is the new wave and this is how the big properties are going to be handled in the future, so you're going to miss out on them.'

One thing I do remember is that Peter Schwed of Simon & Schuster was the last holdout. Many years later he called me one Sunday at my house after we'd excluded him from several auctions, and said, 'All right, goddamn it, include me in.'

As everyone now knows, the result was not just a huge reduction in the length of time needed to find the right publisher and make a deal, but a situation in which publishers, bidding against one another (and sometimes bidding simply against the fear of other publishers coming in with higher bids), began offering advances that would have been unattainable through any other method. This was how we became the first in 1970 to obtain a $1 million advance for a writer (from Little, Brown for Norman Mailer) for an unwritten work, which later became the novel, *Ancient Evenings*, and the first in 1980 to obtain a $2 million advance (from Simon & Schuster for Dr Carl Sagan).

The Sagan is a good illustration of how the fact of auctions has changed the climate of publishing even when an auction doesn't actually take place: we'd made several simultaneous submissions of Sagan's outline for his first novel, *Contact*, and Michael Korda was heard from first, with a bid of $1 million. I had the nerve to say, 'Don't insult me,' after which Michael called back ten minutes later with a bid of $2 million, which we accepted. There was no auction, in that the acceptable $2 million offer was made before there were any other offers, but the spectre of other major houses considering the material simultaneously was obviously one of the factors influencing Simon & Schuster to double its bid even without any counter-bidding going on.

Auctions have also become a sort of substitute for the traditional exercise of good publishing judgment; what I mean is that very often the success or failure of the initial auction is the single factor that determines the ultimate fate of the book, rather than any of the traditional things that happen during the long course of development, editing, manufacture, and distribution. As an example, we recently took on a first novel, *Promises to Keep*, by an unknown, unpublished writer, George Bernau. We were quite enthusiastic about the book and decided to auction it. The result was a deal with Warner Books for $750,000, the highest advance ever paid to an unpublished writer. With such an advance, the book's future is already determined. No one at Warner is sitting around guessing about the best way to publish the book; it was determined on the auction day that it would receive a tremendous first printing, ad budget, etc.

The Bernau auction also again demonstrates the psychological impact of the auction process: the bids were $200,000, then $400,000, then $500,000, then $750,000. The huge leaps reflect each house's awareness that if it didn't take a dramatic step, some other house might rush in with an irresistible pre-emptive bid and snatch away the book. This is why you see so many authors turning down exclusive bids from option-holders in order to put their new books out to auction. Remove a publisher's fear that another house may rush in with a higher bid and you give the publisher permission to proceed conservatively; even with a bestselling author with a wonderful bargaining position, the lack of competition sometimes makes it hard to get out of a publisher his very best offer. Going to auction often means one has nothing to lose and everything to gain. Thus, auctions have changed the industry not just by leading to larger advances and removing worry and desperation from the lives of some authors, but by disrupting long-established, continuous relationships. This in turn inevitably affects the writer and thus affects what he writes, with the result being that something that started out as a sales method has had an indirect but profound influence on literature itself.

This is not necessarily a good or bad influence, by the way; it depends on the author, the house, the book, and the situation at the time, whether the author's work is hurt or helped by his undergoing this process. For all of our identification with the auction process, I'm just as pleased by those instances when we could have auctioned a book but chose not to because we felt that not doing so would be to the benefit of the author. For instance, when we decided to take Norman Mailer away from Little, Brown recently we submitted exclusively to Random House. The result was a deal the equal of any that could have been obtained at auction, and a publishing relationship of greater solidity and depth than an auction might have given us. And the result of that relationship is greater freedom, confidence, and the security to do his best work, which will be directly reflected in the quality of Mailer's current novel. But auctions, by giving one the luxury of comparing dozens of publishing proposals simultaneously, can allow one not just to get the best offer but to choose the best relationship. (The highest offer isn't always the one accepted, of course.) So there are times when auction is the right way to go even when one is thinking not just of making the best deal but of finding the best way to foster a writer's doing his best work.

*Appendix B*

# Subsidiary Rights – the American Way

## by Paul S. Nathan

*For over forty years, Mr Nathan has contributed a regular column entitled 'Rights' to the* Publishers Weekly, *New York. This is an edited version of a talk he gave at Radcliffe Publishing Procedures Course in July 1987.*

After many years of reporting on subsidiary rights I still find the subject interesting – and sometimes fascinating. I realise it's a part of publishing that often has nothing to do with literature and thus may seem crass, but in the nature of things it's an important part.

There was a time when subsidiary rights were truly subsidiary. Whatever income they brought in was considered gravy. Secretaries were often assigned to handle them. Then gradually the picture changed. Nowadays the sale of rights may be what keeps a publishing house in business. And the people selling them are quite likely to be vice-presidents earning good salaries.

I think it might be useful here to review these changes; they have helped determine the course of publishing and pretty much made it what it is today. In effect, sub rights, which used to be the tail of the dog, have ended up wagging the dog. Whether this is good or bad is a question to keep in mind as we go along.

In the 1930s Hollywood was a major buyer of subsidiary rights; book clubs – a fairly recent development – had a certain number of slots to be filled every month and an occasional book was excerpted or serialised in a magazine or newspaper or sold to publishers overseas. Broadway, too, was a market; every so often a book was adapted to the stage. But television was not yet a commercial reality and paperbacks in this country didn't get started until 1939.

It was primarily the paperback revolution that caused a revolution across the whole spectrum of publishing and ushered in the era of big bucks. As the softcover houses became more and more successful, they also became more competitive among themselves for desirable hardcover titles to reprint, and so the prices paid for them climbed. I can remember a night years ago seeing a friend who was the agent for William Shirer. She was ecstatic: Shirer's *The Rise and Fall of the Third Reich* had just been sold for reprint that day, for what I think was $415,000. Whatever it was, it was the record up to that time – and it did seem enormous. I should mention that the agent had not made the reprint sale, because that has always been the prerogative of the hardcover publisher; and there is historical justification for this. Before paperbacks came along, certain books did get reprinted in cheaper hardcover editions. These were run off from the original plates, so it was natural for the original publisher to make the arrangements – often to do the new edition himself – and also to receive half the proceeds. Similarly, one of the two major book clubs printed from the original plates, and as smaller, specialised clubs emerged, they often bought their copies off the publisher. Since traditional contracts included no provision for paperback reprint or club sales, it seemed reasonable that the old 50-50 split apply here too. Where dramatic rights are concerned, the publisher often is not cut in at all – especially if the author is represented by an agent; and the publisher's take from first serial or translation rights sales is, at best, relatively small. Thus it was the major softcover reprint sale and once in a while a big-money club sale that the hardcover publisher began to count on for significant infusions of funds.

The hardcover houses, just like the softcover houses, grew competitive for certain kinds of books. These were the titles that could be expected to attract the most money from the reprint houses. This is how the tail wags the dog: hardcover publishers paying high advances for certain books because they think they are good reprint material.

And what is good reprint material? Well, like what's bought for the movies, it is usually something intended to appeal to a mass audience, because paperbacks to be profitable have to be sold in large quantities.

We see other things happening, too. A book called *I'm Okay, You're Okay* sells for reprint for $1 million. E. L. Doctorow's *Ragtime* goes for $1,850,000 – the highest till then for a work of fiction. (Doctorow's agent, by the way, was the same as Shirer's.) Eventually, prices climax with *Princess Daisy*: $3,208,875. Can this guarantee ever be earned back? Bantam Books says yes. Some of us half a dozen years later are still wondering.

As already noted, this emphasis on the blockbuster has its effect on what books get to be published. Editors with their eye on the bottom line look for razzle and dazzle. They want to prove their value to their employers by bringing in what turns a profit. Maybe if they build up a good commercial record, they can be permitted to publish an occasional book of quiet literary quality.

There have begun to be changes in who the employers are. CBS takes over a hardcover house and a couple of softcover houses, shutting down one of the latter. Random House, Knopf and Pantheon are bought by RCA, then sold to the Newhouses who have a newspaper empire. Gulf & Western acquires Simon & Schuster, Pocket Books and related imprints, and Richard Snyder, the head of Simon & Schuster, is heard to say that 'the book business is the software of the movie and television media'. (Gulf & Western owns Paramount Pictures by the way.)

In this rapidly shifting scene the individual entrepreneur has a tough time keeping afloat.

Now for another twist. It is the early 1980s and recession strikes. Everyone looks for ways to cut expenses. The softcover houses discover that it isn't absolutely necessary to purchase reprint rights to hardcover fiction to satisfy reader demand. They can hire writers to produce so-called category novels – romance, action-adventure, occult, et cetera – at very low cost, and the public will buy them.

This leads to something of a crisis for authors, because with the reprint market drying up for mid-list novels – the non-blockbusters – it has become unprofitable for hardcover houses to publish them. The Ludlums, the Sheldons and the Judith Krantzes continue to have no problems in hardcover or soft.

It looked bad for first novelists and 'literary' writers for a while, but after a few years, with the easing of the recession, the reprinters began to show interest again in hardcover titles of the sort they used to buy for $5,000 or $7,500 or $12,500 or $20,000. Perhaps some of the genre stuff was losing its appeal, particularly as cover prices kept going up for books that were hardly distinguishable from one another. In any case, the purse-strings were loosened once more, cautiously. First novels and writing of quality – including short stories, a once-moribund form – have made a comeback. Quite a few are again being published in hard covers and the best usually attract a reprint offer.

Now let's backtrack a bit. Quite a long time ago two publishing houses anticipated something that has become a present-day trend: they acquired both hard- and softcover rights in certain books and published both editions themselves. Simon & Schuster did this with the novels of Harold Robbins, one of the bestselling writers of all time. They set up a special imprint for his books in hardcover, Trident Press, and after a Trident Press title had been out for a year, Pocket Books issued it in softcover. Over at Dell, a hardcover line was launched, Delacorte Press. Any manuscript acquired for Delacorte automatically became a Dell paperback. Today I don't think there is a Trident Press, but Simon & Schuster as such frequently buys a manuscript jointly with Pocket Books; Delacorte and Dell continue to acquire together, and a number of other hardcover houses – St Martin's, for example – have introduced their own mass market lines. I don't know that St Martin's has ever bought something for hard- and softcover at the start, but it is not uncommon for the hardcover part of the firm to sell something to the softcover division as it might sell to any other mass market imprint.

Putnam, by taking over Berkley, which had been owned by another company, gave itself a paperback arm. Random House has absorbed the softcover Ballantine and Fawcett. And so on.

In a reverse play, New American Library, Warner Books and Bantam, which were exclusively softcover, launched their own hardcover operations. Bantam and Warner have been conspicuously successful at this. Bantam, after smashing records with hardcover sales of *Iacocca* and *Yaeger*, has mopped up with them in paperback. Warner has done outstandingly well with non-fiction such as *Mega-Trends* and with the novels of Andrew Greeley and others.

The lines between hard and soft are becoming blurred as more and more of the commercially important books are being bought with both in mind at the same time. One of the peaks was hit last year when James Clavell's *Whirlwind* went to William Morrow and its softcover affiliate under the Hearst banner, Avon, for $5 million plus.

Tom McCormack, the president of St Martin's, who was bidding for this one but didn't go high enough, wrote a piece for *Publishers Weekly* explaining why the price wasn't excessive. I'd like to read you some of what he says:

There's . . . the value of having James Clavell on your list and having it known that you have this kind of money to spend.

. . . I *want* big agents, and big authors to think of St Martin's when they have a big book, so I must wave a big flag, green, with a huge dollar sign in the middle.

For another thing, we have been a mass market publisher for over a year now, and as I write this we have the number three non-fiction mass market bestseller in America, Judith Thurman's biography of Isak Dinesen. But: a rough estimate tells me that 50 per cent of the agents and publishers here and in England still don't realise that we do mass market books.

So I had reasons beyond immediate 'profit' to want the James

Clavell. I wanted to convey that St Martin's is a very prosperous house, with millions to spend, and that we are a 'vertical publisher'. (All commercial publishers in the future will have to be able to offer hard-soft or forget big authors.)

For all of these reasons, 'break-even' on Clavell would have been worth it to us.

One of the things you'll deal with if you handle rights is the relicensing of reprint rights. The term for which the softcover house holds these generally ranges from five to ten years. At the end of that period some books are still selling, particularly if an author has gone from success to success and is building up a following.

There's a story you might enjoy about the licensing and relicensing of books by Pat Conroy. Bantam, which already was the reprinter of his novel *The Lords of Discipline*, decided it would like to have all four of his published works. So it bought his latest novel *The Prince of Tides* from Houghton Mifflin, then advised Leslie Breed in Houghton's New York office that it would like to buy *The Great Santini*. Avon had previously done this in paperback, but the rights had reverted to the author. Since Avon indicated that it was ready to renew its licence on this for another term, clearly an auction was in order. Leslie settled on the kind in which each contender is permitted to register just one bid and hope for the best.

Bantam's editorial director Stephen Rubin was determined not to let any Conroys get away: his offer simply had to be higher than Avon's. So he thought, 'I'll go for broke: $100,000.' Then it occurred to him that, although generous, the amount was reasonable, and Avon might come up with it too. Okay, then, how about $101,000? But what if Avon's thinking paralleled his own? Better make that $101,500. Even now he was afraid that the two companies might be in lock-step. So, just because it was arbitrary, he added $23. The bid Bantam submitted was $101,523. Avon's proved to be $60,000.

There was another Conroy title available, his only non-fiction book, *The Water is Wide*. This also had a paperback history, having been reprinted first by Dell and subsequently by Avon. Rubin decided now was the time to secure this too. He ended up paying another odd amount, $38,385, which covered the price for *The Water is Wide* plus bonuses tacked on for giving Bantam fifteen- instead of ten-year leases on both its new acquisitions.

Such are the games people play in the rights business – and there are those who have a lot of fun playing them.

I indicated earlier that reprint sales are especially important to hardcover publishers because of the 50-50 split with the author. Although book club prices rarely soar to comparable heights, the same kind of sharing is involved. Actually, though, the principle of the even split has been eroded where the authors are of bestseller stature. Aggressive agents and literary lawyers have forced publishers to give 60 per cent or 70 per cent, or sometimes even 100 per cent, of reprint and club income to the top commercial authors or risk losing them entirely – another reason why it becomes increasingly common to buy hard- and softcover rights at the same time. Not that the publisher then receives any of the author's softcover income, but at least he gets the publisher's part.

In the case of new or less popular writers, the publisher can usually demand the traditional split – and since even an unknown author may surprise everyone with a big hit, there is always a chance of the hardcover publisher making an unexpected killing.

Historically, it's interesting that among all the major publishers Doubleday was the only one that insisted on maintaining the 50-50 status quo while others were making compromises. But even Doubleday had to bend. It would sometimes give an author a bonus for letting it be his publisher – or otherwise get around its own rule. Now that this house has been sold to a German company, Bertelsmann, greater flexibility is doubtless in the cards.

As for the prices paid by book clubs, these, too, occasionally get into the big numbers. Book-of-the-Month was said to have guaranteed $1,750,000 for James Michener's big South African novel *The Covenant*, and it paid $500,000 for John le Carré's *The Little Drummer Girl*.

Back in 1947 Raymond Chandler wrote to a friend:

I have always hated the book clubs and I have always thought that the publisher grabbed far too much of the reprint and subsidiary rights to the books he published. The fact that he will occasionally make concessions to an established writer does not alter his practice towards unestablished writers. The publisher could justify himself perhaps, but he won't give any figures out. He won't tell you what the books cost him, he won't tell you what his overhead charge is, he won't tell you anything. The minute you try to talk business with him he takes the attitude that he is a gentleman and a scholar, and the moment you try to approach him on the level of his moral integrity he starts to talk business.

In our own day some negative opinions about clubs have been expressed by Stephen King and Peter Straub. They had co-authored a foreordained bestseller, *The Talisman*, and at the time of its publication they turned to my

320

column to air their views. King as spokesman said, 'Clubs are an integral part of the industry. I'm not out to bust them. But I think the climate that spawned clubs has changed radically.' He explained that he and Straub had been offered $400,000 for their novel by the Literary Guild, had asked $700,000 instead and been turned down. They then elected to launch *The Talisman* without a club adoption.

To quote King further: 'A book club edition is essentially a remainder before publication rather than after . . . The Guild presents a problem for all writers. You are not selling to one club but to four or five.' By way of illustration he cited his *Pet Semetary*, which was a main selection of both the Guild and the Doubleday Book Club and also available through Doubleday's Science Fiction and Mystery book clubs.

> Once your books sell a certain number of copies, you become important as an instrument to bring in future members. Not that present members won't buy your book, but membership turnover is high, and your book becomes one of those where people say, 'I really want to read that book and I don't want to wait for the paperback.' They can join and get four books for a dollar. If the Guild is going to do this, they should be required to pay for it.

(BOMC, incidentally, has a similar introductory deal, with four books for $2.)

As an indication that he was not anti-club King pointed out that BOMC would be offering his *Skeleton Crew*. It had also taken Straub's *Wild Animals*, which brought together three of his novels in one volume.

I invited both the Guild and BOMC to reply to the charges. The Guild declined, but Al Silverman, BOMC president, took the position that the clubs, through promotion and advertising – I quote –

> stimulate sales in all areas . . . In many cases we're taking unknown authors and helping build their reputations. Book-of-the-Month uses first novels – at least one a month.

Well before *The Talisman*'s publication, Universal Pictures had moved to tie up feature film rights for Steven Spielberg. If I've said little about the movies and television till now, it's because from the publisher's point of view they tend not to provide major income. In fact, as noted earlier, the publisher may not share in dramatic rights at all. On the other hand a successful movie or TV show can stimulate sales of the book on which it is based; and a book spun off by the motion picture or TV programme – the so-called tie-in – may sell a great many copies.

Several times lately the movies have paid a million dollars or more for a book. Two of them – *Memoirs of an Invisible Man* and *Presumed Innocent* – were first novels. Assuming the publisher had some participation, even a modest one, in dramatic rights, these deals could be financially quite rewarding.

It might be mentioned here that outright purchases for motion pictures are the exception rather than the rule. The general practice is for a producer to option a book, then shop it around to the studios or financing organisations. If backing is obtained, and if what are called 'the elements' fall into place – a bankable star, director, et cetera – then the option is exercised. Statistics are not encouraging, however. The ratio of options picked up to those allowed to lapse is probably something like one in 150.

Television has expanded significantly over the last fifteen or twenty years as a market for books. James Michener is said to have received $750,000 for mini-series rights to *Space*, and there is an arrangement for the projected three-volume biography of Lyndon Johnson by Robert Caro (the first having been published) which involves total payments of $1 million. While I think many writers would prefer to see their works of fiction adapted as feature films, there are arguments for going with television. On a trip to Hollywood some time ago I talked with Lee Rich, the head of Lorimar. It was he who introduced the mini-series form with *The Blue Knight*, from the Joseph Wambaugh novel. Referring to his subsequent production *Helter Skelter*, based on the book about the Manson murders, he said, 'This won the largest rating ever achieved by a movie made for television – it probably reached more people than any five movies in history. But there are still people who look down their nose at television. Authors say, "I want my book to be a movie." A lot of books are optioned for motion pictures, but how many get made? In television everything you buy gets made.'

There are three more areas in which rights activity has grown appreciably in the last decade or so. One is foreign rights. American books constitute an increasingly large proportion of many foreign publishers' lists, and the prices paid for them are in some instances quite high. Just last month two English companies jointly acquired hard- and softcover rights to two forthcoming novels by the American Barbara Woods with a guarantee of £175,000. And Barbara Woods is not yet in the top echelon of international stars, nor does Britain begin to have the potential number of buyers for bestsellers that we do. Books are one product of which our country sells more abroad than it imports. This creates a cultural imbalance even though it does help keep our publishers solvent.

## Appendix C

## ACQUISITION STATISTICS ON SELECTED QUOTED AND UNQUOTED COMPANIES

*I am greatly indebted to Mr Eric de Bellaigue of CIBC Securities Europe Limited (formerly Grenfell & Colegrave) for kindly allowing me to publish below a condensed version of the statistics he drew up for a recent report.*

*Author*

| Target Company (Predator) | Value of bid (Date) | Post-tax profit Earnings | Multiple Earnings |
|---|---|---|---|
| Addison-Wesley (Pearson) | $283m (March 1988) | $9.5m | 29.8x |
| Associated Book Pub. (International Thomson) | £210m (July 1987) | £4.1m | 51.2x |
| Bell & Howell (Robert M. Bass Group) | $902m (November 1987) | $32.9m | 27.4x |
| Bowker (Reed International) | $90m (September 1985) | NA | NA |
| CBS Educ. Pub. (iii) (Harcourt Brace) | $586m (December 1986) | NA | NA |
| Doubleday (Bertelsmann) | $475m (October 1986) | – | – |
| Grolier (Hachette) | $450m (April 1988) | $15.5m | 29.0x |
| Harcourt Brace (ii) (BPCC) | $1.94bn | $70.5m | 27.5x |
| Harper & Row (iv) (News Corporation) | $300m (March 1987) | $5.9m | 50.8x |
| Richard D Irwin (Times Mirror) | $135m (January 1988) | NA | NA |
| Heinemann (Octopus) | £100m (July 1985) | NA | NA |

*Table continued on next page*

| Target Company (Predator) | Value of bid (Date) | Post-tax profit Earnings | Multiple Earnings |
|---|---|---|---|
| Kluwer (Wolters Samsom) | Fl 1.05bn (June 1987) | Fl 46.4m | 22.6x |
| Macmillan Inc (Maxwell Comm.) | $2.6bn (Nov. 1988) | $70.8m | 36.7x |
| NAL (i) (Pearson) | $65.5m (December 1986) | NA | NA |
| Octopus (Reed International) | £535m (July 1987) | £17.4m | 30.7x |
| Scott Foresman (Time Inc.) | $520m (October 1986) | NA | NA |
| South Western Publishing (International Thomson) | $270m (December 1986) | NA | NA |

*(i)    New American Library operating profits estimated at $7.5m by NAL management for 1986: sales relate to 1985, when operating profit was $10.5m*
*(ii)   BPCC bid withdrawn in July 1987*
*(iii)  Holt Rinehart and Winston and WB Saunders*
*(iv)   1985/86 results excluding discontinued operations*
*(v)    Six months sales to 30/6/1987 of DM 400m annualised*

*Appendix D*

# SELECT BIBLIOGRAPHY

Bennett, Arnold, *Literary Taste. How to Form It*, Hodder & Stoughton, 1912

Bradbury, Malcolm, *Social Context of Modern English Literature*, 1971

—, *Possibilities*, OUP, 1973

Braine, John, *Writing a Novel*, Eyre Methuen, 1974

Brown, A. Curtis, *Contacts*, Cassell, 1935

Canfield, Cass, *The Publishing Experience*, University of Pennsylvania Press, 1969

Davis, Kenneth C., *Two-Bit Culture: The Paperbacking of America*, Houghton Mifflin, Boston, 1984

Fitzgerald, F. Scott, and Max Perkins, *Dear Scott, Dear Max*, Cassell, 1973

Fraser, W. Hamish, *Coming of the Mass Market 1850–1914*, Macmillan, 1981

Gedin, Per, *Literature in the Market Place*, Faber, 1977

Goldman, William, *Adventures in the Screen Trade*, Futura Publications, 1985

Hepburn, James, *The Author's Empty Purse & The Rise of the Literary Agent*, OUP, 1968

Hoggart, Richard, *Speaking to Each Other*, volume II, Chatto & Windus, 1970

Howard, Michael S., *Jonathan Cape, Publisher*, Cape, 1971

Humm, Peter (ed) *Popular Fictions*, Methuen, 1986

Leavis, Q. D., *Fiction and the Reading Public*, Chatto & Windus, 1932

—, *Collected Essays*, CUP, 1983

Lodge, David, *Language of Fiction*, Routledge, 1966

McLintick, David, *Indecent Exposure*, Columbus Books, 1983

Mayersberg, Paul, *Hollywood the Haunted House*, Allen Lane, 1967

Miller, Karl (ed), *London Review of Books* (passim)

Plimpton, George and others (eds), *The Paris Review Writers at Work* series volumes I to V, Penguin, 1982, 1983

Quiller-Couch, Sir Arthur, *The Art of Reading and Writing*, CUP, 1920

Rhode, Eric, *A History of the Cinema from Its Origins to 1970*, Allen Lane, 1976

Richards, I. A., *Principles of Literary Criticism*, Routledge, 1926

Ross, Gordon, *Television Jubilee*, W. H. Allen, 1961

Steiner, George, *Books in an Age of Post-Literacy: R. R. Bowker Memorial Lecture*, Bowker, 1985

Sutherland, J. A., *Fiction and the Fiction Industry*, Athlone Press, 1978

—, *Bestsellers*, Routledge, 1981

Unwin, Sir Stanley, *The Truth About Publishing*, Allen and Unwin, 1926; 8th Edition revised by Philip Unwin, 1976

Whiteside, Thomas, *Onward and Upward with the Arts: The Blockbuster Complex*, New Yorker, 1980

Williams, Raymond, *The Long Revolution*, Chatto & Windus, 1961
—, Writing in Society (Verso)
Wilson, Charles, *First with the News: The History of W. H. Smith 1792–1972*, Cape, 1985
Woolf, Leonard, *Beginning Again*, Hogarth Press, 1964
—, *Downhill all the Way*, Hogarth Press, 1967
*BBC Yearbooks* (1947–1967 inclusive)
*Bookseller* (10 May 1945–12 August 1988 inclusive)
*Writers' and Artists' Yearbook* – various editions (A. & C. Black)

# Index

*Note*. Book titles are entered under the names of their authors. To distinguish between individual publishers and firms the style 'William Heinemann' is used for the former and 'Heinemann (William), Ltd' for the latter.

Ace Books, 117, 118
Ackroyd, Peter: *Hawksmoor*, 67
Adams, Douglas, 185, 186
Addison-Wesley Inc., 141
advances, 21, 182–3, 229, 300; highest, 6, 154–5
advertising, 85, 153, 195, 225–33; colour supplements, 214–15; on television, 213–14, 229–30
agents and agencies, literary, 29, 50–73; on auctions, 311–14; authors, advice to, 23, 66–8, 196–7; earnings and expenses, 192–3, 196; future, 303–5; and new authors, 30, 191–2; newspaper, 225
aggregates, 71, 136, 137–9; *see also* conglomerates
Aitken & Stone, 60
Albatross, 115
Algren, Nelson, 31
Allbeury, Ted, 21
Allen, W. H., Ltd, 141, 279
Allen & Unwin, 141
Allende, Isobel, 160
Amis, Kingsley, 12–13, 32; *Lucky Jim*, 24; *The Old Devils*, 270, 271
Amis, Martin, 9
Annan, Lord, 104
Anthony, Evelyn, 256
Arandar, 138, 139
Archer, Jeffrey, 7, 35–42, 151, 174; interviewed, 36–42; popularity, 257; Public Lending Right, 255; publicity, 229, 230–1; *Beyond Reasonable Doubt*, 36, 39;

*First Among Equals*, 36, 294–5; *Kane and Abel*, 36, 38, 231, 237; *The Prodigal Daughter*, 37–8, 294–5
*Argosy*, 16
Arlen, Michael, 26
Armstrong, Thomas: film rights, 202
Arnold (Edward) Ltd, 137, 141
Arrow Books, 155
Arts Council, 252, 259–66; awards, 262–263; Literature Panel, 260, 262, 263–5
Ashe, Rosalind, 67
Assael, Harry, 125
Associated Book Publishers (ABP), 141, 145, 166, 171, 245
Association of Authors' Agents, 279, 305
Atlantic Awards, 267
Atlantic Book Co., 94
Attlee, Clement, 282–3
Attenborough, John, 84, 91, 240
auctions, 69, 175–8, 184, 311–14; New York, 176, 199–200, 319
audio-cassettes, 296–7
Australia, 15, 16, 232
*Author, The*, 50, 61, 276–7; 1953, 4; letters, 276, 277; surveys, 119–20, 161, 277, 279
Authors' Foundations, 280
Authors' Trust, 165, 299–300
Automobile Association (AA), 141
awards, 262–3, 264, 266–74; tax, 288

Bagnall, Arthur, QC, 239
Bainbridge, Beryl, 255
Bakewell, Joan, 221–2
Balchin, Nigel, 202

Baldick, Robert, 102
Baldwin, James, 66
Ballantyne, James and John, 56
Balleny, William, 82, 240
*Bananas*, 264
Bantam Books, 148, 295, 316, 318, 319
Bantam Press, 27
Barber, Noel, 151, 229
Barker (Arthur), Ltd, 96
Barrett, J. H., 116, 233–4, 262
Barth, John, 32
Bartlett, Gerald, 128
Barty-King, Mark, 169, 171, 173, 175, 178
Bates, H. E., 15, 281, 291
Batsford, Sir Brian, 50
Baum, Vicki: *The Mustard Seed*, 94
Baxter, Walter: *The Image and the Search*, 96
BBC, 231, 275; radio, 228, 272, 273; tv, 214; books programmes, 212, 228; fiction adapted for, 216, 228
Beacon Books (Odhams), 117
Beauman, Sally, 25, 197
Beaverbrook, 1st Baron, 78
Begg, Hugh, 291, 292–3
Bemrose (Eric), 158
Benchley, Peter, 2; *Jaws*, 3, 174
Benn (Ernest) Ltd, 113–14, 213
Bennett, Arnold, 57, 58, 59, 62
Bentley, Richard, 56
Bernau, George, 313
Bernstein, Sidney (later Lord), 142
Bertelsmann, 141, 166, 235, 236–7, 320
bestsellers, 22–33, 187, 198–200; earnings, 187–8; and films, 210–11; lists, 228; sales, 124–5, 126, 129; televised, 220
Better Books, 81, 85
Betty Trask Awards, 272
Bible, 46–7
Black, Sir Cyril, 101–2, 103, 104
Black Swan, 160
Blackwell, Sir Basil, 102, 103
Blackwell's Bookshop, 103
Blake, Fanny, 150
Bland, Margot, 95; *Julia*, 93, 104
'blanket licensing' 253, 277
Blom-Cooper, Louis, 100
Blond, Anthony, 142, 295
Bloom, Ursula, 255
Bloomsbury Publishing, 151, 165, 176, 280, 299–300; Authors' Trust, 165, 299–300

*Blow Up* (film), 208
Blundell, Sir Robert, 101, 102
Blyton, Enid, 10, 306
Board of Trade, 125
Boccaccio, Giovanni: *Decameron*, 96
Bodley Head, 141, 143
Bonham-Carter, Victor, 252–3
Book Club Associates, 141, 166, 234–7
book clubs, 118, 121, 233–8; US, 130, 320–1
Book Marketing Council, 160
Book of the Month Club, 233, 320, 321
*Book Publishing* (survey), 132
Book Society, 111, 233
Booker McConnell: prize, 146, 262, 263, 267–72; tax avoidance schemes, 267, 283–4
Books for Pleasure, 126
*Bookseller*, 71n; 1940s, 110, 111–12, 113, 114, 140, 202, 244; 1950s, 77, 84, 94, 116, 117, 239, 281, 282; 1960s, 85, 86, 126, 227–8, 306; 1970s, 10–11, 26, 87, 126–7, 128, 143, 228, 247, 262; 1980s, 29–30, 136, 137, 144, 153, 157, 159, 161, 162, 166, 237, 238, 247, 254, 307; re Arts Council, 263–4, 266; re PLR, 258
booksellers, 85; liability to prosecution, 94, 100–1, 102–3
Booksellers Association, 125, 234
bookshops: chains, 155–7; newsagents, 117; publishers', 125; US, 239
Bookwise, 159
Boon, John, 128
Boots' Booklovers Library, 110, 121; sued for obscenity, 94
Borrie, Sir Gordon, 236
Bott, Alan, 111, 115
Bourne, Kathleen, 206
Bowen, Elizabeth, 43
Boyars, Marion, 102
Boyle, Andrew, 275, 288
Bradbury, Malcolm, 66
Bradford, Barbara Taylor, 22, 198; television, 210
Bragg, Melvyn, 221–2, 228; novels, 8
Brando, Marlon, 205
Brett, Simon, 258
Brickhill, Paul: *The Dam Busters*, 117, 124
Brimax Ltd, 141
British Federation of Master Printers, 126
British Lending Library, 252
Brookner, Anita, 151, 257, 271

Brophy, Brigid, 250–1, 253, 254, 257, 277
Brophy, John, 251, 257; *Immortal Sergeant*, 117
'Brophy Penny', The, 251
Browne, E. H., 255
Brunton, Gordon, 146
BTR, 144, 149, 150
Buford, Bill, 29, 270
Bullett, Gerald, 156
Bumpus, J. & E., 81, 85
Bunting, Daniel George, 74
Burgess, Anthony, 8, 160, 242, 274, 287
Burke, J. F., 267
Burlingame, Roger, 88
Burnett, Frances Hodgson: *A Little Princess*, 218
Bush, John, 247
Butler, R. A., 284
Butler, Samuel, 225
Butterworths, 141
Byatt, Antonia S., 1–2, 35, 42–9, 182, 260, 305–6; interviewed, 42–9; *Possession*, 45; *Still Life*, 45–6
Byrne, Mr Justice, 99, 100
Byron, George Gordon, 6th Baron, 53, 54, 148

Caine, Hall, 187
Caine, Michael, 269, 270n
Cairns, Sir David, 99
*Cal* (film), 218n
Calder, Liz, 165, 169, 171, 175–6, 180
Calder & Boyars, 102, 103–4
Calder Educational Trust, 264
Calvocoressi, Peter, 128
*Cambridge Review*, 29
Campbell, Hugh, 159
Camus, Albert, 20
Canfield, Cass, 50
Cape, David, 188
Cape, Jonathan, 74, 75, 76, 77, 83, 188; anecdotes, 189
Cape (Jonathan), Ltd: authors, 151; 1950s, 188–9; 1960s, 81–3, 85; 1970s, 128, 142; 1980s, group, 141, 190
Carey, John, 270
Carey, Peter, 178
Carnell Literary Agency, 64
Caro, Robert, 322
Carr, J. L., 255
Carter, Godfrey, 250, 253
Cartland, Barbara, 10–11, 14, 255

Cassell, 26, 27, 60, 130, 141
cassettes, 296–7
Catlin, George, Prof., 102, 103
*Cats* (musical), 297
CBS, 123, 142–3, 317
censorship, 92–106
Century Co., 77, 143, 151, 170
Century/Century Hutchinson, 141, 280
Chandler, Raymond, 320
Chaplin, Charles, 208
Chapman, Ian, 29, 90, 91, 152, 166; lecture to RSA, 143–4
Chapman, Ian, jr, 150
Chapman & Hall, 56
Chatto & Windus, 84, 119, 141; pre-war, 56, 76; 1970s, 143, 171; authors, 151, 182
Chaucer, Geoffrey, 33
Cheetham, Anthony, 143, 170
Cheetham, Rosemary, 169–70; interviewed, 172, 178–9, 180, 184
'cheque-book' publishing, 78–9
Cheyney, Peter, 113, 283
Chichester, Sir Francis, 84
Christie, Agatha, 63, 125, 283–4; novels televised, 218
Churchill, Sir Winston, 106, 282–3
Clark, Charles, 294
Clavell, James, 151; *Whirlwind*, 6, 318–19
Clayton, Jack, 208–9
Cleary, Jon, 15–19, 151; publicity, 232; *The High Commissioner*, 17; *Pulse of Danger*, 17; *The Sundowners*, 226
Cleland, John: *Fanny Hill*, 101
Clode, Timothy, 136
CMA, 208
Coburn, Kathleen, 45
Cockburn, Claud, 25–6
Cockburn, Lord Justice, 92
Coetzee, J. M.: *The Life and Times of Michael K*, 271
Cohen, Richard, 39, 170, 174–5, 176, 179
Cohn, Harry, 213
Cole, Theodore, 139
Coleridge, Samuel Taylor, 45
Collins, Jackie, 198, 237
Collins, Jan, 157
Collins, Norman: film rights, 202
Collins, Wilkie, 57
Collins, Sir William, 15–16, 80–1, 90–1, 108, 118, 157

Collins (William), Sons & Co. Ltd: authors, 151, 158; Pocket Classics, 51n; 1940s, 113; 1950s, 16, 29, 129; 1960s, 80–1; 1970s, 128, 132–3; 1980s, 133, 135, 141, 145, 163, 165, 229; group, 91, 137, 188; and R. Murdoch, 137, 145, 157–9
Colquhoun, Keith, 279
Columbia, 208, 213
commission publishing, 51, 52
*Complete Bestsellers* (series), 291–3
'complete serial rights', 293–5
computers, 126, 149
Conan Doyle, Sir Arthur, 57
Condé Nast, 190
Congdon, Tom, 174–5
conglomerates, 72, 136–52, 195–6, 299; 1960s, 85
Connell, Vivian: *September in Quinze*, 94, 95–6
Connolly, Cyril, 20
Conrad, Joseph, 58, 62
Conran, Shirley: *Lace*, 25, 197
Conran Advertising, 153
Conroy, Pat, 319
Constable & Co., 52
contracts, 278; option clauses, 69–70, 280; *see also* Minimum Terms Agreement
Cookson, Cahterine, 27, 255, 256, 257
copyright: history, 51–4; purchase by publisher, 51, 53–4; and tax, 281–2, 289; *see also* rights, subsidiary
Corgi Books, 27, 116–17, 118, 155
*Cornhill*, 21
Coronet, 171
Costain, Thomas: *The Black Robe*, 113
costs, publishing: 19c., 53; post-war, 112, 114; 1970s, 128, 261; *see also* print costs
Council of Europe, 261
Countryside Libraries, 121
Creasey, John, 9, 11
crime fiction, 3–4
Croft-Cooke, Rupert, 79
Cronin, A. J.: *The Citadel*, 218
culture, popular, 46–7
Curtis Brown, Albert, 59–60, 60–1, 88
Curtis Brown, Spencer, 79

*Daily Telegraph*, 214, 252
Danckwerts, Mr Justice, 281–2
Darwin, Charles, 225

David & Charles, 128
Davies, Peter, 107
Deeping, Warwick, 26
de Graff, Robert, 115
Deighton, Len, 83
de la Roche, Mazo, 75
Dell Publishing Co., 317–18
Dempsey, Michael, 107
Denniston, Robin, 84, 105, 154, 170, 246
Dent, (J. M.) Ltd, 50, 126, 141, 143
Deutsch, André, 128, 130, 142, 166
dialogue, 18, 39–40; realism, 104–6
Dickens, Charles, 21, 41, 51n, 56
Dickson, Lovat, 78, 79
dictating, 22, 194
Digit Books, 117
Dillons, 155
Disraeli, Benjamin, 50, 54
D'Israeli, Isaac, 50
Dobereiner, Peter, 7
Doctorow, E. L.: *Ragtime*, 316
Dodson, Sir Gerald, 95
Dolby, George, 56
Donnelley & Sons, R. R., 131
Doubleday, 130, 166, 235, 320; book clubs, 321
Douglas, James, 93
Douglas, Norman, 265
Drabble, Margaret, 47, 255
du Cann, Richard, 99
du Maurier, Daphne, 27; film rights, 202; *The Scapegoat*, 118
Duffy, Maureen, 219, 250, 254
Duncan, Jane, 14

Eady Scheme, 203
editorial boards, 146
editors, publishing, 19, 21, 72, 74–8, 168–86; early, 74–8; American, 77, 152, 173; authors, influence on, 19, 21, 23, 36, 104–6, 108–9, 171–3, 182; editing of finished typescript, 173–5; effect of conglomerates, 71, 149–52; freelance, 301–2, 304; moving between firms, 68–9, 71, 152, 184–6; education, 43, 205–6; 18th-century writers, 21
Eliot, George, 48
Eliot, T. S., 76, 297
Ellis, Aidan, 153
English language, 298, 305–7
English language rights, 129

European Economic Community, 161, 162, 240–1
Evans, Harold, 142
Evans, Matthew, 297
Evans, Noel, 107
Evans, Philip, 171
*Evening Standard*, 105–6
*Everyman's Encyclopaedia*, 126
exports, 129–30, 307; to US, 4–6, 25, 113
Eyre & Spottiswoode, 15, 77, 213

Faber, Geoffrey, 76
Faber & Faber, 77, 185; auctions, 178; authors, 151; paperbacks, 160; 1970s, 128, 143; 1980s, 297
Farnol, Jeffrey, 80
Farquharson, John, 60, 63, 64
Farrer, David, 77, 78, 87, 184–5, 262, 268
Faulkner, William, 31
Faulks, Sebastian, 262
Feifer, George: *The Girl from Petrovka*, 80–1, 90–1
feminism, 48–9
Film Industry Defence Organisation, 216
film rights, 202–3, 206, 321–2; tax, 282, 284
films, 201–12, 216–17; from novels, 81, 113, 201–3, 206–7; books subsidised, 213; effect on novels, 22, 206–7, 297; sequels, 209–10; on tv, 216–19; US industry, 201–2, 204; writing for, 16, 30, 201–2, 211
Findlater, Richard, 161, 251, 277, 279
Fitzgerald, F. Scott, 17, 18, 20, 32, 88–9
Fleetwood, Hugh: *The Past*, 105–6
Fleming, Ian, 2, 3, 124, 215, 223–4: tax, 283–4
Fontana, 118, 125, 129, 159
Foreman, Carl, 203
Forster, E. M., 30–1
Forster, John, 56
Forster, Margaret, 263–4
Forsyth, Frederick, 23, 24, 72, 293–4; *The Devil's Alternative*, 134, 174; *The Fourth Protocol*, 155
Four Square Books, 116, 125
France: earnings of authors, 4
Francis, Dick, 23, 24–25, 256, 257
Frankfurt Book Fair, 166
Fraser, George MacDonald, 205, 292
Fraser, Helen, 149, 185
Fraser, Lionel, 140

Fraser & Dunlop, 304
Frere, A. S., 96, 130
Fullerton, Alexander, 172
Futura, 170, 228–9

Gallico, Paul: *The Snow Goose*, 226–7
Galsworthy, John: *The Forsyte Saga*, 126, 203, 228,
Gant, Roland, 77, 82, 83
Gardiner, Gerald, QC, 99–100
Gardner, Kate, 150
Garnett, Edward, 74, 76–7, 275
Gedin, Per, 2, 228, 238
Gilbey, Mr (Hatchards), 80
Gill (Claude), 141, 163
Gilmore, David, 40
*Glasgow Herald*, 29
Glidrose Productions, 283
Goddard, Lord Chief Justice, 92, 94
Godden, Rumer, 79
Godwin, Tony, 81, 85–7, 125; Memorial Scholarship, 86, 87
Goff, Martyn, 103, 270n
Gold, Mr (bookseller), 101
Golding, William, 151, 255; *Rites of Passage*, 270
Goldman, William, 16, 73
Goldwyn, Samuel, 201, 204
Gollancz, Victor, 90, 101, 143, 187, 278; advertising, 225; and J. le Carré, 108; paperbacks, 116
Goodman, Lord, 252, 260
Gordon, Giles, 65, 66, 69, 70–1, 71–2, 73
Gordon, John, 93, 94
Gordon, Richard, 227
Gordon & Gotch, 110
Gottlieb, Bob, 149
Gradwell, Leo, 102
Graham, Gordon, 280
grammar, 298, 305–6
Granada, 85, 123, 125, 141, 142, 170
*Granta*, 29
Graves, Robert, 34; *I, Claudius*, 228
Greeley, Andrew, 318
Green, Benny, 271
Green, Sir Owen, 137
Greene, Graham, 20, 273, 287; early career, 7–8, 29, 242; at Eyre & Spottiswoode, 15; novels, 7–8, 15, 22; film rights, 202; *The Quiet American*, 118, 212; *The Tenth Man*, 295
Greene, Graham C., 83

Griffith-Jones, Mervyn, 92, 95, 99, 100–1
Gross, Miriam, 222
*Guardian*, 165, 253, 261
*Guide for the Writing Desk*, 56
Guild Books, 111

Hailey, Arthur, 11–12; novels televised, 217; *Overload*, 154
Hailey, Sheila, 11–12
Hale, James, 170, 184; interviewed, 172–173, 175, 177–8, 179, 180, 181–2
Hall, Radclyffe: *The Well of Loneliness*, 93
Halliwell, Leslie, 207, 216–17
Hamilton, Hamish, 77, 142
Hamilton (Hamish) Ltd, 71, 72, 77, 118, 133, 141, 142
Hamlyn, Paul, 126, 142, 144, 150, 237
Hamlyn Publishing, 141
Hammett, Dashiell, 8, 265
Hansford Johnson, Pamela, 79
Harcourt Brace Jovanovitch, 86, 89, 124, 127, 166
Hardinge, Lord, 268
Hare, David, 221
Harper & Row, 130, 141, 166, 188
Harrap Ltd, 142
Harrap, Walter, 108, 117, 280
Harris, Harold, 88, 170, 173–4, 183, 184
Harrison, Sarah, 172, 197
Hart-Davis (Rupert), 142
Harvey, Wilfred, 79, 285
Hatchards, 80, 138–9
Hatry, Clarence, 137–9
Havers, Michael, QC, 102
Hawthornden prize, 267
Hazell, Watson & Viney, 98
Headline Book Publishing, 151, 164, 280
Hebdon, Peter, 82, 83
Heinemann, William, 50
Heinemann (William), Ltd, 83; bestsellers, 24, 27; and G. Greene, 7–8; mergers, 141, 144, 149, 150, 185, 186; prosecuted, 96
Heinemann group, 136–7, 141, 142, 144
Heller, Joseph, 13, 32
Hely-Hutchinson, Tim, 164
Hemingway, Ernest, 20, 21, 189, 273, 287; and editor, 88
Hepburn, James, 52, 58, 61, 62, 63
Herbert, Sir Alan, 3, 97, 106, 251, 252
Hern, Nick, 147
Herron, Elsie, 84

Hicklin judgment, 92–3
Higgins, Jack, 172
*High Noon* (film), 207
Higham, David, 60
Hill, Carol, 89
Hill, Susan, 47
Hill, Tim, 300–2
Hill & Co. Author Partnership Program, 300–3
Hodder & Stoughton: authors, 151: J. Archer, 40; J. Creasey, 9; editors, 84, 170; Pocket Books, 115–16, 117; publicity, 229; 1970s, 128, 142; 1980s, 29–30, 133, 145, 296; group, 137
Hodder-Williams, Paul, 84, 124
Hodder-Williams, Ralph, 84
Holifield, Chris, 170–1; interviewed, 173, 175, 176–7, 179, 180, 183
Holloway, David, 102
Hollywood, 201–6, 213, 216, 217, 315
Holroyd, Michael, 252
Holt, Rinehart & Winston, 123, 142, 143
Holt, Victoria, 151, 158, 256
Hong Kong, printing in, 131
Horder, Mervyn, 223
Houghton Mifflin, 319
House of Commons: library funding, 248; Obscene Publications Bills, 96–7, 98, 103, 106; PLR, 245, 252, 254; VAT, 161
House of Lords, 104, 161; PLR, 251, 253–4
Household, Geoffrey, 11
Howard, G. Wren, 81, 82–3
Howard, Michael, 75, 76, 81, 82–3
Howarth, Gerald, 106
Howatch, Susan, 164
Hughes Massie, 63
Hulton, Sir Edward, 214
Hulme, Keri, 271
Hurd & Houghton Co., 54
Huston, John, 287
Hutchinson & Co., 10; authors, 10; mergers, 141, 143; NCR Book Award, 273; prosecuted, 94, 95–6; 1980, 133, 141
Hutchinson, A. S. M., 26
Hutchinson, Jeremy, QC, 99, 101
Hutchinson, Walter, 75–6
Hutchinson New Authors, 249–50
Huxley, Aldous, 30, 75, 76
Hyde, H. Montgomery, 101, 102, 103
Hylton-Foster, Sir Harry, 97
hype, 25, 197–8

*I, Claudius* (tv), 228
*Illustrated London News*, 81, 85, 142
Illustrated Pocket Classics, 51n
Independent Television, 212, 213–14, 215, 216, 217, 219
Inland Revenue, 267, 275, 281–9, 300
Innes, Hammond, 151, 158, 285; *The Mary Deare*, 118
International Management Group, 304
International Publishing Bureau, 59
International Thomson, 166
Irish Finance Bill, 286–7
Irish publishers, 107–8
Irvine, Ian, 146
Irwin, Margaret, 203
Ishiguro, Kazuo, 66
Isle of Man, 94

jackets, 110, 118
Jacobson, Howard, 271
Jaffé, Marc, 148
James, P. D., 24, 25, 146, 219; *A Taste for Death*, 160, 219
James Tait Black Memorial Prize, 267
Jameson, Storm, 79
Janson, Hank, 94, 96
Jay, Douglas, 284
Jenkins, Hugh (now Lord), 253, 254
Jenkins, Roy (now Lord), 3, 96–7, 103, 106
Jerrold, Douglas, 77
*John Bull*, 116
Jones, James, 24
Joseph, Michael, 79, 81–2, 107, 113, 299; article by, 140
Joseph (Michael) Ltd.,: 1960s, 81–2, 83, 85, 141; premises, 148–9; World War II, 112–13
journalists as novelists, 21, 173, 223
Jovanovitch, William, 86
Joynson-Hicks, Sir William, 93

Kahn, Hermann, 121
Kaufman, Stanley: *The Philanderer*, 93
Kaye, M. M., 255
Kean, Edmund, 56
Kee, Robert, 108
Keillor, G.: *Lake Wobegon Days*, 178
Kennedy, Jacqueline, 35
Kermode, Frank, 103, 268
King, Mervyn, 286
King, Stephen, 230, 320–1
King Penguins, 153

Kirkus Book Service, 5
Knopf, 149, 186
Knopf, Alfred A., 88, 90, 225
Koestler, Arthur, 27, 46, 73; and editor, 168, 174, 183
Korda, Michael, 33, 89, 312
Krantz, Judith, 317; tv, 210; *Princess Daisy*, 134, 148, 316

Lacey, Robert, 237
Lacy, Dan, 212–13
Laddie, Hugh, 293
Lambert, Eric: *The 20,000 Thieves*, 117
Lancaster, Burt, 211
Landsborough, Gordon, 116, 290–1, 292
Lane, Sir Allen, 82–3, 85, 86, 111; prosecuted, 97–100
Lane, Margaret, 251
language, 298, 305, 306–7
Larkin, Philip, 181
Laski, Marghanita, 101, 265
Lassalle, Caroline, 160
Latham, Harold, 143
Lawrence, D. H., 43, 275; *Lady Chatterley's Lover*, 97–100, 125
Lawrence, T. E., 189
Lawson, Nigel, 161
le Carré, John, 23, 41, 151, 160; audio-cassettes, 296; development, 223–4; films, 208, 209; and Gollancz, 108; publicity, 229, 230; tv, 219, 220–1; *The Little Drummer Girl*, 320; *The Naive and Sentimental Lover*, 224; *Smiley's People*, 134; *The Spy Who Came in from the Cold*, 24, 209, 223, 278
Leavis, Q. D., 1, 298
Lee, Hermione, 221–2
Lee, Jennie, 260, 268
Lee, John, 56
Left Book Club, 233
Lehmann, John, 79
Leisure Circle, 235, 236
Lennon, John, 83
Lessing, Doris, 48
Lever, Jeremy, QC, 162
Levin, Bernard, 221–2
Lewis, Cecil Day, 99, 182
Lewis, Wyndham, 265
libraries: commercial, 110, 121, 246; public, 28, 244–50; 1970s–1980, 134; 'Brophy Penny', 251; PLR, 245, 250–258

Linklater, Eric, 282
Listen for Pleasure/EMI, 296–7
literary advisors, 74–7
literary agents, *see* agents
Literary Guild, 130, 170, 233
Little, Brown, 312, 313
Lloyd George, Gwilym, 96, 97
Locke, W. J., 26
London Films, 206
*London Magazine*, 264
London Weekend Television, 143
Longman, Mark, 107
Longman, Pearson, 139
Longman Group UK Ltd, 141, 145
Lord, Sterling, 65–6
Losey, Joseph, 203, 208
Lovell, F. W., 244
Lowndes, Natalya, 29–30
Luce, Henry, 282
Lucie-Smith, Edward, 102
Luckham, Bryan, 245–6
Ludlum, Robert, 175
Lusty, Sir Robert, 81, 168, 262
Lyall, Gavin, 151
Lynskey, Mr Justice, 96

Macdonald, 27, 79, 164; Macdonald/
    Futura, 133
Macdonell, A. G., 76
Machell, Roger, 77, 185
Machin, David, 150
Mackenzie, Sir Compton, 281–2
MacLean, Alistair, 23, 29, 151, 158;
    films, 208; *HMS Ulysses*, 24, 27, 29,
    118
Macmillan, Alexander, 2nd Earl of Stock-
    ton, 240
Macmillan, Daniel, 107
Macmillan, Frederick, 238
Macmillan, Harold, 1st Earl of Stockton,
    97, 78–9, 81
Macmillan Inc., (USA), 141
Macmillan Publishing Ltd, 133; 19th-
    century, 238; 1970s, 142; 1980s, 133,
    141, 145, 240
magazine format novel publishing, 290–1
magazines, 56–7, 214; Arts Council
    grant, 264; colour supplements,
    214–15; effect of tv, 214; literary, 76;
    serialisation, 57, 296; stories in, 29, 215;
    payment, 16
Magee, Bryan, 102

Maher, Terry, 240
*Mail on Sunday*, 293–5
Mailer, Norman, 22, 125, 312, 313–14;
    The Naked and the Dead, 104
Manchester: bookshops, 156; City
    Library, 75
Mann, Peter, 165
Mansbridge, Ronald, 239
Mansfield, Irving, 232–3
Marek, Dick, 175
market, world, 129–30
market research, 230
marketing, 226–33; hype, 25, 197–8
Marshall Cavendish, 133
marxism, 46, 305–6
Maschler, Tom, 81, 82–3
Master, Simon, 149, 185, 186, 190, 291
Mathew, John, 103
Mathew, Sir Theobald, 100
Maugham, W. Somerset, 20
Maxwell Communications Corporation,
    141
Maxwell, Robert, 102, 125, 158, 166
Maxwell-Fyfe, Sir David, 94
Mayer, Peter, 91, 132, 144, 163
Mayersburg, Paul, 206
Mayflower Books, 101, 154
McColvin, Lionel, 251
McCormack, Mark, 304
McCormack, Tom, 318–19
McCrum, Robert, 171–2, 184; inter-
    viewed, 178, 179, 180, 181, 182–3
McGraw, Hugh: *The Man in Control*, 96
McGraw-Hill, 127, 130
Mehta, Sonny, 149, 185–6
Meredith, Scott, 311–14
mergers, 71, 72, 108, 318; *see also* conglom-
    erates
Metalious, Grace: *Peyton Place*, 125
Methuen, 141, 146–7
MGM, 16, 113, 203, 204, 206, 295
Michener, James: *The Covenant*, 320; *Space*,
    322
Mills & Boon, 24
Milton House, 128
Minimum Lending Rate (1980), 132
Minimum Terms Agreement, 70, 277–8,
    279–80, 303
Mitchell Beazley Ltd, 141
Mitchell, James, 221
Mitchell, Margaret: *Gone With The Wind*,
    143

Monopolies and Mergers Commission, 236, 242–3
Monsarrat, Nicholas, 12; *The Cruel Sea*, 27, 118–19
Moore, Brian, 273, 287
Moravia, Alberto, 78, 182
Morgan, Charles, 79
Morley, Frank, 77, 226
Morrow (William), Inc., 6, 17
Mortimer, John, 215n, 221
Mottram, Eric, 103
Mottram, R. H., 11
Murdoch, Iris, 8, 9, 48, 151; Booker prize, 269
Murdoch, Rupert: and Collins, 137, 145, 157–9; and Harper & Row, 166, 188; News International, 134, 157, 158
Murray (John), 50, 54, 148
Murry, John Middleton, 76

Naipaul, Shiva, 269
Naipaul, V. S., 268–9
*Naked Came the Stranger*, 223
Nashe, Thomas, 20
Nathan, Paul S., 71, 315–22
National Book League, 247, 264, 265, 270
National Book Sale, 238–9
National Graphical Association, 126, 131, 134, 241
Nationwide Book Club, 235
NCR Award, 273
Neill, Patrick, QC, 103
Nelson (Thomas), Ltd, 142
Nesbit, Lynn, 65–6
Net Book Agreement (NBA), 162, 238–44
New American Library, 141
New English Library, 141
New Fiction Society, 261–2
*New Statesman*, 9, 85, 251
New York: auctions, 25, 176, 319; editors, 77, 152; publishers, 86; 1970s, 127
*New York Press*, 59
*New Yorker*, 90
Newby, P. H., 268
Newhouse brothers, 185–6, 190
News International, 134, 141, 157, 158
newspapers: advertising, 225; colour supplements, 214–15; fiction in: agents, 56–7, 59; reviews, 28; serial with, 293–295
Newton, Nigel, 165
Nicole, Christopher, 11

Niven, David: *The Moon's a Balloon*, 204, 291, 296
Nobel Prize, 267, 273
Nolan, Christy, 272
Norman, Frank, 123
Nottingham, bookshops, 156
novelists, 7–19; advice from agents, 23, 66–8, 196–7; British and American differences, 87; definition, 3; earnings: 3, 4, 26–7, 40, 50, 57, 187, 194–5, 196, 277, 279; magazines, 16, 57; tv sales, 210; 1950s, 4, 119–20; 1963, 277; 1980s, 161, 279; and editors, 19, 21, 23, 36, 108–9, 171–3, 182, 185–6; influences, 21–3, 223–4; interviewed, 15–19, 34–49; isolation, 274, 296; motives, 7–8; new writers, 29, 30, 70–1, 72, 178–80 and fictitious example, 190–3, 197; popular novelists, 193–4; production rates, 8–14, 18–19, 39; publishers, relations with, 52–5, 62–3, 108–9, 145–7, 151, 299–303; Code of practice, 279–280; effect of publisher mergers, 145–152, 164, 166–7, 299; moving between houses, 150–2; partnership, 300–3; as shareholders, 300, status, 299–300; stress and life expectation, 20–1; surveys, 119–20, 161, 277, 279; tax and expenses, 288–9; training and technique, 21, 206–7, 298; on writing, quoted, 30–3; writing methods, 14, 17–18, 21–2, 38, 44–5; *see also* bestsellers; copyright; payment
novels: altered by editors, 87–9, 171–3, 173–5, 181–2; categories, popularity, 256; definition, 3–4; first, 178–80; future, 41, 46, 71–2; length, 249; literary, 1–2, 46, 180, 184; in magazine format, 291–3; numbers published annually: 1, 27–8; post-war, 110–11; 1986, 297–8; openings, 22, 206–7; realism in; 104–6; rejected novels, 9, 298; starting new, 17, 44–5; survival, likely, 1–2, 46, 307; unpublished, 298–9; *see also* sales figures; television
Nurnberg, Andrew, 307
Nye, Robert: *Falstaff*, 67

O'Brien, Edna, 83
Obscene Publications Bills, 3, 96–7, 101, 106
obscenity, 91, 92–106

*Observer*, 100, 214, 225, 271
Octopus, 301; mergers, 136, 137, 141, 144–5, 146–7, 150, 237
Odhams Press, 117
Office of Fair Trading, 158, 237
Ogden, Archibald, 202
O'Hara, John, 15
O'Keefe, Timothy, 102, 108
Old Bailey, 94, 95, 96, 99, 103
options, 69–70, 280
Orwell, George: *1984*, 212
Osborne, Charles, 263, 265, 266
Owen, Alun, 221
Owen, Deborah, 294
Owen, Peter, 261
Oxford, bookshops, 155, 156
Oxford University Press: 1970s, 84, 142; 1980s, 145, 147

Pacey, Joe, 125
Pan Books, 13; formation, 115; 1950s, 116, 117, 118; 1960s, 125–6, 154; 1980s, 141, 149–50, 159, 165, 185–6, 291–2
Panther Books, 116, 117, 125
paper: costs, 112; quota, wartime, 109–12, 114; tax, 56–7
paperbacks, 114–22; bestsellers, 27; Guild Books, 111; non-fiction originals, 116; offset from original text, 127; quality novelists, 159–60; rights, 275–7, (US) 315–18; sales, (1957) 118, (1985) 28; 'Top 100', 165; trade, 'B' format, 160; US: 315–18; (post-war) 114–16; (1960s–70s) 124–5, 128–9; (1970s–80s) 153–5, 159–61
*Paris Review*, 12, 34
Parsons, Ian, 119
Paternoster Row, 109
Paton, Grant, 161
payment, methods, 51–4, 299–300; 'blanket licensing', 253, 277; *see also* royalties
Peabody, Kidder, 189
Pearn, Nancy, 60
Pearson group, 131, 137, 141, 145
Penguin Books Ltd: advertising, 153; covers, 118; joint imprint, 115; World War II, 111; 1960s, 81, 82, 85–7; prosecuted, 97–100; 1970s, 127–8, 132, 133; 1980s, 133, 147–8, 149, 159; takeover, 141, 143, 144; group move to Kensington, 163–4

Penguin and Thomson, 141, 143, 144, 147–8, 163–4
*Penguin New Writing*, 111
Pentos, 155
Perkins, Maxwell, 88–9
Perman, Brian, 150, 185
Peters, A. D., 60, 126, 304
Philip (George) Ltd, 141
Philpotts, Eden, 10, 20
photocopying bureaux, 298–9
Pick, Charles, 82, 83
*Picture Post*, 29, 214
Pinker, James Brand, 58–9, 62
Pinter, Harold, 147
Pitman, Robert, 102, 142
Pitman Publishing Ltd, 141
plays: stage rights, 297, 304, 315; writing, 36, 39–40
Plomer, William, 74
Pocket Books (UK), 115–16, 117; US, 317–18
Poetry Society, 264
Pollinger, Laurence, 60
Pollinger, Murray, 60
Pollitzer, Ronald, 227
popular culture, 46–7
pornography, *see* obscenity
Potter, Denis, 221
Potter, Margaret, 258
Pountney, Michael, 166
Powell, Anthony, 75
Powell, Gareth, 125
Presses de la Cité, Les, 235
prices, books, 110; net Book Agreement, 162, 238–44; non-copyright editions, 51n; and royalties, 55–6; US, 239; 1940s, 113–14; 1950s, 120; 1960s, 241–242; 'standstill' policy, 125, 127; 1970s, 128–9, 134; hardcover/paperback, 128–9
Priestley, J. B., 20
Pringle, Maggie, 71
print costs, 298; in US, 128; post-war, 111–12, 114; 1960s, 126; 1970s, 128, 131, 241; 1980s, 161
print runs, 27, 55
printers: earnings, 134, 161; trade unions, 126, 131, 134, 143
prizes, *see* awards
profits: bestsellers, 195–6; post-war, 112; 1970s, 131–2
profit-sharing, 51, 53

Public Lending Right (PLR), 245, 250–8
publicity, 195, 225–33; hype, 25, 197–200; tours, 227–8; *see also* advertising
publishers: authors, relations with, 52–5, 62–3, 108–9, 145–7, 151, 299–303; earnings and expenses, 124, 193, 195; international, 129–31; personality, 107–8, 150–1, 166–7; readers, 181; transatlantic, 129–31, 164–5
Publishers Association (PA), 117, 119, 238; and book clubs, 234; and libraries, 245; and Net Book Agreement, 238–40; paperback group, 117, 291–2; Public Lending Right, 252, 255; and Society of Authors, 275–80; Code of Practice with authors, 279–80
*Publishers Weekly*, 71n, 89, 127, 318–19
publishing: British/American differences, 87; World War II, 109–11; 'cottage industry', 1945–60, 107–22; 1960s–70s, 123–35; 1980s, 136–67; turnover, 28, 155; *see also* costs
publishing houses: early, 74–7; families, 107; fire, 1940, 109; mergers, 71, 72, 136–52; post-war, 77–9; premises, 148–9
Pudney, John, 282
Purnell, 79, 112n, 139, 285

Quennell, Peter, 101
Quiller-Couch, Sir Arthur, 290, 305, 306

radio, 228, 232–3, 272, 273
Rae, Douglas, 207–12
Rainbird, George, Ltd, 141, 147
Random House Inc., 41, 83, 141, 165–6; buys Cape group, 141, 188–90
Rank, J. Arthur, 202
Raphael, Frederic, 221
Raven, Simon, 8
Rayner, Claire, 255
RCA, 317
Read, Piers Paul, 211, 287
readers, 258, 305, 306; women, 25
Reader's Digest, 116, 233
Reed International, 141, 144, 145, 150, 237
Renault, Mary: *Return to Night*, 113
Rendell, Ruth, 24, 219
Reprint Society, 233
resale price maintenance, 162, 240–1

research, 17, 36–7, 45
Restrictive Practices Court, 239–40
Reuben, Valerie, 147–8
reviewing of novels, 28, 44, 105–6, 226, 227; standard, 180–1
Reynolds, Jim, 87
Rhode, Eric, 201, 204
Rich, Lee, 322
Richards, I. A., 26
Richardson, Tony, 160
Rieu, E. V., 125
Rigby International, Australia, 141
rights, subsidiary: handled by agents, 62; and being out of print, 276, 278; retention period, 275–8, 302–3; in US, 315–322; volume, 119, 293; *see also* copyright; film rights; paperbacks; serialisation; stage rights; television rights; translation rights
Robbins, Harold, 317; *The Carpetbaggers*, 125
Robinson, Derek: *Piece of Cake*, 219
Robinson, Dr John, 99
Rockefeller Foundation, 267
Rogers, Deborah, 64, 65–6, 66–7, 68, 69, 70, 71, 72, 73, 153
Rogers, Graham, (Judge) 103, 104
Rolo, Charles, 127
Rolph, C. H., 92
Rose, Innes, 79
Rosenthal, Tom, 148, 298
Roth, Philip, 258
royalties, 54–6; bestsellers, 40, 242; compared with PLR, 257; origins, 54–5; paperback, 120–1; posthumous tax, 283; rates of 278, 302; statements, 276–7, 279, 303; '13 as 12', 61
Rubens, Bernice, 268
Rubin, Harriet, 89
Rubin, Stephen, 319
Rushdie, Salman, 1–2, 270

Saatchi & Saatchi, 153, 213, 229
Safeways Stores, 295–6
Safire, William, 197–8
Sagan, Carl, 312
*Saint, The* (tv series), 216
sales figures, 6, 26–7; discounts, 55; millions, 124–5; paperback, 28, 118; tv effect, 126; 1970, 126–7; 1985, 28; *see also* bestsellers, royalties
Salinger, J. D., 117–18

Salmon, Lord Justice, 104
Sampson, Low, 80
Samuel, Howard, 140
Sanders, Frank, 240
*Saturday Evening Post*, 16
Sayers, Dorothy L., 75, 225
Schaefer, Jack: *Shane*, 116
Schwed, Peter, 312
science fiction, 3–4
Scofield, Michael, 103
Scott, Paul, 24, 269
Scott, Sir Walter, 54, 56
screenwriters, 16, 30, 201–2, 211
Scribner's, 88; (Bookstore) 239
Seaman, Barbara, 233
Searle, Ronald, 85
Secker & Warburg, 77, 78, 141, 265;
   prosecuted, 94–5
Selby, Hubert, Jr: *Last Exit to Brooklyn*,
   102–4
serialisation: advance, 296; 'complete',
   293–5; magazine, 57, 296; rights, 62;
   tv, 126, 207, 209, 210, 212, 215–16,
   217–21, 228, 322
Seymour, Miranda, 105–6
Sharp, Margery: *The Nutmeg Tree*, 203
Shaw, George Bernard, 52, 61, 299
Shaw, Irwin, 7, 12, 32
Shaw, Michael, 65, 66, 68, 69, 71, 72, 73
Sheil, (Anthony), Associates, 65
Sheldon, Sidney, 16, 198, 295
Sheppard, Rev. David, 103
Sheppard, S.: *The Four Hundred*, 198
Shirer, William, 316
Shute, Nevil, 27, 202
Sidgwick & Jackson Ltd, 141
Sillitoe, Alan, 75, 124–5
Simenon, Georges, 9, 10, 11
Simon & Shuster, 116n, 130, 164–5, 312,
   317–8
Sinclair-Stevenson, Christopher, 71, 72,
   242, 278
Sisson, Nigel, 157
Sissons, Michael, 60, 126, 162–3
Smallwood, Norah, 84–5
Smith, Carol, 65, 66–7, 69, 70, 72, 73
Smith, Cortland, 36, 38, 39
Smith, F. T., 177, 185
Smith (W. H.): book club partnership,
   234–5, 236–7; bookshops, 156, 157,
   271; libraries, 110, 121; Annual Liter-
   ary Award, 272–3

Smith, Wilbur, 13, 24, 256, 257
Snow, C. P. (later Lord), 4, 79, 252
Snyder, Richard, 164–5, 317
Society of Authors, 43, 274–7, 279–81;
   Code of Practice, 279; origins, 52; and
   PLR, 252–3, 277; surveys: (1955/57)
   119–20, (1963) 277; (1982) 161, 279; *see
   also Author, The*
Society of Young Publishers, 124, 125
Sogat, 126, 131, 134, 241
Spark, Muriel, 287
Spedding, James, 53
Sphere, Books Ltd, 141, 160
Spielberg, Steven 321
'spoof' novels, 223
Spring, Howard: *Fame is the Spur*, 202
Squire, Sir John, 74, 76, 107
St Martin's Press, 318–19
Stable, Mr Justice, 95
stage rights, 297, 304, 315
Staples Press, 113
Star, 159
state assistance, 251, 259–66
Stationers' Company, 51
Steel, Danielle, 164, 257
Steen, Marguerite, 202
Stein, Sol, 89
Steiner, George, 1, 2
Steward, Alexander: *A Single Soul*, 213
Stewart, James, 205
Stone, Rodney, 291
stories, short, 44; magazines, 24, 29;
   payment, 16
Strahan, Alexander, 57
*Strand* (magazine), 16, 29, 76
Straub, Peter, 320–1
Streatfeild, Noel, 202
Streep, Meryl, 211
Styron, William, 12
subsidiary rights, *see* rights
Sumsion, John, 254
*Sunday Express*, 93; fiction prize, 273
*Sunday Times*, 12, 142, 144, 157, 158;
   colour supplement, 214, 215, on tax,
   286
*Superman* (film), 205
supermarkets, sales in, 295–6
Susann, Jacqueline, 232–3
Sutherland, J. A., 110, 130, 237–8, 246–7;
   *Bestsellers*, 22–3, 220; *Fiction and the
   Fiction Industry*, 5, 7, 8, 221, 243, 249,
   274, 287

Swanson, H. N., 201
Swift, Graham, 71, 183, 257
Swinburne, Charles Algernon, 56, 189
Swinnerton, Frank, 20
*Sydney Morning Herald*, 15
Symons, Julian, 11

taxation, 281–9; avoidance schemes, 267, 282, 283, 300; on awards, 275; EPT, 113; exile, 286–8; highest, 40, 300; and shareholdings, 300; value-added, 161–162, 288
teaching, 43, 305–6
techniques, 21, 206–7
television: advertising, 213–14, 229–30; appearances, 221–2; arts programmes, 228; books programmes, 212, 221–2; effect on reading, 2; effect on writing, 22; films for, 217; films transmitted, 216–19; interviews, 231, 232–3; programmes, 217–18; publishing, 123; rights, 206, 209–10, 212, 213, 215–17, 220; series and serials: 207, 209; from books, 126, 210, 212, 215–16, 217–21, 228, 322; from films, 209; 'spin-off' novel, 213; US, 204, 206; writing for, 16, 212, 221
Television Book Ltd, 212
Temple Smith, Maurice, 55–6
Thirkell, Angela, 75
Thomas, Hugh, 262
Thomson, David, 273
Thomson, Roy, 1st Baron, 81, 85, 142, 157
Thomson group, 84, 85, 123, 133, 141, 143, 144
*Thorn Birds, The* (tv), 228
Thorpe & Porter, 118
Thurman, Judith, 318
Tilling (Thomas), 123–4, 136–7, 140, 150
Tillotson Syndicate, 57
Tilsley, Frank and Vincent: *Seth Makepeace*, 213
*Time* (magazine), 208
*Times, The*, 56, 86, 96, 123, 227, 235, 287
Times Newspapers, 157
Timms, F. A. H., 241
titles, annual output, 162–3; wartime, 110
'Top 100' paperbacks, 165
trades unions, printing, 126, 131, 134, 143

translation rights, 62, 63
Transworld Publishers, 294
Trask, Betty, Awards, 272
Trenhaile, John: *The Mahjong Spies*, 229
Trevor, Elleston, 126
Trevor, Jonquil, 126–7
Trident Press, 317–18
Trollope, Anthony, 54
Tucker Committee, 284
turnover, 28, 155
Twain, Mark, 52
typewriters, 14, 17–18, 21–2

Ullman, James Ramsay: *The White Tower*, 202
United States: authors, 77; their earnings, 3, 4, 26–7, 40, and in UK, 227–8; films, 201–6, 211, 213, 216–17; hype, 199–200; magazines, 16; market for British books, 4–6, 25, 113; novels in British market, 25; novels published, numbers, 28; prices, 239; printing in USA, 128; publishers buy British companies, 165–6; in British market, 129–31; subsidiary rights, 62, 202–3, 315–22; *see also* New York
Universal Pictures, 321
unsolicited manuscripts, 29–30
Unwin, Sir Stanley, 75, 189; *The Truth about Publishing*, 76, 108, 241
Uris, Leon, 209

value-added tax, 161–2, 288
vanity publishers, 52
Vaughan, Samuel, 197
Vernon-Hunt, Ralph, 117
vertical integration, 153–4, 163–4
Viaduct Publications, 291, 292
Victor, Ed, 65, 66, 68, 69–70, 71, 72, 73, 198; reported in *Sunday Times* on changes in personnel, 185
Vidal, Gore, 13, 32–3
Viking Press, 35, 36, 131, 149
volume rights, 119, 293
Vonnegut, Kurt: *Jailbird*, 134

Wain, John, 33
Walker, Alan Gordon, 150
Wallace, Doreen, 202
Wallace, Irving, 22
Wambaugh, Joseph, 322
war stories, 227

Warburg, Frederic, 78, 182; prosecuted, 95; *An Occupation for Gentlemen*, 78, 130
Warne (Frederick) Ltd, 141
Warner Books, 313, 318
Warner Brothers, 204
Warren, Robert Penn, 31
Waterstone, Tim, 240
Waterstone's, 155–6
Watt, Alexander Paterson, 57–8, 178
Watts-Dunton, Theodore, 56, 189
Waugh, Alec, 61
Waugh, Evelyn, 14, 21–2, 55, 75
Webb, K., 95
Webb, W. L., 268
Webb's Bindery, 111
Webster Group, 141
Webster, T. B. L., 34
Wedgwood, Dame Veronica, 75
*Weekend Novel* (series), 290–1, 292
Weidenfeld & Nicolson, 86, 87, 141
Weldon, Fay, 183, 221, 255, 296
Wellard, James, 79
Wells, H. G., 234
Werner Laurie, T., 15, 16, 138–9, 213; prosecuted, 94–5
Wesley, Mary, 219
West, Dame Rebecca, 48, 99, 268
West, Morris, 213, 229–30
Western Press, 98, 100
Whitbread Literary Awards, 262, 263, 272
White, Pat, 159

Wilder, Thornton, 31
Williams, Shirley, 240
Wilmott, Chester, 227
Wilson, Alfred, 85
Wilson, Angus, 12, 32, 66
Wilson, Guthrie: *Brave Company*, 117
Wilson, J. G., 85
Wilson, Mary (Lady) 271
*Winchester 73* (film), 205
Winnington-Ingram, John, 293
Winsor, Kathleen: *Forever Amber*, 110
Wodehouse, P. G., 20
Wolfe, Thomas, 88
Wolfe, Tom, 290
*Woman* (magazine), 296
women: publishers, 124; readers, 25; writers, 35, 43, 47–9
Woods, Barbara, 322
Woolf, Leonard, 26, 189–90
Woolf, Virginia, 20, 26, 76
word processors, 17, 18, 298
World Publishing, 130
World War II, 109–11
Wren, P. C., 26
Writers' Action Group, 250–4, 274
*Writers' & Artists' Yearbook*, 63, 64, 77, 254, 266–7, 275
Writers' Guild, 250, 263, 265, 274–5, 277–8, 281, 303
writing instrument, 14, 17–18, 21–2
Wyatt, Woodrow, 252

Ziegler, Philip, 129